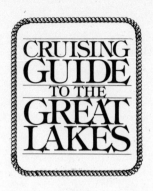

CRUISING
GUIDE
TO THE
GREAT
LAKES

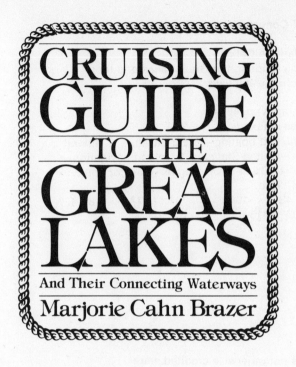

CRUISING GUIDE
TO THE
GREAT LAKES

And Their Connecting Waterways

Marjorie Cahn Brazer

CONTEMPORARY
BOOKS, INC.
CHICAGO

Library of Congress Cataloging in Publication Data

Brazer, Marjorie Cahn.
 Cruising guide to the Great Lakes and their
 connecting waterways.

 Bibliography: p. 487
 Includes index.
 1. Boats and boating—Great Lakes. 2. Inland
navigation—United States. 3. Inland navigation—
Canada. 4. Great Lakes Region—Description and
Travel. I. Title.
GV776.G74B7 1985 797.1'0977 85-427
ISBN 0-8092-5415-8

All photos not otherwise credited were
taken by the author.

Copyright © 1985 by Marjorie Cahn Brazer
All rights reserved
Published by Contemporary Books, Inc.
180 North Michigan Avenue, Chicago, Illinois 60601
Manufactured in the United States of America
Library of Congress Catalog Card Number: 85-427
International Standard Book Number: 0-8092-5415-8

Published simultaneously in Canada by Beaverbooks, Ltd.
195 Allstate Parkway, Valleywood Business Park
Markham, Ontario L3R 4T8 Canada

To Helen
For a lifetime of sharing

CONTENTS

AUTHOR'S NOTE

As anyone knows, who has made return visits to a port, marinas have a disquieting tendency to appear, change name and character, or disappear within a short period of time. Marina information compiled here is as accurate as personal visit and telephone follow-up within two years of publication could make it. If readers know of new marinas or yacht clubs, name changes, or closures in their home waters, a note addressed to me, in care of Contemporary Books, 180 North Michigan Avenue, Chicago, Illinois 60601, will be very helpful in the preparation of subsequent editions of this book—and bring us a little closer together.

M.C.B.

PREFACE

The preface gets written last—a retrospective on the process of writing a book. For me this has been a personal journey, to favorite haunts and to new discoveries. In sharing it with you my purpose is to present the word pictures and concrete information that will help you decide where to cruise and why. To that end I render some judgments in the pages that follow, tell you why some places are more desirable than others, describe in some detail the best of them, report tersely in neutral words what is least interesting, and warn you of the pitfalls. Although I have striven for fairness, the view of the lakes and what they have to offer is candidly filtered through my eyes and preferences. But this is a guidebook, not a prescription—the choices are yours.

Writing a cruising guidebook can be a treacherous enterprise. On the Great Lakes most of the natural landscape stays put, but the harborscape shifts constantly. No sooner is one marina nailed down in a port than two more and a yacht club rise up around it. Restaurants come and go in a twinkling, and tourist attractions wax and wane with the vagaries of public taste. To gather material for this book I have visited almost every port on the lakes, by boat or by car, within the past two years. What I saw should still be recognizable when you get there.

In my travels I have met some warm and helpful people at marinas and yacht clubs, in the towns and the countryside. To all of them I am grateful for their time, their interest, and their extra efforts in providing information. To the editors of *Waterway Guide* and *Lakeland Boating* I offer thanks for permission to use some material previously published by them. I am especially appreciative of the help given to me by David G. Brown, Editor of *Lakeland Boating*, in obtaining new material for this volume.

In writing this book I reflected much on the world of the past, but I operated in the world of the future. My words were "penned" on a personal computer. When the magic pen wrote awful things like "Error Message," or its green lights went out on the screen, Hal Varian rescued me from panic. To guide me along the perilous path to an optical character reading printout, David Rogers gave generously of his time. To both of them my warmest thanks. And to my husband, Harvey, who risked entry into dubious harbors, accepted long digressions from our course to check a port, endured leftovers and loneliness in the writing stage, I can offer only the gratitude of love.

M.C.B.
October 1984

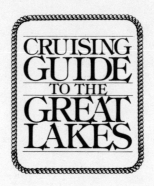

CRUISING
GUIDE
TO THE
GREAT
LAKES

1
MEET
THE GREAT
LAKES

To the European explorers of the 16th and 17th centuries the notion of a vast continent between their familiar Atlantic Ocean and the countries of the Orient was hard to conceive. They expected every river they probed to lead them quickly to the Western Sea. The St. Lawrence, which Jacques Cartier discovered and penetrated for 600 miles in 1535, seemed to offer the most promise. Indian tales of the "great sea" beyond raised hope even higher. Yet 80 years would pass before Samuel de Champlain reached that sea, tasted it, and, to his astonishment and disappointment, found it sweet. It would be another half century before all of the Great Lakes were revealed, and 150 years after that until they were accurately mapped.

Buried in the heart of the continent, our inland seas are unique. No other network of natural waterways on earth even resembles the five Great Lakes and their four connecting rivers. Spanning 8 degrees of latitude and 16 degrees of longitude, and encompassing 95,000 square miles of water, they account for one-fifth of the world's surface fresh water supply. Oceanic in size, even on the smallest of them the sailor loses sight of land as the horizon slips beneath the earth's curve.

Together the Great Lakes form an ecological system, a weather system, and a transportation system. Yet for all their similarities and the intimacy of their relationships, each has a personality of its own—in scenery, in mood, even in the dominant color of its waters. Lake Ontario, small and deep, is arrayed in the darker tones of blue. Erie, shallow and turgid, glides from paler blues to taupe and tawny shades. Color Lake Huron the green of emeralds. Michigan is slate blue and silvery. Majestic Superior wears the royal purple.

For their fleet of several million pleasure boats the lakes offer an enormous diversity of cruising experiences. There is a choice between protected coastal cruising and blue water sailing. For landfall there are choices that range from glittering metropolis, through sophisticated resort, quiet working city, and rural harbor, to trackless wilderness. Mountains and marshes, forests and beaches, archipelagos of rock and high dunes of sand, deep water and shoal, narrow channel and open water, currents and placid pools, storm and sun, brisk wind and gentle calm, fog and ice—the Great Lakes present a sampling of cruising the world over, except for the tropical, and if you went back a few million years, you would find that too.

That was before the lakes were even born. Lakes, like people, pass through a life cycle, and ours are young. The first came to life less than 15,000 years ago, and someday they will all die, mainly from an overdose of silt and vegetation. But at present they are frolicking children. Parented by the glaciers that advanced and retreated across North America for dozens of millenia and the older stream valleys that the ice gouged further, the lakes are as alike as siblings, and as different. Each has survived many incarnations. Their emergence, their size and shape and height above sea level have varied with the waxing and waning of the ice sheets and the flow of meltwater. At each stage in their complex development the lakes have discharged through different outlets, and geologists have assigned different names to their earlier configurations.

In their current mode Erie is the oldest, the first to take on its present appearance, followed soon afterward by Lake Ontario. Then another glacial advance, which didn't reach as far as these southerly lakes, delayed birth of the twins, Michigan and Huron, for several thousand years. By then, about 9,500 years ago, all four lake basins were emancipated from their parental ice. With the burden of crushing glacial weight removed from the land it began to rebound along the northern lake boundaries. Rising elevation, which continues even today, became the dominant influence in lake formation. It blocked off older outlets for the upper lakes, and Michigan and Huron evolved into their present form about 3,200 years ago. Superior, youngest and largest member of the family, followed suit a few hundred years later. For 2,500 years now the lakes have changed little. Man's impact has been their strongest influence. Yet, despite his most strenuous efforts to denude the shores, disembowel the substructure, tame the soil, pollute the water and regulate its flow, the Great Lakes maintain their integrity, their beauty, and their awesome power.

The power of the lakes speaks to the small boat mariner as challenge, as inspiration, as love, and occasionally as fear. The inspiration and the love derive from the lakes' endearing personalities, the challenge and the fear from the nexus of physiography and weather.

THE IMPRINT OF NATURE

When the glaciers finished their work, and all the vacillations in configuration were resolved, the Great Lakes emerged as a gigantic staircase. Lake Superior, named by the French as literally the upper lake, stands an average 602 feet above sea level. Its 31,800 square miles of water funnel into St. Marys River to fall 21 feet to the level of Lake Huron and Lake Michigan. Their combined water surface of 45,400 square miles discharges into the St. Clair River, to drop another 6 feet to Lake St. Clair. This "little lake" in the chain adds merely 500 square miles to the flow entering the Detroit River and a 3-foot drop to the 572-foot level of Lake Erie. Erie adds only 9,900 square miles of surface water before four lakes' worth plunges 325 feet down the Niagara River, more than half of it in one dramatic leap from the escarpment. From Lake Ontario, at 246 feet above sea level and 7,500 square miles in area, the St. Lawrence River assumes the burden. Throughout the journey the flow has gathered momentum. The 75,000 cubic feet of water discharged per second from St. Marys River now rushes down the St. Lawrence at the rate of 234,000 cubic feet per second until it reaches tidewater 265 miles downstream. From there the fresh water, which entered the system up to 1,500 miles inland, must flow yet another 800 miles before attaining the destination of all lakes and rivers, the open ocean.

The turbulence that the staircase phenomenon implies is actually encountered at only a few strategic places—at the rapids of St. Marys River, bypassed by the world's largest parallel lock system; at the confluence of Lake Huron and the St. Clair River, where an underpowered pleasure boat struggles upstream; and at the falls of the Niagara, overcome by an extensive canal and lock system located some 10 miles away. Otherwise, the lake surfaces are influenced mainly by wind and weather. Although there is obviously considerable current in the connecting rivers, only weak circular currents have been detected along the shorelines of the Great Lakes themselves.

Yet, assuredly, the water does move. It oscillates not only in wave patterns, discussed a little later on, but fluctuates vertically as well. It is inflow and outflow of the system that determines these vertical movements, recorded as changes in lake level relative to chart datum. The average height of each lake above sea level is measured with respect to a particular reference point—the gauge located at Point au Père, Quebec, on the lower St. Lawrence River. That also provides the reference plane for depth soundings on the Great Lakes charts, or chart datum. The surface heights of the lakes actually vary by small increments from day to day, but it is the monthly and annual fluctuations that are important for mariners.

The melting of the ice sheets filled the lake basins originally; what keeps them filled is essentially the amount of precipitation that falls within their drainage basins. Surprisingly, there are no large rivers that empty into the Great Lakes. The heights of land that surround the lakes—those barriers from which water flows in opposite directions on each side—are rarely more than 75 miles from the shore. These shallow drainage basins shelter hundreds of small streams and rivers, however, and the Great Lakes region as a whole is endowed with generous rain and snowfall. Thus, on the average over time, the enormous outflow from the lake system and the high evaporation rates from its large water surfaces are balanced by the inflow from direct precipitation, feeder streams and groundwater seepage. But within that overall balance fluctuations of up to several feet can occur from one year to the next, in an irregular cyclical pattern over the course of several years to a decade or more. From the early 1950s to the mid-1960s, for example, there was a severe downward trend in lake levels, while during the following decade they generally rose.

Monthly, or seasonal, variations are more regular and more predictable. Like the streams that feed them, the lakes are usually higher during the late spring and early summer and drop to their lowest monthly level during the early winter. Lake Ontario shows the largest seasonal difference and typically attains its highest level in June, as does Lake Erie. Huron and Michigan high water tends to arrive a month later, in July, while Superior, with the least seasonal variation, doesn't usually see high water until September.

Sustained high winds and/or sudden changes in barometric pressure can cause erratic changes in water level, varying from a few inches to several feet. These are likely to occur at the extremities of the lakes and in deep bays where the waters become constricted by land forms. The wind causes a greater volume of surface water to pile up at the leeward end of the lake than can be handled by return subsurface currents. The water level rises dramatically here, sometimes within a few minutes' time, while it falls precipitously at the windward end of the lake. After the causal conditions have actually diminished, a seiche may occur, wherein a return surge of water rushes from the high end to the low. Then an imbalance occurs in the opposite direction, and the surge reverses. This sloshing back and forth may continue, with diminishing force, until the lake comes to rest again.

The Great Lakes lie squarely in the path of the North American continental weather system, whose main feature is the passage of alternating cyclonic low pressure cells and anticyclonic highs, borne on prevailing westerly winds. Precipitation rates increase as weather moves eastward, with Lake Superior measuring the lowest annual amount, and Michigan, Huron, Erie and Ontario each receiving more, in that order. But the lakes are so large that they modify the weather as it crosses their expanse, and Lake Superior is capable of producing a weather system of its own.

It often seems to Great Lakes residents that the low pressure systems, with their dreary rainy or snowy weather, are more frequent and last longer than the fair weather highs. Whether or not that is true, quick succession and fast-moving systems are an observed phenomenon in this region that has been described as "a climatological battlefield." The contestants are the polar and the tropical air masses that meet and clash over the Great Lakes at the times of the equinox, spring and fall. These are the seasons of the most severe storms on the lakes, but in summer the polar air is usually in retreat. The lakes' influence derives from the simple fact that water heats and cools more slowly than land.

When the severe weather of early spring gives way to the warm, southerly breezes that heat up the land the lake water is still very cold. Warm air passing over these cold surfaces condenses into fog. The cold expanse of the lakes, interrupting the flow of warm air, also delays the warming of the land beyond, on the leeward side. Spring comes a little later on the eastern and northern shores than it does south and west of the lakes. By summer the lakes have warmed up, but there is still a big contrast between the daytime temperature of the water and the land, less at night. This gives rise to the sea-breeze phenomenon, whereby air currents move off the cooler lake to the warmer land during the day, while at night, when the more volatile land temperatures have fallen closer to the more stable lake level, the breeze may be reversed. This happy circumstance brings relief to landlubbers during summer heat waves and ensures balmy nights to sleeping boat crews.

While much of the summer weather on the Great Lakes is agreeably warm and sunny—less rain falls on the lakes than on the surrounding land—they do lie directly in the path of continental thunderstorms generated from the southwest. In this case, too, the lakes moderate the weather. Cool water and strong lake breezes tend to suppress the typical late afternoon thunderstorm activity, although at night the lake effect may actually amplify it. Thus thunderstorms are most likely to occur in the late afternoon or early evening on shore, while on the water they are likeliest to descend at night.

When fall brings another season of severe low pressure systems the warmed-up lake waters add fuel to the incoming storms. They also generate tempests of their own directly overhead, as warm air rises off the surface to meet colder masses moving in. Late fall can be a time of terror on the lakes, especially when the threat of ice is added to the severity of the season's gales. Small boat mariners are ill-advised to venture far from home port later than mid-October, especially on the upper lakes.

The extent to which each of the Great Lakes moderates the weather and the climate of its surrounding shores depends in part on its directional orientation. Three of them—Superior, Erie and Ontario—are oriented with their longest dimension on an east-west axis, while for Michigan and Huron the long axis is north-south. Summer thunderstorms generally slam in from the southwest, and Lake Erie often takes the brunt, with severe squalls that run unobstructed down its length. Lake Michigan, on the other hand, seems to be the most adept at suppressing thunderstorms, perhaps because of its orientation. Winter storms, coming from north and west, usually hit Lake Superior first, where its enormous size intensifies their impact as they move on to the lower lakes. The seiche phenomenon is also more common in Lake Erie than in the others, partly because it is the shallowest lake and partly because of its long east-west fetch.

All of the lakes influence the climates of their leeward shores. Because the thermally stable lake waters modify the temperature of the air masses passing over them, the downwind coasts are cooler in spring and summer and milder in fall and winter than the upwind side. Vineyards and orchards thrive far north of their customary habitat under protection of this gift from the lakes. Regardless of their orientation or their shape, the northern and eastern shores of all the Great Lakes, bathed by south and southwest breezes wafting across the water, are cooler in summer than the opposite shores.

But orientation does make a difference to cruising sailors. They can usually count on a reach or a run eastward on Superior, Erie and Ontario and be almost certain of a beat on the return. On Michigan and Huron conditions are more uncertain, and the point of sail will depend upon the relative proportions of south and west or west and north present in the prevailing wind. Furthermore, any of the lakes can fool you with unexpected easterlies, or take the wind out of your sails altogether for long periods of summer doldrums. There is always wind on these inland seas—but it may not be where you are.

If it isn't, power boaters will enjoy a flat calm, for on the Great Lakes it is the currently blowing or recently abated wind that generates waves. Their height, length and frequency are the net result of direction, strength and duration of the wind, combined with fetch over the lake. Lake Erie, for example, is known for its short, steep chop in a brisk wind with any west in it, longer but even steeper at the eastern end of the lake in direct proportion to the duration of the blow. Similarly, a strong south wind piles up on the shoals and reefs of Lake Michigan's north end in a vicious surf, although the fishermen idling off the Indiana Dunes at the southern end may hardly be rocked. When the wind is in the process of shifting direction it may seem to die for a short time while seas are confused, until both settle in from the new quarter. The aftermath of a big storm or lengthy gale on any of the lakes may see a period of rough or swollen leftover seas. But only Lake Superior is large enough to develop a true swell that closely resembles the ocean roll.

Fog can occur at almost any time on all the lakes, but it is most likely in spring and early summer, and decidedly most frequent and heaviest on Lake Superior. On any of them, however, the northern and western coasts are more vulnerable than the others. Fog is generally a phenomenon of early morning, and in summer it usually burns off by noon.

Weather on the Great Lakes is about as accurately predictable as it is anywhere else, but the lakes' meteorologists employ a unique way of informing the maritime public of what to expect. It is a MArine FORecast in succinct code, designated MAFOR. Updated and broadcast every six hours around the clock, the MAFOR predicts separately for each lake the wind direction and strength, and weather conditions for the following 3, 6, 9, 12, 18 or 24 hours, depending upon how changeable conditions will be. An encoded message might read 13420, which translates as follows: 1 = the message is beginning; 3 = valid for the next nine hours; 4 = wind from the south; 2 = wind speed of 17 to 21 knots; 0 = visibility of more than three miles. This might be followed by 14436, meaning that for the succeeding 12 hours the wind will continue to blow from the south, but at a speed of 22 to 27 knots, with rain. A final three-hour forecast will complete the code, followed by an estimated average wave height over the period and an English language synopsis of the movement of weather systems across the entire Great Lakes area during the next 24 hours. The wind speed estimates of the MAFOR apply to the open lake, not the coastal areas. Because of much lower surface friction over water, the wind is stronger in mid-lake than near shore; on Lake Ontario the differential has been measured at 30 percent in summer, 100 percent in winter.

MAFOR broadcasts are issued in the United States from commercial marine radio stations on a fixed schedule (see Appendix A for the list), which requires that you tune in at the right time and place. National Oceanic and Atmospheric Administration (NOAA) continuous forecasts are broadcast in plain English on dedicated VHF channels 1 to 4 from 22 stations distributed around the lakes. In addition to marine forecasts these report conditions on land for the benefit of the citizenry at large, with special attention to farmers and tourists. Consequently, the marine information is not as extensive or as useful as the MAFOR. But it does have the advantage of being accessible at any moment. At an intermediate level, the Coast Guard issues routine weather broadcasts at three-hour intervals and storm warnings as they arise, on channel 22A from six stations each on a different schedule but announced on channel 16. (See Appendix A.)

In Canada the continuous weather broadcast, issued on different channels in different areas (see Appendix A), includes the MAFOR code, along with near shore information for the benefit of small boat operators, and the latest measurement of lake levels. But the Canadians do not estimate wave height, and their synopsis—important for the long-range information it imparts—is not as inclusive and therefore not as useful as the American. Perhaps some day each government will adopt the best procedures of the other, and Great Lakes mariners will bless them both.

There is an additional category of weather information available by radio, LAWEB, LAkes WEather Broadcasts. These are reports from ships in transit around the lakes and from selected land stations, such as manned lighthouses. They identify their location and transmit information about wind direction and strength, sea conditions, and visibility at that time and position. These are broadcast on the commercial marine radio frequencies in the United States and included with the continuous weather in Canada.

THE HAND OF MAN

From the earliest days of unrecorded history the Great Lakes have provided a highway for men and women to pursue their work, their pleasure, their destiny. Sometime beyond human memory the Indians of the lakes invented the birch bark canoe—a quantum improvement on the old hollowed log—that could carry large payloads safely and efficiently over long distances on the open water or through the tumultuous feeder rivers. After white men arrived on the scene they began to launch a succession of craft propelled by various means, ranging from human muscle through sail and steam to diesel power; nuclear propulsion will doubtless arrive soon. As the power source has grown more sophisticated the ships have grown larger, and the newest lake freighters measure 1,000 feet in length. Until a mere 150 years ago boats plying the lakes and the rivers that feed them were the only means of access to the land. In some places they still are.

At first the lakes were entirely a French domain. In 1763 they were won in war by the British, who only 20 years after that were compelled to share them with the new United States of America. It took another 40 years of survey and diplomatic negotiation following the signing of the 1783 Treaty of Paris before the 1,150-mile marine boundary was finally certified and mapped through the middle of the lakes and their connecting waterways. The United States received Lake Michigan in its entirety, but Canada, heir to Great Britain, got the best scenery.

The Saint Lawrence River is the natural outlet of the Great

Lakes, but over the years men have created artificial passages to meet their economic or political needs that connect the lakes with the rest of the world by several routes. The Erie Canal, joining Lake Erie to the Hudson River and Atlantic Ocean, was renovated some years ago as the New York State Barge Canal. Canada built two canal systems emanating from Lake Ontario— the Rideau leading ultimately to the St. Lawrence via the Ottawa River, and the Trent-Severn Waterway to Georgian Bay. The old canals connecting Lake Erie to the Ohio River have fallen into ruin, but in 1900 Chicago restored pro-glacial Lake Michigan's outlet to the Mississippi River system through its Sanitary and Ship Canal. All of these waterways are interesting cruising grounds that lie beyond the scope of this book, except insofar as they convey visiting boats to the Great Lakes.

Both the United States and Canada early recognized the need to facilitate navigation on the lakes, at first with lighthouses at the most treacherous spots, then with dredging of rivers and harbors, the placement of floating aids, accurate charting, radio aids, and so on. The lakes were demilitarized by treaty in 1842, and treaties and agreements since then have reaffirmed full rights of access for the citizens and vessels of both nations. Every summer thousands of pleasure boats "go foreign" across the invisible boundary. Both governments require that foreign visitors report to a customs or immigration official immediately on arrival at the first port of entry.

There is a strong element of cooperation between the agencies of the two national governments that are responsible for navigation functions. For example, to eliminate costly duplication only the United States produces charts for the connecting rivers, although each government independently charts its own lake-shores. And LORAN-C navigation relies entirely on American signal broadcasts in the lakes region.

Canadian and American buoyage systems differ somewhat in style, but both follow the same principles of color, placement, numbering, and periodicity of lights. Canada, especially on the upper lakes, makes more extensive use of spar buoys than of the nuns and cans favored by the United States, and Canadian buoys tend to be smaller in size. Ranges, both lighted and unlighted, are also more commonly used in Canadian waters, at harbor entrances. These ranges usually carry conspicuous day-markings and are very helpful in finding a harbor on an otherwise featureless shore. On the other hand, the larger size of American lights and buoys is an advantage on that side of the border.

There are also some variations in chart style between the two countries, but the differences are inconsequential on recent editions. For the more remote sections of the lakes, however, Canada is still issuing older-style charts that utilize different graphics, refer to an obsolete chart datum, and show soundings in fathoms rather than feet. Within the next few years these are likely to be replaced by up-to-date charts consistent with current binational style. A new, and more significant, divergence may be expected as Canadian charts are shifted more rapidly to the metric system. So far only a few Great Lakes charts are printed with soundings and elevations shown in meters and distances measured in kilometers (distances on the Great Lakes have traditionally been measured in statute miles, rather than nautical miles), but as new editions are produced the conversion will proceed at an accelerated pace until it is complete. The National Ocean Survey is also producing some metric charts for United States waters, which are offered in addition to the English measure charts; these do not display a mileage scale. Ultimately, the United States will also "go metric" but is likely to do so more gradually than Canada. Whether measured in meters or in feet, depths and elevations on both nations' charts are shown with reference to the International Great Lakes Datum, adopted in 1955, as mean water level at Point au Père, Quebec. And both countries are overprinting new editions of their coastal charts with LORAN-C chains.

Great Lakes charts generally come in four levels of scale: an entire lake presented at a scale of 1:400,000 to 1:600,000; segments of coastline at 1:80,000 to 1:120,000 on the American side and 1:40,000 to 1:100,000 in Canada; harbor or small area charts ranging from 1:5,000 to 1:30,000 U.S. and 1:6,000 to 1:18,000 Canadian; Canadian small craft folio charts printed at 1:20,000, and American small craft charts spiral-bound into books at an assortment of scales. Most of the American harbors are charted in the larger scale as insets to the coastal charts, while Canada prints a collection of harbors on a single large sheet entitled "Plans of Harbours in Lake...." Idiosyncrasies in the charting of each lake will be discussed as needed in the chapters that follow.

Except in major harbor and shipping areas, the Canadian Hydrographic Service tends to issue new chart editions much less frequently than the National Ocean Survey, but when you order charts directly from the government they are hand-corrected to the date of mailing to you. In the United States new editions are not corrected subsequent to issue; the purchaser must insert his own corrections from the weekly Notices to Mariners, available free of charge upon request from the Ninth Coast Guard District. Canadian Notices to Mariners are also free from the Hydrographic Service. (See Appendix C for ordering information.)

Chart numbering follows a different pattern in each country. In the United States a five-digit code is used. All Great Lakes charts are designated 14 for the first two digits. For Lakes Erie, Ontario, and Huron and their connecting waters, the Straits of Mackinac and St. Marys River the third digit is 8, followed by two final digits ascending in that lake order. Lakes Michigan and Superior are coded with 9, and their charts, too, are numbered in ascending order from the smallest scale to the largest within each lake. Canada uses a four-digit system, with the first two digits designating the lake: 20 for Lake Ontario, 21 for Lake Erie, 22 for Lake Huron and 23 for Superior. In general higher numbers in the second pair are assigned to larger-scale charts, but the pattern is not consistent.

Although the charts display a wealth of navigational information, piloting on the Great Lakes requires attention as well to several other important publications. *United States Coast Pilot*, Volume 6, and *Sailing Directions, Great Lakes*, Volumes I and II, published by the Canadian Hydrographic Service, provide descriptive narratives of the coasts and harbors that include important information not amenable to graphic display. Similarly the Canadian *List of Lights, Buoys and Fog Signals* and *Radio Aids to Marine Navigation* and the United States Coast Guard *Light List*, Volume IV, which includes information on radio aids, are indispensable for their detailed descriptions of all of the fixed and floating aids to navigation. In addition to visual aids there are some 70 radio beacons operated by the United States and Canada that cover virtually all lake waters. LORAN-C is provided for both countries by American transmitting stations. Lakes Superior, Michigan and Huron are covered by chain 8970, Erie and Ontario by 9960. Both governments publish additional materials that are helpful to the navigator, listed in their annually issued chart catalogues that can be ordered free of charge. (See Appendix C.)

Although the lakes are tideless, seasonal or annual fluctuations in water level can be critical in navigating certain areas. You may find that rocks and shoals you clear with ease in a high water year are lurking just beneath the surface to grab your keel or propeller when the water drops another year. The problem is most acute in the wild anchorages of the upper lakes and in the intricate channels of Georgian Bay's east coast, but it can also exacerbate the difficulties in entering dredged or man-made harbors whose sand bottoms tend to shift or silt up. It's a good idea to keep track of water level broadcasts as you cruise.

Despite the most careful navigating and piloting, boats do occasionally get into trouble. Except for the most remote wilderness areas, help is rarely far away. The United States maintains 51 Coast Guard stations around the lakes and their connecting waterways (listed in Appendix B). Each monitors the international calling and distress radio frequencies, but the type of equipment available for assistance—cutter, launch, helicopter, etc.—varies among stations. Needless to say, one should be circumspect about calling for assistance at the scene, not only because of the burden of public expense imposed, but also because it usually takes a Coast Guard vessel a long time to arrive and their personnel are not the gentlest with a boat in tow. Furthermore, the service is getting more hard-nosed about answering distress calls from careless mariners and will not respond to an out-of-gas situation unless there is genuine danger to life. They now screen all radio calls to determine the severity of the problem and respond with dispatch of personnel only if there is a threat to life and/or there is no commercial towing service that can reach the scene. If they do take you in tow, the boat will be brought to the nearest harbor, not its destination or origin. In any event, the Coast Guard will act as radio intermediary to send help. In many areas the Coast Guard Auxiliary, a private organization dedicated to boating safety, provides valuable assistance and can often reach a boat in distress much sooner than the Coast Guard. Its members usually monitor Channel 16 when they are aboard their boats.

Canadian rescue operations are handled through the Rescue Coordination Centre at Trenton on Lake Ontario. A distress call to the nearest VHF radio station will be relayed to Trenton, where appropriate action is taken through one of the four Coast Guard bases on the lakes. (See Appendix B.) In addition to the nine cutters operating from these bases, there are seasonal mobile rescue units located in eight areas of intense pleasure boat activity. These are high-powered inflatable boats that can be trailered for launch close to the distress scene for quick response to a call. They are staffed by specially trained college students, who are capable of giving medical first aid and CPR, as well as doing simple boat repairs and towing of very small craft. Government assistance is supplemented by the highly effective Canadian Marine Rescue Auxiliary, a voluntary association of private boat owners under contract to the Ministry of Transport to serve in assigned areas. Like their American counterparts, these dedicated citizens monitor channel 16.

Clearly radio plays an important role on the Great Lakes. There are three categories of broadcast facilities, two American and one Canadian. In the United States two private networks broadcast the MAFOR and LAWEB weather reports, notices to mariners reporting recent changes in and any temporary dysfunction of navigational aids, and urgent marine information as received from the Coast Guard. Lorain Electronics, Inc., broadcasting from WMI Lorain, Ohio and 14 additional sites around the lakes, and Central Radio Telegraph Company's WLC Rogers City, Michigan, with three remote transmitter sites, also handle duplex telephone calls between ship and shore. Each transmitter is assigned one or more working frequencies for placement of calls to and from boats within their calling range. WMI Lorain and all of the WLC stations should be hailed in the usual manner on the working channel for the station nearest your location. The remaining Lorain Electronics stations are now automated and are hailed on the working channel by depressing your transmit button for 15 seconds and momentarily after you hear each ring until the call is answered by voice. Some other private communications companies can be hailed on assigned frequencies to make telephone calls; they are identified in the *Light List*.

In addition to its weather reports, the U.S. Coast Guard's radio network broadcasts local notices to mariners on a regular schedule throughout the day. The nearest Coast Guard station can be called directly in emergencies, but if for some reason they cannot be reached, the commercial stations will assist in a distress call. All are identified in Appendix A.

In Canada all radio communications are handled by a single system, Canadian Coast Guard Radio. Their taped, continuous weather broadcasts go out on dedicated frequencies, leaving their working channels free to handle urgent marine information, notices to shipping and duplex telephone calls. They can be hailed on one of their working channels as well as channel 16. It is important, when cruising the lakes, to have your VHF radio equipped with all of the working channels used by the three sets of broadcasters as well as all the continuous weather channels.

THE CRUISING LIFE

The variety of Great Lakes cruising opportunities enables you to plan an itinerary to suit any crew's taste, from city lights to tranquil wilderness, on wide-open water or through meandering rivers and channels. You can focus on one extreme or the other or taste a sampling of all the variations in between. Whatever your choice, it's important to plan for safety—distances can be long and bad weather sudden—and for enjoyment, knowing what to expect when you arrive.

Each lake offers a range of choices, or, depending on the time at your disposal, you can visit parts of several. You can cruise back and forth across the United States–Canada border, but remember that each time you do you must report into customs and immigration. Canada and the U.S. share the most amicable border in the world, but both have rules and import prohibitions that you need to know. For example, you may bring into Canada only 40 ounces of alcohol or wine per person and no firearms except sporting rifles and shotguns. The United States permits one liter of alcohol but no citrus fruits. Most of the major ports on the Great Lakes, and many of the minor ones, are customs ports of entry or customs reporting stations for their respective countries. On both sides of the border a telephone call from the dock will either bring an officer to your boat or give you verbal clearance and a number. Both nations issue temporary permits for your boat, which you obtain from the customs officer in Canada, an immigration officer in the U.S., and both require that their nationals report back in upon reentering the country.

Planning a Great Lakes cruise is essentially a balancing act. Inevitably some parts of any itinerary will be less interesting than others. One hopes to confine these to overnight stops or alternative destinations in case of bad weather or boat troubles. Vacation time, average boat speed (including sailors' allowance for windless days and willingness to motor), and the number of hours each day that your crew likes to run, will determine both your ultimate destination or turn-around point and intermediate destinations where you'll spend some time. In between you'll estimate each day's passage according to the availability of congenial overnight stops. Your cruise plan must also allow for weather days—stormy, too windy, or too rough. Is there a law that these occur when we're holed up in the least interesting or comfortable harbor on the whole itinerary? Whether there is or not, that's a good enough reason for planning overnight stops as carefully as destinations.

Cruise planning must also take into account logistics of supply for hungry crews who dirty a lot of clothes. Many of the nicest harbors on the lakes are in rural places with little or no shopping available. And there is often a long distance between Laundromats. If you point your bow to the wilderness, these services are even scarcer. If, on the other hand, you're moving from town to town along a highly civilized coast, laundry facilities are readily available and it's often more fun to acquire foodstuffs in some other town's gourmet shop or supermarket than it is to bring them from home. You'll also be dining out more in these circumstances than you will in farm or wild country.

Availability of spare parts for the boat also may depend upon sophistication of the harbor, although skilled craftsmen and mechanics are often found in out-of-the-way places. One item of boat supply can be hard to locate no matter where you cruise. If you cook with propane, it's rarely available at a marina. You will have to depend upon refilling tanks either at campgrounds or, in cities, at a depot located in an industrial district. In either case you'll need motorized transport to carry your tanks to the source of supply—marina courtesy car or taxi.

Where you dock or anchor and what you do ashore is only half the fun of cruising, or even less. It's the boating that you're out there for, and the enjoyment of sea and sky, wind and sun, fish and sea birds. On coastal passages there is the bonus of scenic interest, and on the Great Lakes that's a big bonus. There are the natural extravaganzas like the Pictured Rocks of Lake Superior or the Sleeping Bear Dunes on Lake Michigan or the Thirty Thousand Islands of Georgian Bay. Much of the lakeshore is bordered by pleasant farms and orchards, set on rolling hills or lakeside bluffs, with towns and villages sprinkled in between— not exciting, perhaps, but soothing to the spirit. For excitement there is the awesome spectacle of America's industrial muscle along the Detroit River, at the south end of Lake Michigan, at the western end of Lake Ontario, and on parts of Ohio's Lake Erie shore. There is also the soaring grace of a metropolitan skyline— Chicago, Detroit, Cleveland, and Toronto. The view from the water yields a perspective on man and nature that distills the essentials from the clutter of detail. Mood and meaning are conveyed unhindered to those who gaze upon the scene from the deck of a small boat.

In almost any part of the lakes you'll share the waterway with many other types of craft. Pleasure boats run the gamut from canoes and rowboats through small motorboats out for the fishing, sailboats of all sizes out for the racing or simply a day on the water, to the cruising yachts, power and sail, that range from 20 feet to 200. Putting out from ports large and small on all five lakes are the uniquely styled commercial fishing tugs. To cope with the cold of these northern seas in the spring and fall seasons Great Lakes fishermen cover their boats with a rather square-cut housing that contains a large "barn door" aft. Through this opening the nets are set and hauled, while between stints at the nets skipper and crew can keep to the warmth of the ship's stove just behind the steering station.

And then there are the lake freighters, those majestic long ships that carry the riches of prairie and iron mine from the lakehead on Superior to the hungry people of the world and the voracious steel mills of the lower lakes and beyond. Some bring limestone to the mills from the enormous beds on Lake Huron. On the return voyages some carry coal from Appalachia to electrical generating plants all around the lakes; others carry a variety of bulk cargoes in several directions. Lakers are unmistakable on the horizon. Head-on from a distance they look like huge buildings on the move; in profile their sleek mid-sections, hundreds of feet long, lie low in the water while at either end a superstructure rises six or eight decks into the air. They move fast in open water, throw a huge bow-wave and a boistrous wake, but their powerful engines are deeply muffled and they seem to glide along in dignified silence. Anyone who cruises the lakes is soon captivated by the romance of these graceful ships. Some of them become old friends as you recognize names after several passing encounters, and true boat watchers can identify ownership by the distinctive marking on the stack.

In contrast to the lakers the salties seem puny. These are the ships of many nations that cross oceans to reach Great Lakes ports via the St. Lawrence Seaway. Their cargo holds and superstructures are grouped more conventionally, with unloading cranes silhouetted against the sky amidships. Many kinds of workboats ply the lakes—ferries, barges, dredges, tugs, and a few that are hard to define. For all this large maritime population congestion is found only in a few narrow channels, mostly in the rivers, and in some harbors. On the open lakes you need never be in the way of a big ship or a busy workboat, but in those harbor entrances, narrow channels and rivers the pleasure boat skipper must be the one to watch out. The line of sight from the bridge of a large ship is obscured from anything close by, and neither the helmsman nor the deck officer could see you if you were in harm's way. Even if they could, it takes a mile or more for a ship even to slow down appreciably, let alone stop. Hug one side of the channel in the connecting rivers—often there's enough water depth for you just outside the channel—or stop, if you must, to let a ship pass; then be prepared to ride a tumultuous wake.

The kind of harbor in which you will moor at day's end depends largely on which part of the lakes you are cruising. When the glaciers completed their work they left a sharp dichotomy between the extremities of the lakes they created. The shorelines in the southern latitudes were smoothly contoured, while in the north the coasts were ragged and broken. Thus Lake Ontario, Lake Erie and the southerly reaches of Lakes Huron and Michigan have few natural harbors along their unbroken shores, while northern Lake Michigan, northern Huron and Georgian Bay, and most of Lake Superior are broken up by islands and embayments. Custom, latitude and height above sea level have emphasized this natural difference by designating Erie and Ontario as the lower lakes and Huron and Superior as the upper lakes. According to the lake level criterion Michigan is an upper lake, but the latitude and smooth coasts of its southern reaches make it also "lower"; in effect it's a hybrid. Another characteristic carries the dichotomy one step further. The lower lakes are largely urban and metropolitan, while the upper are largely rural or wild.

Consequently, when you are cruising the lower lakes your destinations and way-stops will be primarily at docks in man-made harbors; many are dredged out river mouths. (This is true for parts of the upper lakes as well, of course.) Most of the transient dockage is at privately operated marinas or yacht clubs, but there are two important exceptions. The State of Michigan, in collaboration with the Army Corps of Engineers, has sponsored a harbor of refuge program that ultimately will provide a chain of yacht harbors "such that a small boat will never be more than 15 shoreline miles from safety." Within those harbors The Michigan Waterways Commission has built marinas to high standards of construction that are usually turned over to the local government to operate. They go by a variety of individual names relating to local management, but because they are consistent and identifiable in style we refer to all of them as Waterways Commission Marinas. In a few instances the Commission runs the marina directly. This program, almost 40 years old, has given Michigan some of the best equipped yachting accommodations on the lakes.

In Canada the government dock is a venerable institution. In order to encourage maritime industries—shipping, fishing, recreational boating—the federal government has constructed a network of wharves and docks on all of the country's navigable waterways. This program was begun in the last century, with most of the wharves built for the use of ships and commercial fishing tugs. A few, of more recent vintage and more appropriate size, are clearly intended for recreational use. But pleasure craft have the right to dock at any federal dock, unless it has been entirely leased (as in a few cases) to a private user. There will be one in virtually every town, and even a few nontowns, on the Canadian shore of the Great Lakes. It may be simply a wharf to tie up to without any services, or marine services may be provided by a private or municipal concessionaire who collects the docking fee for the government. The government dock is likeliest to offer services where it is the only facility. In places that have several private marinas the unadorned government wharf may be buried in obscurity among them, but it is, nevertheless, available for inexpensive docking.

In large urban areas, or on stretches of coastline where the harbors are far between, the cruising boat may encounter some difficulty in finding dock space. On the lakes, as on the seacoasts, the explosion in pleasure boating has elevated the demand for dockage far above supply. You may arrive in a port to find all the dock space rented for the season by local boats, or all the transient spaces filled. In some of these harbors you will find helpful harbor masters who are willing to welcome everybody—and raft boats to the rafters, if necessary. Others are not so accommodating, although you won't be turned out to sea in a storm. If your arrival is predictable an advance reservation is always a good idea, and many American marinas monitor channel 16. Canadian law restricts radio watch by commercial establishments to channel 68.

In some of the larger artificial harbors it is possible to anchor as well as to dock your boat. Permanent moorings, set by yacht clubs, marinas, or municipalities, are becoming more popular on the Great Lakes, so anchoring room in these harbors is diminishing. You may even find, when you request dockage upon arrival, that you are assigned to a mooring, with or without launch service to shore. There was a time when a boat could travel large segments of the lakes without a dinghy, but with the expansion of moorings to supplement dockage there is a greater risk of getting stranded out in the harbor.

To cruise the islands and wild coves of the upper lakes a dinghy is, of course, essential. The only docks in these places are a few Canadian government docks. And since the primary purpose in visiting these areas is to approach nature on her own terms, anchoring is the preferred mode anyway. Depending upon place and time of summer, you may often find yourself alone in these harbors. That is the fond objective of most mariners who come here for the undisturbed sights and sounds of the natural world. For that reason, when a harbor is shared by two or more boats it is important to their mutual enjoyment that they anchor as distant from one another as space and bottom configuration permit. This may sound antisocial, but in practice those who want to get acquainted can easily dinghy back and forth, while those who prefer solitude have that option. Even more critical to the environment of the wild anchorage is mutual observance of noise courtesy. Voices, radios, generators and outboard motors carry farther and louder over water than over land, especially after sundown. At dusk, when the birdsong is sweetest and an ethereal hush falls over the harbor, the raucous intrusion of these noises can be painful. And after dark they can be severely disturbing to sleep.

In addition to sharing an anchorage with other boats, you may find cottagers in residence on shore. Many of these people, especially those in isolated locations, have chosen this site for the same values that brought you here and deserve the same consideration. Try not to anchor in their front yards, and when you go ashore respect the privacy of their property. There is often an undeclared tension between cottagers and boaters, and noise is part of the cause. Even when boaters try to be nonintrusive, cottagers seem to burst forth in a frenzy of outboard activity at sunset, zooming noisily back and forth in total disregard of the havoc caused by their wakes as they pass within inches of anchored boats. The more thickly settled the anchorage, the worse the problem. For this reason the most desirable anchorages are those with few or no cottages; in the chapters that follow we report that status.

Another category of visitor to wild anchorages is the camper. Depending upon location, he may arrive on foot or in a small boat or canoe. While many campers are sensitive to the environment, as their numbers increase litter is a growing problem in the once pristine wilds. But campers aren't the only ones to blame. The holding tank laws for boats are, regrettably, turning beauty spots into privies; every year more toilet paper is in evidence. If we want to continue to enjoy the untrammeled natural world we seek, all of us—boaters, cottagers, campers— must take great care to pack out *all* of our trash to public disposal sites.

Fire is the other human menace to the wild country. A cookout ashore is one of the pleasures of wilderness cruising, but it should be arranged only on open rock or beach; there are plenty of both on the Great Lakes. There is also plenty of driftwood for fuel, so there is no need to hack at living trees for this purpose. The fire, well away from trees, should be confined to a ring of stones, and if you take care to scatter those stones after you have thoroughly doused the coals, the next party to arrive will have the fun of building their own little hearth in the wild. There is nothing quite so disconcerting as to arrive on a wild shore and find it pock-marked with other people's fireplaces and the remains of their cookouts.

PLAN OF THE BOOK

Wild anchorage or sophisticated metropolis, small town or pastoral setting, dramatic scenery or placid, the Great Lakes have it all, and each lake has some of it. The chapters that follow present a lake-by-lake description of the coastline and cruising conditions peculiar to that body of water, and a harbor-by-harbor description of yachting facilities, commercial services and tourist attractions.

A word about definitions. The term *cruising boat* refers to decked vessels, power and sail, of 20 feet or more with a draft in excess of 2½ feet. Decked power boats of any size with draft less than 2½ feet and sailboats capable of reducing draft to that level are designated as *shallow draft boats*. Open, hand- or outboard-powered craft with minimal draft may be referred to as *small boats* or *runabouts* or *dinghies*.

In describing coastlines and harbor approaches only the most significant shoals, currents or hazards are mentioned. I assume you consult the chart and *Coast Pilot* or *Sailing Directions* for full details. Aids to navigation are treated similarly. The landmarks and major navigation lights and daymarks that identify a harbor approach are described in general terms (refer to the *Light List* for details), including the courses defined by ranges. Wherever possible we report channel depths of less than 20 feet and depths at the docks in marinas and yacht clubs or in anchorages. Where those depths are preceded by the word *controlling* they refer to chart datum or low water. Where no such qualification appears they are depths self-reported by marina operators in 1984, a high water year. You should deduct one to three feet, depending on the lake in question, to arrive at chart datum. In some cases this will leave little or no water to float a boat; presumably such harbors will be dredged before water levels reach bottom again.

The radio stations operating on each lake are identified in Appendix A. Radio beacons are not discussed at all, however, because drastic changes have been proposed by the United States Coast Guard for the entire system. Radio beacons were first established on the lakes in the 1920s. During the past 30 years radar and, more recently, LORAN-C have virtually replaced their use by commercial vessels. For a number of reasons the system as it stands is not as useful as it might be for recreational craft. Under the new proposal the system would provide at least one line of position everywhere on the lakes, two where traffic is heavy, would maximize homing capability by placing the beacons at ports rather than offshore islands and coastal points, and make all beacons continuous instead of sequenced as they are now. The Coast Guard is presently awaiting comments from the public before undertaking the revision, which will, of course, be coordinated with the Canadian Coast Guard. Meanwhile, during this transitional period I omit reference to the radio beacons; they are described in the *Light List.*

For each harbor I have tried to present as complete a list of relevant marine facilities as possible. Because this book is addressed mainly to cruising boaters, however, only marinas and yacht clubs that accept transient boats are identified. Especially in heavily populated areas there are many that provide only seasonal dockage or moorings; condominium "clubs," in which membership is a qualification for dockage, are growing in size and number. And all over the lakes there are hundreds of marinas, large and small, that cater to small, outboard-powered boats used for fishing, day-boating, or transportation for cottagers. Rarely do these offer transient dockage, even to their own kind. For easy reference, marinas and yacht clubs that offer transient services are set in bold face type the first time they are mentioned. Public docks without any services are not so highlighted, nor are yacht clubs without dockage. If in some harbors you see marinas that are not mentioned here, it is either because they do not accept transients (as of 1984—marinas change their minds), they cater only to small boats, it's new, or, inadvertently, I missed it.

Marine accommodations fall mainly into three categories—full service boatyards, commercial marinas with dockside services to resident or transient boats but no repairs, and yacht clubs. In the text no distinction is made between the first two, except in the services reported. *Dockside services* is a collective phrase that includes the following: electric power, drinking water, gasoline, diesel fuel, ice, holding tank pumpout, shoreside heads and showers. To avoid tedious repetition a marina or yacht club is said to provide "all dockside services," or "the usual dockside services," adding exceptions where necessary. Laundromats are provided so rarely that they are always specified. In addition, for service yards the type and maximum capacity of haulout equipment, the types of repairs they perform, and the presence of a marine store are reported. That, too, carries a specific definition. It refers only to a store that carries a full line of marine equipment, parts and accessories—a real chandlery— not the supply-room kind of store, with paint and cleaning supplies, that most marinas operate. Finally, launch ramps, ancillary commercial facilities, such as a restaurant, and any other information that distinguishes a particular enterprise is included.

Yacht clubs also fall into two categories—those that extend hospitality to cruising boats when space is available and those that accept only boats from "reciprocating" or "recognized" yacht clubs. Those two words are used interchangeably to avoid monotony. Precisely what they mean depends upon the policy of the club you're visiting. Each of the Great Lakes has an umbrella yacht racing organization. They, in turn, as well as some individual clubs, belong to the United States Yacht Racing Union or the Canadian Yachting Association. Therefore, one criterion used for recognizing or reciprocating club membership is affiliation with one of these organizations. But not all clubs belong to an association. Many of them exchange visiting privileges only with a select list of their own. Whichever criterion each club uses as a condition for transient accommodation, it is stated here as reciprocity or recognition. Services, facilities and amenities offered by yacht clubs are reported in the same style as for marinas.

You may assume that all marinas and yacht clubs accommodate both powerboats and sailboats, unless otherwise specified. You should also recognize that most of them are already filled with resident boats (although a few, especially public marinas, maintain some visitor docks or moorings) and that they can and will accommodate a transient only in the place of a seasonal boat out for the night or longer. Somehow the game of musical boats plays most of the time without leaving anyone out. Size of these enterprises is reported only at the extremes, that is, very large (say 500 boats or more) or very small (fewer than 25 spaces). Dockage fees are not reported because they change with great frequency. Generally speaking, public marinas charge less than commercial operations; some yacht clubs do not charge a dockage fee; others do.

Another word about marinas that do not accept transient boats. Many of them have excellent repair facilities and will, of course, accommodate a cruising boat that requires service. These are mentioned only in harbors where there are no repairs available at the facility offering overnight dockage. In addition, there is a whole spectrum of marine services obtainable in the large cities, and even some of the smaller towns, that are not part of marina operations. These include chandleries, electronics sales and service, canvas shops, engine repairs, sail makers, and so on, often located away from the waterfront. They are outside the scope of this book, but if you need that type of service while cruising, you can inquire at the marina or club where you're docked.

What is in a town? Sometimes a lot, sometimes not much. In the large cities there is usually a great deal to see and do, and most of it is accessible from a marina by bus or taxi, although rarely in walking distance. In the small and medium-size towns marinas are more likely to be centrally located, enabling the crew of a cruising boat to become acquainted in a way that they never could if traveling by car. Most North American places of these sizes comprise two different towns—the "anywhere America" of the chain-bound highway strip, and the original downtown that may be dead or dying but at least has a character to call its own. Furthermore, many of these old downtowns are being revived with new shifts in urban taste and awareness of individual heritage. Just strolling the streets can be interesting, and you can often walk to the special sights you want to see. Smaller towns may or may not have a bus system for more distant roaming, but most have taxis. In some towns car rental may be the only way to reach a site of particular interest that lies on the outskirts or in the countryside, or even several such places. Where there is no commercial rental agency you can usually make a deal with a local auto dealer.

Whichever way you get there—by foot, bike, bus, taxi or rental car—the places to see and the activities to enjoy are included in each harbor description. Obviously, for the very large cities we can offer only a sampler, but for most of the smaller places the rundown is representative, if not complete. Neither hours of operation nor admission fees are listed because they, like dockage charges, change too frequently. But telephone numbers are included for museums, historic sites, theme parks, legitimate theaters, etc., so that you can call to inquire before hot-footing it over. Most attractions are open all day and some extend into the evening hours during July and August, with shorter hours June and September. Commercial attractions and many public ones charge admission; those that don't appreciate voluntary donations. In the large cities, and many of the medium-size ones, consultation with the daily newspaper or the weekly or monthly "city" magazine will tell you what's going on when and where. Even in little towns the weekly newspapers can give you useful information, while providing entertainment in themselves; the country weekly is a unique form of journalism.

Dining out is a popular form of recreation on any cruising boat. Much as this galley slave enjoys it, I have been able to sample only a small fraction of Great Lakes near-shore restaurants over the years. Some of them I can and do recommend heartily; about others I keep tactfully silent. But for your convenience, all marina-associated restaurants and yacht club dining rooms, plus a few others at waterfront that are well known locally, are mentioned—without comment if I have no firsthand information.

In addition to fun facts some necessary mundane information is included in each harbor description: customs reporting, food shopping and Laundromat proximity, availability of a hospital, rail and/or scheduled air transport for crew changes.

Lake Huron, specifically Georgian Bay, was the first of the Great Lakes to be seen by white men, and Lake Erie was the last to be "discovered," some 60 years later. We have chosen here not historical sequence, however, but one that roughly follows population, from the most urbanized lower lakes to the wilder upper ones. More precisely, we follow elevation, beginning with Lake Ontario and moving up the staircase to Superior. The direction of circumnavigation has been selected arbitrarily; it could as easily have gone the other way around. The reader, who may launch his or her boat from any port on the lakes or beyond, can plunge into any section and navigate the book from there. Any way you go, it's good cruising.

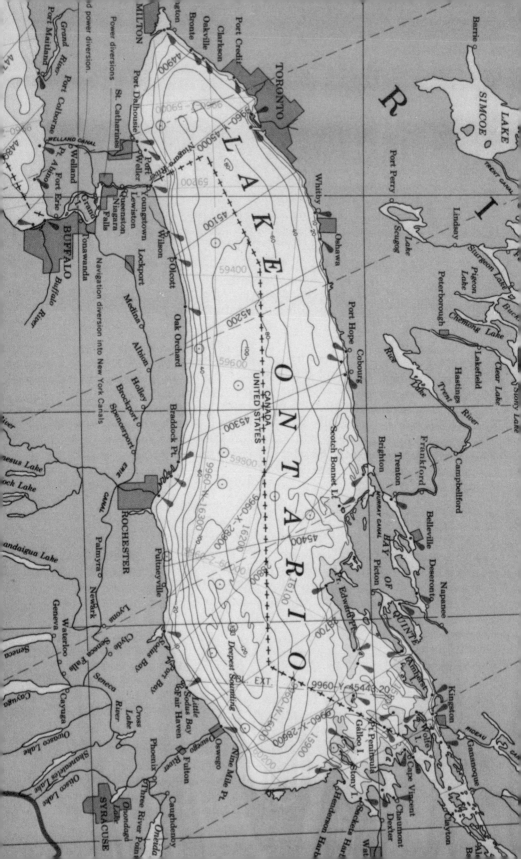

2
LAKE ONTARIO: BIG-CITY SOPHISTICATION, SMALL-TOWN INTIMACY

Lake Ontario has seen its share of tumult, in weather and in war, but today enjoys peace, prosperity, pride and self-confidence. Those qualities apply to the people and the towns, of course. The lake is above such human judgments. Although the smallest of the Great Lakes, Ontario is deep, in keeping with its strategic responsibilities as the gateway lake that receives the entire flow of the other four and passes it on to the St. Lawrence River for transport to the sea. It is also the crossroads lake. Four canals radiate from its shores—the Rideau and the Trent-Severn to the north, the Oswego and the Welland to the south.

Its strategic placement determined the course of events on Lake Ontario from the beginning of European presence. Samuel de Champlain, Governor of New France, was the first visitor of record, in 1615, and the result was disastrous for the French. He crossed the lake in company with his Huron allies to make war on the Iroquois, who inhabited its southern shores. In so doing he incurred the hatred and the unremitting warfare of the most highly organized and successful military machine in native North America. The Iroquois effectively barred the French from the lower lakes for most of the 17th century. By the early years of the 18th, however, the British appeared on the lakeshore and built a post at Oswego in 1722. The French reinforced their Fort Frontenac, built in 1673 at the site of Kingston, and in 1727 they anchored the other end of the lake with Fort Niagara.

Lake Ontario, where the French and the British faced each other directly in the west, saw heavy action during the battle of those giants for supremacy in North America. During the American Revolutionary War, which opened less than 15 years after the British Conquest, Lake Ontario was still a wilderness with essentially the same three forts. It played a less conspicuous role in the later conflict, but the outcome was momentous. Many New Yorkers were loyal to the Crown and after the war took refuge across the boundary waters, to found the towns and cities that rim the lake today. The Province of Ontario dates her birth to the arrival of the United Empire Loyalists in 1784. But peace didn't settle yet on the Lake Ontario frontier. During the War of 1812 both sides had more to lose in the new settlements. Naval sparring between fleets based at Kingston, Ontario, and Sackets Harbor, New York, continued throughout, while bitter battles were fought on the heights above the Niagara River.

With the Treaty of Ghent, peace came at last to Lake Ontario, and the people on both sides of the border finally began their nation-building. In New York it took off in earnest with construction of the Erie Canal. Oswego might have seemed the logical terminus, but with memories of war still fresh, a safer, all-interior route was followed to a Lake Erie terminus. Although Oswego did get a connecting canal in 1828, the New York shore of Lake Ontario never urbanized like the other American Great Lakes coasts. Except for Oswego and Rochester, it remains rural today, while the Ontario side is Canada's most populous and urban corridor. The contrast enhances a Lake Ontario cruise.

One hundred ninety-three miles long, and 53 miles across at its widest, the elliptical lake is oriented almost precisely on an east-west axis. In the prevailing west to southwest winds of summer this can mean a hard beat for sailors bound west, though cross-lake passages can be made on a comfortable reach. Summer winds are often light, with little wave action resulting. When a gale does blow the lake roughs up quickly with steep seas. A funnel effect at the east end can make that a dangerous place to be. Mexico Bay is especially notorious. Thunderstorms brew out of the south and west from late afternoon through the night, occurring most frequently in August.

Fog isn't a severe problem on Lake Ontario. It is most likely to occur in late spring and usually dissipates before noon. The great depth of the lake—maximum 802 feet, average 283—minimizes wind-induced fluctuations in lake level; despite the east-west orientation, seiches are rare. But an easterly current has been measured down the lake at about 8 miles a day, strongest along the south shore.

There are U.S. Coast Guard stations at Niagara, Rochester and Oswego (seasonally at Sackets Harbor and Sodus Bay), but only the station at Buffalo on Lake Erie maintains continuous radio watch on channel 16 and broadcasts weather and notices to mariners on 22A. The Canadian Coast Guard Rescue Coordination Centre, serving the entire Great Lakes, is located at Trenton, on Lake Ontario. There are cutters based at Kingston, Cobourg and Port Weller, with a mobile rescue unit at Trenton.

Summer is a pleasant time on Lake Ontario. Daytime temperatures average in the upper 70s and 80s, dropping into the 60s at night; by mid-season the near-shore water temperature rises as high as 70 degrees. The boating season spans five months, May through September, although hardier souls extend it at either end to more than six. Boating is a major pastime among lakeshore residents—predominantly sailing, although in some of the south shore harbors near rich sport fishing grounds the motor boat fleet dominates. During recent high water level years there has been a great expansion in marina facilities; if water levels should drop drastically again, many berths may become inadequate for cruising boats, if not dried out. Despite this expansion, every harbor is crowded with seasonally moored boats, and in some of them there is little or no space available for transients. The cruising skipper would be wise to schedule his planned stops for those ports that do have transient docks. If you visit the others, on the chance that an absent seasonal boat's space may be available, be prepared to move on without berthing.

Lake Ontario has the smoothest shoreline of all the lakes, with very few natural harbors and anchorages. Most of them are at the northeastern end of the lake, near the St. Lawrence River. That's also where the lake's handful of islands are located. Nor do the shorelines rise very high. There are interesting bluffs along some stretches, but for the most part the coastal scenery is placidly level or gently rolling. It is the towns and their people (and the sheer pleasure of boating) that make Lake Ontario an inviting cruising area, rather than any display of natural phenomena. Our voyage in prose, counter-clockwise from the east end of the lake, begins at one of the most interesting of these.

Kingston

Charts 1459, 2005; U.S. 14768

As Fort Frontenac, a log outpost built by the count of the same name and Governor of New France in 1673, Kingston was the first European settlement on Lake Ontario. Five years later it was granted as a seigneury to René-Robert Cavelier, Sieur de La Salle, who built the first sailing ship on the Great Lakes here. For the next hundred years the outpost was a neglected wilderness backwash until a group of United Empire Loyalists from New York settled in 1784 and conferred an English name that expressed their political allegiance.

Kingston's strategic location at the confluence of Lake Ontario and the St. Lawrence River determined its history, and its history has shaped its character. Proximity to the hostile United States induced the British to establish a major naval base here. The decisive naval battle of the War of 1812 was fought not here, however, but on Lake Erie.

Kingston had another locational advantage that was put to good use. It sits on the west bank of the Cataraqui River, which rises in a chain of interior lakes that connect with the Rideau River, which flows into the Ottawa, which, in turn, reaches the St. Lawrence at Montreal. A few engineering improvements, some locks and canalization, and Canada had an internal military and commercial shipping route safe from American gunboats and shore batteries. Thus was born the Rideau Waterway in 1832. It served its original purpose only briefly before demilitarization of the lakes and enlargement of commercial vessels beyond its capacity rendered it obsolete. Pleasure boats are the grateful heirs to 19th-century military strategy.

Once embarked on a military career, the momentum was sustained in Kingston. Fort Henry, hastily constructed of logs during the War of 1812, was rebuilt in imposing stone in 1836. Twelve years later a rank of four stone Martello towers was constructed across the face of the harbor to enhance the town's protection. Happily, none of these fortifications ever saw action. After confederation in 1867 Canada needed to train its own military officers. What more appropriate location for their school than Kingston? The Royal Military College opened in 1876, Vimy Barracks army camp in 1937, and the National Defence College in 1948.

But Kingston's importance hasn't been all martial. It was the first capital of Canada, specifically of the United Provinces of Upper and Lower Canada, from 1841 to 1844, and the birthplace of Canada's first post-confederation prime minister, Sir John A. Macdonald. In the year that Queen Victoria designated the city as her provincial capital, she also chartered the university named Queen's in her honor, today one of Canada's outstanding institutions of higher learning.

All of these important public institutions and its long tradition of national stature endow Kingston with an aura of civic dignity, exemplified by its imposing limestone buildings and gracious landscaping. This city of 62,000 people, mostly occupied in education, health and government, has successfully preserved its architectural heritage as it has grown and modernized. Much of the historic is visible from the lake as you approach the harbor—Fort Henry and the Royal Military College high on their respective bluffs, the Martello towers (so named for their Corsican origin), neo-classical City Hall with its dome and clock tower, among others.

Take care not to focus on the city skyline so intently that you miss what lies at your feet. The lake near Kingston is studded with shoals. And for a little extra excitement an area of magnetic disturbance surrounds the harbor. You cannot rely on your compass here, but must carefully observe the ranges and buoys. If you're coming up the St. Lawrence River, your course is relatively clear, with a flashing red light at the end of Cedar Island, but only unlighted spar buoys to mark the east channel opening between Point Frederick Shoal and Carruthers Shoal. From the open lake there are two choices of approach.

The main light-buoyed channel from southwest passes east of Amherst Island toward Carruthers Point on a fixed red range of 046° with an orange and black daymark. At the quick flashing red off Carruthers Point you swing eastward to follow the coast inside the lighted buoys to the heavily buoyed west channel leading into the harbor. *Note:* the approach to Kingston is buoyed as if coming in from the sea on the St. Lawrence River; when you approach from south and west you leave reds to port and greens to starboard until you actually enter the harbor at Carruthers Shoal, where red-right-returning takes over. An alternative approach from the south takes you past Nine Mile Point on Simcoe Island, leaving the red buoy on Snake Island shoal to port, to the flashing green on Penitentiary Shoal where you enter the main channel.

Along the main channel from Carruthers Point you come first to **Portsmouth Olympic Harbour**, developed in 1976 when Kingston hosted the Olympic Sailing Games. A handsome example of Kingston's architecture, the 1833 federal penitentiary with its colorful blue tower tops, is a conspicuous landmark, and a fixed green light on a white tower marks the end of the breakwater entrance. Take care to come in at the correct angle parallel to the jetty; groins recently installed to dampen surge in the harbor have not yet been placed on the chart.

Although occupied by a large fleet of resident boats, both sail and power, the Harbour does have some transient dockage at floating slips with 12-foot depths. All dockside services are offered, but not all the slips are equipped with electric power. There are two launch ramps, engine, hull and rigging repairs, but only a small crane on site for haulout; a large one can be brought in if necessary. Grocery shopping and a Laundromat are in the village a few blocks away, but on the premises there is a marine store, the Harbour Restaurant and a snack bar. If you want to take a busman's holiday, the *Island Queen* excursion boat docks here. And since 1976 this is where the annual Canadian Olympic Regatta Kingston, CORK, takes place at the end of August.

Portsmouth was an independent village prior to its incorporation into Kingston in 1952 and has some beautiful limestone buildings of its own to admire as you stroll. Next door to the marina—although it's a longish walk between doors—is Lake Ontario Park, a spacious tract with rides, games and miniature golf, as well as a lakefront beach. The biggest disadvantage of the Portsmouth Olympic Harbour is its distance from the attractions of downtown Kingston, 2½ miles away. There is good bus service on King Street at the marina entrance and taxis are available, too, of course. If you and your crew are walkers, however, there is an array of interesting places to see all the way along the King Street route.

The first you'll come to on the way downtown is Bellevue House National Historic Park on Centre Street (542-3858). Sir John A. Macdonald lived briefly in the atypical Italianate house when he was a young lawyer in Kingston. A little farther on, the campus of Queen's University is a block or so north, with its collection of architectural styles and its art gallery (547-6551) and geological museum (547-2798) open to the public. To reach the campus you'll pass by the 1833 building on the grounds of the Kingston General Hospital that served as the Parliament Building when Kingston was the capital of Canada. (The hospital is associated with the University Faculty of Medicine, and the place to go if you have a medical emergency.)

On the lake side of King Street in Macdonald Park one of the remarkably constructed Martello towers, known as the Murney Tower, has been carefully preserved as a museum (542-4687). Still closer to downtown, on Ontario Street, which now follows the lakeshore, are two more unusual museums. In the Pumphouse Steam Museum the massive machinery of Kingston's 1849 water pumping station is still in working order, supplemented by models and exhibits that explain the age of steam (546-4696). The Marine Museum of the Great Lakes, Kingston's

PHOTO COURTESY OF THE GOVERNMENT OF CANADA

Full sail, Kingston, Ontario.

newest, not only salvaged the dry dock buildings of the old Kingston Shipyard, but displays artifacts that tell much of the Great Lakes maritime story (542-2261). Now you're just about downtown, but the impressive parade of 19th-century homes continues along Ontario Street all the way to City Hall.

If you followed King Street by water, you would reach the **Kingston Yacht Club**, about a mile and a half up the channel from Portsmouth Olympic Harbour. The breakwater is marked by four fixed red lights, and the dredged basin carries 6 feet. The club is more convenient to downtown but can accommodate a transient only in place of an absent member boat, either at a floating dock or on a mooring. At dockside there are the usual services, with a dining room in the attractive clubhouse. The yacht club is in a residential neighborhood, with shopping and Laundromat a bus or cab ride away.

Unless you are in need of fuel or repairs the marina of choice for a visit to Kingston is **Confederation Basin**. The mouth of the Cataraqui River, Kingston's main harbor, is flanked on the starboard side by the leafy, limestone campus of the Royal Military College and on the port side by the imposing neo classic City Hall, its dome and clock tower dramatically flood-lit at night. Underneath that landmark, in Confederation Park, is the municipal Confederation Basin Marina. A flashing green light on the end of the breakwater and a fixed red light at the end of the next wharf upriver guide you into the basin, which carries 6 feet of depth, except close to the Martello Tower where it shoals almost to 5.

At the floating finger docks there is electricity and water. Ice and pumpout are also available, but there is no fuel. On the streetside edge of the park the dignified old railroad station now houses the Chamber of Commerce on the main floor, with heads, showers and Laundromat to serve the marina below. Step into the Chamber office and pick up some of the helpful literature they have on the attractions of Kingston. The Real Estate Association puts out an especially nice leaflet of walking tours. From here a tour train begins its 10-mile circuit of the town to give you an easy and impressionistic look at the many faces of Kingston. A more authentic kind of train provides regular passenger service to Toronto and Montreal, making Kingston a convenient place to change boat crews.

Shops, services, restaurants, night clubs and movies are all within a few blocks of the marina. The Farmer's Market, set up on Tuesday, Thursday and Saturday behind City Hall, is a venerable and beloved Kingston institution. The Firehouse Restaurant, in the old firehouse of course, and the Schooner Restaurant in the quaint Frontenac Hotel both exude old-time atmosphere. For excellent French food in a gracious setting L'Auberge would be your choice. Three major hotels are located on either side of the marina, offering live evening entertainment as well as restaurants. Live theater and dance thrive in Kingston, some of it associated with Queen's University, some sponsored by independent groups. To find out what's playing while you're in town, consult the daily newspaper, *The Whig-Standard,* or the small magazine, *Kingston This Week.*

If you're still exhibit-minded after checking out the museums already mentioned, you can take a guided tour of the 1843 City Hall that watches over you in Confederation Basin. And by bus or taxi from downtown you can cross the river for a thorough look at military history. The Fort Frederick Museum is in the Martello Tower on the grounds of the Royal Military College (549-1333). The Canadian Forces Communications and Electronics Museum at the Vimy Barracks (545-5395) traces military communication from ancient times. Old Fort Henry (542-7388) was discontinued as a military post in 1890, although it housed military prisoners in two world wars. It exemplifies Kingston's military heritage as a living museum, with docents role-playing military life of the 1860s. Wednesday and Saturday nights a staged retreat includes a fife and drum concert, parade drill and mock battle before the final ceremonial flag lowering. Kingston is the town that gave birth to organized hockey in 1885, when the Royal Military College Cadets played the first game against Queen's College. That event and much more is commemorated in the International Hockey Hall of Fame and Museum, also reachable by bus or taxi toward the western outskirts of town.

The Bay of Quinte
Charts 2005, 2006, 2007, 2031, 2064, 2069

Departure from Kingston may carry you up the Rideau Waterway and off the pages of this book. Or you may head westward to the Bay of Quinte, where you'll find a decided change of pace. The Z-shaped waterway, extending almost 60 miles along its ribbon length, but only 3½ miles across at its widest, is Lake Ontario's only sheltered cruising ground—prized by locals and visitors alike. The erstwhile peninsula of Prince Edward County, with its deep bays and indentations, protects the mirrored bays and indentations of the mainland coast from the sweep of Ontario's big waves. Quinte's reaches are broad and unobstructed enough for good sailing, while its sheltered waters are rarely raised into big seas.

In 1889 the 6-mile Murray Canal was cut through the neck at the western end to transform Prince Edward County into an island, known as Quinte's Isle. Even that slim detachment from the mainland was enough to ensure that the island and the mainland would go their separate ways in development. The north, mainland side of the bay has followed the march of urban and industrial progress across the flatlands of Ontario—although there are rural pockets, to be sure. Quinte's Isle remains a pastoral haven of rolling farmlands, dotted with small villages and its low-key county seat, Picton. The crew of a cruising boat has many choices for anchorage in the more scenic eastern part of the bay and among marinas, urban and rural, throughout its length. Note that chart 2064 shows soundings in fathoms to an obsolete chart datum that requires one foot to be added to all depths displayed.

The North Channel

The approach to the Bay of Quinte from Kingston follows the North Channel separating Amherst Island from the mainland. The channel is buoyed as if a westward passage is proceeding from seaward, with reds on the starboard side. Be sure to pass northward of The Brothers Islands, which are connected to Amherst Island by a shoal known as Amherst Bar. If you get a late start, Collins Bay provides a good harbor for the night about 2 miles in. Centre Brother Island, with its flashing green light, lies off the entrance. The **Collins Bay Marina**, located in a pleasant country setting about a mile from shopping, has 7 feet at the dock and the standard list of services, although fresh water is available only at the gas dock and there is no diesel fuel.

There are some conspicuous industrial installations among the farms along the mainland shore between Collins Bay and the village of Bath, about 10 miles west. In the little cove east of town and northeast of the flashing red light buoy that marks Bath Point Shoal is the inviting **Loyalist Cove Yacht Club**. Behind its protective breakwater depths range from 4½ to 15 feet. The fixed and floating docks have the usual services, except diesel fuel. The new clubhouse has a very attractive dining room and bar, and there is a swimming pool. Although located in a residential area a long distance from town, this is a very pleasant stop.

Amherst Island is well developed with suburban and summer housing along its North Channel shore, but there is the remains of only one village, and there you will find a popular anchorage. Stella Bay presents some problems in that it is open to the northeast and the bottom is both far down (25 to 35 feet) and weedy. But if the weather is settled with favorable winds, and you put out plenty of scope on a heavy anchor, you should spend an easy night there. The bay is a little hard to spot from the east, but the ferry dock, ½ mile to the west, is a fairly obvious landmark. Kerr Bay, a mile west of Stella, is even more exposed to north and east, but your anchor can find depths of only 12 feet here; mind the rocks close to each shore.

Adolphus Reach

Upper Gap forms the 2-mile-wide opening between Amherst Island and Quinte's Isle and leads to the first of the bay's long, narrow passages, 12-mile Adolphus Reach. This is where a boat might enter directly from the open waters of Lake Ontario, following the lighted buoys between Main Duck and False Duck Islands. The Gap, too, is buoyed and lighted. As you turn the corner around Indian Point—swing wide to avoid the shoal extending in all directions from the point—to head southwest down Adolphus Reach, Prinyers Cove opens up 2 miles farther along on the port shore. This is a popular anchorage, likely to be crowded on summer weekends. Best holding is on the northwest side; the very end of the bay is weedy.

The remaining anchorages on Adolphus Reach are on its north shore toward the western end. One is behind Lyons Island, with plenty of water if entered from the western side of the island. The provincial park with launching ramp on the north side of the bay may make this a livelier spot than you might care for. Somewhat more seclusion can be found in the passage between Glen Island and the mainland about 3½ miles farther on. You can anchor toward the eastern end of that passage in 10 to 15 feet or move on into Carnachan Bay. The north side is developed with cottages, while the south shore is more wooded, but the bay gets more surge from southwest winds than the pass behind the island does.

At the western end of Adolphus Reach a ferry shuttles between Youngs Point on the mainland and the village of Glenora. Docking is not permitted at either of the ferry wharves, and the marina indicated at Glenora on the chart is suitable only for very small boats.

Picton and Long Reach

You arrive at the first zig in the Z a little past the narrows between Youngs Point and Glenora. Long Reach runs almost north and south. A turn to port carries you between the bluffs of Picton Bay for about three miles to the "metropolis" of Prince Edward County, Picton. There are a couple of mining and cement-making installations on the west side of the bay, while the east shore continues to be residential. A dredged and buoyed channel leads into the quiet harbor, which is safe for anchorage in 10 to 12 feet.

There are a couple of choices for dockside accommodation. The **Prince Edward Yacht Club** is on the west side of the bay, at the narrows formed by Brick Kiln Point. Adjacent to the club there is a government dock with floating slips in 12-foot depths, where electricity and water are provided. The club's facilities— docks, showers, dining room and bar—are open to members of recognized yacht clubs. At the end of the bay, in a park setting close to downtown shops and restaurants, is the **Picton Municipal Marina**, with floating slips, all dockside services and a launch ramp. A Laundromat and food stores can be found within a few blocks, but the beer and liquor stores are located on the outskirts of town. There is taxi service available.

Picton, with a population of about 4,300, is a customs port of entry and, as the principal town of the area, has a large and attractive downtown shopping district. In earlier days it was an important port; its residential streets are graced with the handsome Victorian mansions that speak of the fortunes made here. The Prince Edward County Museum, at Church and Union streets (476-3833), occupies an 1823 church and includes the rectory next door. One of the period's most imposing structures is almost adjacent to the town dock. Villeneuve Castle was an ordinary Ontario farmhouse when it was built in the first decade of the 19th century. Then, in 1860, the prominent lawyer who had bought the property transformed it into a French Gothic chateau and named it for his wife's cousin, the admiral who was defeated by Nelson at Trafalgar. Today it is a restaurant, serving well-prepared food at lunch and dinner. Reservations are necessary.

Picton is a quiet town, representative of its surroundings, but there is one lively annual event that has been taking place since 1937. On Canada Day weekend the Gold Cup powerboat races attract contestants from all over North America; the prizes run to five figures.

Long Reach extends for some 10 miles northward from Picton Bay. Its west side is high, much of it densely wooded and, beyond the cement plant, pleasant anchorage can be had in several of the indentations when the wind blows northwest through southwest. Hay Bay opens to the northeast between Thompson Point and Shermans Point and extends some 10 miles into low-lying farm and cottage country. The shoal making out from Shermans Point is marked by a spar and readily avoided. A half-moon anchorage east of Witlow Point affords protection from all except north winds in 15 feet. In moving up the bay, stay close to the black spar buoys near Ram Island, in order to avoid the 5-foot spot east of it; then anchor on the northeast side of the island. This is obviously not a good place if the wind is northeast. The fishing in Hay Bay, as in most parts of the Bay of Quinte, can be very rewarding. Yellow pickerel, walleyed pike in American parlance, is often plentiful, along with large- and smallmouth bass.

Deseronto

At its northern end Long Reach widens into Mohawk Bay and on the north shore is the village of Deseronto. At the turn of the century it was the site of a flourishing lumber and match industry, but today it is a rather forlorn, old village with about 1500 people and mostly vacant stores. Desoronto does have friendly **Quinte Marina**, however, with full service and repair facilities as well as the full range of dockside services. The old wood finger docks are not too inviting, but there are newer floating slips, in 11 feet of water. Be sure to stay precisely in the buoyed channel leading to the marina, as there are submerged cribs on either side. If you need a haulout, there is both railway and travelift to 30-ton capacity. Grocery shopping and Laundromat are not far away, once you cross the tracks and climb the hill. Although the town has little to commend it, you can take a pleasant side trip up the buoyed Napanee River for about 6 marsh-bordered miles to the town of Napanee. The controlling depth is 5 feet, but the government dock at Napanee reports only 4 feet alongside.

Telegraph Narrows to Belleville

The Bay of Quinte zags again at Deseronto and continues a generally westerly course to its far end. The intensively buoyed channel at Telegraph Narrows, enlarged on a chart inset, should give you no trouble at all. Just remember that you are proceeding from the sea when you move westward. In fact, the rest of the bay is rather heavily buoyed; unlike the reaches you've been cruising, this part has many more shoal areas. The land also tends to be more low-lying. The north shore becomes increasingly nonscenic, while the Prince Edward County side continues pleasant and pastoral.

About 5 miles beyond Telegraph Narrows the waterway widens into Big Bay. On the south shore about where this occurs there is an appealing country marina on Big Island. A flashing red and green light on the end of the wharf marks the entrance to **Baycrest Marina**. The harbor is man-made and Baycrest was one of the first marinas to grace the Bay of Quinte when it was built 40 years ago. The wooden finger slips are in good condition, with 7 foot depths alongside, and all dockside services are available except diesel fuel. Full repair services are offered, with haulout capacity by both travelift and railway to 40 tons. The yard specializes in wood, and you can order a custom-made teak or mahogany wheel for your boat. The friendly proprietors will provide transportation to Picton, if necessary (the closest place for shopping, 12 miles away). If you like to walk, there are enticing country roads to wander.

Belleville

From Big Island it's a little over 7 miles to Belleville, and back to a bit of city life. With 35,000 people, Belleville is the largest town on the bay and earns its living through a remarkable variety of manufacturing and processing enterprises. Are you a fan of Black Diamond cheese? Here's where it comes from— along with Pampers and tennis rackets and a few dozen other things. Belleville's waterfront does not present a grimy, industrial scene, however. Except for a collection of oil storage tanks at the entrance, the harbor is devoted mainly to pleasure boats.

From the east a big plant about a mile and a half out of town is a good landmark, and from either direction the new, high bridge at the west edge of the city will tell you when you're there. When approaching from the west, take special care not to shortcut the buoyed channels; the harbor is fronted by shoals. The harbor buoyage is traditional, reds to starboard on entering. When you reach the flashing red light buoy that marks the approach there are three ways to go. The easternmost channel, carrying 12 feet, leads to a public wharf with a fixed green light on a white tower at the end of the rubble breakwater extending from it. Inside that breakwater a dredged basin is under development as a city marina. When completed it will have floating slips and all dockside services, but its location is inconveniently distant from downtown.

If you follow the next channel westward into the main harbor, it divides at the tip of a peninsula, forming Victoria Park. The starboard channel leads to a long basin dredged to a depth of 6 feet. On the port side, near the outer end of the peninsula, is the **Bay of Quinte Yacht Club**. It has a little alongside dockage in 7 feet, but no other services except its friendly dining room and bar. The remainder of the basin is occupied by city dockage, with both fixed and floating slips, electric power and water, heads, showers and laundry facilities. On the east side of the basin **The Pilots Marine** supplies gas, diesel, pumpout, water, and ice, and has a full marine store. They do not have overnight dockage.

The westernmost of the three channels leads into the mouth of the Moira River. Do not attempt to cross between the channels inside the buoys—a nasty shoal makes out from the peninsula dividing the river and the basin. The buoyed river channel, with a least depth of 7 feet, leads to **Morch Marine**, with 8 feet of water at the slips and all dockside services. The travelift has a capacity of 25 tons. This is where sailboats transiting the Trent-

Severn Waterway can get their masts stepped or unstepped, as there are no commercial facilities for it at Trenton. On the same property are Bob McKie Marine, which specializes in engine repairs; C. Keeble sailmakers, who do all kinds of canvas work; a marine store; and The Wheelhouse Restaurant. On your way to Morch you passed the handsome **Four Seasons Hotel** on the port side. It has dockage that entitles the visitor to the hotel privileges of pool, sauna and tennis courts. The hotel's dining and cocktail facilities with live entertainment are, of course, open to the public.

All of the dockage described, except the outermost east basin, is within a few blocks of downtown shopping, restaurants and movies. Tuesday, Thursday and Saturday mornings there is a farmers' market behind City Hall. Trotting and pacing races take place every Friday night at the Quinte Exhibition and Raceway, located at the west end of town. There is a bus system in Belleville, but you may need a taxi for the races. The Hastings County Museum, an 1883 mansion at 257 Bridge Street East (962-2329) is within longish walking distance of the harbor. Belleville is a convenient place to change boat crews, as it is served by both rail between Toronto and Montreal and inter-city bus. It also has a hospital.

Trenton

It's a dozen miles from Belleville to Trenton, a town of 15,000 people that, like all the others in this neighborhood, was founded by United Empire Loyalists crossing over from the United States in the 1780s and 1790s. The main attraction of Trenton for most cruising boats is the Trent-Severn Waterway that begins here to wind 240 scenic miles to Georgian Bay. The city's marine facilities are at the mouth of the Trent River, below the series of bridges that cross the waterway.

The approach to Trenton, from either direction, is fraught with shoals. It is essential to note all channel buoys and stay within their confines. From the east you will pass through The Narrows, close to the Prince Edward County shore; from Way Point the channel into Trenton, marked by both lighted and unlighted buoys, will open up. If you're coming from the west, take care to pass close along the steep Prince Edward County shore south of Indian Island and Indian Island Bank before you head for the Trenton channel from the Onderdonk Point flashing red light buoy. The channel charted west of Indian Island carries three feet or less in heavy weeds and is not recommended to strangers.

Remember as you approach the harbor after you pass Onderdonk Point that you are returning from the sea and that red buoys will be left to starboard.

There are two quite new and well-built public marinas in Trenton. On the starboard side, just before you enter the river, is **Centennial Park Marina** behind its own breakwater, with floating slips, electricity, water, heads and showers. There is 6 feet in the entrance, 4 in the basin. An attractive setting in a large park that includes childrens' playground, picnic grills and tennis courts, and an elaborate fireworks display on Canada Day, it's a long distance from any commercial services, but a pleasant overnight stop.

Just into the river, on the port side, **Fraser Park Marina** is located in a small park setting, right in the downtown area. It has steel floating slips in 8 feet and all dockside services. This is the preferred location for access to stores, Laundromat, restaurants and the movies. Trenton is a customs port of entry, has a hospital and a passenger station on the Toronto to Montreal rail line. There are no marine haulout or repair services. Nor is there a great deal to do or see, except to walk the pleasant streets of the town.

Trenton has a number of manufacturing and food processing enterprises, but it's most well-known establishment is the Canadian Forces Base at the east edge of town. Built as an air base during the Depression, this was the main training center for pilots and aircraft crews of the Royal Canadian Air Force during World War II. Now it is the largest Air Transport Command in Canada, although it no longer performs a training function. It is also the home of the Rescue Coordination Center that means so much to boating safety on the Great Lakes. Once a year, in late August or early September, the base is opened to visitors and the RCAF mounts a spectacular air show, with participants from U.S. and European air forces as well. If you're in town at this time (392-2811 for information), you can get a taxi out to the base.

Better yet, be right on the premises with a stop at the friendly **CFB Yacht Club**, where you can get all of the dockside services, except diesel, at either a fixed or floating slip with 5½-foot depths. There are also moorings, which have no electricity, of course. The club is located in the cove on the north side of Baker Island, identified from offshore by the big water tower with a revolving light on top. A buoyed channel, carring 5½-feet, leads to the breakwater sheltering the basin. The clubhouse has a lounge for sociability, and for sailboats transiting the Trent-

Severn Waterway there is a do-it-yourself mast-stepping crane that can handle a spar up to 45 feet.

The Murray Canal and Presqu'île Bay

A few miles past Trenton the 5-mile, lake level Murray Canal leads to Presqu'île Bay and harbors west. Entrance from the Bay of Quinte, via the southside channel from Onderdonk Point to Twelve O'Clock Point, is straightforward. The canal entrance is marked by flashing white Twelve O'Clock Point Light on the north pier; a similar light marks the western end at Sherwood Point. Three swing bridges cross the canal, and each of them shows a red light when closed, green when open. The railway bridge near the eastern end is usually left open, and the bridge tenders at the two highway bridges are so alert to oncoming boats that you rarely have to rouse them with the official three-blast whistle signal. Pass on the south side of each bridge opening, irrespective of your direction of travel. That's where you'll find the 7-foot controlling depth of the canal and its approach channels. In a stiff west wind there can be a strong current through the narrow pass at these bridges.

The canal is operated by Parks Canada from mid-May to mid-October, from 0830 to 2030 late June to late August, shorter hours earlier and later in the season. It affords a valuable shortcut for boaters cruising between the Bay of Quinte and westward harbors, but there is one sometimes serious disadvantage. Presque'île Bay at its western terminus suffers a stubborn weed problem. A variety of measures have been taken by the government to keep the buoyed channels clear, but don't stray beyond them. Nor is anchorage advised in the bay.

For an overnight stop in Presqu'île Bay there are a couple of choices. At the western end of the canal there is a tie-up wall, convenient for boats arriving too late in the day to transit the canal eastbound. After you follow the buoyed channel westward from the canal for about 4½ miles you will turn on the Brighton range—an isophase white front light backed by a fixed red rear light, both bearing orange and black daymarks. Entering Presqu'île Bay from the open lake, this conspicuous range brings you in on a course of 295°. If you turn in this direction from the canal channel, you will enter the buoyed channel with 6-foot depth that leads to the **Brighton Marina**. There are floating docks with 4 feet at low water, and all services are offered, including Laundromat, a travelift, and repairs. There is a convenience store and the Galley Restaurant on the premises, but the marina is several miles from the village of Brighton and additional commercial services.

If you exit Presqu'île Bay after leaving the Murray Canal, you will turn to port on the reciprocal of the range, a course of 115°, and follow a well-buoyed channel to the red and white Mo(A) sea buoy off Presqu'île Point. There is a narrow squeak between Salt Point on the peninsula side and the wide shoals making out from the Prince Edward shore. A flashing red light on a white tower marks Salt Reef. Presqu'île Bay is buoyed like the Bay of Quinte and the Murray Canal, with reds on the starboard side heading westward. *Note:* the entrance to the bay from open Lake Ontario is also buoyed that way. Thus on the exit you are "returning from the sea," but if you're cruising eastward along the lake, you will leave the reds to port on entering Presqu'île Bay. If you've just crossed the lake from the American side, there is a seasonal customs officer at the government dock west of Salt Point. A 7-foot channel leads to it, but there are no services.

A Strand of Harbors

Charts 2058, 2060, 2061, 2070

The Bay of Quinte is more than a delightful cruising ground to play around in. For boats passage-making on Lake Ontario's north shore between the Kingston/Thousand Islands area and the mid-lake or western harbors it is a vital connecting waterway. It's only about 25 miles from Presqu'île Harbour to Cobourg, the next port west, but from Kingston to Cobourg on the outside of Prince Edward County the distance is over 100 miles. The only feasible places to put in along this outer route are near the eastern end of it. Local boats anchor behind Waupoos Island on the north side of Prince Edward Bay. Approach from the south and move up the west side of the island in 12 feet, to anchor on the northwest side in 10. At the eastern end of Long Point is a small harbor used by commercial fishermen. There are depths in the harbor of 5 to 7 feet, but the tricky channel leading to it, between Point Traverse and Prince Edward Point, shoals to 2 in places. The Long Point area is well marked by aids to navigation, as islands and shoals extend eastward from it into the shipping lanes. False Ducks Islands Light, a red and white banded tower on the east point of Swetman Island, displays a flashing red light and has a fog horn. On Prince Edward Point there is a white skeleton tower with a flashing white light. East and south of these lights buoys mark some of the shoals.

This area is not recommended to strangers, and if you are making a long passage from (or to) the eastern end of the lake, you would be wise to give a wide berth to the outer shores of Prince Edward County. The coastline itself is low and swampy, with no harbor for a cruising boat to put into, yet there are offlying banks and shoals to skirt. Point Petre Light, a flashing white displayed from a red and white banded tower and equipped with a fog horn; Scotch Bonnet Island Light, flashing white from a white skeleton tower; and Proctor Point Light, flashing yellow from a white tower with red top, are all helpful guideposts to trace from offshore. Once past Proctor Point you can coast the even shoreline of Lake Ontario almost all the rest of the way around.

Cobourg

Cobourg is an important harbor for cruising boats because it is one of the few ports on this stretch of coast that combines a well-found marina with easy access to supplies and services. Furthermore, it's an attractive town. A collection of oil storage tanks on the west side of the harbor and a handsome clock tower rising above the trees help to identify Cobourg from offshore, as does a range of fixed red lights displayed from white, orange and black painted masts on a course of 007°. The artificial harbor is protected by two lighted breakwaters, and an inner breakwater, with a flashing white light on the *T* pier opposite, offers additional protection to **Cobourg Marina**, which lies in the northwest corner of the inner harbor. Operated by the town, the marina has both fixed and floating slips and offers all dockside services, including a Laundromat, but no haulout or repairs. Cobourg is a customs port of entry for boats crossing Lake Ontario.

Although the town of 11,000 people is a manufacturing center, there is little evidence of this at the waterfront. You'll recognize the largest employer if the wind is blowing right and carries the nostalgic aroma of Jell-O. A couple of blocks' walk from the marina leads to the heart of downtown, with full shopping, including a supermarket and specialty food stores, restaurants, and the movie theater. There is also a hospital.

Cobourg is a town for walking, and the Local Architectural Conservation Advisory Committee has published a walking tour guide (available at the marina office) to its treasury of handsome 19th-century buildings. Victoria Hall was one of the most impressive buildings in Canada when it was dedicated in 1860 by no less a personage than the Prince of Wales, later crowned King Edward VII. In addition to serving as the town hall and local courthouse (the courtroom is a replica of London's Old Bailey), it also houses artifacts of the town's history and the collection of the Art Gallery of Northumberland (372-0333). A recent multi-million-dollar renovation of the still impressive building has restored the original opera house as The Grand Hall that will seat 300 people for all kinds of meetings and performances. Only a few blocks from the marina, it is well worth a visit.

There is a remarkable theatrical tradition in Cobourg. Marie Dressler was born here in 1868, an actress who went on to Broadway fame and the 1931 Academy Award for Best Actress in films. The 1833 house in which she grew up, an easy walk from the marina, is now a fine restaurant. In the same tradition another famous comedienne, Beatrice Lillie, who later became Lady Peel, was born in Cobourg in 1898. And the woman who was honored for decades as the first lady of the American theater, Katharine Cornell, spent her childhood summers at her Buffalo family's summer home here. It is said that she participated in local theater groups then, and local theater groups continue to flourish. Check the newspaper for performances scheduled during your visit.

For outdoor recreation Victoria Park, a few blocks along the waterfront from the marina, has a sand beach, swimming and wading pools, a children's playground, lawn-bowling green, and band shell where the Cobourg Concert Band performs on Tuesday evenings. A lovely floral clock graces the grounds. A few blocks farther east is Donegan Park, where the first Saturday in July the annual Highland Games encompass a variety of competitions and performances. Canada Week includes fireworks, and the special events of August consist of sidewalk sales downtown, along with games and children's rides, during the first week, and the Quench Run, sponsored by General Foods, on the third Saturday.

Port Hope

The 19th-century architecture of Port Hope is even more exquisitely preserved than that of Cobourg, but for the maritime visitor the allure of the town of 10,000 people is obscured by its industry-wrapped waterfront. Part of the harbor is a man-made basin, and part is the dredged mouth of the Ganaraska River; both are lined with concrete bulkheads. The river side, where the public marina is located, can be restless when there is a strong flow, and both parts of the harbor suffer from surge in a south wind, as well as a silting problem. For all these reasons, plus the noise of surrounding plants and trains rattling across the waterfront bridges, Port Hope is not a place to head for, except as necessary overnight shelter.

On the approach from the east there is one hazard, Peter Rock, partly awash a half mile offshore and connected by a white tower with red top. Port Hope itself is lighted by a range on 320° shown from white, orange and black towers with an isophase green front light and a fixed green rear light. The front light is on the west breakwater opposite a flashing red light on the east breakwater.

Contrary to appearances on the chart, the east arm of the harbor, the Ganaraska River mouth, has been dredged to six feet in its lower reaches. This is the location of the **Port Hope Marina**, which has dockage alongside the concrete bulkhead in a very narrow basin. There is gas, electricity and water. In the north-east corner of the west basin, also dredged to about 6 feet, is the **Port Hope Yacht Club**. Visitors may be accommodated at along-side dockage on the concrete bulkheads surrounding the basin or on one of the moorings that fill the center. The pumpout is in this basin and the small clubhouse has heads and showers. Port Hope has a hospital, is a customs port of entry and also a stop on the passenger rail and inter-city bus lines. Once you walk under the two railroad trestles and highway bridge there are two large supermarkets a few blocks from the harbor; downtown is about a half mile away.

Newcastle

The clay banks that began to rise along the shore at Cobourg are elevated into bluffs west of Port Hope that continue more or less unbroken to Toronto. They form the lakeshore edge of a flat, mostly agricultural plateau. About 15 miles from Port Hope little Graham Creek cuts through the bluff. The entrance has been improved to lead to a dredged basin just west of the creek, where a channel between the two breakwaters has been dredged to 6 feet or more. The channel is rather narrow and has a dog-leg to port, designed to eliminate surge in the basin of the **Port of Newcastle Marina**, dredged to 6 to 8 feet. (Take care not to run straight into Graham Creek; you'll run out of water.) On the west breakwater a flashing yellow light is displayed over a rotating one. The harbor is not easy to spot from offshore, but the cement plant 6 miles west gives a clue.

The marina is a relatively new one, with all dockside services except pumpout. There is an open-ended travelift of 15-ton capacity, but no repair services on the premises. The Newcastle Yacht Club, which uses the marina facilities, has a clubhouse with snack bar. And there are two tennis courts and children's swings on the property. The setting is one of appealing rural lakeside isolation for overnight stops, if you don't need shops or other commercial services located in the pretty village of Newcastle a couple of miles away.

Port Darlington

The cement plant referred to above is an even better landmark for Port Darlington, only 4 miles west of Newcastle. Here Bowmanville Creek has been dredged to 6 feet and jetties extend into the lake. A white tower with black top on the west breakwater shows a flashing green light. The rather narrow channel is buoyed for the ½-mile passage upstream to the **Port Darlington Marina Hotel**. Here there is accommodation for a fair number of boats at slips with 6- to 8-foot depths and all dockside services except fresh water and diesel fuel, but including Laundromat. The complex includes storage, hull and engine repair facilities, and the travelift can haul out up to 20 tons. The hotel has an attractive dining room and bar, a small swimming pool and a volleyball court, all available to boat guests. From here it's several miles to the nearest town, Bowmanville, for shopping, so Port Darlington, too, is best considered as an overnight stop.

Oshawa

With General Motors of Canada headquartered here, Oshawa is an auto town, but the city of 117,500 has a number of other industries as well, and its port is one that continues commercially active. Nevertheless, there are excellent facilities for pleasure boats at the **Port Oshawa Marina**.

It's less than 10 miles from Port Darlington to Oshawa, but the coastal bluffs have lowered to beach and marsh by the time you get there. The harbor can be spotted from offshore by the oil storage tanks flanking the entrance between breakwaters. A range on the west pier bears 327° between white, black and orange towers that display an isophase green light from the front and a fixed green from the rear. The front light is also equipped with a fog whistle. The 30-foot-deep channel is buoyed to the marina, entered from the northwest corner of the harbor.

In addition to all dockside services and slips with 6- to 8-foot depths, Port Oshawa Marina is a full service yard, including rigging and sail repair, with an open-end travelift capacity of 40 tons. There is a launch ramp, marine store, snack bar, children's playground, small swimming pool, and picnic area. The Oshawa Yacht Club, tenants of the marina, invites members of recognized yacht clubs to the lounge and bar of their clubhouse on one of the pierheads.

This assortment of facilities at the marina offsets in part its three-mile distance from downtown. There is bus service on Simcoe Street, one block from the harbor, however, and taxis are also available. The nearest food, liquor and hardware shopping is at a mall 1 mile away, and the marina can arrange a courtesy car for you to get there. But Oshawa is a city with several interesting places to visit in town by bus or cab.

For car buffs there is not only the Canadian Automotive Museum at 99 Simcoe Street South (576-1222), but General Motors gives plant tours. Call 644-5000 to make arrangements. Parkwood, the palatial mansion and gardens of the man who founded General Motors of Canada in 1918, Colonel Robert S. McLaughlin, at 270 Simcoe Street North (579-1311), is well worth a visit. You can take lunch or tea there at the Teahouse in the Italian Garden. (On a more somber note, the hospital is adjacent to the Parkwood estate, if you need medical service.) Two other historic house museums are closer to the marina on Lakeshore and Simcoe (728-6331). The McLaughlin Art Gallery in the Civic Centre downtown features contemporary Canadian art (576-3000).

For entertainment there are a number of restaurants, cocktail lounges, movies, concerts, and a little theater group. Consult the daily *Oshawa Times*. There is a weekly band concert in Memorial Park at Simcoe and John streets downtown, and Fiesta Week in June is a multi-ethnic fair of food, crafts and performances. For outdoor recreation Lakeview Park, a couple of blocks west of the marina (though a bit of a walk around to it), has a beach, swimming pool, and tennis courts. Oshawa is a good place to change boat crews. Not only is there long-distance passenger train and bus service, but also the Go Train into Toronto.

Whitby

If you'd like a more rural setting for an overnight stop, Whitby harbor, just 5 miles from Oshawa, is a good alternative. The tall chimney of the Ontario Hospital west of the harbor is a conspicuous landmark, and a fixed red range on white, orange and black towers on the east pier leads you in at 353°. There is also a flashing green light on the port breakwater extension. The east side of the outer part of the harbor is used as a ship repair yard, but a buoyed channel leads beyond that to the **Port Whitby Marina** at the north end of the harbor or the **Whitby Yacht Club** on the south side. Be sure to stay in the channel, with about 13 feet of depth. The floating docks of the marina are also in 13 feet, and all dockside services are available, including launch ramp. A travelift can haul out up to 35 tons. There are no repair facilities on site, but personnel can be called in; there is a big boatyard across the street.

The Whitby Yacht Club has both floating docks and moorings available to members of recognized yacht clubs. All dockside services are offered, and the clubhouse dining room is open weekends and Wednesday evenings. The club is in a remote location at the end of the sand spit enclosing the harbor, but there is a beach to play on.

Whitby's harbor is several miles from town, but less than half a mile from the marina there is a convenience store and restaurant. Half a mile the other way is Iroquois Park, with tennis court and swimming pool. There is a hospital just beyond it.

Frenchman's Bay

Frenchman's Bay, about 8 miles west of Whitby, may come as a surprise to strangers. It is a spacious body of water that accommodates some 1,200 boats, yet there is no chart enlargement of the harbor and only one sea buoy and one unusual light to let you know you're there. The reason is that the entire harbor, including the lake bottom, is privately owned. Nevertheless, it is not hard to locate from the big nuclear power plant less than a mile to the east, a conspicuous tower on the west side, and the red and white Mo(A) sea buoy a mile offshore. The harbor is formed by sandbars from which parallel breakwaters extend lakeward. Head straight down the middle between the breakwaters on entering, as the remains of old piers extend from the ends just beneath the surface. A white skeleton tower with orange daymark sits at the base of the east pier and displays an isophase white, red and green light. When the white sector is visible to you you're on the proper course of 358° to 001°; if you see red, you're too far east, and green indicates that you're too far west. This harbor, like most of the others, has a silting problem, but the owners dredge through the channel periodically to 6 to 8 feet.

Three marinas are lined up on the east shore of the bay. The first is **Keen Kraft Marina**, with older wood finger docks and all dockside services, including Laundromat. The open-end travelift has a 35-ton capacity. All hull repairs are taken care of on the premises; Merlan Marine next door is called in for engine work. **Moore Haven Marina** is next, with steel floating docks, 6 feet alongside, electricity, ice, pumpout, gas and diesel. There is a 35-ton open-end travelift, but no repairs are offered on site. Lastly, **East End Marina** has both alongside docking and floating slips, with depths ranging from 4 to 8 feet. All dockside services are offered, except fuel, which is supplied by Moore Haven next door. The travelift here has a 15-ton capacity; as at Moore Haven, craftsmen are called in for repair work. The Pickering Yacht Club is associated with the marina and has a small clubhouse open to members of recognized clubs. On Liverpool Road, within half a mile of the marinas, is a convenient little shopping center, with a Laundromat and, among others, Massey's attractively trendy and informal restaurant and bar.

On the west side of Frenchman's Bay, in a residential area remote from any commercial services, is the **Frenchman's Bay Yacht Club**, with dockage, electricity, water and heads. There is a natural wooded area adjacent to the club, if you like to walk.

Toronto

Charts 2062, 2085

One of the most dynamic and cosmopolitan cities in North America spreads its arms wide in welcome to visitors by boat. Toronto has adorned its 20 miles of lakefront with parks that host 15 marinas and yachts clubs and has transformed its downtown waterfront into a movable feast of cultural and recreational amenities, with ample attention to the waterborne tourist. Add to this a superb public transport system that whisks you quickly and pleasantly to the myriad attractions and activities throughout the nation's largest city from any of its harbors and you have a cruising destination par excellence.

One of the first things you'll hear about Toronto is that it wasn't always such an exciting place. A mere 25 years ago it was Dullsville, a joke among travelers. But Canada's rising post-World War II prosperity, coupled with its hospitality to throngs of immigrants from all over the world—many of them sophisticated urbanites before they came—projected the staid old city into the post-modern world and beyond. The miracle of Toronto still leaves some of us gasping, and the ebullience of its futurism is almost palpable on the city's streets. *New* is the single word that comes to mind—new buildings, new ideas, new concepts of urban lifestyle. Yet the most remarkable feature of the city's renaissance is that it has not discarded its heritage in a rush to the future. Rather, it has retained its neighborhood quality and many of its historic places; even the explosive downtown developments that thrust dramatically skyward seem to organize themselves into identifiable neighborhoods. Consequently, Toronto is a city to walk in—by neighborhood.

Heart of downtown is the City Hall complex. The turreted 1899 version, with gargoyles modeled after the city councillors with whom the architect quarreled, faces the 1965 ode to glass and steel across the landscaped expanse of Nathan Phillips Square. Here all Toronto gathers to meet, stroll, listen to band concerts or watch ice skating, according to whim and season. A couple of blocks away is the crystal palace of Eaton Centre, a vaulted glass dome enclosing the four-level Galleria of artfully staggered shops, embellished by fountains and live shrubbery, with access to Eaton's, the famous department store. Between and around these landmarks the skyscrapers soar and purposeful people pursue the city's and the nation's business. In the interstices some historic buildings remain, and sprinkled throughout is a selection of excellent restaurants.

Toronto is a feast, both figuratively and literally. Its recently established, yet already hallowed, gastronomic tradition is exemplified in each of its neighborhoods, where every ethnic dining experience can be sampled from Argentinian to Vietnamese. A stroll through the several ethnic neighborhoods affords interesting shopping of all kinds, as well as eating. Not the least fascinating of these is Chinatown, centered on Dundas Street just a few blocks west of Eaton Centre, where the succulent roast ducks hanging in the shop windows and the aroma of exotic creations emanating from restaurant kitchens make it hard to focus on sights. Yet the excellent Art Gallery of Ontario is located here (977-0414), and within its grounds The Grange, a graceful 1817 mansion, presents a refreshing contrast to the sleek modernity a few blocks away.

There are, in fact, a number of fine house museums to visit. The most dramatic is the extravagant 98-room, 1914 gothic castle, Casa Loma, complete with secret staircase (923-1171). This requires a subway ride to a residential location, but you should take at least one ride on Toronto's subway anyway. Among the variety of other museums to visit, one of the most outstanding is the Ontario Science Centre (429-4100), with hands-on displays that delight children and adults. Unfortunately, it involves a longer subway and bus ride from the waterfront, as does Toronto's splendid zoo (284-0123). The Royal Ontario Museum, on the other hand (978-3692), with its immense natural history displays and fabled Chinese collection, is close to downtown in another specialized neighborhood. This is Queen's Park, the seat of provincial government, where you can tour the pink Romanesque Parliament Buildings (965-4028). Close by is the shaded campus of the University of Toronto, known as Varsity to its aficionados. The next neighborhood north from Queen's Park is Yorkville, between Avenue Road and Yonge Street, just north of Bloor. Once an independent village, it is now a colorful enclave of townhouses, boutiques, art galleries, sidewalk cafes and some of the city's most appreciated restaurants.

After you've gawked, shopped and eaten your fill, Toronto regales you with an infinite variety of entertainments. In addition to the many night clubs with live entertainment, there are some 40 professional theater groups in the city. The venerable Royal Alexandria Theatre and the sleek St. Lawrence Centre are but two of the many locales for theatrical productions of all kinds. Roy Thomson Hall is the new home of the Toronto Symphony Orchestra, although 1894 Massey Hall, with its excellent acoustics, continues in active use. O'Keefe Centre is where the National Ballet and the Canadian Opera Company mount their performances. All of these auditoria are centrally located, along with many movie theaters. To find out what's going on while you're in town consult *The Toronto Star, The Globe and Mail, The Toronto Sun*, or the monthly magazines *Toronto Life* and *Key to Toronto*.

There is so much to do and see in Toronto that only a small sampling can be presented here, and that relates only to the most central portion of the city. The waterfront is an extravaganza in a class by itself. It will be included in the sequence of harbor descriptions. Clearly one could spend an entire cruising vacation in Toronto, but no matter how long you decide to stay, you should stop in at one of the city's tourist information centers and pick up some of the informative literature and maps that will enable you to make the most of your time. The main office is in Eaton Centre, but there are summer centers in Nathan Phillips Square, at the CN Tower, and on Queen's Quay at the ferry docks. Or you can write in advance to Metropolitan Toronto Convention and Visitors Association, 220 Yonge St., Suite 110, Box 510, Toronto, Ontario M5B 2H1. Be sure to ask for the Toronto Transit Commission *Ride Guide*. It's an excellent map of the downtown and regional transit system—an exact fare system, by the way, so carry the right change. The commission also publishes a handy booklet explaining how to reach each of the city's major attractions; it's entitled *Exciting Toronto by TTC*. If your time is very limited, you might want to consider one of the various bus tours operated by Gray Line (979-3511) or a trolley tour on a vintage streetcar (869-1372.)

Now to get you there by boat. The land begins to rise again west of Frenchman's Bay to reach the 380-foot heights of Scarborough Bluffs. At the foot of the cliff is the easternmost of Toronto's parks at Bluffers Bay, about 5 miles from Frenchman's. The artificial harbor is enclosed by the arms of a landfill. While government authorities created the harbor and developed the parkland, the marine facilities were fashioned through an unusual cooperative federation of four yacht clubs, much of the labor contributed by the members themselves. The Scarborough Sailing Club is a dry land club for small boats, but the other three offer hospitality to visitors. The dome of St. Augustine's Seminary high on the bluff is the conspicuous landmark for the harbor. The entrance channel is dredged to 8 feet and buoyed, but the harbor is so new that the navigation lighting is not yet permanently in place.

Dockage for the three yacht clubs is arranged in a fan around two lobes of a peninsula thrusting from the north shore. The closest to seaward, on the west side, is **Bluffers Park Yacht Club**, which welcomes members of reciprocating clubs. Visitors are accommodated at alongside berths, with 6 to 8 feet of depth, electricity, water and pumpout. There is no fuel, but there are heads, and ice is available. The clubhouse that will contain showers is still under construction. **Highland Yacht Club**, next door, has completed its clubhouse with heads and showers and a members' lounge and supplies electricity, water, ice and pumpout at dockside. On the east arm **Cathedral Bluffs Yacht Club** offers all dockside services, except fuel, at finger slips with 10 feet of depth. Its clubhouse is still a temporary structure.

Bluffers Park is in the suburb of Scarborough, which became part of Metropolitan Toronto in 1953. It is 9 miles from downtown, with bus service on Kingston Road. The trick is to reach Kingston Road, a long, steep climb up the cliff that can raise the pulse rate of even an avid mountaineer. Unless a kind club member opens his car door for you, don't plan on leaving the harbor by land when you dock at Bluffer's Bay.

At Ashbridge's Bay Park, another 5 miles west, the scenery is not so impressive, but the location is somewhat more convenient. From here on, however, you may find dock space hard to come by. All of the Toronto area harbors are crowded, and it is wise to make advance reservations if you can. The bluffs you've been tracing along the lakeshore now give way to the low, flat terrain of Lake Ontario's west end. Ashbridge's Bay, too, is an artificial harbor, created from landfill. It is identifiable from offshore by the tall chimney of the sewage treatment plant on the west side. The **Ashbridge's Bay Yacht Club**, open to members of recognized yacht clubs, is located in a basin behind a lighted spit of land close to the entrance. Twelve- to 14-foot depths carry to the club's docks, both finger slips and alongside docking, where all services are offered, including Laundromat. There is also a railway that can haul to 35 feet, but no repair services on the premises. The clubhouse is large and attractive, with dining room and bar. The surrounding park has a public launch ramp and tennis courts, and farther up Coatsworth Cut into the park the **Toronto Hydroplane and Sailing Club** has floating docks for the smaller boats of reciprocal club members. It's a bit of a walk to the park entrance, but there is local shopping within half a mile from there and a streetcar on Queen Street, one block away, to whisk you downtown.

At Ashbridge's Bay the commercial and industrial sector of Toronto's harbor begins. So effective is the planning in this federal city of over 2,000,000 people that virtually all of these facilities are now concentrated in a 5-mile stretch of harborfront. As part of the long-term redevelopment program a landfill has been built southwestward from the eastern end of the main harbor area to form a large outer harbor. The inside of this Outer Harbour East Headland (also known as the Leslie Street Spit) is under gradual development as Aquatic Park. A few local sailing clubs use it, but there are no transient facilities yet.

Coming from the east, it's necessary to head offshore a bit to skirt this peninsula. It is well marked by navigation lights along its outer fringes. At the end of the Headland, marked by a flashing red light on a white tower with red top, is the Main Harbour Channel, well buoyed and ranged with isophase red lights on towers that display brilliant orange and black daymarks on a course of 002°. Eastern Gap leads from the Outer Harbour through a walled passage, lit at both ends, to the large Inner Harbour. From here ships proceed to the piers on the north side or move eastward through the Ship Channel to a long stretch of berthing facilities.

Inner Harbour is enclosed by a group of islands, the largest of which was attached to the mainland until an 1858 storm cut the umbilical spit. Now they comprise another of Toronto's people-pleasing treasures. All 13 are parks in which automobiles are prohibited. True to the city's love affair with sailing, there are five major boating facilities on the islands.

At the eastern end of Algonquin Island, a short distance from Eastern Gap, is the **Queen City Yacht Club**, extending hospitality to reciprocating club members. There is a problem with silting near the entrance, so favor the Ward's Island side of the buoyed channel, but keep out of the way of the ferry that docks on Ward's across the way from the club. A submerged barge with two orange lights at the bow shelters the club slips, where docking is Mediterranean style, bow in to the bulkhead with the stern tied off to rings. With practice it's not too hard for the less agile among us to get on and off the boat. Dockside services include electricity and water at some slips, ice, pumpout, heads and showers, and there is a pleasant dining room and bar. The club provides launch service to the mainland. Ward's Island, just across the channel, has the last of the private housing on the Toronto Islands, pleasant walking, including a boardwalk, and bicycle rentals. Algonquin Island has a golf course.

The next facility to the west, open to members of recognized clubs, is the **Royal Canadian Yacht Club** on a group of islands bearing its name. Here, too, the mooring is Mediterranean in 6 to 8 feet, but there are short, triangular docks to step off to at the bow. There are also moorings. A buoyed channel directs you through the club's lagoon, and the large white clubhouse is conspicuous. All dockside services are provided, except fuel. There is also an open-end travelift to 8 meters, some engine repair available on site, and a small chandlery. The dining room of the club is formal in that it requires skirts and jacket and tie, but there is an informal snack bar as well as the cocktail bar. A swimming pool, four tennis courts, lawn bowling, and a children's playground round out the recreational amenities. There is, of course, launch service from the moorings and to downtown Toronto. The club monitors VHF channel 9 for advance inquiry about space.

Next along the island shores is **Toronto Island Marina**, a large public facility on Centre Island. Call on channel 68 to arrange for dockage at one of their floating slips in 5 to 10 feet. This is a full service marina, the only one in the Toronto harbor, and includes a Laundromat, snack bar, convenience store, marine store, engine, hull and rigging repairs. The open-end travelift can haul out up to 15 tons. There is a marina launch to the city as well as the public ferry across the park. The small, friendly Harbour City Yacht Club is on the premises with a floating clubhouse. Centre Island has two special attractions for children, the Far Enough Farm, with animals to look at and ponies to ride, and the Lagoon Puppet Theatre, which gives hourly performances in summer (367-8375). For all the family there is Centreville, a small amusement park, designed as a 19th-century Ontario village (363-1112).

On the west side of Muggs Island **Island Yacht Club** offers accommodation to members of a specific list of reciprocating clubs at slips with 10 feet or more alongside. All dockside services are available, except pumpout. The club's recreational amenities include dining room, cocktail bar, snack bar, four tennis courts, swimming pool, and a children's playground with supervised day care. There is also launch service to the mainland.

Finally, on Toronto Island at Hanlan Point, across from the Island Yacht Club, there is a public tie-up wall, with electricity, water, heads, showers and picnic tables. First come, first served.The ferry docks nearby, for easy access to downtown. Now you are close to the Western Gap into the Inner Harbour,

PHOTO BY FRANK GRANT

Toronto skyline from Toronto Islands.

which is how you would enter if you were cruising eastward along the lakeshore. Boat traffic is thick here, so keep a careful watch and proceed slowly. At the inner edge of the Western Gap channel, next to the most easterly hangar at the Island Airport, there is a custom's reporting dock if you've just crossed from the United States.

In the midst of a big city the Toronto Islands exude a remarkable away-from-it-all atmosphere that is cherished by its resident and visiting boaters alike. At ease in your cockpit, you can contemplate the glittering towers of metropolis across the bay, while enjoying the sights and sounds of nature's creatures at your elbow. But if you prefer to be where the action is, the mainland calls with another whole set of facilities.

Fronting the Inner Harbour, where 10 short years ago there were only bleak warehouses and industrial installations, is Toronto's newest extravaganza. Appropriately called Harbourfront, it's a hard-to-define collation of cultural, recreational, retail, service, and marine facilities that incorporates renovated older structures along with imaginative new ones, woven by open spaces and enlivened by a diversity of events that retain the human scale. Call it another of Toronto's captivating neighborhoods. Harbourfront is only half finished, but right about center is **Pier 4 Marina**, a small one, where 12 of the floating slips are reserved for transient boats on a first come, first served basis. Depth is 22 feet and all dockside services are available except fuel and pumpout. This is the closest accommodation you can possibly get to the attractions of downtown along with the fascination of Harbourfront. Future plans call for a larger full service marina in the yet-to-be-developed section of Harbourfront, but demand may continue to run well ahead of supply.

Adjacent to Pier 4 is a complex of marine chandleries, including the "fully found" bookstore, The Nautical Mind, and the excellent Pier 4 Storehouse Restaurant. The open space next door to this complex is the scene of the Summer Weekend Antiques Market. Within walking distance, across a broad swath of roadways—Queen's Quay West, Gardiner Expressway, and Lakeshore Boulevard—is the soaring symbol of Toronto. The CN (Canadian National) Tower is the world's tallest freestanding structure, rising 1,815 feet to pierce the sky with its needle tip. Although beloved by Torontonians for its symbolic significance, its revolving restaurant and spectacular view from the world's highest public observation deck, the tower, completed in 1976, was built for a pragmatic communications purpose. It carries radio and television antennae for both educational and commercial broadcasting.

On the east side of Pier 4 at Harbourfront is York Quay Centre, a complex of art and craft galleries and studios. A Tourist Information Center is conveniently located here, as is the Harbourfront Box Office, where you can buy tickets to the many cultural events in person or by telephone (869-8412). On outdoor stages at either side of the studio building a variety of performances take place, including the Canadian Opera Company's Summer Festival and a full theater season by Equity Showcase Productions. Next along the Quay is Queen's Quay Terminal, an imaginatively renovated warehouse with two levels of sophisticated shops and restaurants and the new Premiere Dance Theatre. Altogether, more than 3,500 events are scheduled annually at Harbourfront. Also distributed around the complex are a number of educational enterprises, including no less than five sailing schools.

If you're docked at or near Harbourfront, you are also as close as you can get to meeting the mundane needs you might have to start thinking of about now. There's a convenience store on the Quay, but the nearest supermarket is at Yonge and Temperance. A bit of a walk farther east, to Front and Jarvis streets, brings you to the Farmer's Market, which is best on Saturday but operates Tuesday through Friday as well. Not only can you obtain fresh goodies, but you can shop for them in an historic building, Toronto's first, 1844, city hall. The newer market building is across the street. And if you walk one block north, you'll reach St. Lawrence Hall, reminiscent of Cobourg's monumental meeting hall and about the same vintage. St. Lawrence Hall was built in 1850, but its initial glory faded as the center of city life moved west, and before its rescue in the 1960s it had degenerated to a flophouse. Take a look at the Grand Hall, beautifully restored. You might as well munch on a bit of history with your tomatoes and cucumbers.

Close by Harbourfront, but entered through the breakwater outside of Western Gap, are two more yacht clubs side by side. Using the preferred eastern pass through the breakwater, marked by flashing red and green lights you'll come first to the **National Yacht Club**, which will accommodate visitors from recognized yacht clubs. It has a little alongside docking in seven to nine feet, where all dockside services are available except fuel, but most of its boats are on moorings. The club has a dining room and bar. Right next door the **Alexandria Yacht Club** is in the northeast corner of the basin. It offers the same dockside services, also to members of other yacht clubs, and its small clubhouse has an informal lounge. The crowded basin in which these clubs are located can make turning difficult for boats in excess of 40 feet. Stana Marine, also in the basin, has no dockage but offers engine repairs. Both yacht clubs are convenient to public transportation on Lakeshore and Bathurst streets, and the Molson's Brewery nearby has a handy retail outlet. For parents of young children this part of the harbor may be a dream come true. Bathurst Quay has two unusual supervised playgrounds: Creative Playground, with wading pool, giant blocks, paints, and so on for children under eight; and Adventure Playground, where youngsters can let their architectural imaginations roam with tools and lumber.

The site of the last downtown marina is in some respects the most outstanding and the most representative of the spirit of Toronto. First, Ontario Place is an island locale, three man-made islands, in fact. Second, it is futuristic in design, with a huge sphere that complements the CN Tower as a symbol of the city. Structures called *pods*, as well as more conventional buildings, hover over the water with only the slenderest of attachments to the land. Third, it is a multi-purpose cultural, educational, commercial, and fun-filled complex with scenes and activities to delight Torontonians and their visitors of every taste. Its offerings include the Cinesphere, where continuous films are projected on a six-story curved screen with 66 stereo speakers; Future Pod, a showcase of high technology; the Forum, where stars of the entertainment world, including the Toronto Symphony, present the entire range of classical and popular musical and dance performance over the course of a season; the Children's Village, with its circus of clever play equipment including water play and a special area for tots; bumper boats, social dancing under the stars, mini-golf, a dozen restaurants and a whole village of shops, all in a tastefully landscaped setting. The crew of a visiting boat can keep so busy right here that they might never want to leave.

The very large **Ontario Place Marina** is an integral part of the complex. Entrance is directly off the lake, with a flashing yellow light at the end of the line of three grounded freighters that act as a breakwater. With steel floating docks, minimum depths of 15 feet, and all dockside services, including Laundromat but excluding fuel, the marina is well equipped, but, as you might guess, an extremely popular destination. Call ahead for space information at 416-965-7676. Be aware, however, that the park is open until 1:00 A.M., although various attractions close earlier, and it may not be the quietest location in town. There is a launch service to the parking lot, and from there a short walk to the bus.

If Ontario Place doesn't keep you busy enough, right across

Toronto, Ontario Place.

Lakeshore Boulevard is the Canadian National Exhibition grounds, the site of Ontario's famous century-old fair, running from mid-August to Labor Day. But there are special events and shows going on here all through the summer, and it's where the Toronto Blue Jays play ball (595-0077). The Hockey Hall of Fame and the Sports Hall of Fame are here (595-1345), and so is the Marine Museum (595-1567) that tells the story of Toronto Harbour and the waterways of central Canada. You can have lunch at the museum in an old waterside tavern.

A concrete sea wall continues as a breakwater from Ontario Place to the Humber River, 3 miles west. About halfway along there are two openings fairly close to one another. The eastern one, with flashing red and green lights defining the entrance, leads directly to **The Boulevard Club**. (The western one has a hazardous concrete block in the fairway.) Stay carefully in the middle of the channel as you approach the club, where visitors from reciprocating yacht clubs can be accommodated on moorings in 12 to 20 feet if space is available. The usual dockside services are available, as well as a launch service on weekends, but no fuel. The handsome clubhouse has a formal dining room, informal snack bar and cocktail bar. There is also a swimming pool and supervised children's play area.

There is one more suburban park harbor before departure from metropolitan Toronto. Just west of the Humber River, identified by a tall apartment house, landfill has created the west basin of Humber Bay Park. The basin is entered from the west side. A pair of fixed red lights, the front one on a white metal structure, the rear on a white tower with red top, define a range of 011° to locate the harbor entrance but do not lead through the channel, which has a depth of 15 to 20 feet. To starboard of the entrance is the **Etobicoke Yacht Club**, a new facility with floating slips, electricity and water at most of them, ice, pumpout and heads. An informal clubhouse is under construction. There is a launch ramp in the park.

On the adjacent arm of the harbor, facing the entrance, is the **Mimico Cruising Club**, with floating slips in 15 to 20 feet and all dockside services except fuel, but including Laundromat. The handsome new clubhouse has a snack bar, a cocktail bar and a game room. Humber Bay Park is in a residential area and there is neighborhood shopping about half a mile from the two clubs.

THE WEST END
Charts 2062, 2067, 2070

Canada's most densely populated megalopolis begins at Toronto and continues around the western end of the lake to culminate in Ontario's "second city," Hamilton. Between them industrial enclaves alternate with old and new residential suburbs, all interconnected by one metropolitan transit system. From Humber Bay to Hamilton the harbors are no more than 12 miles apart. The lakefront shows an almost continuous skyline of buildings along its flat shores—tall apartment houses, mansions all but hidden by trees, boxy industrial plants with high stacks and sometimes with projecting piers, neat small homes, and in between the open spaces of parkland.

Port Credit

Hard on the border of metropolitan Toronto the once independent town of Port Credit is now part of the sprawling industrial city of Mississauga. Yet near the waterfront the townscape retains the quiet nostalgic appearance of the 1920s and 30s, with one-story commercial buildings and a venerable red brick post office. And for the first time in 80 miles there are marine accommodations close to all your daily shopping needs.

Port Credit is identified from offshore by a large generating station with four tall stacks a couple of miles east and a tall chimney on either side of the harbor entrance, the western one often flaring. The end of a submerged pipeline extending half a mile offshore is marked by three lighted cribs. The main harbor was artificially created by two breakwaters and a grounded lake freighter, whose bow displays a quick flashing red light from a white tower with a red top. The west breakwater opposite shows a flashing green light from a white tower with a green top. Until 10 years ago this harbor was the domain of the Canada Steamship Lines, and their warehouse is still the main building of the **Port Credit Harbour Marina**. This is a large full service marina in every respect except, oddly, fuel. Most of the floating slips, with 20-foot depths, have electricity, and all the other dockside services are available, including Laundromat. There is a launch ramp, a travelift with 35-ton capacity, engine, hull, and rigging repairs and Mason's Ship's Chandlery with an extensive inventory. There is also Lucas Galley Restaurant on the premises.

Beyond the entrance to the artificial harbor the channel into the Credit River begins at the flashing red light on a white tower with red top at the elbow of the west breakwater. The curving channel is rather narrow but well-buoyed for the short distance to the basin of the **Port Credit Yacht Club**. The club is open only to members of reciprocating yacht clubs, but its fuel dock, selling gas and diesel, on the west side of the basin opposite the clubhouse, is open to the public. Approach at a sharp angle, as the west side of the river is very shallow except where it has been dredged to about 5 feet. The club's wood finger docks are aging, but they have electricity and water (pumpout at the gas dock), and the handsome clubhouse has heads and showers as well as dining room and bar. Both the yacht club and the marina are within a couple of blocks of the shops on Lakeshore Road.

Oakville

Oakville is a town with two harbors and a multiple personality. The original 1827 village was founded on the banks of Sixteen Mile Creek, Oakville Creek on the charts. That part of the town of 77,000 people that surrounds the creek retains much of the low-key elegance of a wealthy residential community. The industry and commerce that support it are oriented to the highways farther inland. The more sprawling, newer residential development surrounds Bronte Creek, the harbor that anchors the southwest end of town 4 miles away.

Oakville Harbour, a customs port of entry, is identified from seaward by two church steeples and a high mound with a flagstaff on it. A pair of spars identify the entrance channel and the east breakwater has a fixed red light on a white tower with red top and a fog horn. Keep to the southwest side of the 7-foot-deep channel. On the port side is the sailboat-filled basin of the **Oakville Yacht Squadron**. There is some guest dockage alongside the wharf for members of recognized yacht clubs, or a place might be found at a member's dock where the boats are moored bow in and stern tied to floating tires. Water, ice and electricity are available at dockside, with heads and showers in the attractive clubhouse that has a lounge and snack bar on weekends. Just north of the Squadron's facilities is a public launch ramp, and beyond that the **Oakville Harbour Club**, where members of reciprocating clubs may find dockage, both alongside and at floating slips, with all dockside services except fuel. The clubhouse has a dining room and bar, sauna and Jacuzzi, and squash courts. All of these facilities are located in a park at the base of the steep-sided ravine that forms the creek bed with water depths in excess of 10 feet. At the top of the hill you are rewarded for your climb with excellent shopping, restaurants and a movie theater.

Directly across the creek from the Yacht Squadron is the **Oakville Club**, in a charming building that evokes the easy grace of turn-of-the-century recreation. Built as a warehouse in 1878, it was acquired and remodeled in 1908 by the Tennis Club founded five years earlier. Today tennis is still the main function, but there is some dockage with basic services for members and guests from recognized yacht clubs. The Oakville Club is adjoined on the landward side by the town's beautiful historic district, including the Erchless estate, the Customs House, the Merrick Thomas House, and the 1835 post office, all part of the Oakville Museums (845-3592).

Just beyond the Oakville Club there are a few floating slips belonging to the town, where any visitor is free to tie up, but there are no services. Up the creek, beyond the two fixed highway bridges, is the **Oakville Power Boat Club**, with all dockside services offered to members of reciprocating clubs at both alongside dockage and floating slips in 6 to 8 feet. There is gas, but no diesel. The informal clubhouse has a bar, and there are tennis courts in the park adjacent to the club. Up the hill is the Oakville Centre, with a summer theater program (842-2555), and the Centennial Art Gallery located in the library building (844-4402).

Two tall chimneys identify Bronte Harbour from the lake, and a flashing red light from a white tower with red top on the end of the north breakwater, equipped with a fog horn, helps to guide you in. Leave the black can just inside the entrance well to port and hug the north side as you proceed up the creek that has 4 to 6 feet of water at chart datum. Not only is this harbor subject to silting, it also has a strong outflowing current at times. The creek narrows as you move upstream, accentuating the congestion of moored boats.

Metro Marine is the first facility you come to, on the starboard side just around the bend. All services, except showers, are offered at the aging dockage, as well as hull and engine repairs with a travelift capacity of 15 tons. Beyond, at the head of navigation, the small **Bronte Harbour Yacht Club** accepts visitors from reciprocating clubs. Dockage here is also bow in, stern tied to tires. The clubhouse has showers and a bar. Both facilities are surrounded by a pleasant park and are convenient to shopping on Lakeshore Road.

Hamilton

The far western end of Lake Ontario is closed off by a sandbar that stretches 4 miles across to create a natural harbor 12 miles square. Always known as Burlington Bay, it is now officially Hamilton Harbour. The industrial city of almost half a million people, Canada's steel-making capital, dominates the southern part of the bay. On the north shore is the mainly residential city of Burlington, with beautiful homes lining the waterfront.

The single access to Hamilton Harbour is the Burlington Canal, cut through the sand barrier. It is spanned by the high arched bridge of the Burlington Skyway, 120 feet above the water, and conspicuous from far out in the lake on a clear day. The twin towers of the combined highway-railway vertical lift bridge and two pylons on the beach close to each entrance pier also help guide you to the canal. There is a red and white Mo(A) light and bell buoy about a mile seaward of the canal entrance, and the canal itself has a lighted range, showing an isophase yellow front light from a white square tower with a fog horn and a fixed yellow rear light from the lift bridge tower, on a course of 233°. In addition, the north canal pier is lighted at both ends, and the south pier on the inner end from white circular towers with the appropriate top colors. You aren't likely to get lost transiting the canal, but you do have to take care among the freighters you might encounter entering and leaving. The lift bridge, with only 10 feet of clearance when closed, comes first on a passage into the harbor. It is opened for pleasure craft on the hour and half hour around the clock. It's best to contact the bridge tender on channel 16, call sign XL146, but you can sound three long blasts of the horn as a signal.

Because of heavy ship traffic through a confined area, there are strict regulations governing the canal. A boat over 50 feet must wait for the green signal on the lift bridge before even entering the canal, while one under 50 feet may move to within 300 feet of the bridge, wait to starboard if necessary, and proceed through on a flashing blue signal light. Sailing in the canal is prohibited, and there is a speed limit of 10 miles per hour throughout the harbor.

Once through the canal, the bay is clear and deep almost throughout. Just inside the canal on the north side of it is the Canada Centre for Inland Waters, the federal agency responsible for Great Lakes research. There are large piers for the research vessels and at the north end of the wharf space for small craft, if you'd like to pay a visit. Almost directly across the bay, on the northwest Burlington shore, is the **LaSalle Park Marina**, sheltered behind a floating tire breakwater mounted with yellow warning lights, and a red and a green at the opening. The marina has floating docks in 10- to 25-foot depths; some of them have electricity and water. There are also heads and a big launch ramp. The Burlington Boating and Sailing Club has a crew lounge in its clubhouse. LaSalle Park has picnic grounds, a wading pool and playground for children, and nature trails. It is located in a residential district, with neighborhood shopping about three blocks away.

Hamilton's facilities for pleasure boats are clustered close to the southwest corner of the bay; all the rest is industrial, but worth a circuit just to view the power and brawn of steel-making. First on the approach from the canal is the **Hamilton Harbour Commission Marine Dockyard**, a large, full service marina with both alongside and finger docking in 15 to 30 feet, all dockside services and repairs, and a 50-ton travelift. Ulmer sail loft is one block away. The harbor police are located here, so don't panic if you hear their siren scream for 10 seconds to warn pleasure boats that the patrol boat is about to get under way at top speed.

Next door to the Harbour Commission Dockyard is the **Royal Hamilton Yacht Club**, where members of recognized clubs can obtain all dockside services except fuel and enjoy a handsome clubhouse with dining room, bar and swimming pool. A small boat marina comes next, and then the **Macassa Bay Yacht Club**. Dockage here is alongside in 10 feet, with electric outlets, ice and showers. The informal clubhouse has a friendly bar.

These marine accommodations are at the base of a fairly steep hill in a very modest older residential neighborhood, whose local stores are several blocks away, but there is bus service to downtown. Hamilton has not undergone the same kind of transformation as Toronto. It is still a candidly industrial city that retains the pace and atmosphere of traditional Ontario dignity.Yet the central, downtown area is urbane and pleasant, with excellent shops and many restaurants. Hamilton Place is a handsome performing arts center that is home to the Hamilton Philharmonic Orchestra and Opera Hamilton. Next door is the Art Gallery of Hamilton. The Canadian Football Hall of Fame and Museum is downtown near City Hall (527-1158), and throughout the city there are historic sites and buildings open to the public. Hamilton, too, has its fantastic castle, called Dundern, where you can not only admire the architecture, furnishings and gardens, but also enjoy lunch and an afternoon concert. But perhaps Hamilton's most spectacular attraction is the 2,000 acres of the Royal Botanical Gardens, most conveniently reached by taxi from marina or yacht club. You can lose yourself here for hours amid the formal displays, natural areas and hiking trails that meander among woods and marsh. If you like to hike, the Niagara Escarpment runs in back of the city, with its famous Bruce Trail that follows the ridge for 480 miles from Niagara Falls to the tip of the Bruce Peninsula in Georgian Bay. This is as close as you'll get to the trail from the lower lakes. A bus or cab to one of the suburban entry points can provide a pleasant hike for as long as you care to keep going.

Niagara

Charts 2043, 2063, 2070; U.S. 14806, 14816

About four or five hundred million years ago, give or take a few, this part of the world lay under warm, salt seas. In that ocean lived billions and billions of tiny lime-shelled organisms. When they died their shells compacted with other mineral deposits to form a great barrier reef on the ocean floor. Later, over the course of another few hundred million years, the sea receded, the land uplifted and eroded, and four waves of continental glaciers engulfed it before leaving three great lakes in their train—and still that reef survived, battered but recognizable. It stretches in a mammoth arc from near Rochester, New

York, on Lake Ontario through Ontario, Michigan, and Wisconsin almost to Milwaukee. We call it Niagara.

Over this stubborn ridge of limestone the waters from four of the Great Lakes plunge 326 feet, 167 of them in a single drop at what is probably the world's most visited natural phenomenon, Niagara Falls. Nature's boon to the aesthete and the tourist presents an impenetrable barrier to mariners who seek passage between Lake Ontario and Lake Erie. Modern engineering has overcome the obstacle with a canal and locks a few miles west of the falls, while the beautiful 37-mile-long Niagara River can be enjoyed by boaters in part, from either one end or the other.

As the smokestacks of Hamilton recede in your wake you enter another kind of Ontario, the peaceable kingdom of vineyard and orchard. The Niagara Peninsula, wafted by the moderating breezes of two great lakes, is Canada's fruit belt. Especially rich is the sheltered ground between the Niagara Escarpment and Lake Ontario. That steep bluff wavers in its distance from the shoreline between Hamilton and the Niagara River, but it's always there, in the background.

Fifty Mile Point

Fifty Mile Point itself, 8½ miles southeast of the Burlington Canal entrance, is a low-lying peninsula surrounded by shallows that used to be something to avoid. Not any longer. Just west of it a pair of rock-topped breakwalls protect a new harbor created by the Hamilton-Wentworth Regional Conservation Authority. On the east wall a white tower with a green top carries a flashing white and green sector light, which helps identify the entrance channel, 60 feet deep. A dog-leg approach leads you past a peninsula extending from the west shore of the harbor into a large new marina. The floating slips have 20-foot depths and there is electricity and water at about two-thirds of them, along with all other dockside services. There is a triple launch ramp, including a special basin for trailered sailboats, but there are no repair services. The 200-acre park has picnic grounds, playground, bicycle track, and beach with concession stand. While there is no shopping nearby there is a licensed restaurant just outside the park.

Grimsby

Four miles farther on, the harbor at Grimsby is entered between two breakwaters. At the end of the eastern one there is a white tower with black top and a flashing green light. Eight

massive radio towers just west of town provide offshore identification. The artificial harbor and channel suffer a severe silting
problem, but if you veer immediately to port on entering, you
should have no trouble maintaining the 6-foot channel. In a
basin on the east side is **Lakecourt Marina**, with floating slips in
8 feet of water and most dockside services. Water is available
only at the gas dock, and there is no diesel pump, but some is
kept on hand for emergencies. A 35-ton crane can lift boats for
hull repairs, in which the marina specializes, but there is no
engine repair on the premises. There is a launch ramp and a
snack bar called The Galley. At the base of the harbor **Foran's
Marina** has slips in 5 feet of water and offers all dockside
services as well as motor repairs. They haul out with a 10-ton
forklift. By and large sailboats tend to use Lakecourt closer to
the harbor entrance, while Foran's is better suited to powerboats. The shops of Grimsby, a city of 15,000, are located half a
mile to a mile from the marinas.

Port Dalhousie

Port Dalhousie has seen more important days. It had the honor
in 1829 of being selected as the Lake Ontario terminus of the
Welland Canal (more about the canal later). In that role it
flourished for 100 years as a major shipping center, while
steamboats and railroads brought summer visitors to its lakeside beaches. Then, just as the Great Depression was getting
under way, the terminus was moved three miles east. Port
Dalhousie languished, until its recent revival as a tourist attraction, with boutiques and restaurants in its well-preserved 19th-
century buildings. It is part of the city of St. Catharines, three
miles inland.

For most of the 13 miles from Grimsby to Port Dalhousie the
shore is fronted by clay banks of varying heights. The Brock
University tower and a large textile mill, west and southwest of
the harbor, respectively, help to identify it from offshore. There
is a fixed green range at 177° on white towers; the front light is
on the east breakwater and is equipped with a fog horn. The
west breakwater is quite low, and parts of it are often submerged in strong west and northwest winds. The harbor is an
attractive one, surrounded by bluffs, but unfortunately it has
some natural disadvantages. North winds cause a strong surge,
and the normal outflowing current of one knot is increased to
three or more when Ontario Hydro opens the sluice gates at the
southern end. In these conditions docking and sleeping can be
difficult.

Port Dalhousie Yacht Club, open to visitors from recognized clubs, is at the end of the channel on the east side. It offers all services, including Laundromat. There is alongside dockage and slips on both sides of the harbor in 14 feet. The attractive clubhouse on the east shore has a dining room and bar. There is also a city dock on the west side of the harbor, with alongside tie-up and washrooms. The shops and restaurants, many of them in historic buildings, are on the west side of the harbor, and there is a general store about a quarter of a mile from the docks on that side.

In Lakeside Park on the west side of the harbor not only can you enjoy the beach, but you and your children can ride on a carousel hand-crafted in 1838—one of two remaining in the world that carries four horses abreast—and it's still only a nickel. On Canada Day weekend there is a big carnival in the park, culminating in a spectacular fireworks display. Across Lakeshore Road at the head of the harbor, Martindale Pond is the site of the Royal Canadian Henley Rowing Course. Regattas take place throughout the summer, but the first week in August is the Royal Henley Regatta, a major international event.

Downtown St. Catharines is 3 miles away from Port Dalhousie, but there is regular bus service. In addition to full shopping, commercial services and a hospital in this city of 125,000, there is a historical museum (227-2962), Rodman Hall, home of the original Welland Canal builder and now an art center (684-2925), and a walking tour of the city published by the Local Architecture Conservation Advisory Committee. A farmer's market operates Tuesday, Thursday and Saturday in the square at the old Court House, King and James streets.

If you carry bicycles on board, The Merrittrail will take you 14 miles into the heart of the Niagara Peninsula, following parklands and waterways along the first 21 locks of the Second Welland Canal. A handsomely illustrated guide that will inform you about the history and the natural environment of the trail is available; check with the Chamber of Commerce (684-2361) about where to get it. There are some other special attractions in the area around St. Catharines, for which you might want to consider renting a car. Stokes Seed Farm, Canada's largest seed supplier and over 100 years old, welcomes visitors to its beautiful trial gardens (688-4300). Winery tours are a natural in wine country. Barnes Winery (682-6631) and Jordan and Ste. Michelle Cellars (688-2140) conclude their tours with a wine-tasting. Happy Rolph Bird Sanctuary and Children's Farm has walking trails and picnic sites in addition to the farm animals and waterfowl on display. And, of course, if you're renting a car, the spectacle no one tires of—Niagara Falls—is but a dozen miles away.

St. Catharines' second harbor, Port Weller, will be described in connection with the Welland Canal. As you pass it by, keep a watch for ship traffic bound in and out of the canal. Stay about a mile offshore beyond Port Weller to avoid the small arms firing range a few miles east. The limits of the range are marked by small buoys, and red flags are displayed on shore when firing is in progress, but it's easy to avoid the area altogether.

About 12 miles beyond Port Dalhousie the Niagara River flows into Lake Ontario. It is placid here, compared to its middle reaches, but still carries a two-knot current, making it slow progress upstream for a low-powered boat. But on either side there are places to visit. The Niagara Frontier has always been important in the affairs of men and nations. Bitterness reigned at this international border for many years after the American Revolution, when United Empire Loyalists crossed the river from New York to settle on the Canadian side. This narrow river saw some of the fiercest fighting of the War of 1812, and while emotions have cooled since then the monuments of war are everywhere apparent. From far off in Lake Ontario you can see the 200-foot memorial column erected in 1856 over the gravesite of the fallen British leader, General Isaac Brock. It pierces the sky above Queenston Heights where he died in battle. But the river mouth isn't so easy to spot from a distance. It is flanked by the battlements of Fort Mississauga on the west and Fort Niagara on the east, but only Fort Niagara is conspicuous from the lake.

The river's flow carries sand and silt downstream to create a delta at the mouth that trends northeasterly; the shoals are marked by several lighted and sounding buoys. Each of the forts carries a light, flashing red from a white tower with red top on the Ontario side, and occulting white from a gray octagonal tower with yellow top on the New York shore. There is also a fixed red range on the west side bearing 149° between two white towers with red tops. The range is sometimes hard to maintain because of the easterly set of the current beyond the river mouth. You should also be aware that strong north winds in conflict with the river current create eddies and rips just off the mouth.

A short distance inside the river the entrance to Niagara-on-the-Lake is between the two range lights. This is one of the prettiest ports on the lake, but regrettably is very short on dock space. Nevertheless, the **Niagara Sailing Club Marina** extends such hospitality as it can in accommodating visitors at members' vacant slips or alongside. All dockside services are provided, engine repairs are available at Gillingham Yacht Sales, and Murray's Boat Repairs will take care of your hull—with "yacht surgery," if necessary, as the sign informs you. Canada Customs is adjacent to the marina.

Niagara-on-the-Lake has been a gracious resort for generations and retains its historic charm in vintage homes and hotels. The main street is called Queen's Parade-Picton, and about halfway through the village there is suddenly a nonfunctional clock tower in the center of it. The atmosphere is reminiscent of Gilbert and Sullivan, although the fine shops are modern enough in their merchandise, and it is George Bernard Shaw who sets the theatrical tone. The Shaw Festival is a renowned May through October banquet that has been served annually since 1962. Three theaters present a galaxy of plays by other 20th-century masters in addition to the accent on Shaw. Advance reservations are a good idea. You can either write to the Shaw Festival Box Office, PO Box 774, Niagara-on-the-Lake, Ontario LOS 1JO, or telephone at 416-468-3201.

The Niagara Historical Society Museum (468-3912), oldest local history museum in the province, will tell you much about the area's colorful past. Fort George, part of the Niagara National Historic Park at the edge of town, shows you where some of it happened, and the Niagara Apothecary downtown is an authentic remnant of an older day. The Chamber of Commerce publishes a walking tour. Most commercial services are in easy reach, including food, drug, and hardware stores, and medical service can be obtained at the hospital. The Laundromat is on the outskirts. There are a number of restaurants in town; Oban Inn serves fine food in a venerable and gracious setting (reservations required).

Across the river and slightly upstream (about a mile from the river mouth) the New York village of Youngstown is also a pretty one. Like its Canadian neighbor its limited marine accommodations are strained by the demand. The **Youngstown Yacht Club** accommodates visitors from reciprocating clubs at its moorings, or temporarily alongside at the dock in 18 feet, for the usual dockside services, except fuel. The clubhouse has an attractive dining room and bar. Gas and diesel fuel are supplied by **Pierce Marine**, a little farther upstream. They can haul out on a large crane and provide hull and engine repair services, but rarely can supply dockage. Between the yacht club and Pierce there is a village dock, which is usually crowded with rafted boats but is the only accommodation on the New York side open to non-yacht-club members. Note the regulations posted that often change from year to year. There is no longer a customs officer in Youngstown, but you can report in by telephone.

The village is only a block or two from the docks, but it's at the top of a steep hill. On the way you pass Sailors Supply, Inc., a large and complete chandlery, with electronic service and a sailmaker. There is basic food shopping in the village, but no Laundromat, and there are tennis courts in the park. The major sight to see is Fort Niagara, built in 1726, a pleasant 1-mile walk away.

The Niagara River is navigable for 7 miles upstream from the lake; it makes for an enjoyable day trip. The current is strongest in midstream, and by hugging the shoreline you can avoid most of its effect. The river is deep to within 30 feet of the shores, which rise to steep bluffs just beyond the mouth. Lewiston, New York, and Queenston, Ontario, mark the head of navigation, but neither has accommodations for cruising boats. Just where the Brock Monument dominates the west bank the Niagara Gorge, seven miles long, contracts the river's flow to a whirling maelstrom. The shores have become more urban as you approach the twin cities of Niagara Falls, especially on the American side, but there is no way for you to visit the main attraction by boat. As neither Niagara-on-the-Lake nor Youngstown has any transportation services the only alternative is an expensive taxi called from one of the cities of Niagara Falls. You'll probably want to save the falls for a land-based vacation.

A Trio of Little Towns
Charts 14805, 14806

Try to be stocked with necessities when you leave the Niagara area as shopping will be less than convenient for the next 75 miles along the south shore of the lake. The escarpment continues to trace your easterly course at varying distances from the lakefront, although its ridges may be obscured by the low bluffs of the shoreline. But the climate and topography of the Niagara Peninsula continue into the fruit and wine belt of New York State. While there are resort communities along this pleasant coast, it is mainly agricultural. It is also smooth and free of obstructions; you can cruise within a mile of shore.

Wilson

Twelve miles from the Niagara River the east branch of Twelvemile Creek widens at the mouth to form Tuscarora Bay. From offshore the harbor can be identified by three silos about 2 miles west of town. Between parallel breakwaters, a channel, dredged to a controlling depth of 5½ feet, leads into the bay, whose natural depths average only 2 feet. The west pier has a flashing red light on a red tower, and the channel through the bay is marked by daybeacons on pilings. Notice that just inside the entrance the channel hugs the east shore; don't bear to starboard too soon or you'll hang up on the shoal making out from the west side.

The harbor has been used by pleasure craft for a long time and is crowded with boats; much of the dockage is aging wood. But it's a hospitable and convivial place. Don't tie up at the place marked Public Dock on the chart until you obtain local information about the state of bottom in front of it; rocks dumped there some time ago may or may not have been removed. The first marina you come to doesn't take transients, but immediately beyond it the island on the east side of the channel is the home of the **Tuscarora Yacht Club**. Depth at their slips ranges from 5 to 10 feet, and they supply electricity, water, ice, heads and showers to visitors. The clubhouse has a lounge, and the grassy island has a lot of play area for children, as well as picnic tables. Next door the **Wilson Yacht Club** slips have electricity, water from a long hose, and heads.

Beccue Boat Basin, almost at the end of the harbor, is a full service marina with alongside docking and finger slips. All dockside services are offered and all repairs, including rigging and sail, with a 30-ton travelift for haulout. There is also a launch ramp. The Island Yacht Club rents dockage from Beccue; its dining room and bar are open to members of reciprocating clubs, Thursday through Sunday. Beyond the marina Tuscarora State Park has a few slips, without services, and a launch ramp. Or you could anchor in this part of the bay, safely and comfortably in about 8 feet over mud.

The village of Wilson, population 1,200, is from three-quarters of a mile to two miles from the harbor, depending upon where you moor. It has basic supplies, but there is no transportation to get there.

Olcott

The next port east is Olcott at the mouth of Eighteenmile Creek, 6 miles from Wilson. This harbor, too, is entered between parallel piers with a flashing red light and red daymark on the west one. Controlling depth in the dredged channel is 7½ feet, but it is subject to silting. From offshore a water tank marked "Olcott" indicates the whereabouts of the entrance. This harbor is not blessed with a widening of the creek into a bay as Wilson is, and a heavy surge comes in when strong winds blow from northwest through northeast. Nevertheless, there are two marinas and some public docks.

Hedley Boat Company is on the east side immediately past the entrance. It is a full service marina with all dockside services, a launch ramp, a travelift with capacity for 50-foot boats and repair services. Across the harbor the Olcott Yacht Club has no dockage of its own, but a pleasant dining room. Beyond Hedley's on the east shore, **McDonough Marina** has dockage at floating slips in 15 feet, with electricity, water, ice, heads and gas. It can haul out up to 24 feet on a ramp, and do engine, hull and rigging repairs. Across the channel from McDonough's there are **Town Docks** with about 5 feet of depth, water, electricity and heads.

You can continue up the channel in about 10 feet beyond the marinas, keeping close to the east shore to avoid the mid-channel shoals marked with small buoys. If you can clear the overhead power line at 56 feet and the fixed highway bridge at 52 feet, there is a pleasant anchorage beyond the bridge; pass through the starboard side arch.

The marinas on the east shore are closest to the limited grocery supplies available in the village of 1,500 people. And only a block or two away the lakefront park has a beach, playground and tennis courts.

Point Breeze

If you're coasting the south shore, it's 27 miles to the next harbor at the mouth of Oak Orchard Creek. It is called by the creek name about as often as the name of the hamlet of 140 people on its east bank. From offshore you can spot it by the water treatment plant west of the entrance and the four silos on the east side. The creek mouth is protected by a detached breakwater across its face beyond the typical parallel piers extending into the lake. This makes the harbor a quiet place to lie, but the unusual arrangement sometimes confuses strangers. The detached breakwater is marked by three lights, all flashing white, while the entrance piers are marked by flashing red and green lights on the west and east jetties, respectively. You can go around either end of the detached breakwater; the controlling depth from the west end is 5 feet, only 4 on the eastern approach.

Where the channels meet between the piers the depth increases to 8 feet, maintained into the creek. But the channel is narrow, with the west side more shoal. Favor the east shore beyond the marinas.

Norm's Marina comes first, with finger slips in a row along the shore and 15-foot depths. New ownership has recently taken over, however, and they are planning to change the dockage to a system of floating slips, which may be in place by the time you read this. All dockside services are provided, and there is a snack bar. A travelift can haul out up to 25 tons, and there is hull repair on the premises, with mechanics called in for engine repairs. **Harbor Breeze Marina**, just beyond Norm's, has the same docking arrangements in 8 feet, all dockside services, a 25-ton travelift and minor repairs. Both of these are the informal, family kind of establishment that is becoming scarcer on the waterways. Beyond the twin fixed highway bridges with 54-foot clearance the **Oak Orchard Yacht Club** accommodates visitors from reciprocating clubs at their slips, which project into the channel from the shallow west bank and are connected to it by a walkway. There is electricity, water, heads and showers. The clubhouse dining room, at the top of the bluff, is open Thursday through Sunday. There are neither shops nor sights to see in Point Breeze.

Rochester
Charts 14804, 14815

Rochester is the largest American city on Lake Ontario. With fewer than a quarter of a million people, it is also one of the most habitably urbane on the Great Lakes. Its history of creative industrial and civic leadership has given it prosperity and cultural amenities, which, combined with the natural attractions of river glen and lakeshore, make Rochester a delightful place to visit. The harbor marine facilities are 6 or 7 miles from downtown (which grew up around the Erie Canal above the falls of the Genesee River, rather than the lakefront) but the city's good transportation system, by bus or taxi, makes its central attractions relatively easy to reach. They are well worth the effort.

The land at lakeside begins to rise as you approach Rochester, about 35 miles east of Point Breeze, and the interesting contours of hills and ravines will follow your course for a considerable distance eastward. There are no particular hazards along this coast, and Rochester is easily identified by its stacks and a tall apartment house. Two long parallel breakwaters extend north-

Rochester skyline.

easterly into the lake at the entrance to the Genesee River. The Rochester Harbor Light is displayed flashing white from a red tower on the west pier and is equipped with a fog horn, and the east pier light shows fixed green. The river channel is wide and deep, to accommodate commercial vessels almost to the head of navigation 5½ miles upstream, but very few ships call anymore. Strong northeast winds can send a bad surge into the harbor, making it difficult to maneuver, especially if the river current is running hard at the same time.

Just before the railroad swing bridge, which remains open most of the time, a sharp turn to port takes you into the basin of the **Rochester Yacht Club**. Dockage is available to members of reciprocating yacht clubs, with 8-foot depths at the slips and all dockside services, including a Laundromat, but not fuel. The attractive clubhouse has a dining room and bar, swimming pool and tennis courts. Next door to the club, beyond the swing bridge, is **Shumway Marine**, a large full service marina that, in addition to all dockside services at its slips with 8-foot depths, has a launch ramp, a 40-ton travelift and offers all engine, hull and rigging repairs. Shumway's marine store is one of the most extensive chandleries on the lakes. The Genesee Yacht Club is next beyond Shumway's, but has no transient dockage, and past the club is **Voyager Boat Sales**. Here depth at the slips averages 6 feet, with electricity, water, ice, heads and showers offered. There is a launch ramp, a 14-ton travelift for haulout, and all engine, hull and rigging repairs are available. Within a couple of blocks of all these accommodations there is a shopping center with supermarket, drug store, bakery, Laundromat and movie theater among other enterprises. Across the street from the center is Haarstick Sail Loft. The bus for downtown is also close by. Rochester is a customs port of entry.

On the west side of the river **Pelican Bay Marine** is just above the swing bridge opposite Shumway's. Dockage is available both alongside and in slips, with depths ranging from 6 to 12 feet. Dockside services include electricity, water, ice, heads, gas and launch ramp. A travelift can haul out up to 14 tons for engine and hull repairs. Beyond the facilities described the Stutson Street Bridge is a bascule span with clearance of 24 feet. It opens on the hour and half hour, except during weekday rush hours; the signal is one long and one short. Past the bridge on the west side of the river is the **Riverview Yacht Basin**. Its slips are in 8 to 12 feet and all dockside services are provided. There is a launch ramp, marine store, travelift to 40 tons and full engine, hull and rigging repairs. The Charlotte Yacht Club is located on the premises, with a bar open to visitors from other yacht clubs. Buses run downtown from this location as well.

You can take your boat several miles up the river to the Ridge Road fixed bridge, 160-foot clearance. Beyond this there are unmarked shoals for the short distance before the rapids below the dam would impede your progress anyway. There is some industry along the shores, but most of the scene is natural, and as the river narrows the steep walls of the gorge close in.

Rochester was founded in 1803 when a man by that name bought a thousand acres along the Genesee River. Settlement began in earnest a decade later and the town continued to grow and thrive through the 19th century, milling flour, raising nursery plants, manufacturing optical goods and shoes, educating university students. Then in 1884 an inventive genius named George Eastman set up shop to manufacture photographic film. He soon projected Rochester onto the world stage. Kodak, a word Eastman invented, became almost a generic name for both camera and film, and his inventions brought the art of photography within the reach of Everyman. Kodak Park, on Ridge Road in the northwest section of the city, is a 2,000-acre campus, where almost 30,000 people are employed making film; two other plants in the area produce cameras, lenses and all manner of other equipment. Each of them offers tours. Call 722-2465 for information about Kodak Park tours and 726-3426 for the others.

After his fortune was assured, Eastman built a 50-room mansion in 1905 on the city's most fashionable street, East Avenue. Today it is the acclaimed International Museum of Photography (271-3361), displaying both artifacts and a fabulous collection of important photographs; the Dryden Theatre shows classic movies from the museum's archive. East Avenue is a treasure trove of magnificent mansions and fascinating museums. Just a walk down the street is interesting enough, but you can also choose from among the Rochester Museum and Science Center (271-4320), its associated Strasenburgh Planetarium (442-7171), the Rochester Historical Society (271-2705), and one block off East Avenue is the Memorial Art Gallery of the University of Rochester (275-3081). The city's newest museum is one of its most remarkable. Margaret Woodbury Strong was an insatiable collector from childhood and the artifacts she assembled tell the story of American culture and popular taste from about 1820 to 1930. Of particular interest to children is her fabulous collection of dolls and toys at the Margaret Woodbury Strong Museum (263-2700).

George Eastman gave much of his fortune to the cultural life of the city, and the Eastman School of Music of the University of Rochester is world famous. The university's Eastman Theatre downtown is a superb concert hall, where the Rochester Philharmonic Orchestra performs, as well as the several ensembles of the Music School (454-7091). There are also many theater groups in the city. It's best to consult one of the daily newspapers, the *Democrat and Chronicle* or *The Times Union*, to learn what's going on while you're in town. By the way, Gannett Newspapers, which owns both, gives tours of its plant by appointment (232-7100, ext. 3341). All of these suggested attractions are centrally located.

To complement this cultural activity there are several excellent shopping districts in the city. And to top it all off Rochester has some first-rate restaurants; especially recommended is McGuire's on Alexander Street, Rochester's restaurant row.

Trio Number Two

Charts 14803, 14804, 14814

The small-town harbors east of Rochester by and large offer better boating accommodations than those west of the city. They are also more scenic, as each is cradled by wooded bluffs.

Sport fishing, a major pastime along the entire New York coast, is especially prominent here, with a charter fishing fleet in almost every harbor.

Pultneyville

Pultneyville is a private harbor with a hospitable yacht club 25 miles east of Rochester. Formed from the dredged mouth of Salmon Creek, it is a bit tricky to get into. Long ago the hamlet of Pultneyville, population 400, conducted business on the lake and its harbor entrance was graced with a pair of jetties. Now those piers are submerged beneath the surface and constitute a hazard. Nevertheless, the way around them has been well buoyed with two ranges to guide you—once you've identified Pultneyville from offshore, which isn't all that easy to do.

There is a lakefront power plant about 6 miles to the west, and Fairbanks Point is about 2 miles east. When you've spotted occulting white Pultneyville Yacht Club Light on the point northwest of the entrance, a southerly approach will carry you between two pairs of red and green flashing light buoys on a fixed green range that lines up at 189°. The range is on shore, and the front light is equipped with a white diamond-shaped daymark. After passing the second set of buoys the entrance opens up to starboard with another range at 259° showing white and red daymarks and fixed red lights. A third pair of red and green light buoys helps you keep the 5-foot channel. It's best not to attempt this harbor in a blow from the northeast, when heavy seas build up at the entrance.

Once inside the harbor a turn to port leads you up the creek to the **Pultneyville Yacht Club**. There you will find slips and along-side dockage, with gas, pumpout, heads and showers in the clubhouse. The club is a small and informal one with a kitchen, picnic tables and a play area for children. Nor does the village up the road offer much more. There is a general store, a few antique shops, some well-preserved 19th-century homes and an old church now called Gates Hall, where local thespians perform through the summer. Pultneyville is a harbor for escape from the sleek to the quaint.

Sodus Bay

Sodus Bay is almost the opposite. Here, in the best natural harbor on the south shore of the lake, you will find a large sailing fleet and extensive yachting facilities. Though there aren't many bright lights and sights to see in the resort community of Sodus Point, its focus is definitely nautical. The 10-square-mile bay has good water almost throughout and offers a choice of lovely anchorages in addition to the commercial facilities in the northwest corner.

About 11 miles east of Pultneyville a high white bluff shows up to identify the east side of the entrance to Sodus Bay. The dredged channel leading into the bay is protected by a pair of parallel breakwaters, and the group flashing white light displayed on the west pier forms a range at 109° with the flashing green light on the east pier, to assist your approach from the west. The channel, with a controlling depth of 10 feet, is further buoyed and lit. To get around the shallows and submerged ruins off Sand Point just inside the harbor you head southeast after passing through the breakwaters; the flashing white light north of the point has a red sector to warn you if you stray into danger.

The 1,200-person village of Sodus Point and its marine accommodations are clustered around the northwest corner of the bay and out along Sand Point. **Sodus Bay Marina** is the first one you come to on the south shore of Sand Point. With both moorings and dockage at steel-based floating slips in 8 feet, this is a full service marina with all dockside services, repairs, a 20-ton hoist and a marine store. An unusual feature is the antique shop associated with the marina. Next comes the **Sodus Bay Yacht Club**, with alongside and finger dockage in 4 to 6 feet, in addition to moorings. The club's full dockside services, except for fuel, are open to members of reciprocating clubs; the dining room and bar are open weekends.

Sill's Marina, around the curve of the bay behind its own sunken barge breakwall, is the largest establishment, with slips in 12 feet, all dockside services except showers, a 100-ton crane for haulout, full hull, engine, rigging and sail repairs (there is a sailmaker on the premises), marine store and launch ramp. Next door is **Trestle Landing Marina**, with dockage in 10 feet, all dockside services except ice (available nearby), full repairs and a 30-ton travelift. **Arney's Marina**, on the outskirts of town (although here the outskirts aren't far from the center), caters mainly to power boats with slips in 3 to 10 feet, the usual dockside services except diesel and showers, launch ramp, motor repairs and haulout capacity to 30 feet by crane and ramp.

There are several other docks along the busy village waterfront, but they are private and accommodate mainly charter fishing boats. Sodus Point wears the attractive air of an old seafaring village; grocery and hardware stores and a Laundromat are all handy on Bay Street. If you like beer, this is a good place to be. The Sodus Point Malt House for Genesee Brewing Company is across the street from Trestle Landing Marina, and the attractive old stone brewery building has been incorporated into the newer one. Captain Kelly's Lighthouse Inn on the waterfront has good food and offers you no fewer than 17 choices of beer—eight on tap and nine imports. They also have dockage for diners.

If the bustle of Sodus Point exhausts you, you can find peaceful anchorage at several pretty spots around the bay— northwest and southeast of Eagle Island, a restaurant with dockage at Connelly's Cove, the bight east of Thornton Point, or the south end of the bay. On the way you'll find **Oak Park Marina** on the east shore, with floating slips in 6 to 8 feet, all dockside services, a 40-ton travelift, engine and hull repairs, and a picnic area. In approaching the marina, take care not to cut across the point at Bonnie Castle, which shoals out, but proceed down the bay to a point opposite the marina, then turn sharply.

Port Bay

Eight miles east of Sodus Bay Port Bay, about one by two miles, is accessible from the lake through a privately maintained channel. It is lit by flashing red lights on each end of the short west breakwater and two flashing green lighted buoys in the channel, which is dredged to 5 or 6 feet. A gravel pile on the west side of the entrance helps to identify it from the lake. The bay is largely undeveloped with respect to marine services, and its entrance is insufficiently protected to attempt in heavy weather, but there are some good anchorages under the wooded bluffs. These are quite obvious from the convenient inset enlargement on chart 14804.

Little Sodus Bay

Another 7 miles along the scenic coast brings you to Little Sodus Bay, less than half a mile wide by two miles long. This bay, like its big brother, is surrounded by wooded bluffs dotted with attractive summer homes. Most of the marine facilities are clustered in the southwest corner, almost a mile and a half from the rather nondescript village of Fair Haven (population 850) on the east shore.

The channel between the familiar parallel breakwaters extending into the lake has a controlling depth of 7 feet along the east side, but shoals to 4 feet (at chart datum) along the west. Flashing white and green lights are displayed on the piers. A strong current sets easterly across the entrance in high west winds. There is shoal water on both sides immediately inside the breakwaters, so continue on for another 100 to 150 yards before changing course.

A turn to port brings you to **Fairhaven Beach State Park**, where there is alongside dockage for about a dozen boats in 6 feet. There are no services, but there are washrooms in the park, a picnic area and, of course, the beach. If you turn to starboard after clearing the breakwater shoal area, you will see **The Boathouse**, a marina that caters mainly to sail boats. There is alongside dockage and floating slips in 4 to 12 feet, as well as moorings. All dockside and repair services are offered, and the travelift has a 40-foot capacity. There are picnic grounds with grills and swimming from either the bay side or the lakeside beach. This is about as far from the village as you can get, but a very pleasant spot.

As you move down the bay, be aware that Grass Island near the northwest corner is largely submerged in high water. Approaching the southwest cove of the bay, **Fair Haven Yacht Club** is the first accommodation, with 2 to 12 feet at the floating docks, water, ice, heads and showers, for members of recognized clubs. Next is **Chinook Harbor**, with 6 to 10 feet at the slips and all dockside services except pumpout and diesel. They also have a restaurant. The public launch ramp is next door. A buoyed channel leads to **Harbor View Marina**, with 5 feet at low water, the same depth at the older dockage in slips and all dockside services except fuel and pumpout. Some engine repairs are offered, and a 10-ton travelift is available for haulout.

Across the bay in the southeast corner, **Frost Haven Marine Service** has alongside dockage in depths to 11 feet, with all dockside services and a launch ramp. This is a cottage resort with campsites and a picnic area. The **Pleasant Beach Hotel** on the east shore has dockage with electricity, water, gas, restaurant and bar. These two places are closest to the village grocery, hardware and gift shopping and the Saturday night band concerts in the park. There are several sheltered coves for anchorage around the bay, all quite obvious from the enlargement on chart 14803.

The East End
Charts 14802, 14803, 14811, 14813

The coastline continues scenically hilly and fairly steep-to beyond Little Sodus Bay, with one danger spot where Ford Shoals reach out almost a mile. A flashing white light buoy marks the outer extremity.

Oswego

This city of 24,000 people was the first New York settlement on Lake Ontario and has always been an important port. Although not the major lake terminus of the Erie Canal, the Oswego River and Canal was a busy 24-mile connection between Clinton's Ditch and Lake Ontario almost from the beginning. It still does a brisk trade in pleasure boats, even if fewer commercial vessels now ply its waters.

Oswego is easy to spot from offshore by locating the Niagara Mohawk Power station with its two immense stacks 1½ miles west of the harbor and the twin towers of Nine Mile Point Nuclear Power Station 7 miles east. The arrangement of break-waters off the river mouth, designed to reduce harbor surge, can be a bit confusing to a stranger. The piers that project outward into the lake are not parallel, as at most of the other New York harbors, but converge at their outer ends. A detached breakwa-ter lies at a slightly northwest by southeast angle across the pair. You can enter from either side of the detached breakwater, but in strong westerly winds a hefty current runs eastward. There can also be a river current up to five knots coming out of the harbor when the river is in flood. The detached breakwater is marked with a flashing white light at the west end and a flashing red at the east. The occulting red light on the west pierhead has a fog horn; the east pierhead is marked by a flashing green light. There are additional lighted and unlighted buoys to guide you into the harbor and from there into the Barge Canal (as the venerable Erie is now known).

Oswego, 13 miles from Little Sodus Bay, is a customs port of entry with reporting by telephone. You can tie up along the public east wall of the harbor, without services, or you can turn to port to enter the basin of the **Oswego Marina.** The service dock, providing gas, diesel, ice and pumpout, is on the outer wall. The slips in the basin have depths in excess of 8 feet, and there are heads, showers and Laundromat. The marina hauls out on a very large overhead crane and offers full engine and hull repairs. Most important for sailboats transiting the canal, there is mast stepping and unstepping here. The Chart Room restaurant is on the premises.

This marina is the only one in town and is a convenient half mile over the bridge to all the downtown stores, restaurants, movies and hospital. Oswego is a historic city and it retains that appearance, with some well-preserved industrial, commercial and residential buildings in a setting that hasn't yet been sanitized by excessive restoration. The historical museum is in the Richardson-Bates House on East Third Street, and there is a marine museum on the west side of the river. Oswego's early history was far from peaceful; its strategic location was contested in every North American war (except the Mexican). The present Fort Ontario, a few blocks from the marina on the lakefront, was built in 1759 as a successor to other fortifications that were raised here as early as 1727. It was rebuilt in 1839 and was most recently used as a temporary shelter for European refugees after World War II. It has been restored to Civil War period appearance and is worth a visit (343-4711).

North Pond

The bluffs of the south coast recede from the shore after you pass Nine Mile Point and enter the potentially treacherous precincts of Mexico Bay. Here the coast makes an abrupt right-angle turn northward and becomes a dangerous lee in heavy weather. There is no major harbor to break the 40-mile distance across Mexico Bay from Oswego to Henderson Bay, but if you're caught out in worsening weather, there is a refuge halfway between.

North Pond is a beautiful bay, 3½ by 2 miles, surrounded by bluffs, with creeks and marshes in between that shelter wildlife. It is quite shallow, however—about 12 feet at its deepest—and the narrow shifting channel between sand dunes, 3 feet deep at low water, makes entrance difficult. Local residents place red and black buoys to define the channel, but it is not easy to spot from offshore, where the coast seems featureless. A chart enlargement helps. North Pond is a popular fishing ground, and a number of marinas cater to the small boat and charter needs of fishermen. Gas is available, but little or no transient dockage. Your best bet is to anchor in one of the coves along the spit south of the harbor entrance.

Henderson Bay

As you move northward along the east coast Lake Ontario's single chain of islands appears on the horizon. Between the easternmost, Stony Island, and Stony Point on the mainland is the passage that leads from southward to the three lovely bays that make up this corner of the lake. Stony Point Light, an isophase red on a white tower, and a flashing red light buoy off the northeast end of Stony Island help to show the way. Approaching from the west, you pass between this light buoy and the flashing green off Point Peninsula northeast of it. Henderson Bay is entered at Lime Barrel Shoal, also marked by a flashing green light buoy. Leave this buoy to port and swing wide around Six Town Point to avoid its shoals, but mind the long shoal making out from Gull Island. Once you've passed these hazards the bay is clear and deep as you move southward. In high water years the spit on either side of Association Island is submerged; take care not to be misled by what looks like good water. There are two special anchorage areas in the bay, each marked by flashing white light buoys at their four corners.

There is no real village in Henderson Bay, but at the place marked Henderson Harbor on the east side of the bay there are two places to dock. **RCR Yachts** has dockage in 6 to 12 feet, with electricity but not water, diesel fuel but not gas, pumpout, a travelift capable of hauling to 46 feet, hull, engine and rigging repairs. Next door **West View Lodge** also has dockage, with electricity, water, gas, ice and a restaurant.

In the southeast corner of the bay the **Henderson Harbor Yacht Club** extends hospitality at vacant moorings, alongside docks or small slips with 4- to 5-foot depths with all dockside services except fuel. The attractive clubhouse has a dining room and bar, and the grounds have picnic tables and grills. Connell's Marina next door sells gas, has a 10-ton crane and provides repairs but no dockage. To reach it for service you must make the entrance to Graham Creek by coming in on its fixed green range at 117° in order to avoid the rocks and shoals that impede the approach.

In the southwest corner two marinas with aging dockage cater to powerboats. **Harbor's End** has slips in 4 feet, with electricity, water only at the gas dock (no diesel), ice, heads, engine repair and a 15-ton travelift. **Lake Ontario Marina** also has 4 feet at its slips and supplies all dockside services, haulout by crane up to 36 feet, engine and hull repairs, and a launch ramp.

Henderson Bay is a fishing center and is crowded with boats

seeking bass, lake trout and salmon in their seasons. Sail is not much in evidence here. For cruising boats the nicest anchorage is in Whites Bay on the west shore.

Sackets Harbor

Black River Bay lies just northeast of Henderson Bay and can be reached from Henderson through a deep water passage between Bass Island and Horse Island. Boats coming in from the lake approach from the north end of Stony Island, leaving its flashing red to starboard and heading for the flashing white Sackets Harbor Light on Horse Island. Shortly past Horse Island flashing white Navy Point Light guides you into Sackets Harbor. Give the point a wide berth as you come around; the water is shallow up to 200 feet from it.

On the south side of the peninsula **Navy Point Marina** is a full service facility with 6 to 13 feet of water at its slips, all dockside and repair services, including Laundromat, a 20-ton open-end travelift and a marine store. There is also a picnic ground with grills. Across the small harbor the town provides alongside tie-up at Market Square Park, with electricity, water, heads and a launch ramp.

Sackets Harbor is a quaint village of 1,200, whose interesting history is being carefully preserved. It was at one time the major American naval base on the Great Lakes, a critical shipbuilding center during the War of 1812 and the site of the first exchange of fire in that conflict. Two battles were fought here, and Battlefield Park is posted with signs and maps to explain the action. An annual reenactment of the Battle of 1812 takes place in July. The Pickering-Beach mansion, an 1817 summer home at the end of Main Street next to the battlefield, has been handsomely restored as a historical museum (646-2052), as has the Union Hotel. All of these are close to the marina and the public dock, Sackets Harbor being a small place, and there are other lovely old buildings to admire in the village. Necessities can be obtained at the general store and bakery, and there are taverns and restaurants.

Chaumont Bay

The third bay of the triumvirate in northeast Lake Ontario is also approached from that useful flashing red buoy off Stony Island. In this case you aim for flashing white Cherry Island Light, passing between Point Peninsula and Pillar Point. To reach the village of Chaumont and its marine facilities, leave Cherry Island to starboard, minding the shoal that makes out from the light, and coast along Point Salubrious (I wonder who conferred that name), leaving Johnson Shoal flashing green light buoy and the red and green off Independence Point to port. At the Chaumont Harbor Light, fixed green on a white tower, you enter Sawmill Bay.

On the port side, almost at the end of the bay, is the **Crescent Yacht Club**, with alongside dockage in 4 to 12 feet for members of reciprocating clubs. There is electricity, water, heads and showers, and the clubhouse has a dining room and bar. Next door **Crescent Marine** has older dockage in 8 feet, with all dockside services except showers and diesel fuel, haulout up to 60 feet on a marine railway, hull, engine, and rigging repairs and a launch ramp. The village of Chaumont, about half a mile away, has a look of faded gentility about it, but essential shopping is available.

Much of Chaumont Bay is smooth-sided and exposed for anchorage, but shelter can be found in the cove adjacent to Long Point State Park on Point Peninsula. Chaumont is the last harbor on our circumnavigation of Lake Ontario. Twenty miles around Point Peninsula and Grenadier Island is Tibbets Point, the southeast entrance to the St. Lawrence River.

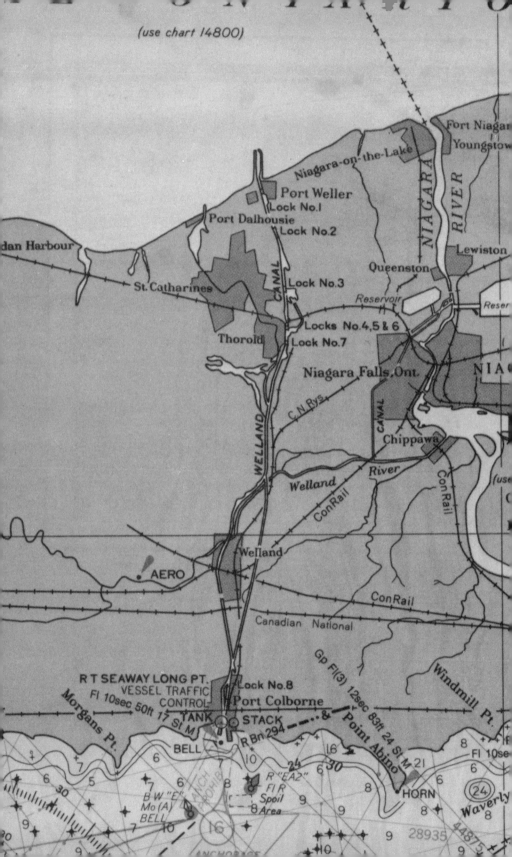

3
ENTR'ACTE:
THE WELLAND
CANAL

Chart 2042

The geography of North America imposed barriers to westward migration from the English-speaking nations on the seacoast—the Appalachian Mountains by land and the Falls of Niagara by sea. Americans solved the problem by building the Erie Canal across a gap in the mountains to Lake Erie in 1825, to create a through water route between the Great Lakes and the Atlantic Ocean. For Canada Niagara Falls was the major impediment to continental access via the St. Lawrence River and the Great Lakes.

The First Welland Canal across the Niagara Peninsula opened in 1829, just four years after the Erie. It was privately built, but government soon recognized its strategic importance and took over for enlargement and improvement into the Second Welland Canal in the 1840s. The number of locks was reduced from 40 built of wood to 27 and built of stone. The Third Canal was constructed between 1875 and 1887; the Fourth, and latest, Welland Canal was begun in 1913 and opened in 1932. This was the most massive reconstruction, in which, among other changes, the Lake Ontario terminus was moved from Port Dalhousie to Port Weller. The number of locks was reduced to eight. Improvements continue. Between 1938 and 1973 three tunnels were burrowed under the canal to prevent bottlenecks on important land routes. At one of them cars, trains and ships can bypass one another without conflict. During this period there was also some straightening of the canal, allowing old routes to be used as recreational waters.

The Welland Canal is a critical segment of the St. Lawrence Seaway. It readily accommodates ocean freighters—1,385 of them transited in 1982 along with 3,837 lake boats—but once more it's too small for the largest lakers. The maximum allowable ship length is 730 feet, and a growing part of the lake fleet well exceeds that size, up to 1,000 feet. There is talk of a Fifth Welland Canal. For pleasure boats transit of this segment of the seaway is a remarkable experience, but it requires some advance preparation of both vessel and crew.

Port Weller

Because commercial traffic takes priority in the canal, transit for a pleasure boat can take up to 12 hours. Once you're in it you must keep on going; partial transit is prohibited, except in emergency such as a breakdown. There isn't any place to dock or anchor anyway along the 27½ miles of the canal's length. Therefore, you want to get an early morning start on your passage. The canal functions 24 hours a day, but night passage is ill advised for pleasure boats. If you spend the night preceding a southbound transit at Port Dalhousie, you are 5 miles from the Lake Ontario entrance; from Niagara-on-the-Lake and Youngstown it's 9. But you can lay over at a pleasant marina just around the corner from the canal entrance, which is called Port Weller, and across the levee from the canal itself.

St. Catharines Marina is protected by a breakwater with a flashing red light on a white tower with red top. Entrance is made from the south, so you must move down into the bay east of the Port Weller breakwaters until you can make the approach. Note the low narrow strip of land extending eastward near the outer end of the eastern land spit forming Port Weller. It is marked by a red spar. Otherwise the bay is clear and deep. Port Weller is located from offshore by the radio tower, the flashing red light on a red skeleton tower equipped with a fog horn on the west breakwater and the range lights on a course of 180° with orange and white daymarks on the structures. The front light is a fixed yellow, the rear a yellow, red and green sector light. The marina offers slips in 3 to 10 feet of water, but there is only 4½ feet at the fuel dock in low water. All dockside services are available, as well as engine and hull repairs and a 10-ton travelift. It is several miles to town and shopping. For boats making the transit from Lake Erie there is only one place to stay the night before, Port Colborne, discussed a little later.

Locking Through

The strategic importance of the Welland Canal dictates strict rules and regulations, applicable to pleasure boats and giant ships alike. But for the recreational craft there are a few special considerations. The nicest one is that it's cheaper, $4 per lock. The toll can be paid only to the lockmaster at Lock 3, so have your $32 ready in national currency, or you can order tickets in advance from the Seaway Authority (see Appendix C for addresses). Boats less than 20 feet in length, or without motors, are prohibited. Because it is more difficult to lock up than to lock down, boats making the transit from Lake Ontario to Lake Erie are required to have a minimum crew of three. For cruising couples it is usually possible to hire a local young person as a third crew member by making inquiry through the marinas at Port Weller and Port Dalhousie. (If you're unsuccessful in finding someone this way, telephone the lockmaster at the first lock for assistance.) He or she will be with you only through the first seven locks, which are concentrated in the first 7½ miles of the canal. You'll still be in the city of St. Catharines when your crew member departs, so he'll have little trouble finding transportation home.

Locking lines are supplied to pleasure boats by the lock tenders. The most important equipment you must carry are the fenders that will protect your hull from the rough lock walls. Ordinary plastic fenders, no matter how large, are likely to be destroyed when pressure from a filling lock presses your boat to the wall and it scrapes upward. Horizontal fender boards are equally useless, but very stout (four by four) vertical boards extending well above and below the deck line will do the job, as will bags stuffed with hay, which you may be able to obtain at the marinas at each end of the canal. You will be required to moor to lock walls on either side, so it's best to fender both sides of your boat before you start. There is little time between locks to switch fenders. After the boat is decked out in fenders, every crew member is required to don a life jacket.

There are two ways to begin your transit. When you've entered between the outer piers of either Port Weller or Port

Colborne harbors you can call VDX-22, Seaway Welland, on channel 16 or 14 (to which you'll switch for working traffic) to receive instructions about how to proceed. Or you can tie up at the pleasure craft dock on the port side just before Lock 1 or Lock 8, about a mile from the entrance pierheads, and use the special telephone there to call the lockmaster. In either case, you must keep your radio on and tuned to channel 14 throughout your transit.

There is an elaborate system of light signals at the locks, basically red for a closed lock not ready to open, a series of flashing yellow lights if a lock is being filled or emptied to accommodate a waiting vessel (it takes 12 minutes to move an average of 21 million imperial gallons of water into or out of a lock) and green for "go" into the lock. There are also three stages of "Limits of Approach" before each lock that are equipped with lights. Whenever you see red, stop and wait by the side of the canal for instructions or a change in light color. There are tie-up walls at each lock, but they're meant for ships and require a high leap to reach the bollards. Most pleasure boats circle out of the way.

Pleasure boats are sent into the lock chamber first when they are locked through with a ship. (Small craft are not permitted to lock through with certain cargoes, so you may have to wait quite a while for your turn.) They are usually directed up to the front of the lock, where the lock tender will drop bow and stern lines to waiting crew members. These should be turned around a strong cleat *but never made fast.* The motor should be turned off while locking, and as the boat rises in the chamber your line tenders will take up the slack. Turbulence varies from lock to lock, and it can be difficult to hold the boat close to the wall in some locks or keep it safely off in others. All you can do is stay alert and use your strength as judiciously as possible. When several pleasure boats are locking through together the lockmaster often instructs them to raft. The largest boat will be placed against the wall, and the others will raft up against it in descending order of size. Keep hold of the locking lines until instructed to cast them off, then proceed out of the lock expeditiously. Remember that the helmsman of the ship behind you cannot see your boat from his bridge. The order of passage is maintained through the canal, so adjust your speed accordingly and observe the canal speed limit of seven miles per hour.

There are some characteristics of the several locks that you should know about. When the locks are being emptied there are sometimes eddies and cross-currents near the Limit of Ap-

Welland Canal lock.

proach. If Lock 1 is your first experience, you have 1½ miles to catch your breath before Lock 2 repeats the process, then 2¼ miles between Locks 2 and 3. You want to maneuver smartly in Lock 3 because it's a popular St. Catharines tourist attraction, complete with viewing stand. The first three locks lift you a total of 139 feet to the foot of the Niagara Escarpment. One mile past Lock 3 you enter the double flight locks. Four, five and six open directly from one to the next for another 139-foot lift up the face of the escarpment in a distance of half a mile. There are two sets of these steps, enabling vessels to pass in both directions simultaneously. Another half mile farther on, Lock 7 overcomes the final 46½ feet to the average level of Lake Erie. The following tabulation shows which side you moor to in each lock:

	Upbound	*Downbound*
Lock 1	Starboard	Port
Lock 2	Port	Starboard
Lock 3	Port	Starboard
Lock 4	Port	Port
Lock 5	Port	Port
Lock 6	Port	Port
Lock 7	Port	Starboard
Lock 8	Starboard	Port

After you exit Lock 7 you will have a placid passage of about 20 miles through the Niagara countryside, with only one city of any size, Welland. There are 10 opening bridges on the canal. Most of the tenders see you coming, but they also use red and green light signals and you may have to circle at the edge of the channel to wait. Much of the canal is tree-lined, not just for aesthetic reasons, but because the trees act as a windbreak for the passing ships and also help to hold the banks against erosion. At some side channels and old waterways there can be a cross-current.

Lock 8 is in Port Colborne, the Lake Erie terminus of the canal, and usually amounts to nothing at all. It is there because of the enormous fluctuations in water level that sometimes occur in Lake Erie, as much as 11 feet at Port Colborne. Most of the time there is little change in level, and sometimes both gates are open and you simply pass through the lock chamber. This is an agreeable way to begin a downbound transit, which is easier all along the way.

Port Colborne

A city of 20,000 people, Port Colborne can be more than just an overnight stop on the way into or out of the Welland Canal. Its grain elevators and a couple of plant chimneys make it conspicuous from offshore, and from the red and white Mo(A) sea buoy all the way into the harbor there are numerous lights and light buoys. Note that the harbor is buoyed as if coming from the sea via the Welland Canal, with reds on the port side entering from Lake Erie and greens to starboard. The breakwaters are parallel to the shoreline, with a wing projecting lakeward near the east end of the west breakwater. It has a fixed red light with a fog horn. Immediately after passing between the breakwaters, at the flashing white light on the west breakwater, a buoyed channel leads northwestward. This one is colored conventionally and leads around the west side of the elevator wharf to **Port Colborne Yacht Harbour**. There are floating slips in 5 to 10 feet, with all dockside services (not all slips have water faucets), a launch ramp, a small travelift, and hull and engine repairs. Next door **Marlon Marina** caters mainly to smaller boats in slips with 4 to 5 feet, but has all dockside services except diesel fuel.

These marinas are pleasantly situated about half a mile from downtown shopping. Close by is a park with children's playground and Sunday evening band concerts. Downtown shopping is convenient and includes a Friday morning farmer's market. The Port Colborne Historical and Marine Museum on King Street (834-7604) is a complex of buildings that includes a tea room in a restored 1913 cottage. There is a walking tour published by the Local Architectural Conservation Advisory Committee, and several restaurants in town. Rathfon Inn, part of which dates to 1794, is an attractive country resort 3½ miles along the lakeshore; they will pick you up for dinner if requested when you call for reservations.

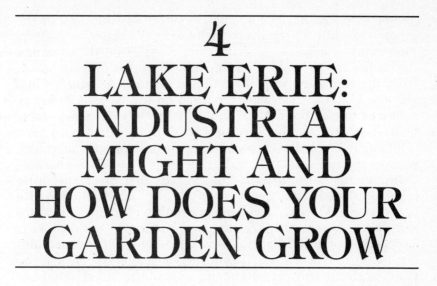

4
LAKE ERIE: INDUSTRIAL MIGHT AND HOW DOES YOUR GARDEN GROW

In many respects Lake Erie is the flip side of Lake Ontario. It, too, is set on a fairly level plain of rich soil. But here the industrial towns and cities march along the southern, American shore, while the north side rims the agricultural "sun parlor" of Ontario. Erie also has few natural harbors, but in contrast to its sister its island group lies at the western end of the lake. Where Ontario is deep, Erie is shallow. It is, in fact, the shallow depth of this 240-by-55-mile body of water, that nowhere exceeds 210 feet in depth and averages 62 feet, that conditions its character.

Although it lies on the same east-west axis as Lake Ontario, Lake Erie is more vulnerable to sudden wind-driven changes in water level and seiches that can measure up to 10 feet and last as long as 12 hours. Sustained strong winds, usually from the west, drive forward a volume of surface water too large to be returned through the shallow layer of reverse currents beneath the disturbed level. Consequently, the harbors at the western end of the lake drop drastically in water level, while it piles up at the eastern end. Harbors along the middle ranges do not experience such extreme changes.

Lake Erie weather is not radically different from that of the other lakes, but its relatively shallow depths generate its infamous short, steep seas in strong southwest or northeast winds. And it lies in the direct path of thunderstorms moving across from the southwest. Squalls on Lake Erie can be sudden and vicious. The strongest wind recorded on the lake, at 87 knots, occurred during the famous squall of July 4, 1969, when many boats were lost. Weather forecasts are especially important here.

If Lake Erie's shallowness causes some problems for mariners, it also confers the lake's greatest blessing. The fish population, both commercial and sport, far exceeds that of all the other lakes combined. The "death of Lake Erie," much publicized a few years back, was a decidedly premature obituary. There are shifts in the species that are abundant, to be sure, but the lake is a sport fisherman's delight, as its vast fleet of small and medium-sized motorboats testifies. If Ontario is a sailor's lake, Erie is the realm of the motorboat (although plenty of the "other" kind can be found on both lakes, of course). And the relatively warm water (average 73° in August) that supports the fish combines with sand beaches to make Erie a good swimming lake now that industrial pollution is largely controlled. The cruising season here is a good six months, May to October.

The wealth of the lake is responsible for two types of man-made hazards you should watch out for. Fish nets are liberally placed all around its shores, with stakes to mark them. And off the Canadian shore, mainly at the east and west ends, there are underwater gas wells, some equipped with towers that display a quick flashing white light and fog horn. The charts indicate the areas of greatest concentration of both kinds of hazards.

If trouble does arise, there are United States Coast Guard stations at Buffalo, Erie, Ashtabula, Fairport, Cleveland, Lorain, Marblehead, and Toledo; a Canadian Coast Guard cutter is based at Port Dover.

Lake Erie was the last of the Great Lakes to be seen by white men. So effective was the Iroquois menace in closing off the lower lakes to the French that they weren't even sure it existed until two exploring priests traced its shores from eastward in 1669. In one of those extraordinary coincidences of history, they met another Frenchman, Adrien Jolliet, coming the other way with an Indian guide. Ten years later René-Robert Cavelier, Sieur de La Salle, built the first sailing ship on the lake at Cayuga Creek near Buffalo. The *Griffon* made a successful passage all the way up the lakes to Green Bay in Lake Michigan, where she took on a load of furs intended to finance La Salle's exploration of the Mississippi. On the return voyage she disappeared—the first of many lake vessels simply to "sail away." Her fate remains one of the unsolved mysteries of Great Lakes lore.

Lake Erie began to play a significant role in the fur trade during the 18th century, and the Niagara Portage was a critical pass in the battle between France and England for supremacy in North America. There was less action here during the American Revolution, but the War of 1812 saw one of its most critical engagements in the naval Battle of Lake Erie. Staunch Indian resistance to American settlement had kept the Ohio frontier in turmoil until General Anthony Wayne's 1794 victory at Fallen Timbers near Toledo ended the Indian Wars. Nine years later Ohio became a state.

The opening of the Erie Canal in 1825 was probably the most important event in Lake Erie's history. It became the high road to western settlement and the return east of the produce those settlers harvested from the rich soils of Ohio and the Mississippi Valley. Except for Leamington and Port Colborne at either end of the lake, the Canada shoreside farming and fishing settlements moved sleepily from the 1820s to the 1980s. Across the lake it was a different story. Settlers continued to pour into the region. More canals were built, connecting Lake Erie to the Ohio River, and all along the lakeshore port towns sprang up to serve them. Today all the Ohio canals are gone, save a couple of historic restorations, but increasing wealth brought continuous industrial and commercial growth to these towns as the 19th and 20th centuries moved on. Some became and remain important metropolitan centers—Buffalo, Cleveland, Toledo—where illustrious names in the robber baronage established empires in steel, oil, glass and shipbuilding. Others faded into small industrial city status—Ashtabula, Lorain, Sandusky. Others never grew beyond quaint small towns.

Lake Erie's historical contrast continues—industrial prowess strides across the southern shore opposite the tranquil gardens of the north coast. But each of the industrial harbors has a place for recreational craft, for pleasure boating dates back many years in the region's past. Consequently, there are not a few elderly marinas, although there is a growing number of newer, modern ones as well. And between the industrial harbors are residential towns with extensive marine facilities. There is quite a lot to choose from on the American side of the lake, bordered by New York, a corner of Pennsylvania, a great swath of Ohio, and a piece of Michigan. The Ontario side is almost entirely rural and its marinas are of the simplest kind, but there is a quieter, more away-from-it-all atmosphere here.

Lake Erie is a paradox. Its shores are not dramatically scenic, the harbors on the American side are congested and often industrial, those on the Canadian side are lacking in amenities, the lake has a deserved reputation for being cranky and difficult to deal with at times. Yet its rich marine life, with the vast bird population related to it, and the sheer joy of being on the water, keep thousands of resident boaters utterly devoted to it. For the crew of a cruising boat there are some very special places to visit.

The East End

Charts 14822, 14823, 14832, 14833

Maritime visitors to Lake Erie still come from the east by the old Erie Canal route or the almost as old Welland Canal. For convenience, we will circumnavigate counterclockwise from the Welland.

A run eastward of about 20 miles from Port Colborne, along a shore lined with summer cottages, brings you to the Niagara River. Halfway along you will round Point Abino, marked by a group flashing white light and a fog signal. In the curve of Abino Bay, about 1.8 miles north of the point, the large, white Gilded Age clubhouse of the **Buffalo Canoe Club** is prominent on the shore. A long pier extends into the lake, with another large white building on the end. Although it may have been a canoe club when it was founded in 1882, the friendly club is now devoted to sailboats and powerboats. Visitors are accommodated on moorings in depths up to five feet, with a launch service summoned by three blasts on the horn. The spacious old clubhouse has showers, a dryer for sailors' gear, though no washer, a very attractive lounge area, dining room and bar, a snack bar and outside three tennis courts and a beach. From here it's about ten miles to the river or the Buffalo Harbor entrance.

Niagara River

From its broad entrance in Lake Erie the Niagara River looks deceptively placid, especially on a wind-quiet day. One might never suspect that the thunderous cataract is just 20 miles downstream. In fact, however, the river's descent begins right at the entrance and will drop 10 feet before it reaches the falls. The 2- to 3-mile current in the first couple of miles increases to 8 or 9 miles per hour in the 2-mile-long narrows between the Peace Bridge and the foot of Squaw Island. Then the river widens again before dividing into two channels around Grand Island, where the currents run only 1 to 4 miles per hour. About a mile beyond the junction at the north end of Grand Island the waters gather momentum into the swirling rapids that lead to the precipice of Niagara Falls. But no vessels are permitted to get that far; the channel junction is the effective head of navigation.

There is a quiet passage around the upper river's turbulence via the Black Rock Canal close along the American shore, reached from the open lake via the North Entrance to Buffalo Harbor. Buffalo is, of course, conspicuous from the lake, with its industrial stacks and office towers. From the red and white Mo(A) sea buoy entrance can be made south or north of the three-mile-long enclosing breakwater. The South Entrance leads to commercial and industrial piers, the North Entrance to the Black Rock Canal and the industrial Buffalo River. Numerous lights and lighted buoys line the channel, and the Buffalo Harbor Light, a tall white tower with a flashing white light, is equipped with a fog horn. The canal will be described a little later. Meanwhile, for those who have a powerful motor or two, and need no more than 22 feet of overhead clearance, we will follow the natural course of the river.

In addition to the current there are unmarked shoals in the stretch south of the Peace Bridge, although those in mid-stream are covered by at least 6 feet of water. Middle Reefs, right at the entrance, are marked by an abandoned lighthouse and a flashing red lighted buoy on the Canadian side. And it is on the Canadian side of the invisible boundary that you will make your passage. Stay at least a quarter of a mile offshore to avoid the rocks and shoals along the coast and remember that moving downstream on the Niagara River is "proceeding from seaward"—reds are on the starboard hand. For passing under the Peace Bridge the fourth span from the U.S. side is recommended, but be prepared for powerful eddies and the swiftest current right here. A mile and a half below this high bridge the International Railroad Bridge is fixed at 22 feet; the swing span you may notice at the east end no longer opens.

Along this stretch of the Ontario shore you are passing the city of Fort Erie. You may get a glimpse of the historic old fort, which has been handsomely restored, but there are no small craft docking facilities in town. Buffalo's industrial panorama stretches along the starboard shore on Squaw Island and across the ramparts of the Black Rock Canal. Where the river divides around Grand Island the Chippewa Channel on the Canadian side becomes a broad stream, curving for 9½ miles around suburban and rural shorelines, fronted on both sides by scenic parkways. The controlling depth is 9 feet. About 4 miles below the International Bridge the **Niagara Parks Commission Marina** is an attractive one, with floating slips in 10 feet and all dockside services. There is also a snack bar and a Canada Customs service. There are no other services within several miles, however.

Almost directly across the channel on the Grand Island, New York side, is the **Beaver Island State Park Marina**, a very attractive new facility, with 8 feet at the slips, all dockside services except fuel, a picnic ground and restaurant. The entrance is protected by breakwaters, marked with flashing red and green lights. The park is a large one, with a big recreation building near the marina that is reminiscent of Independence Hall, playgrounds, picnic grounds, beach and golf course.

When turning around the lower end of Grand Island near the limit of navigation it's advisable to take the channel between Navy and Grand islands and enter the United States' Niagara River Channel just below the North Grand Island Bridge, a fixed span at 46 feet. There are some lighted breakwaters and cribs relating to the industrial installations at this Niagara Falls end of the channel. Along this side of the river is where most of the Buffalo area marine facilities are located, interspersed with the industrial. Many of them do not accommodate transients, however.

La Salle Yacht Club on the mainland accommodates visitors from reciprocating yacht clubs at slips in 8 feet with all dockside services, except fuel; the clubhouse has a dining room and bar. Two fixed red lights help identify the club from the channel. A short distance east, in Little River, **Smith Boys Marina** has slips and alongside docking in 6 to 25 feet; all dockside services except showers; haulout by travelift up to 30 tons; full engine, hull and rigging repair; a marine store; and spacious grounds with grills and picnic tables. Essential shopping is a five-minute walk, and rental cars are available to take you to the splendor of Niagara Falls, the city lights of Buffalo, or both. Across the river on Grand Island a buoyed channel leads to **Sandy Beach Yacht Club**, with a quick flashing white light at the end of the T-shaped dock. Members of recognized yacht clubs are accommodated in slips with 20 feet and the usual dockside services except fuel.

The clubhouse bar is open on weekends, and there is a large lawn here, too, with picnic facilities.

The Niagara River Channel is extensively buoyed, with a controlling depth of 12 feet. Remember that the buoyage will be reversed as you move south. About 7½ miles upstream the Erie Canal, officially the New York State Barge Canal, terminates at the Niagara River via Tonawanda Creek. About 4 miles farther upstream, just above the Interstate 90 fixed bridge with 99-foot clearance, is **Marina Bay Club**, with 3½ to 6 feet at its slips, electricity, water, ice and heads. The travelift can handle 20 tons, with engine, hull and rigging repairs available, and mast stepping and unstepping for transit of the Erie Canal. Ripples Restaurant is located on the premises in an otherwise industrial neighborhood. A mile and a half farther, on the Grand Island side, **Anchor Marina** offers all dockside services, except pumpout and diesel, at its slips with 6-foot depths. The travelift here has a 15-ton capacity, and mast-stepping, engine, hull and rigging repairs are available. Next door the **Buffalo Launch Club** offers reciprocal privileges to power boats and a public restaurant. There are no commercial services nearby.

The Black Rock Canal

Just off the entrance to Anchor Marina you begin the approach to the Black Rock Canal, with a pair of fixed red range lights with white daymarks displayed a couple of miles upstream on a course of 139°. The American side of the river is not navigable from this point south. Just beyond those range lights is **Jafco Marina**, one of Buffalo's largest, with all dockside services in 10 to 12 feet of water at the slips; a 30-ton hoist; full engine, hull and rigging repairs; and a large marine store. The marina also has a restaurant and bar.

Half a mile beyond Jafco the Federal Lock will lift you 5 feet to the level of Lake Erie. Pleasure craft are locked upbound on the half hour and downbound on the hour, but commercial traffic is given priority, so it is advisable to call the lockmaster in advance on channel 12 or channel 16, call sign WUD-21 Black Rock Lock. Red and green lights at the lock gates indicate their closed or open position. There is a speed limit of 6 miles per hour in the canal. It is crossed by two bridges with closed clearance of 17 feet that open on a signal of one long and one short blast, followed by the high level Peace Bridge. To transit the canal from Lake Erie you enter Buffalo Harbor through the North Entrance, pass the Buffalo River entrance channel, where you might encounter considerable cross currents, and at flashing green light buoy "1" begin your turn to port into the canal entrance channel.

Not far above the Peace Bridge you can pull off the canal at the **Buffalo Yacht Club**. Dockage at either fixed or floating slips is available for members of recognized yacht clubs, with all dockside services. The attractive clubhouse has a fine dining room and bar. The 3½-mile stretch of canal from the lock to Buffalo Harbor is bordered mainly by industry and Interstate 90, but toward the upper end there is a large redeveloped area of waterfront, backed by the tall buildings of downtown Buffalo.

Buffalo

Just before the turn to exit the harbor, or at the turn into the canal if you're coming from Lake Erie, Erie Basin opens up, with a flashing red light on a white tower at the end of the enclosing pier. **Erie Basin Marina**, part of the impressive multiuse redevelopment of this waterfront area, is an attractive facility with fixed and floating slips in 21 feet of water and all dockside services. There is a launch ramp, but no haulout or repairs. The Hatch restaurant is on the property, with others nearby, and a supermarket is located in one of the apartment houses across the highway. This is the place from which to explore downtown Buffalo, with a bus stop near the marina entrance and taxis available as well.

In addition to the usual downtown amenities of any large city (Buffalo has almost half a million people)—restaurants, theaters, shops—Buffalo has an exceptional historic district, where both conducted and self-guided walking tours are available. The city was among the nation's largest in the latter years of the 19th century, and its prosperity was articulated in the stone and brick of splendid mansions along Delaware Avenue and adjoining streets. Two native sons were sent to the White House during the halcyon years, Millard Fillmore and Grover Cleveland, and a third had the honor to be assassinated here while attending the Pan American Exposition of 1901. William McKinley lingered almost a week after he was gunned down. His vice president, Theodore Roosevelt, staying at the home of prominent attorney Ansley Wilcox, took the oath of office as successor in the Wilcox library on September 14. The house at 641 Delaware Avenue is now the Theodore Roosevelt National Historic Site (884-0095) and the centerpiece of the Allentown Historic District. It is here that you can arrange a walking tour (884-0330). There are interesting shops as well as houses to see. If you're here the second week in June, you can enjoy the annual Allentown Art Festival at the same time.

Farther out from downtown, along Elmwood Avenue, are two excellent museums, the Albright-Knox Art Gallery (882-8700), with an outstanding collection of contemporary art, and the Buffalo and Erie County Historical Society Museum (873-9644), the only structure remaining from the Pan American Exposition. If your interest in architecture isn't yet sated there is a Frank Lloyd Wright house owned by the state that can be toured by appointment (636-2901). For an unusual experience you can visit the world's oldest and largest player piano roll manufacturer. QRS Music Rolls, at 1026 Niagara Street, conducts two tours a day (885-4600). Finally, at the foot of Main Street there are two World War II naval vessels open to visitors and the Museum of Naval History is nearby (847-1773).

Dunkirk

It's 35 miles from the red and white sea buoy at Buffalo to the next harbor southwest on Lake Erie at Dunkirk. Although there are no major hazards along the way, bear in mind that this is a lee shore in prevailing westerly winds. The pretty bluffs along the coast are cut by ravines carrying small streams down to the lake, and vineyards reach inland from the bluff tops. Cattaraugus Creek is the largest of the streams, and its mouth is a harbor of refuge for small, shallow draft boats. Its tricky, shifting entrance has recently been improved with breakwaters, and the channel is now marked by daybeacons.

The big Niagara Mohawk power plant at the entrance to Dunkirk harbor identifies it from offshore; the three chimneys are floodlit at night. From the flashing red buoy off Point Gratiot, which is marked by a big white occulting light, enter the harbor on a southeast course between the pierhead and the detached breakwater. Flashing red and green lights flank the entrance, and a buoyed channel leads to a pair of inner breakwaters. The west one is marked by flashing red lights, and you will pass around the western end of it to approach the only facility for transient boats, the hospitable **Dunkirk Yacht Club**. Controlling depth in the channel and the yacht basin is 5 feet. The club has good slips and all dockside services except fuel. There is a dryer in the informal clubhouse, but no washer, and there are barbecue grills in the waterfront park in which the club is located. Stefan's, east of the club, has gas, but ask about water depths before you approach.

Dunkirk is an old town, and now a very quiet one, with 15,000 people. The yacht club is at the foot of Central Avenue, the main street, and convenient to the downtown stores, including groceries, a few blocks away. There are also restaurants nearby. Many of the older towns on Lake Erie have cleared their waterfronts of warehouses and industrial buildings, often not replacing them, so as to give a rather bleak, if spacious, look to the waterfront area. Dunkirk is one of these. But you can learn something of what the city was by a visit to the Historical Museum on Washington Avenue; the hours are severely limited, so call first (366-6352). On July Fourth weekend the town sponsors a Harborfest in the park.

Barcelona

Barcelona is a small harbor of refuge 17 miles southwest of Dunkirk, with depths in the entrance channel and basin ranging from 5 to 8 feet. Although enclosed by a pair of converging breakwaters, it is not adequately protected from north to east winds, and in westerly winds there is often a bad surge. The breakwaters are marked by flashing red and white lights, and a white building with red roof helps to identify it from the lake. The old lighthouse on the hill back of the waterfront gives Barcelona its claim to fame, as this was the nation's first to be serviced with gas, in 1830. Thirteen burners lighted the mariner's way until the light was decommissioned in 1859.

Monroe Marina in the southwest corner of the basin is a friendly, family establishment with steel docks in 5 to 8 feet, all dockside services except pumpout, a 10-ton travelift, all repairs and a marine store. There is a grocery store a block away, fresh and smoked fish for sale at dockside and a harbor front restaurant. But Barcelona is not a village as such; it is the harbor for the town of Westfield a couple of miles inland.

Erie
Charts 14824, 14835

The canny Revolutionary leaders of the new state of Pennsylvania foresaw the future importance of the Great Lakes and bought their state a 45-mile stretch of Lake Erie frontage shortly

PHOTO COURTESY OF NEW YORK STATE DEPARTMENT OF COMMERCE

Barcelona, New York.

after the War of Independence. They chose wisely and well, acquiring one of only two natural harbors on the lake. The city that began to grow up there after settlement of the Indian wars in 1794 became a rich port and industrial center, making it an interesting place to visit today. But its place in American history will be forever secured as the construction and assembly site for the fleet of little warships with which the young Captain Oliver Hazard Perry swept Britannia from Lake Erie in 1813. His flagship, *Niagara*, still sits proudly where she was born, raised from the bottom of the bay in 1913 to celebrate the centennial of his stunning victory. Lake Erie folks have, in fact, been celebrating Perry and his victory ever since it occurred. As you enter the harbor you'll see the first of several monuments to the event, and Perry's name has been conferred on places in virtually every town and hamlet on the south coast.

In addition to its strategic value, Pennsylvania's "Erie Triangle" is a scenic bit of real estate. The handsome old city is set on the line of bluffs that continues along the coast for the 28 miles from Barcelona. And the encircling arm of the Presque Isle Peninsula that forms the harbor is a beautiful natural area of woods, marshes and lagoons, a 3,000-acre state park. Tall stacks identify the city from the lake. In coming from the east you simply continue on a southwest course to the buoyed channel and entrance range of fixed green lights shown from white towers on a course of 235°. If you are coming from the west, big Presque Isle Light on the northwest side of the peninsula displays a flashing white light. The 4½-by-1½-mile harbor is entered between a pair of piers, with an occulting red light with a fog horn on the north jetty and the front range light on the south pier. The buoyed channel in the harbor leads to the commercial wharves, but most of Presque Isle Bay is sufficiently deep and clear for pleasure craft to navigate without difficulty. Anchorage is not advisable, however, as the sheltered spots are shallow.

There are three locations for dockage. **Presque Isle State Park** has a fine marina, reached from the center of the harbor on a range of 340° formed by fixed red lights with white and black daymarks. Lighted buoys further outline the entrance itself, where a turn to port brings you to the docks with 6- to 9-foot depths and all dockside services except diesel fuel. There are picnic tables at the marina, and the large park has beaches, hiking trails and a nature center. But the shape of the peninsula is such that these attractions are a long distance from the marina. In fact, the marina's isolation is a severe disadvantage, as the city buses do not run out here and it's about an 8-mile cab ride to downtown. On the other hand, if you're a fisherman, this is a good base for angling the productive waters of Presque Isle Bay. Many species are landed here; in recent years smallmouth bass and steelhead trout have been especially abundant.

In the southwest corner of the bay the **Erie Yacht Club** extends hospitality to members of reciprocating clubs. Its basin is completely enclosed by a breakwall with an occulting white light marking the northeast corner, red and green entrance lights, and fixed red range lights on a course of 150° through the entrance. There is 10 to 12 feet of depth in the channel and the basin. Dockage for guests is alongside, and all dockside services are offered. The attractive clubhouse has a dining room and bar. The club is located in a charming residential neighborhood, but it, too, is inconveniently distant from downtown. Because Erie is built on a bluff cut by ravines, it is not an easy city in which to move around. From the yacht club the route downtown is a rather roundabout 2½ to 3 miles.

There are three marinas and one yacht club downtown, however, that offer dockage to transients on a space-available basis. They are, as might be expected, older facilities than the others. The Public Dock is a large cross-shaped pier, and behind the arms on either side of the main stem is a sheltered area called the Canal Basin. In the west basin **Gem City Marina** has

PHOTO COURTESY OF THE NEW YORK STATE DEPARTMENT
OF COMMERCE

Lakeshore at evening.

slips and alongside docking in 10 feet, with gas, ice, heads and showers; dockside electricity and water were being installed in 1984. Engine repairs are available and a travelift up to 25 tons. Next door to the marina the **Presque Isle Yacht Club** accommodates members of recognized clubs in slips and alongside, with depth of 10 feet and the usual dockside services, except pumpout and fuel. The clubhouse has a bar.

In the east basin **R. D. McAllister Sport Boat Center** is a venerable marina that has been in the same family for 50 years. Docking is alongside in 10 feet, with all dockside services except ice, pumpout and showers. Catering almost entirely to powerboats, engine and hull repairs are offered, and an unusual method of haulout—an 80-ton capacity elevator, constructed in 1926. There is also a marine store. Just east of the Canal Basin **Bayshore Marina** is in the process of being rebuilt and enlarged under the name **Bay Harbor**. At present there is alongside dockage in 10 feet with all dockside services, marine and convenience store, Laundromat, engine and hull repairs and a railway for haulout up to 30 tons.

When you step ashore at the Public Dock you immediately step back into Erie's history. There, docked nonchalantly alongside the sporty little pleasure craft, is Perry's brig *Niagara*, open, of course, to visitors (871-4596). You're on historic State Street, and a couple of blocks beyond the pier is the Cashier's House

(454-1813), built in 1839 for the cashier of the United States Bank of Pennsylvania located in the Greek temple next door, later used as the Customs House (871-4597). A block or so away, at Second and French, is the 1809 Perry Memorial House, an inn that hosted famous people such as the Marquis de Lafayette and sequestered runaway slaves before the Civil War (459-9393). Continue up State Street another block or so and you'll reach tree-shaded Perry Square, surrounded by imposing public buildings. Note especially the elegant Georgian public library. Turn right through the park, then walk down West Sixth Street for as long as you continue to enjoy admiring the impressive mansions built by Erie's elite in every fashionable architectural style of a hundred years ago and more. The one at 338 houses the Erie Art Center (459-5477), and next door at 356 is the Erie Historical Museum (453-5811). A slight detour down Chestnut Street to Fifth brings you to the Firefighters Historical Museum (456-5969).

Although Erie's historic streets and buildings fascinate, it's also a handy place for more practical matters. The city of 117,000 people is a customs port of entry, has good medical facilities, and a downtown shopping mall is reasonably close to the harbor at Eighth Street. It's a good place for crew changes, as it has a commercial airport, and is served by Amtrak as well as inter-city bus lines. Beyond the central historic district, the town is rather spread out, however. There are two restaurants near the Public Dock, and many others around the city; Serafini's on West Twelfth Street offers good Italian cuisine. There are also night clubs with live entertainment, and the restored Warner Theater, at State and Eighth streets, shows classic movies in summer (452-4857). The Erie Playhouse (454-2851) mounts live theatrical productions. For kiddies' active recreation there is Waldameer Amusement Park at the entrance to Presque Isle Park, a cab ride from anywhere. Finally, there are several wineries in the surrounding countryside that offer tours and tastings. The Erie Chamber of Commerce makes sightseeing easy for you through a variety of group tours that include many of the attractions mentioned above and more besides. Call them at 454-7191.

The Western Reserve

Charts 14824, 14825, 14826, 14836, 14837, 14839

Connecticut was as smart as Pennsylvania and after the Revolution held on to part of the land grant conferred by King Charles II that she called her Western Reserve. It stretched from the Pennsylvania border halfway across the lakefront of present-day Ohio, and jurisdiction wasn't finally settled until Ohio became a state in 1803. Connecticut families, and easterners in general, seeking new opportunity came in growing numbers after 1795 to farm the rich soil and to build little towns along the rivers that empty into Lake Erie.

Conneaut

Just inside the Ohio state line, and about 30 unobstructed cruising miles from Erie, the Conneaut River flows into Lake Erie. The land profile southwest of Erie lowers somewhat to wooded hills, which continue for many miles, interspersed with towns and villages. Conneaut can be identified from the lake by green water tanks west of the harbor entrance. Two converging breakwaters with flashing green and white lights extend almost a mile into the lake to create a large harbor beyond the river mouth. The west light is equipped with a fog horn. From here a wide channel, dredged for ships, leads upriver to the big Pittsburgh and Conneaut loading docks, where the lakers call to unload iron and limestone and pick up coal. Another pair of lights, red and green, are set on the ends of the inner breakwaters that delimit the freighter channel. When you're approaching from the east, take care not to confuse these lights with the outer breakwater. Just to the west of the inner piers an enclosed basin in the outer harbor accommodates the **Conneaut Boat Club**. There are fixed red and green lights at the entrance to the Boat Club, which has 8 feet at its slips, the usual dockside services, except pumpout and diesel, and a bar in the clubhouse.

Southwest of the boat club is the municipal pier, reached by a dredged but unbuoyed channel from the outer harbor. There is some dockage here, too, but it is not a desirable accommodation and depths are uncertain. This part of the waterfront is recreational, with parkland west of the public dock. A Fourth of July Festival takes place annually in Lakeview Park, and the larger township park several blocks away has tennis courts, picnic facilities, playground and beach. There is also a restaurant or two near the waterfront, but the neighborhood's old, red brick commercial buildings have rather gone to seed. It is 2 miles from the harbor to downtown Conneaut. If you find a way to get there, the Railroad Museum in the old New York Central Depot is worth a visit. Conneaut is a customs port of entry combined with Ashtabula 13 miles southwest.

Ashtabula

Ashtabula is bigger and busier than Conneaut, but it is also more interesting, with a choice of berthing facilities. Power plant stacks east of the harbor and silos to the west identify it from the lake. Converging breakwaters enclose an outer harbor off the mouth of the Ashtabula River. A fixed red light on the west pierhead and a flashing green on the east are backed up by Ashtabula Harbor Light, a flashing white on a white tower with a fog horn 600 feet in from the end of the west breakwater. Buoys, both lighted and unlighted, mark channels to industrial slips across the face of the harbor and to the river mouth at the west side. You will head for the river mouth and proceed upstream under the awesome 100-foot-high conveyor and through the Fifth Street Bridge, with a closed clearance of 11 feet. The bridge opens for pleasure craft on the hour and half hour, on a signal of one long and one short. Ashtabula gives you a splendid opportunity to watch the lifeblood of the lakes flow through the massive loading and unloading apparatus of docks and lake freighters. It may be a bit noisy at times, but the show is worth it. Just be sure to keep out of the way of maneuvering lakers.

On the starboard side, past the bridge, is **Sutherland Marina**, with alongside dockage in 14 feet and all dockside services except pumpout but including cable TV hookup. A crane lifts out up to 15 tons; there are full engine and hull repairs and a marine store. Next upstream the **Ashtabula Yacht Club** has both alongside dockage and slips in 6 to 8 feet. The usual dockside services are available, except pumpout and fuel. The clubhouse is informal with a lounge area, picnic grounds and playground for children. Groceries and a Laundromat are a couple of blocks away.

The area in which these two establishments are located is on the edge of Ashtabula's heavy industrial district, and the 19th-century commercial neighborhood adjacent is in an interesting stage of restoration. Shops of various kinds, including several antique stores, restaurants and taverns, evoke the earlier days of the city's life without being cutesy or pretentious. The main part of town is 2 miles south at the highway.

Fairport

Twenty-seven miles southwest of Ashtabula the Grand River flows into Lake Erie. Its dredged mouth and breakwater-enclosed outer basin form the harbor that serves the city of Painesville, 3 miles inland. Most of the commercial facilities are on the east side of the river in the village of Fairport Harbor, while the even smaller village of Grand River, 2 miles upstream on the west bank, has accommodations for pleasure boats.

Once again, stacks and tanks identify the harbor from offshore, but the breakwater arrangement here is different from most. A long seawall extends eastward from the inner end of the east breakwater to parallel the shore for about a mile; there is a flashing white light on its eastern end. Watch out for it if you're coming from the east. There's enough water for pleasure boats to enter the harbor this way, and in rough weather you might want to do that. But under ordinary conditions it's advisable for strangers to proceed to the main entrance between two breakwaters thrusting into the lake. The east pier has a flashing green light opposite the west breakwater light showing occulting white with a fog horn. An extension on the west breakwater has a fixed red light. The river mouth is directly south of the harbor entrance, with another set of lighted piers, fixed red and green. Occasionally there is a strong current at the river entrance, and the speed limit in the river is 10 miles per hour.

About a mile and a half upstream the first marina you come to on the west bank is **Winfield Marina**. Some of their floating slips, with 10 feet of depth, have electricity and water, and there are shoreside heads. Gas is available, as well as engine, hull and rigging repairs, a launch ramp and marine store. The open-end travelift has a capacity of 24 tons. Next up the river is **Rutherford's Landing Marina**, catering to power boats in an attractive setting with both alongside dockage and slips in 8 to 10 feet. Most dockside services are provided, except pumpout, heads and showers. A travelift can haul out up to 40 feet for engine and hull repairs, and there is a launch ramp and snack bar. Next door is the **Grand River Yacht Club**, with slips in 12 feet and all dockside services, except ice and fuel. There are swings and a swimming pool on the club grounds, but the lounge is for members only. Near all three establishments is a small shopping mall that includes a canvas shop and several restaurants.

Across the river the **Fairport Harbor Yacht Club** has slips in 4-to 5-foot depths and all dockside services except pumpout and fuel. Its informal clubhouse has a lounge, and there is a children's play area. Farther upstream, beyond the fixed bridge with 18-foot clearance, the **Western Reserve Yacht Club**, a power-boating organization, offers dockage to members of recognized yacht clubs, with all dockside services except pumpout and fuel. Its small clubhouse is informal in a pretty river setting.

There isn't much to do or see in Fairport, and it is rather a long haul from the lake to the marine accommodations, but it provides a welcome harbor in the long distance between Ashtabula and Cleveland, as the next two are very crowded, may not be able to accommodate visiting boats and are difficult to enter in rough weather.

Mentor Harbor

Five miles beyond Fairport, Mentor Harbor is actually a set of lovely residential lagoons. The thorn on this rose is the entrance, which is inclined to silt up, form sandbars both offshore and inside the channel and churn up breaking seas in heavy northwest through northeast winds. As this is a privately owned harbor you can call the harbor master at the Mentor Harbor Yacht Club on channel 16 to inquire about the state of the channel. From offshore you can locate the entrance about halfway between Fairport's stacks and those of the big power plant at Eastlake. The parallel breakwaters have fixed red and green lights with white daymarks, and there are fixed white range lights on white pilings to guide you through the channel at 142°. Depth is dredged regularly to 8 to 10 feet, with the east side of the channel less vulnerable to silt.

Immediately to starboard past the entrance is one of the loveliest yacht clubs on the lakes. Like a resort in its setting and in the Spanish architecture of its large clubhouse, the **Mentor Harbor Yacht Club** extends hospitality to members of reciprocating clubs. There is 8 to 10 feet of depth at the slips, with all dockside services. In addition to the dining room, bar and snack bar in the clubhouse there is a swimming pool, tennis courts, children's playground, beach, sundeck, picnic area and launch service for boats docked opposite the club grounds.

If you turn to port past the harbor entrance and follow the north lagoon, you reach **Mentor Harbor Lagoons Marina**. This is an older-style marina in a natural setting, with narrow wood docks in 8 feet of water. Drinking water is available at the gas dock (no diesel), and there is electricity at the slips, pumpout, heads, and engine, hull and rigging repairs, with travelift haulout of up to 50 feet. Mentor Lagoons Yacht Club, using the marina docks, extends clubhouse lounge and shower privileges to members of reciprocating clubs.

The city of Mentor is several miles away along U.S. 20, but there is a small grocery about three-quarters of a mile from the marina, and a few small stores a mile and a half from Mentor Harbor Yacht Club. Taxis can be called from Mentor for transport to additional shopping, restaurants, and Lawnfield, the historic home of President James A. Garfield.

Chagrin River Harbor

The twisting, shallow Chagrin River enters Lake Erie 5 miles past Mentor, just east of a big power plant with very tall stacks. This harbor is even trickier to enter in good weather and should not be attempted at all by strangers when northwest to northeast winds are blowing above 20 miles per hour. The problem here is a sandbar that extends well offshore, which, combined with bulkheads and rip-rap placed along the shore to prevent erosion, can develop a vicious chop and breaking seas off the river mouth. Despite regular dredging, the sandbar can build up after northeast storms and late in the season to depths as shallow as 6 inches. Despite these disadvantages, the harbor is busy and crowded, mostly with powerboats, and you can usually hail a local boat to inquire about the state of the channel or request depth readings via radio as he precedes you through the entrance. In any case, it's advisable to stay offshore for about 300 yards until you make your approach along the west pier, lining up its fixed red lights on each end of the pier as a range at 145°. When leaving the harbor, stay on the reverse course until the 12-foot contour before turning east or west. *Note:* don't mistake the power plant breakwater, with its occulting red light on a red column half a mile east, for the Chagrin River entrance.

Once inside, the **Chagrin Lagoons Yacht Club** lagoon opens up on the starboard side. This is as far as most sailboats can go. There is 5 to 6 feet at the slips, alongside tie-up for members of recognized yacht clubs and all dockside services except diesel. The clubhouse has a bar, and the dining room is open Wednesdays and weekends. Up the curving river between the bluffs the **Chagrin River Yacht Club** and the **West Channel Yacht Club** face each other on opposite sides. Chagrin River on the east bank accommodates members of recognized yacht clubs at slips and alongside tie-up in 4 to 5 feet, with electricity, water, heads and showers. The clubhouse is an informal meeting room. West Channel has 3- to 6-foot depths at its slips, with all dockside services except fuel and pumpout. The clubhouse atmosphere is casual, and there is a swimming pool.

Beyond the West Channel Yacht Club **South Shore Yacht Supply** has floating slips in 6 feet, for powerboats only, with all dockside services except pumpout and fuel. The travelift can accommodate 30 tons and engine and hull repairs are available, as well as a marine store. Beyond the fixed bridge with 17-foot clearance **Lake Shore Marina** has alongside docking in 4 to 5 feet for boats up to 23 feet and offers ice, heads, gas, engine and hull repairs, and haulout by ramp and crane. There is a restaurant on the premises, and it is about three-quarters of a mile to a grocery store and Laundromat. The village of Eastlake is several miles away.

Another Pair of Yacht Clubs

About 10 miles southwest of Chagrin River the **Wildwood Yacht Club** is in an artificial basin at the mouth of Euclid Creek, marked by flashing red and green lights on the pierheads. There is 8 feet through the channel entrance and 4 to 8 feet at the slips and alongside tie-up, with the usual dockside services except fuel.

A mile and a half beyond, the **Northeast Yacht Club** is in a similar setting, with fixed red and green lights on white piles marking the entrance between its breakwaters. Depths of 7 feet carry through the channel and at the slips, but the club accommodates only boats up to 35 feet. The usual dockside services are available, plus a travelift up to 40 feet and repair by arrangement. The clubhouse is an informal gathering place. Both of these yacht clubs are in Cleveland suburbs.

Cleveland

Although many cities grew up on Lake Erie during the past 200 years, Cleveland early became the queen. As the terminus of the Ohio and Lake Erie Canal, which opened in 1827, her future was assured in shipping, shipbuilding, and later steel-making, oil refining and scores of other industries. Although she has fallen on hard times in recent years, the city's lake and Cuyahoga River front still display a staggering panorama of industrial configurations, a stream of ships plies in and out of the harbor, and the cultural legacy of her captains of industry, combined with new ventures in multi-ethnic enrichment and historic restoration, make Cleveland worthy of an extended visit.

Industrial and commercial installations still dominate the lakefront behind the 5 miles of protective breakwater that creates the harbor. Yet Cleveland boaters have managed to tuck seven large yacht clubs and marinas into the interstices. All of them are cut off from the main part of the city by roaring expressways, railroads, industrial establishments and decaying commercial neighborhoods, with only taxicabs for access and egress by land to the many places you will want to visit. But some will require shorter cab rides than others. Most of them are enclosed by locked, cyclone fences, topped with barbed wire, for security.

A city like Cleveland is hardly difficult to spot from offshore, of course, but its symbol and most famous landmark, the Terminal Tower, does give you a line on the location of downtown, the Cuyahoga River and the Main Entrance through the breakwater opposite the river mouth. The Cleveland Stadium, at water's edge near the river mouth, is another helpful landmark. At the Main Entrance two converging pierheads extend lakeward from the breakwater. The west one has a big white tower with an alternating red and white flashing light and fog horn, the east pierhead an isophase green light on a white tower. The ends of the long breakwater are also lighted with flashing red and green lights, and the pierheads enclosing the river mouth opposite the Main Entrance are similarly marked with fixed red and green lights. If you're coming from the east, you can enter the harbor behind the east end of the long breakwater, which is marked with a flashing red light on a tall white tower. A buoyed channel then runs 4 miles along the inside of the breakwater to the Main Entrance. Most of the marina facilities are located at this end of the harbor.

First comes the **East 55th Street Marina**, a large city establishment with floating slips in depths of 7 to 14 feet, electricity, water, heads and showers. Flashing red and green lights on steel piles mark the entrance to the basin, sheltered by breakwalls. Behind an enclosing peninsula just east of the Municipal Light Plant the **Forest City Yacht Club** offers dockage in slips with 9 to 12 feet to members of reciprocating clubs. An illuminated sign indicates the club's location. All dockside services are available, except diesel, the clubhouse is informal with lounges and kitchen and there is a small playground for children and picnic tables on the grounds. Between the Municipal Light Plant and Burke Lakefront Airport the **Lakeside Yacht Club**, open to members of recognized clubs, is enclosed in a basin with isophase red and green lights defining the entrance. All dockside services are offered here, at floating slips in 10-foot depths. The clubhouse has a dining room and bar. This group of facilities is closest to downtown.

The airport, the stadium, the river entrance and a few other installations interrupt the succession of marinas until you reach the west end of the harbor. There the long breakwater ends in an elbow projecting shoreward, with a pierhead extending westward again to the lake. Between that pierhead and the shore city-operated **Edgewater Park Marina** and the **Edgewater Park Yacht Club** share an enclosed basin. If you're coming from the west, you can enter Cleveland harbor and then the basin through this western end. In heavy winds and seas, however, the breakwall is sometimes submerged and hard to see, and at night the lights are easily confused with city lights. In these conditions it's best to go 1 mile farther to the Main Entrance and then return westward to the basin. The western entrance is marked with a flashing green light on the east breakwall and a group flashing red on the west breakwall; the basin entrance has a flashing white light on the port side.

At Edgewater Park Marina, the older of the two municipal marinas, docking is modified Mediterranean style, with stern to the dock and the bow tied off on poles in 20 feet. There are the usual dockside services, except pumpout, a travelift to 50 tons, and hull and rigging repairs available. There is a public launch ramp next door. The Edgewater Yacht Club on the opposite side of the basin has slips in 10 to 15 feet, with all dockside services, and a bar in the informal clubhouse. In strong northwest through northeast winds there is a surge in the basin.

It's best to arrive in Cleveland adequately stocked with food and clean clothes, as ordinary grocery shopping and Laundromats are not handy. But there is a venerable Cleveland institution you may want to visit both for fun and for enhancement of the galley stores. Farmers have been bringing their produce to Market Square at West 25th Street and Lorain Avenue for almost 150 years. At first they came to an outdoor market, since 1912 to the massive yellow brick West Side Market building, with an Italian campanile on one corner. On Monday, Wednesday, Friday and Saturday 180 merchants offer an enormous range of farm-grown and ethnic foods. From there, take a stroll down Lorain Avenue. Westward from 25th Street it's known as

Antique Row, for the abundance and variety of shops selling anything and everything that is old and collectible.

Closer to downtown, on the east side of the river along Old River Road at the foot of Superior and St. Clair Avenue, is the old warehouse and mill district known as The Flats. Now obsolete for their original use, these buildings are being converted into trendy shops and restaurants and are already a popular place to shop. This is where Moses Cleaveland, the Connecticut Land Company's surveyor, first came ashore in 1796, and there is a replica of the log cabin built here by the first permanent white settler, Lorenzo Carter. For shopping in a totally different vein The Arcade, at 401 Euclid Avenue in the heart of downtown, is a fantasy in glass, marble and brass, with elegant shops lining balconies around a central atrium on five levels. It was an avant-garde architectural creation when it was built in 1890—and it still is.

While downtown there is much to see and admire in the array of early 20th-century skyscrapers and handsome public buildings. A convenient way to take it all in is on a two-hour guided walking tour, arranged by calling 781-8819. There are also horse-drawn carriage tours from the 1929 Terminal Tower on Public Square, Ohio's tallest building and at one time the largest outside New York (621-0050). Three-hour bus tours (232-4450) are available as well. When you step into City Hall, at 601 Lakeside, you can see the original of a painting you've been looking at all your life in books, Clevelander Archibald Willard's *The Spirit of '76.*

Euclid Avenue is the city's main street, and beyond the downtown office buildings Cleveland's theater district has been rescued from imminent death and restored to vibrancy. The cluster of movie palaces built in the 1920s and known as Playhouse Square was completely dark by 1969, after half a century of popularity. Demolition for a parking lot was announced in 1972, when volunteer theater lovers and history buffs organized to save the complex. Now Playhouse Square shines again, with the summer Great Lakes Shakespeare Festival performing in the Ohio Theater (771-7000), and the Cleveland Opera and Cleveland Ballet planning to take up residence in the State Theater, while the Palace will stage contemporary music festivals and vaudeville. You can tour the complex by appointment; call 771-4444.

Cleveland has a large number of museums, many of them clustered in the unique University Circle area—a complex of cultural, educational, research, medical, residential and supportive commercial institutions that grew up around the original 1880 campuses of Case Institute and Western Reserve University (now merged). Located four miles from downtown out Euclid Avenue, most of the institutions are set in and around a spacious, bluff-top, landscaped campus, from which Rockefeller Park winds down a ravine to the lakeshore. You can get there by cab, bus or rail rapid transit from the Terminal Tower. Among the traditonal museums are the Museum of Art (421-7340), the Museum of Natural History, which includes a planetarium (231-4600), and the Western Reserve Historical Society, whose 20 period rooms portray life in the Western Reserve from 1770 to 1920 (721-5722). More uncommon is the Crawford Auto-Aviation Museum, with a collection of over 2,000 classic cars, bicycles, motorcycles and airplanes (721-5722). Two unusual museums devoted to health are the Cleveland Health Education Museum, at 8911 Euclid Avenue (231-5010), which has operating models and exhibits of all aspects of the human body, designed to appeal especially to children, and the Howard Dittrick Museum of Historical Medicine, on the third floor of the medical library building at 1100 Euclid Avenue (368-3648), where objects are displayed relating to medical, dental and pharmacological practice since ancient times.

Back at the waterfront there is one more exhibit you might want to take in. The USS *Cod*, a World War II submarine, is docked just west of the airport (566-8770). If you're tired of walking and want to be entertained, the Cleveland Indians play at the Stadium on the lakeshore (861-1200). For evening entertainment Cleveland has, of course, many restaurants, night clubs and movie theaters; the Shakespeare Festival mentioned earlier; and the Cleveland Opera Theater that performs outdoors in summer at the Cleveland Institute of Music (791-5165). To find out what is going on in town, check the weekly arts/ entertainment supplement in the Friday edition of *The Cleveland Plain Dealer*, or call the Visitors Bureau on its 24-hour line, 621-8860.

Finally, if you want to take a busman's holiday, you can get a fascinating tour of Cleveland's industrial might by following the Cuyahoga River for about 5 miles, with a number of bridges to blast and wait for, or the Old River with one bridge for 1 mile. Up the Old River, by the way, is Cuyahoga Boat and Engine Company, with complete engine and hull repair service. Or you might leave the driving to the captain of the *Goodtime II*, which departs from the East Ninth Street Pier on two-hour tours of the

Cuyahoga, complete with informative commentary (531-1505 or 486-6350).

Special annual events in Cleveland include July Fourth fireworks at Edgewater Park, and the Indy car race at Burke Lakefront Airport and the Labor Day Weekend National Air Show, also at Burke Lakefront Airport (781-3500).

Rocky River

Although Cleveland has seven yacht clubs in its harbor, the one called Cleveland Yachting Club, one of the nation's oldest, founded in 1878, is in the suburb of Rocky River, 6 miles west. The harbor is the dredged mouth of Rocky River, which courses down a steep ravine to the lake. It is best identified from offshore by a large apartment house with an illuminated *W* about 3 miles west and a spire on the hill above the entrance. The club's white race course buoys surround an offshore area several miles in diameter. Entrance is made between a cliff on the west and a breakwater on the east, lighted by a flashing green at the outer end and a fixed green at the inner end, which form a range at about 133°. In a blow from the north the entrance can be very choppy. There is also a current in the river that can flow either way, so take account of it when docking. The channel has a controlling depth of 6 feet to the head of navigation about a mile upstream.

Below the first fixed bridge the **Cleveland Yachting Club** is situated on an island off the west bank. It offers all dockside services to members of recognized yacht clubs, including a Laundromat. The gracious clubhouse has a bar and a dining room where skirt or jacket and tie are required for dinner, a picnic area, swimming pool, and a playground for children.

Three fixed bridges and a power line cross the river, all with 49-foot clearance. On the east bank under the highway bridge are two marinas catering mainly to powerboats. At **Captain Krumreig and Sons** dockage is between pilings with short side docks in 8 feet. There is electricity and water at some of the docks, ice, gas, an 8-ton travelift and engine repair. **Emerald Necklace Marina** just beyond has the same kind of dockage, with all services except diesel and showers, a 10-ton hoist, engine and hull repair and a marine store. Rocky River is a residential community, and none of the marine facilities is convenient to shopping or any commercial services. This is a pretty and well-protected harbor for an overnight stop, however.

Firelands

Charts 14826, 14830, 14841, 14843

Connecticut hung on to her Western Reserve as a land of opportunity for citizens burned out by the Revolutionary War. Not all the settlements west of Cleveland were established by victims of war damage, but the region took on the name Firelands. Some of the towns still retain their New England air.

Lorain

Not so Lorain. It may have started out that way, but by the end of the 19th century Lorain was a steel and shipbuilding town. It still is, and there are impressive installations to see along the lower three miles of the Black River. But recent recession has taken a heavy toll and downtown has rather gone to seed in this city of 75,000 people. One of Lorain's less conspicuous enterprises is familiar to cruising boaters—the voice of WMI, Lorain Electronics Corporation, that brings you the MAFOR broadcasts from stations all over the lakes and provides ship-to-shore communication too. Yet there is only one place in town for transient pleasure boats.

The coal docks and stacks on the west side of the harbor help to identify it from offshore. The artificial harbor is enclosed by converging breakwaters extending from shore and a roughly east-west detached breakwater across the entrance. Flashing white lights on white towers mark the ends of the detached breakwater, the western one with a fog horn. The pierheads are marked by flashing green on the east and fixed red on the west, both displayed from white towers. The river entrance from the outer harbor has flashing red and green lights. A short way beyond, past the industrial buildings on the east bank, the municipal **Lorain Yacht Basin** occupies its own dredged enclosure, with depths of 8 feet. The usual dockside services are offered at the slips, except pumpout and showers, and the marina is only half a mile to downtown shopping. Lorain is a customs port of entry.

Of the two major attractions in town the restored Palace Theater, now the Palace Civic Center, offers a variety of music and theatrical performances within walking distance of the marina (245-2323). Lakeview Park is not within easy walking distance, but if you're in town in June, you might want to call a cab to view the spectacular bloom of the 3,000 plants in the Rose

PHOTO BY CHRISTIE PHILLIPS

Great Lakes Historical Society Museum, Vermilion, Ohio.

Garden. While you're there you can enjoy the beach, stroll the long boardwalk, play tennis or lawn bowling and have a picnic. A June visitor can also take in the city's week-long International Festival, featuring ethnic food, music, cultural displays and sporting events.

Lorain's recreational boating harbor is actually four miles west of the city on Beaver Creek. A spit of land jutting lakeward is marked by a fixed green light. Rounding this from the east, or approaching it from the west, you enter the harbor on a range of 124°, identified by fixed red lights on pipes. A fixed green sits on the landward end of the spit opposite the front range light. The channel carries about 8 feet to the **Beaver Park Yacht Basin**, which offers all dockside services, except showers and diesel, at its slips. There is a 30-ton travelift, but no repair service on site. The series of fixed bridges and overhead cables that cross the creek about a quarter of a mile upstream clear only 9 feet at minimum, but **Beaver Park Marina** and **Copper Kettle Marina** beyond them provide most dockside services to the powerboats that can pass underneath.

Vermilion

At Vermilion you are on the threshold of Ohio's recreational lakeshore, the first of the towns that cater to tourists. Less than 10 miles from Lorain, but 150 years apart in atmosphere, Vermilion is mainly a residential community of 12,000, with unique historical connections to the life of the Great Lakes. A handful of towns around the lakes seem to sprout ship captains in quantity and Vermilion is one of them. At one time 42 resided here, and many of their handsome 19th-century homes are well preserved. Commercial fishing was another traditional occupation and there is still some. But as a sign of the times the last substantial fish company was sold for condominium development but six months before this writing. Doubtless they will be tasteful condos, for Vermilion is careful about the nurture of its 19th-century ambiance. Downtown there is an ongoing program of preservation and restoration under the name of Harbour Town 1837, although the shops serve the modern needs of residents and mariners alike for food, drugs, hardware and so on. And there are plenty of mariners; Vermilion is a boating town.

You'll recognize it from offshore by the round water tank with "Vermilion" painted on it. A detached breakwater lies across the entrance to the Vermilion River between two short piers extending lakeward. It has three lights on it, quick flashing white at each end and flashing white in the middle. You can enter around either end through buoyed channels to the pierheads marked by flashing red and green lights. Controlling depth to the first fixed bridge, three-quarters of a mile upstream, is 6 feet.

Your introduction to Vermilion is a series of graceful lagoons just inside the harbor mouth that are bordered by charming homes, most with a boat out in front. At the second lagoon there is a fixed green light, and a turn to port brings you to the **Vermilion Yacht Club**. Both alongside and finger dockage is available to members of reciprocating clubs in depths of 5 to 10 feet, with all dockside services. The clubhouse, which blends nicely with the lagoonside homes, is an informal gathering place, without food or beverage service.

On the west bank of the river, just beyond the waterworks, are the **Public Docks**, with floating slips in 4 to 7 feet, electricity and water. Next door the **Vermilion Boat Club** offers floating docks in the same depths to reciprocating yacht club members, with all dockside services except fuel and pumpout. The clubhouse has a bar, with swimming pool and picnic area on the grounds. Next is **Moes Marine Service**, with floating slips in 4 feet, electricity, water, heads, gas, launch ramp and a 20-ton hoist. All three of these establishments are convenient to downtown shopping and attractions. From most of the others you'd probably want a cab.

Beyond the highway fixed bridge, with 12-foot clearance, there are several establishments for powerboats. The first, in a basin off the east bank, is **Romp's Marine**, with floating and fixed slips, all dockside services except diesel fuel, launch ramp, travelift to 30 feet, engine and hull repairs, marine and gift store, snack bar and mini-golf game. Romp's is within a comfortable walk from downtown, and there is a shopping center nearby. On past the two fixed railroad bridges, with clearances of 21 and 14 feet, a turn to starboard leads to the **Valley Harbor Marina**, with fixed and floating slips in 9-foot depths, the usual dockside services except diesel, a marine, convenience and gift store and some engine repair. Just beyond, and slightly upriver, is **Key Harbor Lagoon Marina**, with fixed and floating docks in 5 to 6 feet, all dockside services except fuel and pumpout, a 20-ton travelift, engine and hull repairs and a picnic pavilion. These two marinas are over a mile from downtown.

Strolling the side streets of Vermilion to admire the old homes gives you a flavor of the town whose heyday antedates the Civil War. You can pick up a walking tour map at the Chamber of Commerce at Liberty and Main. At the foot of Main Street, commanding a sweeping view of the lake, is the Museum of the Great Lakes Historical Society (967-3467). Its fine collection of marine artifacts, paintings, models and documents dramatically portrays the history of Great Lakes shipping. Shopping on Liberty Avenue, the centerpiece of Harbor Town 1837, is an agreeable experience, and there are good dining choices among the Olde Prague for Czech and Hungarian cooking; L'Auberge du Port, French, right on the waterfront a bit upriver from the public docks; and McGarvey's, noted for seafood, on the east bank of the river off Liberty Avenue, with dockage for diners.

Huron

A town of 7,000 people, Huron presents a pleasing blend of the two worlds of commercial lakeport and small-town recreational harbor. Its artificial harbor is at the mouth of the Huron River, 11 miles west of Vermilion. The southernmost port on Lake Erie, Huron is a receiving port for iron ore and limestone and a shipping port for grain. The commercial wharves on the east side of the river are not so extensive as to dominate the scene as they do elsewhere. The village and the pleasure craft facilities are on the west bank.

From offshore the stacks of the Huron Lime Company identify the harbor. Approach cautiously, on the lookout for fish net stakes which are often heavy in this area. The west breakwater extends much farther into the lake than the east, with a flashing red light displayed from a tall white tower equipped with a fog horn. The short east breakwater has a flashing green light, and there is an additional pair of inner lights, fixed red and flashing white.

Almost opposite the Pillsbury Company wharf and elevator is Huron's semicircular **Small Boat Mooring Basin**, a public marina with floating docks and all services except fuel. Next upriver is **Harbor North Marina**, catering mainly to sailboats, with floating slips in 6 to 8 feet, all dockside services, a 10-ton crane, engine, hull and rigging repairs. **Huron Marine Park** close beyond has dockage in eight feet with electricity, water, heads and showers.

Beyond the two fixed bridges, with minimum clearance of 19 feet, are two marinas that cater to powerboats. First is **Holiday Harbor**, an older facility with narrow wood finger docks in 5 feet of water, some supplied with electricity and water. The other standard dockside services are offered, except diesel fuel; there is a launch ramp, travelift up to 40 feet, engine and some hull repair. Next door **Huron Lagoons Marina** is similar, but has some newer floating slips, with electricity and water at all of them as well as the other services, except diesel. The travelift here also hauls out up to 40 feet, and full engine and hull repairs are available. Both of these marinas are located a long distance from town by road, with the closest store about a mile and a half away.

The commercial facilities of Huron are rather spread out, so shopping is not very handy to the "downtown" marinas, although it is accessible. The Showboat and J.B.'s Twine House are popular waterfront restaurants, and there is a bowling alley nearby. Huron Playhouse performs in repertory during July and August, and the Huron Water Festival celebrates Independence Day in style with a four-day event featuring rides, games and entertainment, as well as fireworks. And in August the Rotary Club sponsors an art show at the Boat Basin.

Two and a half miles west of the entrance to Huron harbor, Sawmill Creek flows into Lake Erie. It has been dredged out to accommodate a marina associated with **Sawmill Creek Lodge**, a resort estate that includes golf, tennis and beach, in addition to the hotel with pool, several restaurants and live evening entertainment. In a separate building the 1887 Shops offer a collection of gift and fashion stores.

Sawmill Creek can be difficult to enter in strong winds and rough seas and should not be attempted by strangers under those conditions. There is no breakwater, but about a mile of sheet piling protects the shoreline (and bounces back the waves) and is the most visible landmark. The entrance itself is marked by fixed red and green lights, with a controlling depth of 5 feet. Concrete slips and all dockside services, except pumpout and diesel, in a pleasant resort setting make this a good overnight stop. It is quite a long walk from the docks to the hotel and shops, however.

Mainland Playground

Charts 14830, 14842, 14844, 14845

A glance at the Lake Erie chart will show you that as you move northwest from Huron, Ohio, the lake takes on a different character altogether. Long peninsulas reach out from both north and south shores, with a stepping-stone parade of islands almost connecting them. Within this near enclosure the water is shallowest, abounding with reefs and shoals—the conditions that make this part of the lake a recreational center surpassing all others. It is among the shallows and drop-offs that fish of many species play in astonishing numbers. And on the surface humans play in their multitudes, with the fish, with the wind and with their own recreational ingenuity. But in this part of Lake Erie you must take special care to identify aids to navigation and heed their advice. There are probably more tows and rescues effected here than in any other part of the Great Lakes. And this is where those notorious summer squalls often hit hardest.

Sandusky

There can be no more appropriate entrance to this playground of the lake than the approach from the east into Sandusky Bay around the three-mile-long peninsula of Cedar Point. At its tip, about 10 miles from Huron, is what many consider the finest amusement park in the country—not a theme park, not an expo, not an educational experience, just an amusement park, with equal emphasis on both words. Thrilling rides, captivating games, glittery stage shows, a full range of eateries are set in 365 acres of artfully landscaped grounds and trails, with a long sand beach fronting the lake side. On the Sandusky Bay side is a 1,200-slip full service marina. Cedar Point Amazement Park, as its proprietors like to call it, carries on its 115-year-old tradition at this site with finesse and good taste that in no way inhibit its excitement and fun. For the more sedate the large 1905 Breakers Hotel has been restored to its original grandeur, with two dining rooms and live entertainment in the bar.

The 333-foot Space Spiral ride is the landmark conspicuous for many miles that identifies Cedar Point and the entrance to Sandusky Bay. This shallow bay, 15 miles long by 5 miles wide, is Lake Erie's second natural harbor. The city of Sandusky on the southeast side was once a much more important lakeport than it is now, although there is still some ship traffic. The shallowness and orientation of Sandusky Bay make it a miniature Lake Erie, subject to large fluctuations in water level, ranging up to 8 feet in strong winds. Controlling depth in the bay beyond the area around the dredged deep water channels at the east end is only 2 feet at low water (actual depth has been 4 to 6 in recent years). But other than the three bridges that cross its middle with a minimum clearance of 8 feet, it is relatively free of obstructions. Shallow draft motorboats can pass the entire length of the bay to enter the Sandusky River and motor about 15 miles upstream to the city of Fremont. At chart datum the least depth in the river is 2 feet, but in recent years it has seldom dropped below 4. The entrance to the river is buoyed, but the buoys are not always easy to spot against the low, watery, featureless landscape. The inner bay and river mouth are good for watching waterfowl.

From the tip of Cedar Point a long breakwall extends northeast into the lake, with a flashing white pierhead light on a white tower with fog horn. Mosely Channel, as the approach is called, is buoyed from beyond the pierhead and lighted by a fixed green range with white daymarks at 237° If you're approaching from west or north past Marblehead, you can enter Mosely Channel near its junction with Straight Channel; take care to leave flashing red light buoy "2" well to starboard on the approach. Straight Channel is then followed to where it divides. Ships turn westward into Bay Channel, while pleasure boats either turn eastward for Cedar Point or continue in Straight Channel to Sandusky.

Cedar Point Marina is enclosed in a basin with fixed red and green lights at the breakwater entrance. Concrete slips in 10 to 15 feet; all dockside services, including Laundromat; open-end travelift to 20 tons, engine, hull and rigging repairs; and a large marine and convenience store make this a complete service facility. There are also two restaurants on the premises, a swimming pool and picnic tables and grills. Entrance to the amusement park is adjacent.

In Sandusky itself **Battery Park Municipal Marina** is being entirely remodeled. Its older wood docks are being replaced by floating slips with 9 to 15 feet of depth, and all dockside services will be offered. At present writing there is no electricity or water at the slips. The enclosed basin is currently entered from the northwest near can buoy "15," but when the remodeling is completed the entrance will be moved to the northeast corner, with red and green lights flanking it. The park has tennis courts, picnic grounds, a children's playground and a wave action pool. Next door to the marina, and also on the park grounds, the **Sandusky Sailing Club** is in Sadler Basin. There are some floating docks, but mostly moorings, and heads and showers in the small clubhouse for members of recognized clubs. Sadler Basin is enclosed in its own breakwater with fixed red and green lights at the entrance. Sandusky is a customs port of entry.

Battery Park is at the edge of downtown, and shopping, including a supermarket, is several blocks away. But Sandusky is a pleasant city to walk in. This is a town where much of the old waterfront has been torn down and the property is gradually being redeveloped. Ohio lakeshore viniculture dates back 125 years to when German immigrants brought their wine-making skills to the new land. One venerable establishment still on the waterfront is E and K Winery at 220 Water Street (627-9622). The initiator of regional wine-making, it dates from 1863 and, with a hiatus of about 10 years during the 1960s, has been operating ever since. You can tour, taste and buy not only the firm's wine, but all the equipment needed to make your own, along with advice on how to do it. A block away on Water Street a farmer's market sets up every Wednesday and Saturday.

Sandusky is the home port of several ferry operations. If you prefer to dock in town, you needn't miss the delights of Cedar Point; you can get there by ferry. You can also take a choice of ferry rides to the Erie Islands, described in the next section, where dockage for your own boat can be hard to come by on summer weekends. If you're down at the harbor front on Friday afternoons, there's often a rock concert starting about 4:30.

Marblehead/Catawba

Sandusky Bay is formed mainly by the 14-mile-long Marblehead Peninsula that reaches eastward to form its north shore. Thrusting northward into the lake from about the middle of the north side of this peninsula is Catawba Island. Once it was truly an island, but over the eons sand piling up at its base has connected it to the mainland. In the dip between Catawba and

Marblehead sandbars have created three harbors, West, Middle, and East. Although Middle is undeveloped, the other two shelter a vast fleet of resident boats, mostly power. The west side of Catawba Island is also indented with numerous marinas, and there are a few on the outside of the Marblehead side.

Together with Cedar Point and Port Clinton (a few miles west) one might believe that most of Ohio's 300,000 registered boats are based here. (Actually there are close to 13,000 docks at well over 100 marinas, plus a great deal of rack storage.) Certainly a large proportion of the state's 600 licensed fishing charter captains are. With the enormous demand for seasonal dockage that all this marine activity generates there isn't a lot of room for transients. In fact, only about half the marinas will accept them. You'll also see a lot of dockage that looks commercial but isn't. Condominium dockage is becoming popular, and there are several marina clubs, not yacht clubs as such, but marinas whose services are available only to members. As might be expected, this heavy concentration of resident boats also generates a lot of traffic on the open water in this area, especially on weekends.

Marblehead has a literal name. First settled about 1821, the peninsula began exporting the valuable stone almost from the beginning. It still does, using an impressive overhead conveyor and mobile shuttle to waiting vessels. Marblehead Light, flashing green from a white tower, is the oldest in continuous service on the Great Lakes. Built in 1821, it still guides your passage around the peninsula toward East Harbor, about 8 miles from the Sandusky Bay breakwater. The marine facilities you pass are all private, as are many of those in East Harbor, but several do provide service to transients.

East Harbor is entered between a pair of parallel breakwaters with flashing red and green lights. A buoyed channel carries through the shallow harbor along the south side, where most of the marinas are lined up. The controlling depth is 3 feet at chart datum. The sand spit enclosing the harbor is part of East Harbor State Park, and it is possible to anchor off the beach in eight feet, but you're likely to roll in a southwest wind. This is a good observation area for aquatic birds, and there is a great blue heron rookery nearby. The park has hiking trails as well as beaches.

Just past buoys "7" and "8" **Marine City** offers dockage to transients on a space available basis at slips with 9-foot depths. Some have electricity and water, and the other standard dockside services are offered, except diesel fuel. There is a launch

PHOTO COURTESY OF OHIO DEPARTMENT OF NATURAL RESOURCES

Marblehead Light.

ramp, a 16-ton travelift with engine and minor hull repairs available, a convenience store and a swimming pool. This marina is one of the few that accommodates sailboats as well as powerboats, although in low water years the East Harbor channel may be too shallow.

Two and a half miles northwest of East Harbor is the new entrance to West Harbor. In passing between the two, note two-foot Middle Harbor Shoal, marked by a flashing white light buoy. Converging breakwaters protect the harbor, with group flashing red and flashing green lights on the pierheads. The buoyed channel, with a controlling depth of 7 feet, leads first to **East Harbor State Park Marina**, catering to motorboats. The marina is enclosed in a basin with two entrances carrying fixed red and green lights. All dockside services, except diesel but including Laundromat, are provided at the floating slips with 5- to 7-foot depths. A 10-ton hoist hauls out for engine and hull repairs, and there is a launch ramp, a marine store, a restaurant and a playground. **Anchors Away Marina** is in the next basin with fixed red and green entrance lights. There are depths of 5 feet at the slips, and all dockside services are offered except diesel fuel. The travelift can accommodate 20 tons for engine and hull repairs. There is a snack bar and fish cleaning service. The adjacent Crow's Nest restaurant specializes in ribs and salad.

A little farther down and across the harbor is **Midway Marina** for powerboats, with 5 feet at both fixed and floating slips, all dockside services except fuel but including Laundromat, a 20-ton hoist, engine and hull repairs, a marine store and picnic grounds. Moving up the west side of the harbor, across from Anchors Away, is the **West Harbor Sailing Club**, with floating slips in present depths of about 6 feet, all dockside services, launch ramp, travelift up to 25 tons and engine and hull repairs under arrangement with nearby Walker Boat Repairs. The informal clubhouse has a lounge area and swimming pool. At the widest part of the harbor **Treasure Cove Marina** caters to powerboats at slips in 5 feet, with electricity and water at some, ice, pumpout, heads and gas. A marine railway can haul up to 10 tons for engine and minor hull repairs. There is a launch ramp, marine store and snack bar.

At the top of the harbor on the west side **Fox Haven** is a very large marina for powerboats, with concrete slips and all dockside services. Opposite Fox Haven passage can be made under a fixed bridge with 14-foot clearance to the north end of West Harbor, where **Gem Beach Marina** is located. Gem Beach also has a channel leading directly from the lake through a pair of jetties with flashing red and green lights. This is another large marina catering to powerboats at concrete slips. All dockside services are offered, including Laundromat, a travelift hauls to 35 tons, and there are full engine and hull repairs, a marine and convenience store. There is a roller skating rink and mini-golf on the premises.

On the west side of Catawba Island there are two marinas that accept transient boats. The first one is about 5 miles from the Gem Beach entrance to West Harbor. Opposite Scott Point at the tip of the island is Mouse Island, which was the summer home of President Rutherford B. Hayes, who came from Fremont. Don't attempt to pass between the island and the point, however. **Sugar Rock Marina** is in an especially pretty setting. The harbor should be entered from the south, with care for a sunken breakwall extending out from Sugar Rock Point. In some years some of it shows above the surface. The channel into the marina is usually buoyed with Clorox bottles and currently carries about 4 feet. The same depth is found at the marina docks, which cater mainly to powerboats and offer all services except diesel fuel, travelift to 10 tons, engine and hull repairs. About a mile south **West Catawba Marina** can accommodate powerboats to 30 feet (limited by a narrow turning basin) at docks with 4-

foot depths and all services except showers and diesel fuel. A breakwall jutting due west from the marina displays a row of yellow lights at night. There is a travelift up to 25 tons, but no repair personnel on site. The Nautical Watch Restaurant on the premises is open 24 hours.

Catawba Island settlers began the cultivation of wine grapes during the mid-19th century, the most famous being the Catawba variety. There are still half a dozen wineries left in the area that includes Sandusky and the Erie Islands, although Catawba itself now grows mainly houses, for both summer and year-round residence. Mon Ami Restaurant and Winery, in a handsome 1870 stone building, is one of those six, but its distance from the marinas requires a taxicab. In fact, there is little or no shopping, commercial or entertainment activity convenient to any of the marinas. For cruising boats the Marblehead/Catawba area offers some well-equipped accommodations for overnight dockage, especially to powerboats, but that's about all. For avid fishermen, on the other hand, it offers some of the best perch, walleye and bass fishing anywhere. You might even want to go out on one of the dozens of party fishing boats found in every harbor and at most marinas.

Port Clinton

The urban hub of all this recreational and residential activity is Port Clinton, an attractive little town of about 7,000 people astride the Portage River 7 miles southwest of the tip of Catawba Island. Parallel breakwaters thrust through the shallows from the river mouth, with occulting red and isophase green lights on a white tower and aluminum column, respectively. A stack and a relay tower help identify the entrance point from offshore and form a range for the middle of the harbor entrance at about 200°. But do not follow it up the channel. Controlling depth in the channel is 8 feet through the marina area.

The south side of the river, below the bascule bridge half a mile from the mouth, comprises the town's small commercial dockage area for fish tugs and the ferry to Put-In-Bay, plus a small city dock, without services, for pleasure craft. This is also the location of the downtown shopping area. On the north side of the river, where it turns westward, is the **Port Clinton Yacht Club** in a parklike setting. Either alongside dockage or slips in six feet are offered to visitors from reciprocating clubs, with electricity, water, heads and showers. The small, informal clubhouse has a bar, and on the grounds are two tennis courts, a children's playground and a swimming pool. The club is in convenient walking distance to downtown.

All of Port Clinton's marinas are beyond the bridge, with 9-foot closed clearance, that opens on the hour and half hour in reponse to one long and one short blast. But only two readily accept transient boats, both sail and power. **Jeremy's Marina** is on the north side beyond the sewage treatment plant opposite, about a quarter of a mile from the bridge. At floating docks in 6 feet all dockside services are provided except fuel, there is a travelift and a marine railway "large enough to haul the ferries," engine, hull and rigging repairs. **Clinton Reef Marina** is a quarter of a mile farther up on the north side. A dredged channel leads into a basin with 4 to 6 feet at the slips, electricity and water at some, ice, pumpout, heads and showers, gas, a 40-ton hoist and hull and engine repairs. There are a swimming pool and cocktail lounge on the premises.

Both of these marinas are within walking distance of town, where the most eye-catching building is the Old Island House Inn, serving the public since 1886. It is still a popular restaurant and bar—the mahogany back bar is a classic of the Victorian art form—with live entertainment on summer weekends and has a gift shop as well. Other shops necessary to a boat's well-being are handy, and there is a hospital if you should need medical service.

Two and a half miles west of the Portage River entrance **Lakefront Marina** is reached directly from the lake. Jetties protect the entrance, with flashing red and green lights on them, and a lighted range of fixed reds on skeleton towers at 210° guides you into the buoyed channel that carries 9 to 10 feet. This full service marina has floating slips in 10 feet, with all dockside services, travelift up to 25 tons, engine and hull repairs and a marine and convenience store. Many of the floating docks are joined with a strap about 4 feet below the surface. When arranging dockage sailboat skippers should request a place that avoids this condition.

The Erie Islands
Charts 14842, 14844

There is something enchanting about an island, and Lake Erie's archipelago is her not so secret treasure. Where the bottom configuration of a lake is uneven the top is likely to be so too. The low-profile Erie Islands may be thought of as higher shoals than those still underwater. But five of them are large enough to command a place in the world of viniculture, quarrying and summertime recreation. The three Bass Islands, whose name confirms the piscine fame of these parts, are stacked from south to north from 3 to 10 miles north of Catawba Island. Kelleys is 3 miles off Point Marblehead, while the largest of them all, Pelee Island, lies north of the border in Ontario. Although similar in limestone structure and rural tree and meadow ambiance, each has its individual personality.

South Bass Island

Nobody calls it that. The whole island has taken on the name of its harbor and village, Put-In-Bay. Some say the name is literal—mariners have been putting into its shelter since time remembered. Others say that some 18th-century exploring Englishman thought its shape resembled a pudding bag and careless usage corrupted the name. By whatever name, the island has been attracting summer visitors since the 1860s. At that time it, along with Middle Bass and some other small islands, was owned by Jose de Rivera St. Jurgo, a self-made millionaire who was born to poverty in Spain in 1813, the year Put-In-Bay entered the history books.

On September 10 of that year Captain Oliver Hazard Perry sailed out of this harbor with the fleet that we met a few pages back in Erie, Pennsylvania, to engage the British naval squadron moving out from Amherstburg on the Detroit River. The intense battle lasted only a few hours, but Perry's victory secured the region for the United States. The details of the exploit are quite fascinating, and if you haven't learned about it already, you'll have a good chance on the island, which still takes pride in the young leader's accomplishment. Mr. St. Jurgo left his mark too, with the introduction of grape culture and his 1866 gift to the people of the island, the park at which you will dock.

The next famous personage connected with Put-In-Bay was Jay Cooke, the notorious railroad financier, who built an elaborate home on Gibraltar Island in the harbor just after the Civil War. It is now owned by Ohio State University and used for summer programs in hydrobiology. Elegant summer homes and fashionable resort hotels continued to spring up through the next 30 years, but after the turn of the century, when excursion steamers brought throngs of day visitors from the mainland, Put-In-Bay's eminence began to wane. Fire took its toll as well.

The last of the elaborate hotels burned in 1919, although some of the remaining homes and smaller hotels help retain the island's old-fashioned atmosphere. An important rum-runner's rendez-vous during the 1920s, the island's wine-makers were neverthe-less ruined here, as elsewhere; today there is only one left.

South Bass Island is utterly devoted to recreation, for the cottagers who triple its permanent population of 350, the campers at the state park, the day-trippers who fill the frequent ferries from Catawba and from Port Clinton, and the boaters who swarm in the harbor from all over the western end of Lake Erie. It's not a quiet place to visit, but it is fun. Try to avoid the weekends, though. Both dockage and anchorage are inadequate for the fleet that pulls in Friday through Sunday and on every holiday. Despite rafting six deep, some boats circle the harbor an hour or more looking for a place to lie. A new star-shaped floating dock in mid-harbor with launch service, for short-term daytime use, should ease the situation somewhat. Nevertheless, a cruising boat should plan for weekday arrival.

The monument to Perry's victory is the beacon visible for as far as 25 miles on a clear day. The slender obelisk rises 352 feet from the flat park in which it was raised on the centennial of the battle. At night it displays an isophase white light and is floodlit. Approaching from the north, you can pass between Ballast and Middle Bass islands. From the east three buoys direct you through a narrow channel south of Ballast Island and past the reefs that make out from the northeast tip of South Bass. From the south, Catawba or Port Clinton, the course is between Green Island and South Bass. A couple of buoys mark shallows in the harbor area, and a buoyed channel, dredged to 8 feet at chart datum, runs along the dock faces at the village.

The **Public Marina** is enclosed in breakwaters with a fixed green light on the end of the north pier. Entrance is made from westward. Dockage is alongside, with a great deal of rafting, as we noted earlier. Try to avoid the outside wall, as wash from other boats is heavy there. Electricity and water are available dockside, and fuel is sold at several private docks along the waterfront. Between the village and Gibraltar Island there is a special anchorage area, with 5- to 10-foot depths, where you can drop your hook, but take care not to pick up any of the private mooring buoys with names on them. Toward the southwest corner of the harbor **The Crew's Nest** is a private membership marina that offers its docking facilities to nonmembers from Sunday afternoon to Friday noon. In addition to electricity and water at dockside, there is a swimming pool, tennis courts, picnic area, and dining room and bar with live entertainment in the clubhouse. The marina monitors channel 16 if you want to call ahead for space.

Across the park from the docks you'll find all the shops and restaurants of Put-In-Bay, including a general store for groceries and a Laundromat. There is also an assortment of taverns and cocktail bars, some with live entertainment. Some of the island's attractions are an easy walk, for others you might want to rent a bicycle (the most popular means of transport) or a moped, or take the trolley. The narrated train tour, with a few choice stops, is a good way to get an introduction to the island.

Right downtown there is a restored 1917 carousel to ride, and the Put-In-Bay Museum is in the blacksmith shop. The Ohio State Fish Hatchery on the west side of the harbor is open to visitors on weekday afternoons (285-3701). But the main must-see attraction is the Perry Monument, officially the Perry's Victory and International Peace Memorial (285-2184). This is a National Historic Site, and the park rangers present interpretive talks that tell you about the Battle of Lake Erie and the War of 1812. The view from the top is magnificent on a clear day. Riding along the island's country lanes is a pleasure in itself, but two destinations to aim for are the Heineman Winery, with its tour of both cellar and the Crystal Cave (285-2811), and the state park, with its swimming beach. Next to the park is a par-three, nine-hole golf course with rental clubs; tennis is in town back of the school.

Put-In-Bay goes in for special events. The oldest and most famous is the Inter-Lake Yachting Association Regatta the first week in August. One of the biggest in the country, it dates from those elegant days of 1885. During the 1907 event the first ship-to-shore wireless telephone connection was made aboard the commodore's flagship. Founders Day Weekend, the last weekend in June, is a gala occasion with music, a fair, antique car parade and ox roast. And, of course, July Fourth is celebrated with fireworks.

Middle Bass Island

The other two Bass Islands continue their historic occupation of wine-making. North Bass, owned by the Charles F. Meiers Company, is the largest vineyard on the lakes and is not open to the public.

On Middle Bass Island the Lonz Winery combines business with tourist pleasure (285-5411). The main cellar building is a

Gothic creation that dates from late in the 19th century, although the winery was established in Civil War times. Not only does Lonz offer tours, tastings, a snack bar and a gift shop, but it also provides dockage for visiting boats. There are no services, but restrooms at the winery are open 24 hours.

The approach from all directions is the same as for South Bass Island; the two harbors are only a mile and a half apart. Note that the lighted bell buoy marking the long shoal off the northeast point of the island is quite a distance from shore and don't pass inside it. Similarly, the red nun off the southwest corner of North Bass is more than a mile offshore. On entering the harbor in the southeast corner of the island, follow the channel, with 5-foot depths, to the south basin where you'll find floating docks in 5 feet. In a northeaster there is a surge. Anchorage is possible in the north basin with local knowledge. The harbor has old sunken seawalls and docks; heed the signs that warn you not to moor. There are country roads to wander among the vineyards, but the wine cellar itself is the big attraction. In walking to it you must cross the airfield. Don't be misled by its unused dirt road appearance. Planes can swoop down on you with alarming suddenness.

Kelleys Island

Largest of the American islands, Kelleys lies 4 miles from Marblehead, 10 miles from Sandusky, is served by ferries from both, and exudes yet a different atmosphere. The village of fewer than 100 people exists mainly for the benefit of tourists. On Kelleys Island the limestone quarries and vineyards are all abandoned to the curious gaze of wandering visitors.

Approaches to the island are all clear, provided you mind the very long shoal extending from the northeast end, defined by buoys. The only dockage adequate for cruising boats is at **Seaway Marina** on the south shore, about a mile east of the ferry dock. The basin is entered from the west between a pair of stone jetties with red and green lights, with 15 feet or more in the channel and the harbor. Dockage is alongside with rafting on busy weekends. If you're against the wooden wall faced by bollards, fender boards are more effective than round fenders. The marina has all dockside services, including Laundromat, and offers rental bikes and golf carts for exploring the island. There is a small convenience store, with village grocery and hardware stores about a mile away.

Kelleys Island is named for the Cleveland brothers who

PHOTO COURTESY OF MICHIGAN TRAVEL BUREAU

Kelleys Island beach.

bought the whole place in the 1830s for $1.65 an acre. The handsome stone mansion they built is now a resort, with a dining room open to the public. It sometimes gives tours (746-2273). Grapes were first planted here in 1846, and 25 years later there were reported to be 26 wine cellars; the population peaked at 1,000 people in 1910. A bike tour of the island takes you past many of the quaint carpenter Gothic houses they lived in. But earlier inhabitants left their mark in a different way. The Eriez Indians were in residence here before the whole nation was exterminated in wars with the Iroquois, and some artists among them carved pictographs, probably during the 17th century, that recorded events in their lives. Inscription Rock is not far from the marina.

The natural feature for which Kelleys Island is most well known is on the north shore. You can get to the Glacial Grooves either by a 2½-mile bike ride or by dinghy from your own boat anchored in North Bay. This cove is inadvisable for an overnight stop, as a wind shift to northwest through northeast makes it untenable, but on a day of southerly winds it's a pleasant spot. The state park is located here, and you can enjoy a swim from the beach after you've examined in wonder the evidence of glacial power. Although not as lively or crowded as Put-In-Bay, for evening entertainment on Kelleys Island there are restaurants and taverns. Dirty Don's Casino has dockage for patrons and live entertainment, but the docks are unprotected and the casino is only about half a mile from the marina anyway.

Pelee Island

Just across the international boundary in Ontario, Pelee Island, the largest in the group, lies about 8 miles from the others. In approaching from the south, note Chickenolee Reef off the southeast corner, marked by a buoy. Fish Point, reaching far out from the southwest shore, is a growing sandbar; give it a wide berth. Otherwise the approaches are clear.

About halfway up the west coast there is a wharf for the Sandusky ferry, with a gift shop, liquor store and a Canada Customs office. This dock is completely unprotected, however, inadvisable for overnight and impossible in strong westerly winds. Pelee Island's main harbor is at the village of Scudder on the north coast, and customs will log you in there as well.

The harbor at Scudder is created by an L-shaped western wharf and an eastern breakwater, with a detached breakwater perpendicular to the others. The detached breakwater has a flashing red light atop a white tower with red top. At the end of the west wharf is an elevator with a fixed red light on it. An inner breakwater, extending eastward from the wharf, has an iso-phase red light. All of these structures make Scudder a fairly well-protected harbor, although there is surge in strong northeasterlies. Available dockage is another story. There are slips on the east side of the harbor, but they are almost fully occupied by local boats and party fishing boats. Depths range from 3 or 4 feet at the innermost slips to 5 or 6 feet at the outer ones. There are no services.

Pelee Island is a farming community of about 300 people, with some summer cottage population in addition, but there is little to see or do here. For the cruising boat it is of interest mainly as a convenient overnight stop on a passage across Lake Erie. On the other hand, the paucity of available dockage makes even that advantage problematical.

The West End
Charts 14830, 14846, 14847

The west end of Lake Erie is distinguished by the shallow depths on the lake and the low, marshy shores cut by dozens of small creeks, where land and water seem to merge in an Eden of aquatic wildlife. Much of this terrain is protected in parks and refuges. In uneasy proximity the west end is also flanked by two metropolitan areas, each on its own river—Toledo, Ohio, and Detroit, Michigan. And in each state, rising literally from the verdant marshes to pierce the horizon are the immense cooling towers of two nuclear power plants—Locust Point in Ohio and Enrico Fermi in Michigan. They make good navigational landmarks. Bear in mind as you approach west end harbors that strong westerly winds can temporarily drive down the water level in this regularly shallow end of the lake to even lower levels, well below chart datum. The number of towing services operating in the area is testimony to the frequency of pleasure boat groundings.

In proceeding westward from Port Clinton, where we last left the mainland, the marshes begin almost immediately. In 1907 this seemed like a good lonely place to set up a rifle range and Ohio National Guard camp. Named for the hero of Lake Erie, Camp Perry has served a number of military functions, including prisoner of war camp during World War II. Artillery, anti-aircraft and small arms fire practices are held regularly, endangering an offshore area about 10 miles square, marked by white and orange can buoys. Red flags are displayed from the camp tower and at the targets when firing is in progress, and marine safety broadcasts are issued by the Coast Guard. There is not usually firing on weekends, but it's a good idea to call the Coast Guard to make certain. The whole area is easily avoided, however, by following South Passage between Catawba and South Bass islands, passing outside the light buoy at Niagara Reef, and heading toward the lighthouse on the southwest end of West Sister Island.

If you're looking for an overnight stop in this area, 9½ miles southwest of West Sister Island is the entrance to Cooley Creek and **Anchor Point Boat-O-Minium**. It's not too easy to spot from offshore, but the Toledo Water Intake Crib, surmounted by a large circular building with four quick flashing white lights on each corner of the crib, serves as a convenient guidepost 2 miles northeast. Entrance to the creek is protected on the east side by a low steel and stone jetty, but on the west side the steel pilings are partially submerged and hazardous. Fixed red and green lights with white daymarks define each end of both jetties, however, the greens forming a range at 222° to carry through the channel entrance. Leave the prominent white restaurant to starboard as you proceed up the main channel, carrying eight feet to the marina. All dockside services, including a Laundromat, are offered at slips with 6 to 7 feet of depth. Haulout by travelift and hoist up to 50 tons, full engine and hull repairs, a launch ramp and a marine and convenience store round out the marine services. In addition, there are tennis courts, a swimming pool and the Flying Bridge Restaurant and bar, overlooking the lake in this attractive, rural setting.

Toledo

The Maumee River is the largest river flowing into the Great Lakes. Along its banks and at its mouth sits the city of Toledo. Founded in 1836, the town really began to grow in 1845 with the opening of the Wabash and Erie Canal and took off in giant steps when the glass industry came in with Edward Libbey and later Michael Owens toward the close of the 19th century. Today it is headquarters for three major producers of all kinds of glass, including fiberglass likely used in the construction of your boat. Petroleum refining and a cross-section of manufacturing industry, much of it automobile-related, keep the 350,000 residents of the city busy. But Toledo is more than a smokestack town, and you may find the rather long passage down through Maumee Bay in the southwest corner of the lake worth the time it takes.

Maumee Bay is very shallow and uneven, with large, unmarked, diked spoil areas, so stick to the channel. It actually begins 18 miles northeast of Toledo, where boats coming from the north pick it up. From the east you can enter the channel, buoyed in soldier-straight ranks every mile or so, at the Toledo Harbor Light, only 9 miles from port. This is a three-story buff-colored brick house with a group flashing white and alternating flashing red light, equipped with a fog horn. It's hard to miss. If you're uncertain about it on a hazy day, the Consumers Power Company stacks on the mainland west of the channel are conspicuous. As you approach the city a fixed red range, with red and white daymarks at 237° comes into view. The commercial harbor officially extends 7 miles upstream and is buoyed most of the way. There is sometimes a river current of about 1 mile per hour, and wind-induced water level fluctuations can range from 8 feet above chart datum to 7 feet below.

Although there are loading docks right at the river mouth on the south side, the scene here is quite open and pleasantly nonindustrial. Across the mouth on the north side is Bay View Park, fronted on the river by the Coast Guard Depot and the Naval Reserve Station. Between these two, and sharing the channel, is the entrance to two of Toledo's yacht clubs. Turn to port immediately inside the basin for the **Toledo Yacht Club**, which extends hospitality to members of recognized clubs. The slips have depths of 8 to 12 feet, with the usual dockside services except pumpout and diesel fuel, but including Laundromat. The clubhouse, built in 1885, is gracious and spacious in the style of that era, with dining room and bar, and swimming pool, tennis courts, shuffleboard, children's playground and picnic areas on the tree-shaded grounds. The adjacent park has a golf course. The **Bay View Yacht Club**, also in the park, is located at the far end of the entrance channel. Powerboats predominate in its membership. The docks here are also in 8 feet of water, with the customary services. The less elaborate clubhouse has a dining room and bar. About a mile from the two clubs a neighborhood shopping center called Marina Place has food stores and a drop-off laundry. Downtown Toledo is a 4-mile cab ride. Toledo is a customs port of entry and has railroad passenger as well as airline service for boat crew changes.

A short distance upriver from the yacht clubs, **Harrison Marina** is enclosed in a basin on the north side, but the breakwater is not lighted. The marina is at the edge of Bay View Park in pleasant surroundings. Dockage in slips with 6 to 10 feet of depth, all dockside services, a 30-ton travelift, engine, hull and rigging repairs and a marine store complete the offerings here.

Continuing upstream, the river banks become industrial as you pass through four opening bridges—three rail and one highway, whose closed clearances range from 17 to 38 feet—to the next marina. **Brenner Marine** is on the south, port, side of the river and is the closest to downtown. It has slips in 10 feet, the usual dockside services except diesel and showers, a launch ramp, travelift up to 15 tons, engine and hull repairs and a marine store. The Toledo Sports Arena is next door (698-4545).

A walk across the Cherry Street Bridge from Brenner's brings you to Portside Festival Marketplace, Toledo's brand new harbor front redevelopment, raised in warm wood, cool glass and gracious promenades, where grungy warehouses used to stand. Food shops and stalls, boutiques, restaurants and good things yet to come are featured here. Downtown, with more shops and restaurants, is not many blocks away, although you might want to take a bus. On Monroe Street beyond downtown is Toledo's greatest treasure—her first-rate Museum of Art. The Greek temple and its modern addition (255-8000) house not only fine exhibitions of painting, sculpture, and decorative arts but also a world-renowned collection of artistic glass. The Peristyle Concert Hall in the museum is where the Toledo Symphony and visiting musical artists perform (255-8000). The museum is located in a historic neighborhood of Victorian homes, for which a self-guided walking tour brochure is available (243-9450). The University of Toledo Department of Theatre mounts a summer series (537-2255), but the campus is not within walking distance of downtown or Brenner's. Special events take place in Promenade Park on the river during the summer on Independence Day and during the mid-August Riverfest and Labor Day weekend Toledo Festival.

A cruise farther up the Maumee River will give you more viewing of a piece of America's industrial might, but industry gradually gives way to residential neighborhoods both posh and modest. Two more opening bridges and one 104-foot fixed bridge allow any boat to pass, but the second highway bridge is a fixed span of 45-foot clearance. A couple of islands now appear, and past Clark Island is the **Maumee River Yacht Club**, about 8 miles from the river mouth. To reach it, however, you must proceed past Clark Island to the fixed red Walbridge Park range lights with square daymarks, on a course of 000°. Follow the range almost to shore before turning to the club docks. Accommodation is provided to members of recognized yacht clubs at fixed and floating slips with 8 to 15 feet of depth. All dockside services, except fuel and pumpout, but including Laundromat, are offered. The large, handsome clubhouse has a dining room, bar and swimming pool on the grounds. This club, too, is at the waterfront edge of a park. A walk through the park and across the street brings you to Toledo's excellent zoo (385-4040).

With less than 5-foot draft and 37-foot height it's possible to cruise another few miles, under three more bridges, to the head of navigation at Perrysburg. Unless the Maumee Yacht Club is your destination, there is another engaging way to cruise the river. From the Promenade Park Boat Basin at Portside *Arawanna II* goes out on one-hour excursions (381-1041) and *Arawanna Princess* runs luncheon and dinner cruises (693-2628).

Toledo Beach

A little over 6 miles northwest of the Toledo Harbor Light, about 11 miles north of the Maumee River entrance, the dredged out mouth of Sulphur Creek shelters one of the area's largest marinas and a yacht club. At one time there was an amusement park here, called Toledo Beach, at the end of the trolley line from Toledo. The marina took the name, but its post office address is La Salle, Michigan. The harbor entrance is not easy to pick up; best indicator is the set of Consumers Power stacks 2½ miles southwest. A fixed red range at 290° guides you into the rather narrow entrance between a couple of short, half-submerged piers, with quick flashing green lights on the south pier. This inauspicious approach leads to very large **Toledo Beach Marina**, with all dockside services at the slips in 4 to 6 feet. An open-end travelift can haul to 35 tons, and complete hull, engine and rigging services are available. There is a small marine store and snack bar.

A turn to starboard inside the breakwater leads to **North Cape Yacht Club**, which accepts visitors from reciprocating clubs. Its slips have 8-foot depths, with all dockside services except fuel. The informal clubhouse has a bar and snack bar, and at the sand beach there is playground equipment and picnic tables and grills. Toledo Beach is isolated from any town, but a mile or so up the road leading to it there is a convenience store.

Bolles Harbor

Three miles north from Toledo Beach is Bolles Harbor, where you will encounter the first, but among the most modest, of Michigan's splendid small craft harbors of refuge. A buoyed channel leads through the shallows of La Plaisance Bay into La Plaisance Creek, with 5 feet of controlling depth. A long spit of land encloses the entrance on the north, with a group flashing white light and triangular red daybeacon on the end. Opposite on the south is a short fishing pier. A fixed range at 241° with a quick flashing white front light and an isophase white rear light, is sometimes difficult to detect at night against other lights, and its daymarks are small and difficult to see during daylight hours.

The first facility inside the entrance is the **Waterways Commission Marina** with water and electricity at the slips, gasoline, launch ramp and heads. Next is **Trout's Yacht Basin** with 8 feet at slips and alongside tie-up and all dockside services except showers. A travelift hauls out up to 20 tons for engine and hull repairs, and there is a launch ramp. The **Monroe Boat Club** beyond accepts visitors from reciprocating yacht clubs at its slips with 9 feet, electricity, water, ice, heads and showers. The clubhouse has a bar, game room and marine store, and the dining room is open on summer weekends. There is also a children's playground. Last in line is **Harbor Marine** with both slips and alongside dockage in 8 feet, all services except showers, a 20-ton hoist and engine and hull repairs.

Bolles Harbor is actually the pleasure craft harbor for the city of Monroe, about 3 miles distant. There are two convenience stores within walking distance. Monroe's harbor is entirely industrial.

Sandy Creek

Sandy Creek empties into Brest Bay about 7 miles northeast of the Bolles Harbor entrance. A fixed red range with red day-marks on a course of 303° leads into the creek mouth, with 4½ feet of depth, to the **Detroit Beach Boat Club**. The club has dockage in 8 to 10 feet, all dockside services except diesel, an informal clubhouse with bar and dining room on weekends and a playground for the children.

Swan Creek

A mile and a half beyond the Enrico Fermi Nuclear Plant, with its immense twin cooling towers, fixed green range lights on white piles at 312° lead into Swan Creek. The **Swan Boat Club**, with mainly powerboat membership, offers dockage to members of recognized clubs at slips with 6-foot depths and all dockside services except fuel. The clubhouse has a bar and a dining room open on weekends, with a children's play area on the grounds.

This whole marshy coastline is foul with submerged fish net stakes and should be navigated with great care. At Swan Creek you have arrived at the northwest corner of Lake Erie. For now we will cross the Detroit River Channel and continue on the lake across the north shore.

The Canada Shore

Charts 2100, 2101, 2110, 2181, 2183

Rotate the map of Ontario 90 degrees to starboard and you will see that the southern part of the province resembles an elephant. His trunk, raised high in pachydermian pride, forms the southernmost part of Canada, the Essex County peninsula and the Erie coastline northeastward to Port Stanley. Here the rich soil of the flatland and the moderating climate of the lakeshore combine to produce a cornucopia of garden vegetables in "The Sun Parlour of Canada." (Dumbo's forefoot, planted squarely on the Niagara River, forms the other gentle-climated

Ontario peninsula given to fruit and tobacco culture.) Indeed, the entire north shore of Lake Erie is devoted to provisioning man's larder; citizens who aren't raising crops are harvesting the lake's abundant fishery. Consequently, most of the harbors are working harbors. Pleasure boating is incidental, and you might not care to stay in any one of them more than overnight, unless you're fishing. Unlike the American side of the lakes, Canadian commercial fisheries live amicably with sport fishing.

There is virtually no industry on this coast, and the largest town, Leamington, boasts 12,500 people. The line of march of Ontario urban/industrial progress lies about 10 miles inland along the railroad and the superhighway. Many of the harbors are far from the towns they serve, so don't count on doing much shopping along this coast. In startling contrast to Lake Erie's south shore, the Canada side is monochromatic, slow-paced and rather old-fashioned. Herein lies its appeal for the cruising boater and the summer cottager. If unglamorous, it is peaceful country, a refreshing change of pace.

Kingsville

From the busy shipping lanes of the Detroit River a generally eastward course brings you out of the traffic into Pigeon Bay. Keep a sharp lookout for fish net stakes, as you must throughout this coast, and note the red buoy on Grecian Shoal. Twenty miles from the Detroit River Light a pair of breakwaters protects the mouth of Cedar Creek. A flashing red and a fixed green flank the entrance. Sandbars build up on both sides of the harbor entrance, and though the channel is deeper, the bar limits draft to 5 feet.

Once inside, the creek mouth opening to starboard from the channel forms a pleasant, entirely recreational harbor. Although 3 miles from town, it's preferable to Kingsville harbor if you can get in. On the starboard side the **Township Dock** provides electricity and water. **Cedar Island Yacht Club**, mainly for sailboats, is on the port side, with 6 feet at the slips, electricity, water, pumpout, heads and showers. The clubhouse is small and informal. **Melton Brothers Marina**, just before the bridge across the creek, has finger docks with 6-foot depths, all dockside services except diesel fuel and showers, a launch ramp, trailer or railway haulout up to 40 feet, minor engine repairs and steel hull repair. The township park on the outer side of the creek has a sand beach. There is a summer Customs Office here.

Kingsville, 2 miles east of Cedar Creek, is a very busy commercial fishing harbor, which may or may not have room for a transient pleasure boat. Furthermore, the harbor is tumultuous in strong southeast winds. Otherwise it is quite easy to get into. A water tower west of the entrance is a helpful landmark, and a fixed green range with white, orange and black daymarks leads on a course of 308° past the breakwaters. The west breakwater, passed first, has a flashing green light, the east pier a fixed red one with a fog whistle. The east wharf is entirely taken up by fish tugs and the Sandusky ferry, while the west pier is for loading coal and sand. The finger piers at the far end may have space for you, in 6 feet of water with electricity and water, although silting occurs here as in all the harbors on this coast. Gas, diesel and pumpout are also available. There are two modest restaurants at the harbor front. The village of Kingsville itself, population 5,000, is an attractive one with not a few old mansions adorning its streets. Fortunes have been made here in farming, food processing and fishing.

Point Pelee

The sharply pointed finger of Point Pelee reaches 9 miles southward and together with the Erie Islands all but closes off the west end of the lake. From Pelee's tip treacherous sandbars build up as much as 5½ miles beyond the point, yet it is between Point Pelee and Pelee Island that the only natural deep water channel is found. All ship traffic, upbound and downbound, must squeeze through this pass, making Pelee Passage one of the most congested traffic lanes on the lakes. It is lavishly appointed with lights and buoys. The most important of these are Pelee Passage Light, flashing red on a white square building with black stripes and equipped with a fog horn. Pleasure boats can find enough depth just off the channel to avoid the direct path of the ships, but it's wise not to stray too far.

Point Pelee itself is a national park that protects a remarkable and fragile natural environment of marsh, field and forest. It shelters hundreds of species of bird and animal life, some of them endangered, and is a primary resting place for tens of thousands of migratory birds and monarch butterflies on their incredible semiannual voyages. The park was established in 1918, the first in Canada set aside for its biological value. Visitation by the throngs of nature lovers and beach parties that congregate here is carefully controlled. There are trails, including a boardwalk into the marsh, beaches, and bicycle and canoe rentals. There is no safe anchorage off the park, but there is a small harbor about 2 miles from its landward entrance on the west side of the peninsula, suitable for smaller powerboats.

As of this writing Leamington has no small craft facilities, but a new breakwall has been installed and a large marina is planned. The nearest accommodation to Point Pelee National Park is at Sturgeon Creek, about 2 miles east of Leamington, 11 miles from Kingsville. At Sturgeon Creek, identified by several radio towers east of it, a pair of converging rubble breakwalls is marked by flashing red and green lights. Watch out for an old bridge ruin just inside the entrance. Depths in the creek vary with the shifting sand bottom, but probably average 4 feet or more. The fixed highway bridge a short distance upstream has a clearance of 18 feet. Beyond it, **Sturgeon Creek Marina** has older wood docks in 6-foot depths, with electricity, water, ice, pump-out and gas. It has a launch ramp and offers engine and hull repairs. There is a grocery store about half a mile away, but no public transportation to the park. You can either hike or hitch.

Wheatley

From Point Pelee to Long Point 135 miles east, there is no coastal chart. You must navigate on the general chart of Lake Erie for your passages between harbors, although most of the ports are depicted in large scale on 2183. A dozen miles north of Point Pelee, about 17 from Southeast Shoal Light, Wheatley is an impressive commercial fishing harbor. The big yellow building of Omstead Fisheries Company, reportedly the world's largest fresh water fish processing plant, which also packs frozen vegetables, is a conspicuous landmark. There is also a water tank northeast of the harbor. A long east breakwater, with an isophase red light on a white tower with red top at the outer end forming a range at 342° with a fixed red on the same kind of tower at the inner end, protects the entrance to Muddy Creek. The front light is equipped with a fog whistle. There is a short breakwater on the opposite shore and a detached breakwater about 300 feet off the end of the east pier to help in breaking southeast seas. This one has a flashing red light on it.

The entire harbor is committed to the very large fishing fleet that operates from here. But in an emergency space may be found for a pleasure boat at the docks with 8-foot depths. Hyke Metal Products, on the west side of the harbor, builds the steel tugs that you see and will provide repairs to pleasure boats in need, with an overhead crane for haulout.

A mile and a half east of the main harbor, near the provincial park, the dedicated members of the **Wheatley Yacht Club** have carved out a harbor and built parallel rock jetties to protect it. There is a flashing red light on the east jetty; the channel carries 8 feet, the basin 6½ to 7. The slips have no services as yet, but the clubhouse has heads and a meeting room where the hospitable members gather. The village of 1,600 people is about a mile inland.

Erieau

Thirty miles northeast of Wheatley is the Ontario shore's only natural harbor, Rondeau Harbour. Regrettably it is uncharted and too shallow over much of its 2-by-6-mile expanse to accommodate cruising boats. But there is a well-protected facility for cruising boats in the deeper, charted waters of the harbor entrance, as well as a number of small boat marinas in the bay.

There isn't much in the way of conspicuous landmarks on this low, featureless coastline. Two piers enclose the harbor entrance. The longer west one has a flashing green light on the end, with white, orange and black daymark and a fog horn. It forms a range at 012° with a fixed green rear light with orange and black daymark. The shorter east pierhead has a flashing red light. The water is deep through this channel, but it is subject both to fluctuations and currents that change with the direction of the wind. At the inner end of the west pier a long narrow basin opens to port. This is the location of the **Erieau Marina** with slips in 15 feet, all dockside services, the Slip in Cafe Restaurant and car rental by the hour for your shopping convenience. A travelift hauls out up to 40 feet, and mechanics can be called in. Note that there are pilings both above and below the water at the end of the marina wharf and give them a good berth. Just beyond the north end of the marina basin rubble breakwalls enclose another basin with finger slips, but these are dedicated to the commercial fish tugs operating from the harbor.

Erieau is a resort community of small cottages and camps strung along the long, narrow sand spit that forms the south side of Rondeau Harbour. There is no real village center, but there is a food store a couple of blocks from the marina, and there is fresh fish available if your own luck has been poor. Along the lakeshore south of the marina basin is Kenterieau Park, with a public sand beach. Take your dinghy into Rondeau Harbour to reach its main attraction, Rondeau Provincial Park, which occupies the eastern side. In addition to its sand beaches, the park encloses a primeval forest. The bay itself is good fishing territory.

Port Stanley

The 45 miles from Erieau to Port Stanley is one of the longest stretches on Lake Erie without a harbor of refuge. The shoreline is clean the whole distance, and beyond Pointe aux Pins the clay cliffs rise to present a somewhat more interesting scene. Although the village of Port Stanley is small—about 2,000 people— the harbor is large and has the most accommodation for pleasure craft on the middle and western reaches of the Canadian shore. It is identified from offshore by the oil storage tanks and grain silos inside the west breakwater. The artificial outer harbor is enclosed by converging breakwaters. On the west pierhead a flashing green light, displayed from a white structure with a fog horn, lines up on a range of 341° with a fixed green light with white daymark on top of one of the oil tanks. The east breakwater is marked by a flashing red light from a white tower with red top. Buoys and another light lead through the outer harbor to the dredged mouth of Kettle Creek, lined with wharves for the fishing fleet and tankers that call. Continue on past these installations to the highway bridge, with a closed clearance of 13 feet. It opens on the hour and half hour for pleasure craft that sound three long blasts.

Kettle Creek carries 6 to 8 feet to the railway bridge, another mile upstream. Almost midway on the east bank **Stan's Marina** has dockage in 9 feet, alongside and in slips, with all dockside services. There is a launch ramp, and a crane lifts out up to 50 tons for engine and hull repairs. Shopping is only a few blocks away in the pleasant village. Just below the railroad bridge, on the west bank, the hospitable **Kanagio Yacht Club** has dockage in 9 feet with all services, including Laundromat, a 30-ton crane and engine repair. There are tennis and badminton courts, and the clubhouse has a dining room and bar with live entertainment and dancing on Saturday nights. Downtown shopping is a quarter of a mile away. The Port Stanley Players perform in summer stock at the arena. For powerboats with less than 5-foot draft and 14-foot height, **Port Stanley Marina** is on the west bank beyond the fixed railway bridge and overhead cable. An older marina and trailer park, there is dockage with gas, pumpout, ice and a launch ramp.

The 60 miles of coastline between Port Stanley and the tip of Long Point is a lee shore directly in the path of southwest winds blowing over a long fetch. The three harbors spaced 10 miles apart—Port Stanley, Port Bruce and Port Burwell—can provide some welcome refuge. Port Stanley is, by far, the most desirable, so make sure you have good weather prospects before taking your departure.

Port Bruce

Port Bruce is a small summer cottage resort on Catfish Creek. There are sand bluffs along the shore at this point, and the break in their line is the best means of identifying the creek entrance from offshore. There is no harbor chart for Port Bruce, but the creek entrance is flanked by a pair of breakwaters, the west one extending farther into the lake than the east. On the end of the west pier a flashing green light is shown from a square mast. Note two groups of pilings off the end of the east, corrugated sheet metal breakwater. There is a controlling depth of 6 feet at the harbor entrance, but, despite the breakwalls, it can be extremely difficult to get into in heavy southwest seas.

Cruising boats can tie up along the west wall beyond the inner end of the breakwater in a parklike setting with public washrooms. In strong winds anywhere from south there is a lot of surge here. Depths of 4 to 6 feet will carry up the creek for about a half mile to a small boat marina just before the highway bridge with 16 feet of clearance. There is no village, but there is a fish market and a couple of eateries.

Port Burwell

This is another working, fishing harbor, but the infrequently dredged channel is now so badly silted up that boats drawing more than 3 feet should probably not attempt it. The harbor is easy to find, however, as the village of about 700 people shows up against the bluffs. An oddly shaped west breakwater and pier shelter the mouth of Big Otter Creek from the west, with an outermost flashing white light on a mast and an inner flashing green on a white structure. A much shorter east breakwater carries fixed red range lights, with orange and black daymarks, on a course of 355°. These substantial navigational aids lead to nothing much, however. This was once a shipping port, and there is still tie-up among the fish tugs along either wall, faced with corrugated steel and equipped with big iron bollards. The harbor also piles up the water in strong southerlies and south-easterlies. There is food shopping and a Laundromat on the east side, and a fish market past the highway bridge on the west side. A shallow draft boat or dinghy might enjoy meandering up the creek through the farming countryside.

Long Point Bay

One of Lake Erie's most conspicuous natural features is the long finger of land jutting 18 miles southeastward from the Ontario shore. Appropriately called Long Point, the sand spit created by prevailing southwest wind and wave action is still growing, as it has for the past 4,000 years. It greatly lengthens the voyage of pleasure boats across the north side of Lake Erie, and its shifting bars and currents have been a hazard to shipping since white men launched their first vessel on the lake almost 300 years ago. Since 1799, 163 vessels have been reported wrecked off the point. One of them was counted a blessing to local residents; she carried a cargo of whiskey, which was inexplicably missing when the authorities came to investigate. Today's lakers give the point a berth of 3 to 9 miles on their carefully regulated up- and downbound tracks. One of the lake's tallest, most powerful lights shines flashing white and sounds a warning fog horn here. Lake Erie's deepest sounding, 210 feet, is 7 miles off the point.

Long Point may be an obstruction to mariners, but the bay it encloses is a fisherman's and a naturalist's delight. Like its southwestern counterpart at Sandusky and the Erie Islands, Long Point Bay is the centerpiece of Ontario sport fishing. Only here nature's gift is shared with commercial fishing under mutually respected ground rules. The sportsmen angle mainly for smallmouth bass and yellow perch, while the tugs set gill nets primarily for perch and trawl for smelt in the deeper parts of the bay and beyond its limits.

The point itself shelters a maze of marshes and lagoons, with dunes and forest on the lake side back of the sand and gravel beaches. In fact, when you're coasting along the flat, low point it looks entirely wooded. A large part of the peninsula, primarily the triangle of sand spits, marsh and lagoons in the middle, is owned by the private Long Point Company, a sportsmen's club that was formed in 1866. West of their tract is Long Point Provincial Park, and most of the eastern end has been donated by the company to the Canadian Wildlife Service. Long Point is a haven for migrating and nesting birds; over 320 species have been sighted, and in June hordes of turtles trek from the marshes on the inner bay to the dunes across the spit to lay their eggs.

If you're on a long passage east or west across the lake, anchorage inside Long Point affords a convenient stopover and avoids a long haul in and out to one of the marinas on the bay. The best spot is behind Bluff Bar, about 7½ miles west of Long Point Light. There is a flashing green light buoy near the tip of Bluff Bar that helps identify it. No distinguishing landmarks give you your bearings in this world of watery land; you must rely on the buoy and your depth sounder. The anchorage shoals off quickly, so don't go too far in, but set your hook in 12 to 15 feet over sand. Despite the low shores, you'll be comfortable here in any wind except northwest. In that case the anchorage is untenable. Unfortunately there is no other.

The best alternative is **Turkey Point Marine Basin**, about 10 miles northwest across the bay. This friendly, full service marina is in a spacious sheltered basin with 6-foot depths, about 2 miles south of the resort village of Turkey Point. Alongside dockage and slips, with all dockside services, a launch ramp, travelift to 25 tons, engine and hull repairs, are the marine services offered. The Oyster Pearl restaurant and bar is on the premises, and there are sand beaches nearby. The marina monitors channel 68.

Port Rowan Area

Off the entrance to the Turkey Point Marine Basin a pair of flashing red and green light buoys identifies the channel from the main part of Long Point Bay into Inner Bay. Inner Bay, approximately 5 miles by 7, is very shallow and best suited to powerboats. At the western end there are several marinas in and around the village of Port Rowan, identified from offshore by its church spire and water tank. In the village itself **Kestl's Marina** is at the government wharf, with a flashing red light at the outer end, alongside docking and some older slips in 6 feet of water. There is some electricity available, plus gas, ice, pumpout and a restaurant. The village of 850 isn't much commercially, but there is a grocery store and a Laundromat close by.

South of town **Norm's Bayview Marina** is approached by a buoyed channel with 6-foot depths and can accommodate boats up to 28 feet at alongside dockage in 6 feet. All dockside services are available, except water and diesel. There is a launch ramp, a trailer to haul out up to 30 feet, engine repairs and a convenience store. **Sandboy Marina** is also reached through a buoyed channel with 8- to 10-foot depths; it can accommodate boats to 40 feet, but most are under 25. There is electricity at some of the floating slips, ice, heads, gas, a launch ramp, trailer haulout to 26 feet and engine repairs. The buoyed channel into **Marina Shores** carries 5 feet but there is 12 feet at the slips and alongside dockage that can accommodate boats to 43 feet. Some slips have electricity, and the other dockside services are available, except showers and diesel. There is a launch ramp, trailer haulout up to 25 feet and engine repairs. One mile northeast of Port Rowan, **Bluebell Marina** has an 8-foot-deep buoyed channel and a range of 8 to 10 feet at dockside. All the usual services are available, except diesel fuel, and there is a launch ramp.

Three miles northeast of Port Rowan the hamlet of St. Williams can be identified by a pair of silos and a flashing red light on a white tower with red top at the end of the wharf. **Booth's Harbour** is reached through a buoyed channel with 5-foot depths. The boat wells have short, partial docks but can accommodate boats to 50 feet in 3- to 9-foot depths. All dockside services are available, except diesel; a travelift can haul to 12 tons for wood hull repairs. There is also a launch ramp, marine store, snack bar and small beach.

Port Dover

From the entrance to Inner Bay at Deep Hole Point it's 10 miles to Port Dover, the most interesting port for pleasure boats on the Ontario side of the lake and, reportedly, the largest freshwater fishing port in the world. Certainly there is a huge fleet of fishing vessels berthed here, and some very large plants, including another branch of Omstead's. It's an 18-mile run to or from Long Point Light. Bluffs line the lakeshore along this coast, and a water tank helps identify the entrance to Port Dover at the mouth of the Lynn River. An off-lying shoal area to be avoided southeast of the harbor entrance is marked by a flashing red light buoy. The dredged harbor is entered through parallel piers. The familiar flashing red light on a white tower with red top sits on the east pier, and on the west is an isophase green on a white structure with a fog horn, which forms a range at 021° with a fixed green on a tower with orange and black daymark. Be sure to come in on the range and avoid the submerged ruins just west of the west pier. Controlling depth in the entrance channel is 8 feet, diminishing to 6 up the Lynn River to its confluence with Black Creek half a mile upstream.

Immediately inside the east pier a large, dredged basin opens to starboard, but this, along with the west wharf, is the domain of the commercial fishermen. Pleasure boats proceed upriver, past the bascule highway bridge (closed clearance 24 feet) that opens on the hour and half hour in response to three blasts. Just beyond the bridge **Bridgeview Marina** has slips with 12-foot depths and electricity at some of them. All other dockside services are offered, except showers, a travelift hauls to 20 feet for engine and hull repairs and there is a launch ramp and marine store. Next upriver is **Matthews Marine**, with alongside dockage in 8 feet, dockside services except showers and fuel, a 20-ton travelift, engine and hull repairs. A little farther upstream Black Creek flows into the river; the overhead power line here has a clearance of 66 feet. The **Port Dover Yacht Club** occupies the end of a peninsula in the creek in a pleasant setting, with slips in 6 feet and the usual services except pumpout and fuel. The small clubhouse has a bar.

Port Dover is a lively community of 3,600 people, a customs port of entry, whose downtown shopping area surrounds a pretty village green called Powell Park. On the third Saturday in August there is an arts and crafts show there. Downtown shopping is half to three-quarters of a mile from the marinas and yacht club, but the Laundromat is not convenient. On the way you'll pass the Port Dover Marine Museum, housed in an old net shed (583-2660). There are several restaurants and taverns in town; The Galley is where the local folks gather for breakfast and morning coffee. Along the west wharf below the bridge is an amusement area, with bowling, mini-golf and dodge-em cars. The professional Lighthouse Festival Theatre (583-2221) performs its summer repertoire in the restored Town Hall upstairs theater. A plaque on the outskirts of town tells you that Fathers de Casson and Galinée, the discoverers of Lake Erie, wintered here.

Nanticoke

Nanticoke Creek, 6½ miles from Port Dover, is all but lost between the huge installations of the Steel Company of Canada west of it and the immense Ontario Hydro Generating Station to the east. Both of these have elaborately lighted channels leading to their big wharves. Nanticoke Creek itself is entered between parallel breakwaters built of sheet piling, with a flashing green on the south pierhead and a single station range with fixed white, red and green lights on the north bank, equipped with a fog whistle. The white sector shows the preferred channel, with

6 feet of depth. **Hoover's Marina** offers dockage alongside and in slips, with 8 feet, electricity, water, heads, gas and a popular restaurant.

Port Maitland

At Peacock Point, 4 miles beyond Nanticoke Creek, you officially leave Long Point Bay. (Give the point and its big shoal area a wide berth.) Another 18 miles takes you to Port Maitland. Be sure to skirt Tecumseh Reef on the outside; it is marked by a flashing red light buoy. Its nasty rocks and shoals extend in a continuous swath almost 5 miles from shore.

When it was an outlet for a Welland Canal feeder Port Maitland was an important place. Now it is a moribund suburb of inland Dunnville, with some industrial plants at the harbor, where a few fish tugs moor. For a cruising boat this is strictly a harbor of refuge. The plants make it conspicuous from offshore, and there is the usual pair of breakwaters with a flashing red light on the east pier and a fixed green range with orange and black daymarks at 020° on the west pier. The harbor is dredged from the mouth of the Grand River, and depths at the edge of the channel are sufficient for anchorage. Expect surge in winds from southerly directions, however, and when there are storms from south or southwest, followed by a wind shift, the currents in and out can be fierce.

Another 15 miles brings you to Port Colborne, described in earlier pages, with good facilities for pleasure boats. In this stretch, too, a dangerous set of reefs make out from Mohawk Bay. Take care to pass outside the flashing red light buoy. At Port Colborne we have completed our paper circumnavigation of Lake Erie.

5
INTERLUDE: DETROIT RIVER, LAKE ST. CLAIR AND ST. CLAIR RIVER

The Detroit River—Metropolitan Highway
Chart 14848 or 14853
Small Craft Book

D'Etroit, The Strait, over 30 miles long by 1½ wide at its widest, is one of the most strategic passes on the Great Lakes. No sooner had the French discovered Lake Erie and pacified the Iroquois than they recognized that a military post here would secure the precious fur trade of the North, West and Southwest. Moreover, the trade could be pursued in swifter ships with heavier ladings across the lower lakes than the northern canoe route could handle. In 1701 Antoine La Mothe, Sieur de Cadillac, established Fort Ponchartrain d'Etroit—the first French farming settlement in the West, as well as a fortified trading post. Its name soon shortened, the settlement occupied both sides of the river but grew slowly and fitfully through the 18th century. Nevertheless, it became an important center of the British trade after 1763, and His Majesty held on to it until 1796 when the new United States finally asserted title to the north bank. When faced with a choice of allegiance some of Detroit's most prominent citizens moved across the river to Sandwich, the settlement that changed its name to Windsor in 1834.

The War of 1812 brought invasion and counter-invasion to the towns that faced each other across the narrow strait, and a hostility between citizens that was eventually submerged in the century of progress that followed. After the opening of the Erie Canal, Detroit became a major port for the transshipment of settlers and goods and grew rapidly as Michigan opened up through the 1830s and 1840s. There was no doubt that it was and would remain the new state's preeminent city, the commercial and financial center of a big, rich hinterland. After the fur traders and the lumber barons and the copper and iron magnates extracted their fortunes out of the earth they built their mansions in the city beside the river and its expanding suburbs and settled down to the gracious life. Industry came to Detroit, as it did to every American city, during the closing years of the 19th century, but it wasn't until World War I that the great eruption of smokestacks took place. This was the beginning of Motown, the motor capital of the world, whose very name would become a synonym for automobile.

Meanwhile, on the south shore—here Canada is curiously south of the United States—Windsor and its surrounding villages grew more slowly as farming communities. In 1858 Hiram Walker established his distillery and the village of Walkerville, which he intended to be a model company town; it merged with Windsor in 1935. By the close of the century Windsor, too, was a small industrial city, but its destiny remained bound up with Detroit.

Traffic in people and ideas and a few other things has always been brisk across the narrow stream. Throughout the first half of the 19th century a procession of fugitive slaves found their way to sanctuary in Canada through Detroit's underground and Windsor's open door. During the 1920s and early '30s another peculiar institution reversed the flow—this time it was illicit alcohol that found its way by dead of night from Canada to secret entries on the thirsty American side. Detroit River traffic in bootleg whiskey was probably the heaviest anywhere in the United States.

Ford of Canada assembled its first car in Windsor in 1904, and it, too, has been an auto town ever since, though greatly different from Detroit in character and atmosphere. The bonds of history and friendship between the two cities became visible in 1929, with the completion of the Detroit-Windsor Tunnel, a masterpiece of difficult engineering. A year later the graceful towers of the Ambassador Bridge soared above the river. Today, commuter traffic is heavy both ways on these arteries.

Although Detroit and Windsor are loyal and harmonious neighbors, you must choose sides as you travel up the river that separates them. Each passage offers a different experience of this complex 32-mile waterway—awe-inspiring industrial agglomerations and a glass-towered skyline on the American side; rusticity, parks, some industry and a medium-city skyline on the Canadian, with marine facilities that somehow match the prevailing mood. Each is worth a transit. But remember that wherever your course takes you in the Detroit River you are cruising one of the world's most congested waterways. It is imperative that pleasure craft watch for and avoid the ships that often cannot see and certainly cannot maneuver around them. Don't underestimate the hazards of recreational traffic on the river either. Speedboats dart in and out among sailboats at any place and time, especially at marina entrances. On both sides of the river pleasure boat facilities are found in two clusters, at the lower and upper ends. In between is the world of big-time industry and commerce.

The Detroit River drops three feet from the level of Lake St. Clair to Lake Erie. Consequently currents can run 1¼ to 1½ miles per hour. Two ship channels lead from Lake Erie to convergence at the Detroit River Light, a big white tower with a group flashing white light and a fog horn. Shortly beyond they divide again around a series of islands and shoals. Downbound ships follow Livingston Channel, which crisscrosses the international boundary, while the Amherstburg Channel bordering the Ontario shore is for upbound vessels. At this widest part of the river its biggest island, 8 by 1½ miles, logically named Grosse Ile, lies close off the Michigan side, with deep water Trenton Channel between. Ships can reach it only from upriver, but there is sufficient depth for pleasure boats to cross over from flashing green light buoy "13" just beyond the Detroit River Light.

Grosse Ile

Grosse Ile, Michigan, is a residential island, with three yacht clubs around its southern tip and one farther up the west side. A buoyed channel leads to **Grosse Ile Yacht Club** in a basin between Hickory and Meso islands. It can be reached from buoys "7" and "8" just before the entrance to diked Livingston Channel. Occulting red and green lights mark the entrance. Members of reciprocating yacht clubs can find dockage in slips or alongside, with depths ranging from 3½ to 7½ feet. All dockside services, except fuel but including Laundromat, are available, and the clubhouse has a dining room and bar. North of this club along the same approach channel a fixed green range at 306° leads through a pair of buoys into the **Elba-Mar Boat Club.**. Here dockage, alongside and in slips, with 6 feet, is available to members of recognized yacht clubs, with the usual services except diesel, and a dining room and bar in the clubhouse.

A turn to port from buoys "3," "4" and "5" on the approach channel to these two clubs leads through an unmarked channel that carries 10 feet to the **Ford Yacht Club**. A fixed red range on 015° leads to the east basin, while a fixed red range on 024° leads to the west basin. Both ranges have white daymarks and red and green lights at the entrance to each channel. Visitors should go to the west basin, where members of recognized yacht clubs can find slips with 7 feet and all dockside services except fuel. The clubhouse has a dining room and bar, and on the grounds are picnic and play areas.

Gibraltar

You cannot cross from Grosse Ile at this point to the mainland shore, as the river is very shallow here. The channel along the mainland shore must be approached from flashing green "13" in the ship channel on a course of about 332° for a distance of 5 miles to the tip of Horse Island. Continue another mile and a half, taking care to avoid the rocky shoals at the north end of Horse Island, then favor the port shore, to the entrance range for Gibraltar harbor. Here is the first of the downriver marinas in the southernmost of five Detroit suburbs that are known as the downriver communities. This one is primarily residential. All the marinas on this part of the river cater mainly to powerboats.

Fixed red lights, the front light equipped with a red and white daymark, on a course of 239° guide you into the channel that is Gibraltar harbor. **Gibraltar Boat Yard** is a very large full service marina with both alongside dockage and slips with rather narrow, older wood catwalks, in depths of 4 feet. All dockside services are available, except diesel fuel, the open-end travelift can haul up to 16 tons for engine and hull repairs and there is a marine store. A restaurant and supermarket are across the street. At the gas dock here you will encounter an institution unique to the Detroit River and Lake St. Clair—a convenience store that sells beer and wine. (I have some rather negative feelings about this, as alcohol is as much a menace on a crowded river as it is on a crowded highway. Regrettably, in the name of competition, every marina goes along with the practice.) **Humbug Marina** is the other very large facility at Gibraltar, with slips in 6 to 8 feet, all dockside services, including Laundromat, a hoist to 30 tons, engine and hull repairs and a marine store.

Trenton Channel and a Side Trip to Dearborn

Another mile and three-quarters up the river brings you to the first of the buoys marking the deep water Trenton Channel. Past Calf Island, move over to the Grosse Ile side of the channel as you pass the first of the many industrial installations you'll see on this course. Just beyond the island is the first of two bridges connecting Grosse Ile to the mainland. This one has a closed clearance of 18 feet; the next one, 3 miles up, clears 10 feet. They open on request with one long and one short blast. Short of the first bridge, on the Grosse Ile side, is the **West River Yacht Club**, with 12 feet at the slips, electricity, water and pumpout. There is a swimming pool, golf course, restaurant and bar on the premises.

The contrast between the two shores begins to grow as the homes on the island side are faced by a succession of steel and chemical plants in the cities of Trenton, Riverview and Wyandotte. You'll pass a few marinas that don't accept transient boats. A couple of miles beyond the end of Grosse Ile is **Rick's Cove**, which does. There are 5-foot depths at the slips that accommodate powerboats, with all dockside services except fuel, a 15-ton travelift and engine and hull repairs. Another mile upstream, on a channel inside Mud Island, **Ecorse Boat Basin**, for powerboats, has the usual dockside services at its older wood slips, except showers and diesel, a hoist to 28 feet and engine repairs. There isn't much in the way of commercial services useful to boaters near any of these marinas, but they are on a bus line into downtown Detroit, about 10 miles by road.

One of the region's major tourist attractions is handier to the downriver marinas than it is to the others, about a 5-mile cab ride from Wyandotte. Henry Ford, notorious for his remark that "history is bunk," set out to capture 19th-century America in a village he created with transplanted houses, shops, schools, workplaces, and whatever from all over the nation. He called it Greenfield, after the community on nearby Greenfield Road where he was born. The individual structures at Greenfield Village are authentic—many of them historic, like the Wright Brothers' cycle shop—but it's their juxtaposition in the city of Dearborn that is artificial. Nevertheless, the village is a fascinating place (271-1620).

On the same property is the Henry Ford Museum (same

telephone, but separate admission), an eclectic collection of transportation artifacts, mechanical contrivances, household furnishings and decorative arts, all handsomely displayed. Across the street from both, Dearborn Inn is a gracious resort-style hotel, with an excellent dining room.

Two and a half miles past Ecorse Channel you come to the mouth of the Rouge River, if you can find it amid the welter of stacks, conveyors, tracks, ramps, silos, tanks and gargantuan sheds. The Ford layout, the largest private industrial complex in the United States if not the world, is a couple of miles upstream, if the Rouge, thick with industrial discharge, can be said to flow. Steel and chemicals continue to dominate the Detroit River front, some of the plants falling obsolete and idle as American industry has reduced and shifted gears in recent years. The separate river channels have joined into one where the river narrows to half a mile across. Canadian and American industry now face each other, although the structures are widely spaced and low-key on the Windsor side.

As you approach the high span of the Ambassador Bridge, Detroit industry gives way to harbor terminal facilities, and beyond the bridge the Canada side is all parks and homes and greenery, with one brief exception farther upstream. The Detroit skyline, dominated by the gleaming cylinders of the Renaissance Center, has grown on the horizon for some time now, and soon you're passing the clean architectural lines and greenery of the city's waterfront redevelopment, including Ren-Cen itself. Beyond that more terminal and warehouse installations are backed by a 2-mile stretch of mostly abandoned, obsolete factories. Just as you're tiring of the workaday scene the gem of the Detroit River comes into view, sitting like a pendant at its throat, dividing the strait into two channels again.

Belle Isle Channel

Belle Isle, aptly named masterpiece of park designer Frederick Law Olmsted, has for over 100 years refreshed and inspired urban-weary Detroiters, with its gardens, walks, drives, beaches, playgrounds, golf course, zoo (398-0900), aquarium (824-3223) and Dossin Great Lakes Museum (267-6440). The umbilicus connecting this oasis to the city is a beautiful, but somewhat low-level, fixed bridge, with 32-foot clearance. If you can get under it to reach the spate of marine facilities on the other side, be sure to heed the buoys that surround Scott Middle Ground. If your mast is too tall, you must follow Fleming Channel as the

Jefferson Beach Marina.

ships do around the south side of the 3-mile-long island and
backtrack through a buoyed channel.

On Belle Isle itself are two of the nation's most venerable
clubs, the **Detroit Boat Club**, just past the bridge, and the **Detroit
Yacht Club**, beyond the beach and golf course. Both accommodate visiting boats from recognized yacht clubs. The slips at
Detroit Boat Club have 4- to 12-foot depths, with all dockside
services except fuel. The lovely clubhouse has a dining room and
bar, with a swimming pool and paddle tennis on the grounds.
The much larger Detroit Yacht Club facilities include all dockside services, except fuel but including Laundromat, at the slips
with 5 to 7 feet, a convenience store, indoor and outdoor
swimming pools, tennis courts, picnic grounds and dining room
and bar in the elaborate clubhouse. The slips here are enclosed
behind a breakwall, marked by four red lights on the flagpole at
the entrance.

On the mainland shore, almost opposite the DYC, is the
municipal **Memorial Park Marina**. Double fixed red and green
lights mark the entrance to the basin. The slips have depths of 13
feet, with all dockside services except fuel. The marina is
adjacent to some luxury apartment buildings, and the immediate neighborhood is the affluent Indian Village, a restored
residential community. Jefferson Avenue, a block away, has not
been so elegantly restored, but it has a supermarket nearby and

a bus line. This is the closest facility to downtown on a fairly quick bus ride, although taxicabs are preferred at night. There is 24-hour security at the marina, surrounded by locked cyclone fencing, as there is at most of the others on this part of the river.

Marinas now follow in rather quick succession, and they all have the ubiquitous beer and wine store at the gas dock. Next after Memorial Park comes the **Detroit Boat Basin**, with 15-foot depths at the slips, all dockside services, railway haulout up to 75 feet, engine and hull repairs and a marine store. The next two sets of docks are for restaurants, the Roostertail and Sindbad's. **Sindbad's** is also open to overnight transients, with slips in 8 to 9 feet, electricity and water. Next door is **Kean's Detroit Yacht Harbor**. Here the slips have 8-foot depths, with the standard dockside services, except diesel but including Laundromat. There is a launch ramp; a 30-ton hoist; engine, hull and rigging repairs; a marine and convenience store; and ferry service to the Detroit Yacht Club. Upstairs, above the marina office and store, the St. Clair Yacht Club invites members of reciprocating clubs to their dining room and bar. Just beyond the end of Belle Isle at the head of the river the **Bayview Yacht Club** and **Gregory Boat Company** are side by side. Bayview sponsors the annual Detroit-Mackinac race, for sailors only, with 7 feet at the slips, and offers all dockside services except pumpout and fuel. The very attractive, rather country-style clubhouse has a dining room and bar. At Gregory's there are 15-foot depths at the slips, all dockside services, haulout by hoist up to 56 feet, engine and hull repairs.

If you're at one of these marinas during the right days in July, you'll have almost a front row seat at the annual Stroh Gold Cup Regatta, one of the world's most prestigious powerboat races. The course between the Belle Isle Bridge and the Waterworks is closed on race days, so if you're passing through, you'll be obliged to take Fleming Channel on the Windsor side. This entire group of marinas is located in a part of the city that once was busy, commercial and industrial. Most of that has been cleared away and grass, almost literally, grows in the streets between some shabby residential pockets. There is no shopping nearby, and the Jefferson Avenue bus is far inland. The only transportation to the sights of Detroit is by cab.

Detroit Attractions

Downtown's centerpiece is the riverfront development. The Renaissance Center's four circular office towers surrounding the world's tallest hotel, the circular Westin at 72 stories, reflect the shifting light and scene below their mirror walls. The complex is much more impressive from the outside than from the cold, cavernous interior. The most interesting thing inside is the Money Museum in the National Bank of Detroit, open during banking hours. But there is also an array of sumptuous shops and restaurants. The view from the top lounges and restaurant, after a breath-catching outside elevator ride, is spectacular. In the shadow of this glittering ode to tomorrow is a humble reminder of yesterday—the Mariner's Church, built in 1849 with money willed by two sisters for a church dedicated to Great Lakes sailors.

West of Ren-Cen, Hart Plaza opens a landscaped face to the river. Downtown skyscrapers back it up, and on its flanks are Ford Auditorium (961-7017), the home of the Detroit Symphony Orchestra, and the Veterans Memorial Building, the first outpost on the new riverfront in 1950. This is said to be the spot where Cadillac came ashore to found the city. Beyond it is Cobo Hall, with a busy schedule of conventions and exhibitions (224-1000) and Joe Louis Arena (567-6000). Detroit celebrates its ethnic diversity each summer weekend with a festival in the square sponsored by a different nationality group.

The city is a sprawled one, and you'll bus or cab a couple of miles north along Woodward Avenue to its Cultural Center. On either side of this broad esplanade the Renaissance palazzo of the renowned Detroit Institute of Arts (833-7900) and the complementary Detroit Public Library anchor an oasis in an otherwise declining area. It includes the campus of Wayne State University, the Detroit Historical Museum (833-1805), the Children's Museum (494-1210) and the Detroit Science Center (833-1892). You can rest your feet over lunch in the glass-domed, palm-fringed Kresge Court in the Art Institute.

Another mile or so up Woodward Avenue, the New Center (new in the 1920s) was built as the headquarters for General Motors. The impressive Fisher Building houses Detroit's most elaborate legitimate theater (872-1000) and the surrounding neighborhood is one of fine shops.

The Detroit Zoological Park provides a natural setting for most of its animals on a large tract at Ten Mile Road (counting from the river) in the suburb of Ferndale (398-0900). You can stay on the Woodward bus, but be prepared for a long ride. And still farther out Woodward, at Lone Pine Road (about Sixteen Mile) in the suburb of Bloomfield Hills, the Cranbrook Educational Institutions is a unique place to see. A complex of schools, from kindergarten through graduate study in fine arts, the

exquisite campus was designed by resident architect Eliel Saarinen in the 1920s and 1930s. The entire site is on the National
Register of Historic Places. A walk among the 40 acres of garden,
graced by the sculpture of Carl Milles, is a visual banquet, but be
sure to leave enough time for the Institute of Science (645-3210).
Unfortunately, much of the prized collection of the Academy of
Art Museum was sold a few years ago (it costs a great deal of
money to maintain a national treasure), but its exhibits still show
you some of the finest work of its renowned art faculty and
alumni (645-3312).

For evening entertainment Detroit has its share of night clubs
and restaurants. Many of the good restaurants specialize in
ethnic foods—Greek, Italian, Middle Eastern—but the best for
continental dining remains the London Chop House, oddly
located in a downtown office building. Joe Muer's is a superb
seafood house that has valiantly stood its original ground for
many decades. Despite deterioration of the neighborhood
around it, Detroiters still line up for a table.

Amherstburg

If you choose to come up the river on the Canadian side, you'll
enter Amherstburg Channel at the Bar Point Pier Light "29D,"
flashing green from a white and black tower with a fog horn.
After 4 miles the heavily buoyed channel leads past the village of
Amherstburg. Fort Malden was built here in 1796 after Great
Britain withdrew her troops and government authorities from
Detroit. This is where the British established their naval yard,
from which Commander Robert Heriot Barclay set sail on that
fateful September 10, 1813, to meet Perry's fleet off Put-In-Bay.
The village, a customs port, is still small (about 6,000 people) and
rather quaint, with gift shops, taverns, restaurants, butcher,
baker and probably a candle maker.

Duffy's Dock serves only transient boats at wood slips with big
pilings, electricity, water, ice, pumpout and gas. Duffy's Tavern,
which operates the marina, is a restaurant and bar with live
entertainment. Underneath all the modernization you might
discern that it was built as a private home in 1800. Fort Malden
National Historic Site is only a few blocks away, with mementos
of the area's history in some of its restored buildings (736-5416).
Also in Amherstburg is the North American Black Historical
Museum, which traces black history from African days to the
settlement of refugee slaves in Essex County (736-7353).

Bois Blanc Island, pronounced "Bob-Lo" in local parlance,

across the narrow channel from Amherstburg, has been a retreat for the light-hearted since the beginning of the century. Those were the days when excursions on a river boat were a regular feature of any city dweller's summer evening or holiday, and throngs of Detroiters and Windsorites crowded the ferries to the island amusement park. Miraculously, this pleasure ground, without a bridge to the mainland, has withstood the debilitating vicissitudes of the auto age, the movie age, the TV age, rising costs, and the loss of innocence, not only to stay alive but to embark recently on a multimillion-dollar expansion program. Bob-Lo is still pulling them in by the ferry load, from Memorial Day to Labor Day, but its visitors by private yacht have a special place of their own.

On the west side of the island its **Port-O-Call Marina** has alongside dockage and slips in 6 feet of water with electricity, water, and heads. The dockage fee includes admission to the park and its shows, but the rides are extra. Approach the marina around the north end of Bois Blanc Island, or it can be reached from Livingston Channel through the gap in the dike at isophase red light "20." To reach Bois Blanc is about the only reason one might want to use Livingston Channel; its diked sides make dull cruising. The park, in addition to rides, games, shows and eateries, has expansive grounds around the marina and enticing woods to roam at the north end.

LaSalle

Two miles beyond Bois Blanc Island, Amherstburg and Livingston Channels merge to form Ballards Reef Channel, which leads after a couple of miles to Fighting Island Channel. These are the ways of ships, through the least scenic parts of the river. You can proceed north from Ballard's Reef Channel into an unnamed channel that leads east of Fighting Island—an odd name for an island that has surrendered as a dumping ground for all the hideous wastes that chemical and industrial plants can bestow on it. Take either pass around Turkey Island, but if you're looking for a place to dock, take the channel east of Grassy Island that begins at a red and green buoy. This is a stretch of river shoreline that isn't well known. It's where Windsor's downriver marinas are located in a quiet, grassy, rural, wildlife-rich setting that leads you to question whether you really are on the world's busiest international waterway in the midst of a metropolitan area of 5½ million people. Almost all of these marinas are located on long, narrow inlets from the river, where the slips are lined up on one side and turn-around space is sometimes tight, but depths run to 6 feet or more. Most are small, friendly, family operations. They are from 6 to 8 miles from Windsor, on either side of the village of La Salle.

The first you'll come to is **Acali Place Marina**, with alongside dockage and slips in 6 feet and the usual dockside services except ice and fuel. **Mueller Marina** also has wood finger docks, with electricity and water. **Island View Marina**, catering mainly to powerboats, has alongside dockage and slips in 6 feet, with electricity and water at some of them, ice, pumpout, gas, trailer haulout up to 36 feet, engine and hull repair, launch ramp and snack bar. Next along the line is **Sunset Marina**, with alongside dockage in 8 to 10 feet, all dockside services except showers, and a snack bar. **Holiday Harbour** is a very attractive facility with floating slips in 10 to 12 feet enclosed behind a steel breakwall, with two white lights at the entrance. It offers the usual dockside services, except pumpout and fuel, and there are picnic grounds, play equipment, a swimming pool and a clubhouse with a game room.

Lou's Marina is actually dockage for the Pilot House Restaurant, but serves transients boats at slips with 8-foot depths, electricity and pumpout. The restaurant has live entertainment on weekends. **La Salle Marina** has steel docks at its slips in 12 feet, with the usual dockside services except pumpout, showers and diesel. It has a launch ramp, travelift up to 40 tons, hull, engine and rigging repairs. It is also the most conveniently located with respect to commercial services—variety, liquor, and beer stores and Laundromat across the street. Next door is a park with tennis courts. **Westport Marina** comes next with slips in 12 to 14 feet, electricity and water. An open-end travelift can haul up to 35 tons for engine and hull repairs. **Park Haven Marina**, almost at the north end of the channel, has older wood docks in 6 to 8 feet, with all services except showers and diesel, a launch ramp and a snack bar.

Windsor

After you pass into the main stretch of the Detroit River, described earlier, you'll move 12½ miles virtually to the head of the river beyond Belle Isle before you reach Windsor's marina facilities. Opposite the narrow end of Peach Island, Little River flows into the Detroit River. At their confluence, in the shadow of a large apartment house, a concrete breakwater with red and green lights at the entrance encloses the large, new municipal

Lakeview Park Marina. There are 20-foot depths at the slips, all dockside services, a launch ramp and a restaurant and bar on the premises. Two breakwalls west of it, downstream, the **Windsor Yacht Club** is enclosed in its own basin, dredged to 8 feet, with 6 feet through the entrance. Advance reservation is required for dockage (519-945-1863), with the usual services except pumpout and fuel. The clubhouse has an especially tasteful interior, with a splendid view of the river from the dining room and bar.

There is some neighborhood grocery shopping not far from these facilities, and a bus line downtown. On the way you pass the formerly independent community of Walkerville. Hiram Walker offers tours of the distillery, with reservations (254-5171), and the Hiram Walker Historical Museum on Pitt Street (253-1812) is in the historic, brick François Baby mansion. It was here that invading American forces set up their headquarters in 1812, before the house was even finished, only to withdraw aoross the river a few days later under the nervous leadership of General William Hull. He was later court martialed for his weakness, having subsequently surrendered Detroit to the British.

Downtown Windsor has a lively, compact shopping area, with restaurants and night clubs. But its riverfront parks are the special attraction. Coventry Gardens has a spectacular floating fountain, which showers 34 different-colored spray patterns; Dieppe Gardens offers the most photographed view of the Detroit skyline and the passing ships. The Art Gallery of Windsor, at 445 Riverside Drive West (258-7111), features the work of Canadian artists, including the famous Group of Seven, and has an excellent collection of Inuit prints and sculpture.

Lake St. Clair—Playground at a Million Doorsteps

Charts 14850 or 14851SC, 14853
Small Craft Book

Forming a roughly square, 24-by-26-mile expanse between the St. Clair and Detroit rivers, Lake St. Clair, with maximum depth of 21 feet, is a fisherman's delight and a ship captain's nightmare. The outlet of the St. Clair River forms a broad, marshy delta that makes piloting even worse. Imagine the days of sail, when a vessel might wait days for a fair wind to blow it through those flats and marshes against a current of a knot or more. Father Louis Hennepin doubtless had plenty of time to contemplate the name he conferred on the lake and river, as *Griffon*, the lakes' first sailing ship, inched her way upstream in 1679.

Since the U.S. Army Corps of Engineers made the first channel improvements it's been a little easier. Today a ship strikes off across the lake from the Detroit River for 16 direct, well-buoyed miles to the St. Clair Cutoff Channel, which in turn extends another 6 miles to junction with the natural South Channel. They pass between the big white William Livingston Memorial Light at the end of Belle Isle and Peach Island Light, set themselves on the reciprocal of fixed white Peach Island Range lights, shown from white and red structures at 227° (a front range for downbound vessels) and follow the mileposts. You can do the same, if you're in a hurry. In these pages we'll circumnavigate the shores.

Lake St. Clair resembles Lake Erie in that its shallowness creates some special conditions. Squalls and thunderstorms whip across fast, raising short, steep seas hazardous to small boats. Drastic water level fluctuations and seiching also occur with some frequency, especially in Anchor Bay at the north end. The lake's low, featureless shoreline, combined with the natural and pollution-induced haze that sometimes hovers above, can pose visibility problems. It's important to keep track of your whereabouts. Lake St. Clair may be a backyard playground for Detroit and Windsor people, but it's no toddlers' wading pool.

Ontario Shore

As in other parts of the Great Lakes, the urban and congested harbors are on the American side of the lake. The southern and eastern Ontario shores front a fertile agricultural region with hamlets and summer colonies. It's low country, with streams feeding into the lake and rich marshes that widen toward the north shore—peaceful and pleasant, home to countless fish and water birds. Shallows extend up to a mile lakeward all along this coast, so it's important to follow the buoyed channels carefully from deeper water into the harbors. The bottom is mostly sand, and channel buoys are often shifted from year to year to find the best depths.

The first harbor east from Windsor where transient accommodation can be found is at Pike Creek, a 5-mile run from the flashing green buoy at the east end of Peach Island. A Hiram Walker tank marks the spot from offshore. The creek entrance is protected between breakwalls with flashing red and green lights, and an unlighted, buoyed channel leads in from the lake through 4- to 5-foot depths. A private range of two red lights at about 180° has been set by the **South Port Sailing Club** on the west bank shortly past the entrance. Dockage for members of reciprocating yacht clubs is at slips with very short side docks in 4 to 5 feet, and all dockside services are offered, except fuel and showers. The small clubhouse has a lounge area, with picnic tables outside. On the same side of the creek, just below the highway bridge with 7-foot clearance, **Pud's Place** is a small, older marina with slips in 4 to 5 feet, electricity, water and ice. On the east bank below the bridge **Dudley's Marina** has slips in the same 4 to 5 feet, with electricity and water. These marinas accommodate mostly powerboats and some small sailboats.

Four miles beyond Pike Creek the Puce River enters the lake between two breakwalls with flashing red and green lights. Channel depth here is 4½ feet. **Bell's Puce Marina** has mostly smaller powerboats in residence, but there is 6 feet of water at the slips that line the river front. All dockside services are available, except diesel; there is a launch ramp, a travelift up to 12 tons and hull repair. The Bell Buoy Restaurant and Tavern is on the premises, there is a convenience store nearby, and Bell's rents canoes if you'd like to follow the pretty river for a while.

Belle River looks important from the chart, but the planned federally sponsored marina is not yet a reality. The next mooring place for cruising boats is at the mouth of the Thames River, about 17 miles east of Puce River. A quick flashing green light buoy guides you to the outer end of the 1½-mile-long, buoyed channel into the river mouth. From there a fixed red range, displayed from white towers with red tops, at 148° takes you the rest of the way. The channel is subject to silting but is generally 6 feet deep; favor the west side. At the river mouth there is a community of modest homes built along a network of dredged lagoons, a popular kind of residential development around Lake St. Clair, but there are no stores. Americans can report into customs by telephone.

The first channel to starboard leads to the **Thames River Yacht Club**, a new sailing group with only their dockage and electric outlets yet in place. On the river, just beyond the channel to the club, is **Radlin's Marina**. Although the slips are short, catering mostly to small boats, 20-foot depths are reported (the river is much deeper than its entrance channel) and there are the usual dockside services, except ice and diesel fuel. The Mariner's Restaurant is on the premises. Upstream a short way a big sign directs you to **Luken's Marina**, set back in a side creek carrying 12 feet. This is a large marina, catering mostly to powerboats but with some sail, with 8 to 10 feet at the slips and all dockside services. The open-end travelift can haul up to 15 tons for engine and hull repairs. There are picnic grounds in a country setting.

The elaborate buoyage leading from Lake St. Clair to the Thames River was not originally placed there for pleasure boats. The river, which originates near London, is navigable for 17 miles to the city of Chatham. At one time there was substantial commercial traffic, and occasionally a small ship may still find its way in. All of the bridges open on request and the least depth is 6 feet, although depths run mostly between 10 and 20. A leisurely side trip upstream through farm lands and tiny settlements can be a pleasant diversion from open water cruising; the speed limit is 6 miles per hour. At Chatham there is reportedly dockage at the Holiday Inn.

Mitchell Bay forms the northeast corner of Lake St. Clair, and there is a marina at the little settlement, but it's a bit tricky to reach from the lake. Only shallow draft powerboats or small centerboard sailboats should attempt it. First you take a northerly course on a buoyed channel that leads to Martin Island, where a single station range light, with a white and orange daymark, shows red, white and green; white marks the channel course at 354° to 355°. Close to shore you swing gradually to starboard to come onto a single station range with the same appearance that guides you to Mitchell Bay harbor on a course of 105° to 107°, with a couple of buoys about halfway along. Once at the harbor, the **St. Clair Parkway Commission Marine Park** has very attractive facilities. The side docks at the slips are short, and the bollards for alongside docking are slim, but depths range to 10 feet. At some of the docks there is electricity, ice, pumpout, heads, showers, gas and a launch ramp. There is a restaurant at dockside, and picnic tables and a children's playground in the park. Beyond Mitchell Bay the marshy delta of the St. Clair River, laced by deep channels if you know how to find them, bears more resemblance to southern bayous than it does to northern waterways. It's a watery, grassy world of fish, ducks and nature's nursery.

Michigan Shore

Returning to the stark contrast of the southwestern corner of the lake, Windmill Point divides the poor man's waterfront at the east end of Detroit from the opulence of some of its richest suburbs. Five in a row carry the name Grosse Pointe—one plain, plus Park, Farms, Woods and Shores—and the green lawns and shrubbery of their mansions and estates trace the coast for about 9 miles. Clumps of masts punctuate the scene periodically, where each community has laid out a waterfront park, complete with marina—for residents only. But there are also two yacht clubs where cruising members of reciprocating clubs can find hospitality.

Crescent Sail Club (for sailors only) is on a spit of land about four miles from Windmill Point. A tall, fixed green and white light identifies it from the lake, and fixed red and green lights mark the entrance to the basin. Dockage in slips and alongside carries 8 to 10 feet, with the usual services except ice and fuel. The informal clubhouse has a snack bar. A couple of miles north, the ornate **Grosse Pointe Yacht Club** shows up for a long distance with its Italianate tower topped by a Gothic spire. For further assistance a tall, isophase green light is displayed from a skeleton tower. The large dockage area is protected by a break-wall, outlined by three fixed red lights, with fixed red and green lights marking the entrance. For overnight docking the club will accommodate only members from distant reciprocating clubs, beyond the Detroit–Lake St. Clair area. All dockside services are provided at the slips, with 6 to 12 feet, in addition to the sumptuous clubhouse dining room and bar, swimming pool and tennis courts. These two yacht clubs might serve as a base for visiting the attractions of Detroit, although distances are considerable and would require car rental or a taxicab, as the bus line is not close by.

If you happen to come through the west side of Lake St. Clair on a weekend, you will bear witness to an astonishing scene of maritime activity. For every thousand boats berthed on the American side of Lake St. Clair it seems that 900 of them must be out, virtually carpeting the lake. It's a challenging test of seamanship to maneuver among the darting speedboats, racing sailboats, anchored or idling fishermen and meandering cruisers, power and sail. And the performance continues all the way north, although different types of boats tend to group themselves on different parts of the stage. Sailboats, especially racers, congregate off the Grosse Pointes, and the motor-powered fishing fleet tends to get smaller in size of vessel, but with no diminution of numbers, as you move north.

The Grosse Pointes end at Gaukler Point, fronted by a wide rock ledge that straggles northeastward for a mile and a half. Be

sure to pass outside the quick flashing white light buoy at the
end of it. Behind the shoal is Lake St. Clair's Nautical Mile—a
string of very large marinas that justify the city of St. Clair
Shores' motto as the "Boating Capital of Michigan." The Miller
Memorial Light, flashing white and red atop a tall apartment
building, announces that you're there. All of the marinas are
built on landfill projecting into the lake, with dockage around
series of dredged lagoons. There are generally no navigation
lights marking the entrances, but the gasoline signs are conspicuous, and at each one is the locally customary beer and wine
store.

First from the south is **Emerald City Harbor**, with steel docks
in 3- to 9-foot depths, catering mainly to powerboats. All dockside services are available, except diesel fuel, and a hoist hauls
up to 30 tons for engine and hull repairs. On the premises is a
service not often found at marinas. Len's Prop Shop has been
straightening shafts and smoothing propellers for many a long
year in a picturesque little cabin reminiscent of the old days
before marinas became sleek. **Jefferson Beach Marina** also
arouses a touch of nostalgia, as the site of the old Jefferson
Beach Amusement Park. You'll recognize the fun house-grand
ballroom architecture in the largest marina building. There are
4- to 12-foot depths at the slips here, all dockside services, a 30-
ton hoist, engine, hull and rigging repairs and a very large
marine store. Brownie's Restaurant, with live music and dancing, is on the premises, and a barge in the harbor sells snacks.

Next marina on the line is **Michigan Harbor, Inc.**, with mostly
powerboats at its slips in 4- to 12-foot depths. All dockside
services are offered, as well as a hoist with capacity up to 40 feet,
engine and hull repairs. Last in the row is **Miller Marina**, also
mostly power, with depths to 14 feet at its slips, the usual
dockside services except showers, a hoist to 30 tons, engine and
hull repairs.

St. Clair Shores, like Detroit and all its suburbs, sprawls in
response to life by car. Jefferson Avenue, which fronts the
marinas, is a commercial street with restaurants, but food stores
aren't at all handy.

About eight miles northeast of St. Clair Shores, Point Huron
thrusts into the lake opposite the fingers reaching out from the
delta of the St. Clair River, to set off the northern extremity of
the lake as Anchor Bay. The peninsula back of Point Huron is the
site of **Huron-Clinton Metropolitan Beach Park**, one of the
largest public beaches on the lakes, with a marina included in
the park. At the tip of Point Huron, Black Creek flows into the

lake. The channel leading into the creek should be approached from flashing white light buoy "1" about two miles offshore. A range at 297°, with a flashing green front light and a fixed green rear light, both with white diamond day marks, leads through the buoyed channel with a controlling depth of 5 feet. There is 8 to 10 feet at the slips in the basin to starboard where the creek widens, with all dockside services, except diesel, and a launch ramp. The beach is a long walk across the park.

The Clinton River, 2 miles beyond Point Huron, is, like St. Clair Shores, lined with marinas. But none of them accepts transient boats for overnight dockage. You can obtain fuel, of course, and if you need repairs, dockage is provided during the service period. Controlling depth is 5 feet.

Beyond the Clinton River you are in the main part of Anchor Bay, the domain of the small motorboat and fisherman. The only accommodations for transients are in the far northeast corner at the village of Fair Haven, about 11 miles from the outer channel buoy off Point Huron. This is quite far off the track for a cruising boat, although it's only 4 or 5 miles from the North Channel of the St. Clair River delta if you use that route entering or leaving the river. A couple of unmarked shallow spots, with only 3 feet at chart datum, limits the passage to Fair Haven to boats of that draft or less.

At Fair Haven you're in a country village far from the congestion and sophistication of lower Lake St. Clair. Four of the five marinas that take transient boats are small, family operations with the particular kind of informal hospitality that endears some of us to the fast-fading "Ma and Pa" marina. These are all located on a side channel west of the main body of Swan Creek. A flashing green entrance buoy marks the approach from deeper water to Swan Creek, with fixed red and green lights at the entrance. Additional buoys delineate the 5-foot-deep channel.

The first marina on the port side at the end of the spit separating Swan Creek from the side channel is **Vernier's**. Its slips have 8-foot depths, with electricity, water, pumpout and heads. The setting is spacious and rural, but it's a mile walk to the village. Next up the side creek is **Terry's Marina**, with 5 feet at the slips, electricity, water, heads and showers. **Port Loke Marina** has 4 feet at its slips, with all dockside services except diesel. Finally, at the head of the channel, **Fair Haven Marina** also has 4-foot depths at its slips and all dockside services, except ice and diesel. This marina can lift up to 25 tons on a rail crane and provides engine and hull repairs. It is the closest to the village's modest food shopping and a few restaurants. There is no Laundromat in town. If you follow the main channel of Swan Creek, you reach **Dickie Dee Marina**, also a family affair but a bit larger and more sophisticated than the others, with 6 to 8 feet at the slips, electricity and water at some of them, all other dockside services, a hoist of up to 25 tons, engine repair, a launch ramp and a marine store.

St. Clair River—The Long Ships and the Towns that Crew Them

Charts 14852, 14853
Small Craft Book

To the St. Clair River more than to any other stretch of the Great Lakes belongs the unique tradition of the soft-spoken, giant cargo vessels that carry the wealth of mine and prairie from the upper lakes to the lower. They slip past each other and the shoreline in closest proximity here, where for many miles the waterway is less than half a mile wide. Like the region around Vermilion, Ohio, many a ship's officer and seaman was born and raised or makes his home on the river. Since the early 19th century the life of its quiet, dignified towns has traditionally been geared to the river's rhythm and commerce. And here is where the crew of a cruising pleasure boat can experience the small intimacy of a fellow traveler with the great vessels gliding almost silently past. The throaty call of a laker's horn, as it exchanges signals with one bound in the opposite direction on approaching a bend, is an unforgettably haunting sound. There is a language in those whistle signals; they keep the line moving safely, but sometimes they simply call a greeting to family and friends ashore.

In its 39-mile flow from Lake Huron to Lake St. Clair the river descends six feet. Its current diminishes gradually from the 4-mile-per-hour rush of Lake Huron's waters at the head to 1½ where it begins to spread its broad delta 11 miles above Lake St. Clair. A number of deep water channels course through that delta, although most of the ship traffic uses only one. We'll take them here from west to east.

North, Middle and South Channels

From Anchor Bay two well-buoyed channels lead through the shallows in least depths of 5 to 6 feet, to converge at the deep entrance to North Channel. The more southerly of these has a flashing green light buoy at its outer end. North Channel winds eastward through marshland and summer cottage settlements for about 10 miles to its junction with the main channel of the river. About a third of the way along, on the north side, **Sassy Marina** is a large, new facility in spacious, landscaped surroundings. Two entrances to its basins are flanked by fixed red and green lights. All dockside services are offered at the concrete slips with 7- to 15-foot depths. The travelift can haul up to 120 tons, seoond largest on the Great Lakes, for full services to engine, hull and rigging. There is also a 40-ton forklift for in and out service to cruising boats that might want to "park" for a while. Picnic tables on the grounds and a cocktail lounge on the property complete the amenities. Shopping is about 3½ miles away in the village of Algonac at the junction of the channels. Algonac is a customs reporting station, to which boaters entering the United States can telephone from the marinas.

Middle Channel is entered opposite Point Huron, where Anchor Bay opens off from the main body of the lake. It, too, is approached through a buoyed channel with 6-foot depths, beginning with a flashing green light buoy in the deeper part of the lake. After winding about 9 miles between Dickinson Island and Harsens Island and their straggling fingers, it joins up with North Channel. A mile beyond that junction is **Sunset Harbor** on Harsens Island. Behind a gravel breakwater, and catering mainly to powerboats in slips with 10-foot depths, the usual dockside services are offered, except water and diesel. There is a 30-ton hoist, engine and hull repair, picnic grounds with grills and an adjacent beach. There is also a convenience store nearby.

In the main Lake St. Clair ship channel a quick flashing white light on a red and green junction buoy marks the entrance to St. Clair Flats Canal, leading to South Channel. This was the original ship route before the St. Clair Cutoff was dredged and opened in 1962. As it is a longer way around and not especially scenic, a cruising boat does just as well to use the Cutoff, taking care to stay out of the path of the big boys. Their movement is carefully controlled here through a radio-telephone reporting system, managed by the Canadian Coast Guard to prevent upbound and downbound vessels from meeting in this relatively narrow, 6 mile, heavily buoyed and ranged cut. It joins South Channel at Southeast Bend. Just beyond that junction is **Al D'Eath Marina** on Harsens Island, easy to identify by its candy-striped building. Two basins have slips for boats up to 36 feet with 4- to 6-foot depths. There is electricity at some of the slips, gas, diesel, a 30-

ton hoist, engine and hull repairs. A boardwalk and picnic area provide a good vantage for river watching.

South Channel straddles the border, and the Michigan side of its 9-mile length from Southeast Bend to the main channel of the river at Russel Island is lined with cottages, while the Squirrel and Walpole Island sides in Ontario are quite wild. Walpole Island is an Indian reserve, with only a little summer cottage development. Favor the east side of the channel beyond Russel Island because at this point a strong current sets westward into North Channel from the river.

Chenal Ecarte

A couple of miles beyond the Russel Island junction Chenal Ecarte leads off to the east and southeast. A red and green pair of buoys past flashing red light buoy "36" identifies the entrance, assisted by a fixed red range with orange and black daymark on a course of 138°. This narrow, deep water channel twists through alternately wild and rural landscape for 16 miles to Mitchell Bay in Lake St. Clair. (It can also be entered from the lake through the buoyed Mitchell Bay channel previously described.) Eight and a half miles below its entrance from the St. Clair River it meets the Sydenham River, which can be followed upstream for 2 miles to the attractive town of Wallaceburg, a customs reporting station. An occasional small commercial vessel even finds its way here. Bollards along a low wharf line the placid riverfront for alongside tieup in a parklike setting. There are no services, but shops and restaurants are close by.

Chenal Ecarte below the Sydenham River is limited by an overhead power line to boats of less than 20 feet in height. The only other hazards on this unusual waterway are two private cable ferries a mile or 2 to either side of the Sydenham River junction. Do not attempt to cross their path at either side when the ferries are in motion; the cables rise above the surface as the ferry moves across. The swing bridge at Walpole Island village, 5 miles below the St. Clair River entrance, with a closed clearance of 12 feet, opens on the hour during daylight hours. Speed limit in this waterway is 4½ miles per hour, in order to protect the fragile banks and dykes.

Across from the range lights at the entrance to Chenal Ecarte are two marinas. **McMillan Marina**, serving only powerboats, has slips and alongside dockage in 6 to 12 feet, electricity, water, pumpout, gas, a hoist to 36 feet, engine and hull repairs. **Ecarte Marina** offers all dockside services, except showers, mostly to powerboats, at slips with least depths of 5 feet. There is a 20-ton hoist, engine and hull repairs and a marine store.

Marine City

Continuing up the main stem of the St. Clair River, the tributary of Belle River flows in from the Michigan side at Marine City, 4½ miles above Chenal Ecarte. The town derives its name from its early 19th-century shipbuilding tradition, but today it's just a friendly, unpretentious river community and customs reporting station of 4,500 people. Belle River is easily identified by the big piles of limestone at the mouth. But don't be put off; the stream, with 5-foot depths, is a placid, residential waterway, with three family-style marinas on the west bank below the fixed highway bridge with 13-foot clearance.

The first one is **Del-Dot**, in a state of transition between owners at this writing, and temporarily out of operation. Next is **Belle River Marina**, with 5 feet at its slips, all dockside services except showers and diesel, a launch ramp, a 20-ton hoist, engine and hull repairs.The friendly proprietors will provide courtesy transportation to downtown shopping and Laundromat. The special feature of Belle River Marina is its gem of a fish store, with a few gourmet goodies in addition to a wide variety of fresh fish. **Marine City Marina**, next upstream, has 8 feet at its slips, with all dockside services except showers and diesel, an 8-ton hoist, engine and hull repairs, a launch ramp and a convenience store.

About 4 miles beyond the Belle River entrance Clay Creek flows into the river on the Ontario side, marked by a fixed yellow light with orange daymark. Here the **Driftwood Inn** offers alongside dockage in a protected basin with 4-foot depths. Gas and ice are available, but the main attraction is the restaurant, with outdoor deck overlooking the river, bar and live entertainment.

St. Clair

The stacks and industrial installations that you now begin to see on both banks along the river are either power generating stations or salt mines and processing plants. Also, as the river narrows and curves, with island and shoal areas appearing now and then, there is a marked increase in buoyage and ranges. St. Clair, Michigan, about 8 miles above Marine City, is a major salt producing city. But this town of 5,000 has more than salt to offer the palate of the boating visitor. Its most famous institution is the St. Clair Inn, a gracious hotel on the riverfront, with an excellent dining room and lounge with live entertainment. There is dockage for diners, but boats suffer badly here from the wash of passing ships. The inn will pick up a party at nearby marinas if arrangements are made when you call for reservations. Another fine restaurant, about 2 miles north of the city, Chuck Muer's River Crab, will do the same.

On Pine River, which flows into the St. Clair below the main part of town, there is a **Waterways Commission Marina** with all dockside services. The Diamond Crystal Salt Company helps identify the river entrance. Immediately inside the mouth there is a highway bridge with 13-foot clearance that opens on the hour and half hour to one long and one short blast. The marina is around the first bend in the river, which has a 6-foot controlling depth at this point. It's a half-mile walk to the St. Clair riverfront mall with a variety of shops, including a supermarket, and the downtown movie theater. A boardwalk promenade along the river bank is ideal for ship watching.

A mile and a half upstream on Pine River, in a country setting with a great deal of land, is the **St. Clair Marina**. River depth is 6 to 8 feet, and depths at the docks, both alongside and in older wood slips, is 5 to 8 feet. All dockside services are offered; a 40-ton open-end travelift hauls out for full engine, hull and rigging repairs; and there is a launch ramp and marine store. Propeller and shaft work is also done here. The spacious grounds have tennis courts, a volleyball court, horseshoe pitching and picnic grills. The city dial-a-ride van service provides transportation downtown.

Beyond St. Clair the scene changes gradually from the tree-shaded, residential and small town vista to the industrial complex of Port Huron/Marysville-Sarnia at the head of the river. This time it is the Ontario side that overwhelms, with a phantasmagoria of petrochemical plants and oil refineries. The first commercial oil well in North America was sunk 20 miles east of Sarnia in 1858, and the young settlement's future was assured. Despite the ascendence of Alberta in the oil business, Sarnia, a city of 47,000 people, is still of major importance in the Canadian economy, the terminal of a transcontinental pipeline, and a vital port, as well as a petrochemical processing center. On the American side salt, power generation, and some automotive-related manufacturing represent the local industry; between Marysville and Port Huron there is a stretch of affluent riverside homes.

Port Huron, Black River.

Port Huron

Port Huron extends a warm welcome to pleasure boats, with two private facilities and five well-appointed municipal docking and service areas along the Black River. The harbor master monitors channels 16, 9 and 68; call Port Huron harbor master. A large gravel pile on the south bank identifies the entrance to Black River; the entrance light is a flashing green. Controlling depth in the river is 7 feet for the first mile, then 5 for the next mile and a half. Five bridges cross it in the first mile and a half, two of them railway bridges that generally stand open. The first two highway bridges, with 10- and 12-foot clearances, respectively, open on the hour and half hour from 0900 to 1730, on signal of one long and one short after that. The third opens on signal from 0800 to 2300.

Immediately inside the river on the port side **Blue Water Bridge Marina** is a full service facility, offering alongside dockage in 11 feet, with all dockside services, a launch ramp, travelift up to 25 tons, engine, hull and rigging repairs and a marine store. On the starboard side is the **City Boat Service Center**, with gas, diesel and pumpout. Next to it is the **Port Huron Yacht Club**, devoted to sail, with alongside dock space in 6 feet reserved for guests from reciprocating clubs, with the usual dockside services except showers and fuel. The small, informal clubhouse, with a deck overlooking the river, has a bar and lounge.

Next door to the club is the first of the municipal docking facilities. **Fort Street Dock** has 20 slips with electricity and water (mostly seasonal), and **Quay Street Dock**, on the other side of the first highway bridge, has alongside dockage exclusively for transients, with electricity. These three locations are the most desirable for ready access to the attractive downtown shopping area, restaurants and movies in this city of 34,000 people. Across the river from the Quay Street Dock is the **Southside Dock**, with slips accommodating boats to 30 feet, all dockside services except fuel but including TV hookup. Another half mile or so upstream the slips of the **River Street Dock** line a parklike embankment between the second and third highway bridges. All dockside services are available here, including TV hookup. It's a half-mile walk or bus ride downtown, but there is a bowling alley nearby for amusement, and the St. Clair Community College campus, scene of many of the activities included in the annual Blue Water Festival, is across the street. About 2 miles farther up the river, on the south side at the outskirts of town, is the large **Municipal Marina**, with all dockside services, except fuel but including Laundromat. This is a seasonal facility but is sometimes used for transient overflow.

Transient overflow is most likely to occur when Port Huron hosts the start of the big race to Mackinac Island in mid-July. The race lineup is the climax of the town's week-long Blue Water Festival, which includes such events as an arts show, antique auto show, music festival and twirling contest, in addition to a carnival with rides, games and shows. Other annual events in Port Huron include a polka fest in June and an antique classic boat show in September. The Museum of Arts and History at 1115 Sixth Street, a few blocks from downtown (982-0891), includes displays in natural and marine history and fine arts, as well as regional lore. For evening entertainment the Port Huron Little Theatre (984-4014) offers some summer programming. On a more mundane level, Port Huron is a customs port of entry, has a hospital and daily rail passenger service to Chicago and points in between.

Sarnia

Sarnia also has excellent yacht accommodations, but they are all quite distant from the downtown riverfront shops and restaurants. **Bridgeview Marina** is a very large facility, reached through the old coal dock slip (no coal to soil your boat) at Bay Point, about half a mile beyond the entrance to Black River. A red buoy marks the point. Slips with 4 to 10 feet of water, all dockside services, a 30-ton travelift, launch ramp, full engine and hull repairs, picnic tables, a swimming pool and golf course next door complete the services offered. The marina is associated with an adjacent condominium development, and is very pleasantly situated, but a taxi is needed to reach the nearest shops. Customs can be telephoned from the marina.

The other Sarnia marine facilities are actually located in the suburb of Point Edward on the Lake Huron shore.

The St. Clair River current runs swiftest around the base of the high, arching Blue Water Bridge. It can exceed 4 miles per hour for a mile below the bridge and 5 or more in the narrows above it. Make sure you have enough power on upbound or downbound to maintain control. The current is less strong on the Canadian side than the American.

The Point Edward harbor basin is close east of the river entrance, but there is a good deal of current in the shallows off the basin, so it's advisable to swing gradually around in deeper water and then come in on the Sarnia Yacht Club fixed green range with orange daymarks, at about 180°. If you're approaching from the open lake, come in on the fixed red Point Edward Range, also at 180°. The front light is on a white tower with orange and black daymark; the rear light, with the same kind of daymark, is atop the Blue Water Bridge, which you'll see from many miles out. A big apartment house on the east side of the basin also helps identify it from offshore.

A curved breakwater encloses the harbor on the east, and an L-shaped breakwater extends from the west side. Once through the breakwater, **Lake Huron Yachts** lies directly ahead, a small marina, with boat wells that do not have side docks, but bollards to tie off the stern with bow to the dock. The usual services are available, except pumpout and fuel. A turn to starboard inside the basin leads to the **Sarnia Yacht Club**, with 20- to 25-foot depths at the slips, all dockside services, a launch ramp, a restaurant at the gas dock and a pleasant clubhouse; the weekend bar is open only to members. Point Edward is a residential suburb, but there is a convenience store and a supermarket within half a dozen blocks.

6
LAKE HURON: BEACH AND BLUFF AND A GIFT OF ISLANDS

Lake Huron, like Gaul, is divided into three parts—the main body of the lake, Georgian Bay, and the North Channel. Georgian Bay is where a white man first gazed on the Great Lakes. This was Etienne Brulé, a scout sent by Samuel de Champlain from Quebec to the country of the Ottawa and Huron Indians. Champlain himself followed a few years later, in 1615, and gave Georgian Bay its first name, La Mer Douce. In his wake, up the St. Lawrence, Ottawa and Mattawa rivers to Lake Nipissing, then down the French River to Georgian Bay, there followed a procession of explorers, fur traders, missionaries, soldiers, adventurers, saints and sinners, that made the route a highway to empire and Huron the most important of the lakes for two hundred years. Fur lured most of them. Heathen souls to be saved drew some of them.

The devoted Jesuit missionaries fanned out from the mouth of the French. The fur traders followed a sheltered route through the North Channel to St. Marys River. From there some went north into and across Lake Superior, eventually to the Rocky Mountains and the Arctic Ocean. Others continued westward through the Straits of Mackinac and across Lake Michigan to

189

Green Bay and the Mississippi Valley beyond. They all traveled by canoe—immense 36-footers carrying 6,000-pound payloads across the lakes, smaller craft in the turbulent rivers leading to the interior. The lakes gave entrée to the continent, Lake Huron was the key, and Michilimackinac (today shortened to Mackinac) was the keystone.

For 13 years after settlement of the American Revolution awarded the western part of the lake to the United States, Great Britain held on to Mackinac, as she did Detroit, to protect the Montreal fur trade. And in the War of 1812 fur was a major issue. Some of its most dramatic episodes took place on Lake Huron. A few years later the old fur trade route was abandoned, schooners and steamers on the lakes became the major mode of transport, and Lake Huron entered a new era.

On both sides of the boundary farmers came in to settle the rich soils of its lower reaches, and lumbermen roared through the northern pine forests. Like a scythe in the hand of a wrathful God they leveled the great white pines, first in Michigan, then on the Ontario shores of Georgian Bay and the North Channel. In two or three generations it was all over and the lumberjacks moved on. Some of the mill towns that had stripped the logs into lumber to build two nations turned to different work; others withered and died. Fishing became more important, as did the mining of limestone and gypsum. Lake Huron people have always earned their livelihood from the bounty of the land and the lake. Very little industry, and no city larger than 50,000 people, has intruded on its shores. As a consequence, Lake Huron is the most recreational of the Great Lakes; tourism is its major industry.

For pleasure boats Lake Huron is the destination lake, especially the fabled cruising areas of the North Channel and Georgian Bay. Without large population centers there are fewer residential boats here than on the others (except Superior), but those who cruise far from home on a summer vacation are likeliest to head for Huron. And with good reason. Except for fast track city life, every variety of cruising experience can be found—oceanic open water, sheltered passages and labyrinthine island channels, sand beaches, rocky defiles, small cities and farm hamlets, dramatic cliffs, uninhabited forest, resorts, marinas simple and sophisticated, and wild anchorages to absorb a lifetime of exploration.

Each of the three main parts of this second largest of the Great Lakes presents a cruising personality of its own. The main body, like the lower lakes, has mostly smooth coasts with artificial harbors at the river mouth sites of small towns and cities, and a good deal of sand beach in between. In this respect there is little difference between the American and Canadian sides. Ontario's Georgian Bay is a junior Lake Huron in itself, with towns, resorts, beaches, one of the world's most remarkable island archipelagoes, and a precious corner of wilderness. The North Channel, also entirely in Ontario, offers big cruising ground in relatively sheltered water, farm villages and enchanting groups of islands. Dockside conviviality or remote pine-girt anchorages are the choices here. Each part of the lake also presents different challenges to piloting and seamanship skills. On the open waters of all three the demands are little different from experience on the other lakes, but piloting among the islands of Georgian Bay and the North Channel requires a set of skills not ordinarily utilized elsewhere. These will be detailed in the appropriate place further on in the chapter.

Because of its size, 100 miles by 160 in the main body, and 50 by 110 miles in Georgian Bay, and its north to south orientation, weather on Lake Huron can be quite different between the north and south ends. Generally, as you move northward both days and nights are cooler, but you can swelter in the North Channel and shiver in Port Sanilac if the weather turns perverse. Water temperature also rises over the course of the summer from south to north, reaching its highest level in September. But usually by early July you can swim in a comfortable 68 degrees in even the northernmost shallows.

Fog is more common at the northern end of the lake, especially in the Straits of Mackinac. The complex confluence of land formations and marine currents here brings fog to the straits when it doesn't occur elsewhere. Similar conditions occur in the passage between the main body of Lake Huron and Georgian Bay, off the Bruce Peninsula. Another fog-prone area is the north end of Georgian Bay near Killarney. But even in these areas fog rarely persists past noon in the summer months.

The lake's north to south orientation and the northwest to southeast axis of Georgian Bay are both ideal for sailors—when the prevailing westerlies cooperate. But the long fetches along the main axes can raise perilous seas in a gale, especially at the extremities and on the leeward shores. The heaviest winds are likely to blow from west and northwest. The North Channel, running 100 miles from east to west and up to 20 miles across, is protected from the sweep of Lake Huron by Manitoulin Island, the world's largest in fresh water. Nevertheless, it is big enough for exhilarating offshore sailing and is capable of developing a good chop of its own in high winds. Sailing winds are somewhat lighter and less reliable here than in Georgian Bay, and the orientation of the channel will likely require a beat if you're heading west. But it's easier to crisscross the channel to take advantage of fair winds than it is the other parts of the lake. In all three sections the wind tends to come up mid-morning, lull around noon, then rise to a crescendo as the afternoon wears on, to fall again into an evening calm. This pattern is most conspicuous and dependable on Georgian Bay, where, despite forecasts of light breezes, afternoon sailing can be a real sleighride. Motor cruisers, for obvious reasons, get an early start on Lake Huron and usually put into port by mid-afternoon.

As elsewhere on the lakes, late afternoon and evening thunderstorms come in mainly from the southwest. This makes the southern part of the lake more vulnerable. Occasionally stormy weather will come from the northeast, especially in the Georgian Bay–North Channel area. Also, as on the other lakes, attention to water level fluctuations is important. Here it is not seiching that is the hazard to watch out for, but annual changes in water level that can make the difference between accessibility and untenability in North Channel and Georgian Bay anchorages.

There are United States Coast Guard bases at Port Huron, Saginaw River Entrance, East Tawas and St. Ignace, with a seasonal station at Harbor Beach. Canadian Coast Guard cutters are based at Meaford and Parry Sound, with mobile rescue units at Tobermory, Port Severn, Britt and Whitefish Falls.

When cruising the upper reaches of Lake Huron a cabin heater is a welcome amenity. Warm clothing is, of course, the *sine qua non* of any open water cruising. But on Lake Huron you aren't likely to need much in the way of dress-up clothes. A few of the yacht clubs and some of the Mackinac Island hotels may require skirt, jacket and tie, but almost everywhere else dress is informal. One semi-dress-up outfit for morale on a night out will probably do the job.

The remoter precincts of Georgian Bay and the North Channel present some logistical challenges to the mate or steward on a cruising boat in the galley stock and laundry departments. In those areas there are no giant supermarkets and few Laundromats, but basic foodstuffs and limited selections of meat and produce are available. And in ports throughout the lake there is fish to be had that stops only briefly between the boat that brings it in and your galley—perhaps just long enough to be delicately smoked.

If you're headed up Lake Huron, it is probably the allure of nature that is calling you. Along with all the other gear, pack a few field guides—to birds, to flowers, to trees, to rocks. How you plan a Lake Huron cruise will depend on the time available and your ultimate destination. There are many alternatives for long passages and short hops, so you can vary the routine to take in a bit of each variety of experience that awaits you. Boats bound for the north end, North Channel or Georgian Bay destinations, can run up either shore. The Ontario harbors offer better marine facilities on the lower half of the lake's main basin, and some of the towns are more interesting, while the Michigan harbors are better equipped in the upper reaches. As some sailors do to catch the wind, you can take long diagonal runs to get the best of both sides.

The Edge of the Thumb

Charts 14862, 14863

The lower peninsula of Michigan is shaped unmistakably like a mitten. But before Lake Huron attained its present configuration the thumb of the mitten lay underwater. When it emerged, dripping from the pro-glacial lake, the soil lay rich and thick on the surface, and today the flat fields yield the nation's largest crops of beans and sugar beets. But that came after the primeval crop was swept from the earth. This is where Michigan's great lumbering era began in the 1840s, quietly at first, then at an accelerating pace to supply the growing cities and towns of the vast grasslands to the west. The boom peaked in the Thumb and the Saginaw Valley in the 1870s and 1880s, when some 3½ billion board feet of lumber was towed out of Michigan on barges and rumbled out on trains.

But the Thumb paid a terrible price. During the hot, dry summer of 1871 small fires erupted all over the lake country. On the shore of Lake Michigan they destroyed a thriving young Chicago that would rise from the ashes more splendid than ever. On Lake Huron they merged into a huge conflagration that raged across the Thumb for two long days, destroying villages, farms and immense stands of uncut timber. Miraculously few lives were lost and the settlers rebuilt. A short decade later the tragedy was repeated, with the mass of fallen timber from the previous fire providing seasoned tinder for the new holocaust. This time it claimed several hundred lives and millions of dollars in property across the entire peninsula. The American Red Cross had been organized just three weeks earlier; the fire of '81 was its first relief project.

So overwhelming were these events that local people still talk about them, perhaps because life has been quietly prosperous since then. Nothing so dramatic has occurred since in this serene stretch of countryside. The coast is generally low, rising gradually into flat, sandy bluffs as you move north, fronted by some stretches of beach, with scattered boulders up to a mile offshore. If you're making a long run up Lake Huron, you may want to follow the dredged and lighted ship channel that leads from the Point Edward Range for about 6 miles into the open lake. For ships the funnel shape of this end of Lake Huron and the shoals it encloses can mean disaster in a gale—none worse than the Great Storm of November 9, 1913, which claimed 10 vessels and 235 lives, most of them right here. That's another event that people on both sides of the lake still talk about as though it was yesterday. At the outer end of the channel the red lightship *Huron* used to greet passing boats. Now an impersonal lighted horn buoy does the job, and the venerable lightship rests in a park in Port Huron; no doubt you noticed her as you passed by on the St. Clair River.

Lexington

If you choose to follow the shoreline up the lake, you'll come first to the village of Lexington, 19 miles from the St. Clair River. A rubble breakwater encloses the **Waterways Commission Marina**. The town's water tank identifies its location, and the breakwater entrance is marked by a group flashing white light and flashing green lights. Controlling depth is 7 feet in the entrance, 6 in the slips, where all dockside services except heads and showers are offered. There's little to see or do in Lexington, with 800 people and a few stores, but it's a good overnight stop if a long day is running out on you.

Port Sanilac

Only a dozen miles beyond Lexington, Port Sanilac has a little more to offer. Its harbor was the first to be built for pleasure craft under the sponsorship of the Michigan Waterway Commission, in 1951. This town, too, is identified by its water tank, and the overlapping breakwaters carry flashing red and green lights with matching daymarks. There is also a tall white tower with a group flashing white light back of the harbor. Anchorage is possible behind the breakwater, or you can tie up at the **Waterways Commission Marina** with 9 feet of water at the outer slips, 4 to 5 against the shore, and all dockside services. There is also a courtesy car for downtown shopping several blocks away. If you should need repairs, Port Sanilac Marina next door can haul out up to 20 tons and offers both hull and engine work. The marina is in a park with picnic grills and tables and a children's playground.

The Sanilac Historical Museum, a few blocks from the marina on M25, is the town's main tourist attraction (622-9991). It is in the 1872 mansion built by a pioneer physician, whose lake captain grandson donated it to the county, and has an extensive library as well as a marine, medical and agricultural artifact collection. July Fourth is cause for a big celebration in the park, culminating in fireworks, of course, and the last weekend in July is the Summer Fun Festival, with contests, food, displays, and music at the Barn Theatre. In August the theater mounts a play schedule.

Harbor Beach

When the U.S. Army Corps of Engineers built the harbor in 1877 that changed the town's name from Sandy Bay it was the world's largest made by man. It was designed as a refuge for lake freighters of shallow draft, and still serves that function as well as accommodating pleasure boats. There is a large Detroit Edison power plant, whose 300-foot stack makes the harbor conspicuous from the lake, 30 miles north of Port Sanilac. Three detached breakwaters almost encircle the basin. The main entrance is flanked on the north by an alternating flashing white and red light with fog horn and on the south by a flashing white light. Buoyed channels lead to the two plant piers. Toward the south end of the harbor there is a long pier without services at which pleasure craft can tie up in 4 to 5 feet. A new **Waterways Commission Marina** is enclosed behind its own *L*-shaped breakwall at the north end beyond the industrial installations. The basin, dredged to 8 feet, has only 9 slips at present; ultimately there will be many more. Dockside services are expected to be in place by the 1986 cruising season. The marina is about a mile from the center of town.

Harbor Beach is an attractive town of 2,100 people, with good shopping and a hospital handy to the waterfront. It claims world fame as the birthplace of the late Frank Murphy, onetime Mayor of Detroit, Governor of Michigan, Governor-General of the Philippine Islands, and Justice of the United States Supreme Court. His modest ancestral home and early law office are open to the public.

Beyond Harbor Beach the coastline shoals out farther, with rocks and boulders overlying the sand up to a mile and a half offshore near Pte. aux Barques. A big light, group flashing white atop a white tower, marks the point, and offshore a flashing green light buoy marks the edge of the shoal area. It's a good idea to stay about 3 miles offshore as you round the top of the Thumb.

Port Austin

After rounding Port Austin Reef, with its big buff-colored tower showing a flashing white light, you can head for the mouth of Bird Creek and the harbor of Port Austin, about 30 miles from Harbor Beach. Give the reef a wide berth, as rip-rap and other obstructions surround its base. Bird Creek is shallow and narrow, suitable only for the small boats serviced by several marinas there. But the **Waterways Commission Marina** docks reach into 5- to 6-foot depths in the outside artificial harbor, which is sheltered from the northwest and west by an angled, detached breakwater with flashing red light and red daymark at the end. A buoyed channel leads to the marina west of the creek entrance, which is further protected on the east side by the breakwater that encloses the creek mouth. Nevertheless, in a northeaster the surge can be heavy. All dockside services, except diesel fuel, are available. It's an easy walk to the village stores.

Port Austin is a pleasant summer resort, its lumbering days already past when President James Garfield spent his summer vacations here—before he became president, as he survived only four months in the job. There are still some lovely, old homes gracing its quiet streets.

Saginaw Bay
Charts 14863, 14867

Twenty-six miles across and 52 miles long, Saginaw Bay interrupts the smooth flow of the Michigan shoreline with one of the state's favorite fishing grounds. Legend has it that the sturgeon were once so plentiful that the local folk caught them with spears, pitchforks and clubs. Commercial fishermen might net 80 in one cast, and up to 150 pounds each at that. The sturgeon may be gone, but there are enough bass and perch left in the relatively shallow waters of the bay to crowd its reef contours with sport fishermen any day in the summer, and triple on weekends. In season salmon and trout offer big-game angling thrills. Although the bay is not especially scenic, the lure of the fish has built cottage resorts and small boat marinas around the bay and supports a prosperous charter fleet. And the marshes and shallows of the eastern shore abound with waterfowl and bird life.

But Saginaw Bay is not a body of water to trifle with. It's big enough to kick up quite a fuss, and when strong winds parallel its northeast to southwest axis they can raise or lower the water levels by as much as 4 feet at the southern end. Charity and Little Charity islands and their related shoals in the upper part of the bay, and a couple of shipwrecks off Sand Point, are the only hazards in the middle, other than fish net stakes. But all of the shorelines are shoal up to 3 miles out. At the bottom of the bay is Lake Huron's largest city and only industrial complex; a 15-mile-long ship channel leads to Bay City and the Saginaw River.

Caseville

Eighteen miles from Port Austin, on the northeast side of Saginaw Bay, Caseville is an old resort town that still jumps with activity for all ages, including a fun slide, roller rink, two miniature golf courses, numerous restaurants, and shops of all kinds. It, too, had its summering president in residence— William McKinley. The fate of the two presidents who have favored Michigan's Thumb makes one wonder just a bit.

A dredged channel, marked by buoys, leads to the mouth of the Pigeon River inside a north breakwater that shelters the approach. A fixed red range on a course of 313° helps to guide you in; there is also a flashing green light at the end of the breakwater. Controlling depth in the channel is 6 feet. None of the private marinas accepts transient boats for overnight dockage. The **Waterways Commission Marina**, opposite the entrance channel where the river widens, has 5 feet at the slips and all dockside services, except diesel fuel. The shops and restaurants are handy, but the exciting entertainments enumerated above tend to be farther out along the highway.

Wildfowl Bay is very shallow, but leading to **Bayshore Marina** is a 5-foot channel marked by lighted buoys and a fixed red range at 103°. Alongside tie-up in 5 feet has electricity, water at some locations, ice, showers, gas and pumpout. There is also a 30-ton travelift, engine and hull repairs and a marine store.

Bay City

A pleasure boat can enter the channel to Bay City anywhere north of light buoys "23" and "24." Closer than that you can get involved in unmarked spoil areas. Bay City is conspicuous from far out by its stacks, and its industrial plants loom larger on the approach. If that isn't enough, there's a fixed red range with white daymarks at 211° at the Saginaw River entrance. And the river is buoyed for 19 miles upstream to the city of Saginaw. The whole stretch is considered one port, although between the two cities there is pastoral countryside. Bay City-Saginaw is a customs port of entry, but all the small boat accommodations are in Bay City.

A quarter of a mile inside the river entrance the **Bay City Yacht Club** appears on the starboard side. It has two basins, reached by a channel with 8 feet on a daybeacon range. Visitors from recognized yachts clubs should go to the north basin for slip assignment and all dockside services except fuel. The clubhouse has a bar and there is a playground for children. One and one half miles from the entrance, on the east bank in the suburb of Essexville, is the **Saginaw Bay Yacht Club**. Members of reciprocating clubs may dock in slips or alongside in 6 to 18 feet, with all dockside services except fuel. The clubhouse has a dining room and bar and there are picnic areas and playgrounds. **Bay Harbor Marina**, across from the Saginaw Bay Yacht Club on the west bank, is a large establishment with 5 to 9 feet at the slips; all dockside services; open-end hoist to 60 tons, engine, hull and rigging repairs; and a marine store. These facilities are all about three miles from downtown.

About 6 miles and five bridges (vertical clearances ranging from 7 to 30 feet) up the Saginaw River there are two more marinas. For obvious reasons, they have more powerboats than sail. The two railroad bridges are likely to be standing open, and the others open to one long and one short blast, except during rush hours. Consult the *Coast Pilot* for details. **Parkside Yacht Harbor** has 9 feet at alongside dockage and in slips with all services except diesel. A 20-ton travelift hauls out for engine and hull repair. This is the closest marina to shopping. **Brennan's Marina**, another large one a little farther upriver, offers all dockside services at its slips with 8 to 9 feet of depth; a 60-ton travelift; engine, hull and rigging repair; and a marine store, 1½ miles from downtown. Most of the marine accommodations are quite far from the shopping, restaurants and other services of this pleasant city of 50,000 people, but taxicabs can be called.

Although Bay City and Saginaw now display the panoply of modern auto-related industry, they were launched on the trunks of white pine trees. During the mere 40 years between 1850 and 1890 an estimated 32 billion board feet of lumber was cut from the extraordinarily rich forests of the Saginaw Valley. Saginaw, which ultimately had 74 mills and sawdust piles up to 40 feet deep, was where the jacks raised hell on a Saturday night, and for decades its name was synonymous with sin. Bay City, despite its 36 sawmills, was where the lumber barons built their palaces. Some say the two towns spawned 98 millionaires. Center Street, where many of them built mansions, ranks among the most splendid boulevards of Victorian architecture in the nation. Promenade there under the trees, then visit the Historical Museum of Bay County, at 1700 Center Street (983-5733), to learn more about their story. At the New Wenonah Park on the riverfront downtown there are free concerts twice a week at the Art Shell; the entire range of musical expression is presented over the course of a summer.

It's about 22 miles from the mouth of the Saginaw River to its source at the confluence of the Tittabawassee and the Shiawassee. If you have patience for the bridges—five more opening spans beyond Bay City and six fixed, with a minimum clearance of 18 feet near the end of the run—it can be an interesting side trip, with a minimum depth of 7 feet. In the open places between the industrial centers of the two cities the low, flat land is bare of the forest that once shut out the sky.

The western shore of Saginaw Bay more or less matches the east side—low, marshy, agricultural, but with somewhat fewer summer cottages. About 9 miles from the Saginaw River entrance **Hoyles Marina** is reached through a buoyed channel, with 5-foot depths, on a fixed red range. Most of the slips, in 8 to 10 feet, have electricity and water, and all other services are offered. There is a 15-ton hoist, engine and some hull repair, a launch ramp, a convenience store, picnic and swimming areas.

Au Gres

Twenty-five miles north of the river mouth Point Au Gres reaches out into the bay. North of the point the Au Gres River flows into the bay. Parallel piers protect the entrance, with flashing red and green lights and matching daymarks. A pair of

buoys beyond the piers guides you through the channel with
controlling depth of 8 feet, but the river shallows to 6 for the 2½
miles upstream to the **Waterways Commission Marina**. Two
overhead power lines with 59-foot clearance cross the river
below the marina, which is located just below the U.S. 23
highway bridge. All dockside services are available, except diesel. Down the road from the marina are grocery stores, Laundromat, and restaurants in the village of Au Gres. There is also a
county historical museum in an 1897 two-room schoolhouse.

East Tawas

As you round Point Lookout after leaving Au Gres and move
on up the coast toward Tawas Bay 20 miles ahead, you will see
two sets of lighted ranges leading to elaborate loading structures. The first one marks the nontown of Alabaster, where U.S.
Gypsum loads the useful mineral from its immense open pit
quarry. Three miles farther on, National Gypsum Company
loads at Port Gypsum. These are not places for pleasure craft to
approach closely, but they are interesting to observe from a
distance.

You are now entering Tawas Bay. Although Tawas City has the
more imposing name, East Tawas is the larger town (2,400) and
has the facilities for cruising boats. The elaborately constructed
four-sided breakwater-cum-slips, with two inner curved piers,
assures a calm mooring in any wind at the **Waterways Commission Marina** slips with 12 feet and all dockside services. A
flashing green light marks the north end of the breakwater and
the harbor entrance. But the structure wasn't intended just for
you. Its broad concrete surface is a platform for throngs of
fishermen seeking Tawas Bay perch and trout. At the head of the
dock a city campground is squeezed between Highway 23 and
the waterfront. Between the two, shoreside and dockside jump
with activity most of the summer, and the adjacent beach
swarms with families. There is also a children's playground and
tennis courts.

East Tawas is a lively place, devoted to summer fun. Its
downtown restaurants, shops and Laundromat are all within a
few blocks of the marina. The Iosco County Historical Museum
in a turn of the century house on Bay Street (362-8911) is also
nearby. The waterfront park is the scene of East Tawas's special
events, including the Mariner Fest, a weekend of contests,
games, and displays in mid-July; the July antique and hobby

show; and the early August Art Fair. If you've been sitting on a boat too long, and would like to stretch your legs, the Michigan Shore-to-Shore hiking, biking and horseback riding trail begins here its 125-mile scenic traverse to Empire on Lake Michigan.

If the hubbub of East Tawas city life is not to your taste, you can find a place to rest your boat across Tawas Bay in the protection of Tawas Point. The bay is too open for anchorage, but **Jerry's Marina**, catering mainly to powerboats up to 30 feet, is reached on a fixed green range with circular daymarks, on a course of 128° in 5-foot depth. Daybeacons also flank the entrance to the enclosed basin. Most of the slips, with 5-foot depths, have electricity and water, and the other dockside services are offered, except diesel. Haulout up to 30 feet by trailer, engine repairs, a marine store, launch ramp, two beaches and a grocery store complete the facilities. The **Tawas Bay Yacht Club**, just southwest of the marina, is also reached on a fixed range with red daymarks at 165°.

The Beachfront Coast

Charts 14863, 14864, 14869, 14881

At Au Sable Point, 8 miles northeast of Tawas Point, you officially leave Saginaw Bay. This is also a turning point in the character of the Michigan coast. Where the lumberjacks brought "daylight to the swamp," as they referred to the mowing of the forest, from Saginaw Bay southward they uncovered rich soils that Michigan farmers have been cultivating ever since. But northward to the peninsula's tip the soil cover was skimpy, and subsequent attempts at farming usually ended in heartbreak. Once the magnificent trees were gone this was a bleak and scarred land. Far-sighted leadership began a reforestation program soon after the turn of the century, however, and in 1909 the Huron National Forest was established, covering over 400,000 acres in five counties. Although still logged under careful management, the now mature forest back of the shore-line, laced with streams and dotted with lakes, combined with almost continuous soft, sand beach at water's edge, has transformed this part of the state into a four-season resort area. The view from offshore shows stretches of bluff and deep woods backing up the beachfront, with the almost continuous line of cottages sometimes conspicuous, sometimes concealed.

Au Sable/Oscoda

Five miles beyond Au Sable Point, the Au Sable River flows into Lake Huron. The villages of Au Sable and Oscoda flank the river, which is entered between parallel piers marked by flashing green and white lights with appropriate daymarks and a fog horn on the south pier. Each town has a water tank to help identify the river entrance from offshore. Controlling depth between the piers is 6 feet, shoaling to 3 in the river, although actual depths in recent years have been higher. A control dam upstream sometimes releases a heavy discharge, which creates a strong outflowing current in the river mouth.

Immediately inside the harbor on the port side is a large state four-position launching ramp, and beyond that, below the highway bridge fixed at 23 feet, is **Main Pier Marina**, the only one for sailboats. Depth at the slips and alongside tie-up is 9 feet, with all dockside services, a launch ramp, engine repair and a restaurant. Oscoda is mainly a powerboat port, with a large charter fishing fleet. Beyond the highway bridge, surrounding an island on the starboard side, are three facilities. **Northeast Michigan Marine** has 6 feet at its slips, with all dockside services except diesel, a 15-ton open-end travelift, engine and hull repairs. No information about **Fellows' River Pointe Marine** is available at this time. The **Oscoda Yacht Club** extends hospitality to powerboats from reciprocating clubs with 5 to 6 feet at slips and alongside, electricity, water, ice, heads and showers, two dining rooms and a bar in the clubhouse.

Village shopping is not within handy walking distance of the marinas, but the restaurants will provide transportation. One restaurant and a miniature golf game are on the Au Sable side of the river beyond the highway bridge. The Au Sable River was a major thoroughfare for logs in the lumbering years, and as reforestation covered the nudity of its logged-out banks it became one of Michigan's favorite canoeing rivers. Despite the dams, which require short portages, most of the riverside is wild and beautiful. Canoes can be rented in Oscoda, if you want a change of boating pace. The liveries will transport you and your canoe upstream as far as you like, so that you can paddle the easy way back home. And if you're in town the last week of July, you can watch the finish of the annual Au Sable River Canoe Marathon, run 240 miles from Grayling. The Paul Bunyan Festival tops off the event, with contests of logging skills that recall the old days on the Au Sable, giant-size pancake breakfasts, rides, games, and the usual summer hoopla.

Harrisville

About 18 unobstructed miles due north of the Au Sable is the peaceful village of Harrisville. The small **Waterways Commission Marina**, providing all the usual services, is enclosed by a big breakwater, with plenty of room to anchor, but the bottom is weedy and holding is dubious. In northeasters this harbor has always suffered from surge, but a new extension to the breakwater may now correct that problem. The village water tank identifies it from offshore, and the channel between the breakwaters carries 7 feet. It is entered from the north, marked by flashing red and white lights with daymarks.

Within the harbor enclosure are both a beach and children's playground, but if you're among those who like to walk for miles on clean, open sand, head south from the dock, past the state park, until you get tired. If you get as far as "The Great Black Rock," a lone boulder dropped out of context on the powdery sand, give a thought to the Indians who made sacrifice in its hollowed surface to ensure a safe journey on the mighty lake. Harrisville shopping is only a few blocks from the harbor. If you're in town on a Saturday afternoon, you might catch a band concert on the courthouse lawn, and in August the village hosts an arts and crafts fair.

Harrisville, beach and Black Rock.

Alpena

It's 30 miles from the rusticity of Harrisville, population 500, to the relatively citified atmosphere of Alpena, population 14,000— the most interesting port of call on the western lakeshore. Rocky shoals reach out as much as 2½ miles from shore along this stretch, so don't hover too close, especially as you enter Thunder Bay. Although the bay looks beautiful on a bright, summer day, its bordering shoals and sudden storms have often made it a nightmare for ships, especially in the days of sail. It is one of the lakes' many "graveyards," now the Thunder Bay Bottomland Preserve for the benefit and edification of scuba-diving history buffs. Regrettably, there is no protected anchorage in this pretty indentation of the Lake Huron coast, but **Partridge Point Marina** is in an artificial basin, marked by five white strobe lights and a red buoy. The channel carries mostly 5 feet, but in places may shoal to 3 . There is 9 feet at the slips with all dockside services, a launch ramp and a dive shop.

You'll know you're at Alpena by the stacks, tanks and church spires stretching above the tree tops. Watch out for the many fish net stakes in the bay. The lighted and buoyed channels in the harbor lead to commercial piers in the Thunder Bay River and at the plants north of it. The pleasure boat harbor lies just to the

Presque Isle Light Museum,
Lake Huron.

south of the river entrance, behind landfill enclosures, marked by a flashing red light on a red tower. Entrance is made from the southwest, with a sharp turn to port to head for the gas dock at the inside end. All dockside services are provided at this **Waterways Commission Marina**, with 5 feet at the slips. Arnold Boat Works at the site offers engine, hull and rigging repairs, travelift haulout up to 30 tons, and a marine store. Next door the bar and lounge of the Thunder Bay Yacht Club is a friendly place, and the city tennis courts are adjacent.

Alpena, like its neighbors, began life as a lumber town, but it diversified in the 20th century and is now home to a variety of enterprises, from portland cement through auto carpeting to paper products. If you write letters to overseas family and friends on aerogramme paper, here's where it's made. You can tour several of the local plants; call the Chamber of Commerce at 354-4181. With prosperity, a handsome residential district extended south along the lakefront from the marina location; it makes a pleasant evening stroll from your boat. One entrepreneur, Jesse Besser, who pioneered in the fabrication of cement blocks, returned the fruits of his success as benefactions to the city. The Jesse Besser Museum is a fine example of small city, professional museumship, with displays of Indian culture, lumbering and farming, a planetarium, and an art gallery (356-2202). For boaters it requires a cab ride to the outskirts of town, but the trip is worth it.

Everything else in Alpena is agreeably convenient to the marina. A downtown mall is virtually next door, with additional city shops of all kinds within a few blocks beyond, as well as restaurants and a movie theater. And Alpena has its own excellent resident, professional Thunder Bay Theatre, performing in an interesting restored building at 400 North Second Avenue (354-2267 or 354-2297). On the mundane side, the city is a customs reporting station and has a hospital.

The limestone deposits, hundreds of feet thick, that are found all around the shores of upper Lake Huron begin at Alpena. The cement loading piers here are fairly conventional. But farther up you will see the huge conveyor belts and elaborate, overarching apparatus that bring raw limestone from vast quarries to the waiting bulk carriers that carry it to the steel mills of the lower lakes. The very names of the harbors convey their purpose— Rockport (no longer used), Stoneport, Calcite Harbor and Port Dolomite. Some of the long ships that usually pass on the horizon may now cross your path on their way to these ports.

Presque Isle

From Alpena it's about 55 cruising miles to the next harbor with dockage, but there are a few places to anchor in between. Some shelter can be found between Thunder Bay Island and Sugar Island at the north end of Thunder Bay, but there is likely to be an uncomfortable roll if much sea is running. Enter only from the south and anchor in 6 to 10 feet. A better spot can be found about 17 miles farther on under False Presque Isle. This is open to the southeast, but fully protected from the more commonly prevailing winds of southwest to northwest. Round Thunder Bay Island on the outside to avoid the long bank of nasty shoals lying north of Thunder Bay. If your draft exceeds 4 feet, pass on the outside of Middle Island, with its flashing white light on a white and orange tower. Otherwise you could gradually work your way toward shore from Thunder Bay Island, to coast at least a mile off by the time you reach South Nine Mile Point.

The best anchorage in this part of Lake Huron is at Presque Isle Harbor. There are a lot of cottages on these shores, but most are hidden among the trees. Keep about a half mile offshore when approaching from either north or south, until the fixed green range with red and white daymark opens up at 274°. Keep the range carefully to avoid shoals on both sides, one of which is marked by a red buoy, and you'll carry 10 feet into the harbor. The best anchorage is in the southern part of the bay in about 10 feet, but you might want to take your dinghy over to the north side for a bit of sightseeing.

The white stone lighthouse that you aimed for while coming up the lake is the original Presque Isle Light, built in 1840. Thirty years later the government decided that wasn't a good place for a lighthouse and built a new Presque Isle Light on the north side of the peninsula. This flashing white light, also atop a white stone tower, guided your way if you approached from the north. The old tower and lightkeeper's house lay forlorn for 60 years until the Stebbins family bought it for a summer home in 1930. They not only restored the buildings, but filled their home with antiques, and in 1959 opened both the house and light tower to the public. They have added many artifacts through the years, and offer a warm welcome and a storehouse of information to the museum's visitors. Beach your dinghy near an old marina dock and walk down the road toward the end of the peninsula. Branching off to the right, a beautiful forested track, with a sign, will lead you to the lighthouse museum.

At some time in the future there may be a Waterways Commission marina installed at the site of the defunct private marina. At the moment there is a restaurant there.

If you're downbound on the lake from northward there is an alternative anchorage in North Bay on the other side of the "almost island." Although open from northwest through northeast, in big wind and sea from southerly quarters this may be a preferred spot to wait it out before rounding Presque Isle. Keep to the middle of the bay to avoid shoals from both sides as you head toward anchorage in the southeast corner in about 10 feet. The rear range light in Presque Isle Harbor can be a useful guide on a course of 158°.

Rogers City

Rogers City, 18 miles beyond Presque Isle, extends a warm welcome to cruising boats. Stay at least a mile offshore as you round Adams Point, marked by a flashing white light buoy. Immense piles of limestone let you know you're approaching Rogers City, but they belong to commercial Calcite Harbor southeast of the city. Rogers City itself is identified by its water tank, and the harbor is the small craft basin, enclosed by breakwaters. A heavily buoyed channel guides you southwest from deep water for entrance from southeast between the flashing green and flashing white breakwater lights. The **Waterways Commission Marina** offers all dockside services at slips in 5 feet.

The marina is located in a city park, with beach, playground, tennis courts, and a band shell where you can enjoy a free concert on Saturday afternoon. On July Fourth the park hosts a gala celebration, topped off by fireworks, of course; early August is the Nautical City Festival. As you leave the park to head downtown a quarter of a mile away, the side of a big shed is covered with informative notices of the commercial services available. Rogers City, with 4,300 people, is an attractive town and a customs reporting station. In addition to the usual shops, there are several restaurants and a movie theater. The Laundromat is not within convenient walking distance, but there is sometimes a courtesy car at the marina, and there are taxis. The Presque Isle Historical Society Museum on Second Street (734-4121) is in an old home and has an appealing country exhibit.

If you can negotiate automobile transport (harbor master, taxi, rental car or thumb), a 3- to 4-mile trip to Calcite Harbor and the world's largest limestone quarry is worth the effort.

There are two overlooks. From Quarry View you can observe the open pit mining operation, look at the fossils on display, and perhaps find a few of your own. Then drive around to Harbor View and watch the various grades of limestone being loaded into the ships of the United States Steel Corporation, which owns the harbor. The first cargo was shipped from here in 1912 on the steamer *Calcite*, and when she was retired in 1960 her pilot house was placed here at the scene of its lifework. It is open to the public.

Boat crews that habituate northern Lake Huron and Lake Michigan waters feel a particular fondness for Rogers City, where the familiar voice of WLC originates. It was the first to be heard ship-to-shore on the Great Lakes, back in 1922. The station was then licensed under call letters WCAF. But so few ships were equipped for voice correspondence that the following year the station reverted to wireless telegraphy. In 1941 U.S. Steel applied for a new voice transmission license for its subsidiary company, now Central Radio Telegraph, and WLC, "World Limestone Center," has been heard ever since. The studio is tucked away in obscurity on the quarry grounds at Calcite Harbor.

Hammond Bay

Beyond Rogers City the coastline continues the northwest trend that began at Presque Isle and sweeps gracefully around Hammond Bay. Three miles beyond this indentation, a 20-mile straight run from Rogers City, the **Waterways Commission** has placed a small boat harbor of refuge, known as Hammond Bay. Entrance is from northwest, where the detached breakwaters are marked by flashing red and white lights with appropriate daymarks. Controlling channel depth is 9 feet, with 6 feet at the slips, where all dockside services are offered, except diesel. There is no town or commercial activity of any sort. In fact, the area is quite undeveloped and wooded, with a soft sand beach and dunes, a restful overnight stop except when there is a strong wind and surge from the northwest.

The Straits of Mackinac
Charts 14880, 14881, 14885, 14886
Small Craft Book

Lake Huron and Lake Michigan are Siamese twins that barely miss being separated by a bridge of land near the north end of both. Only the bed of an ancient river, widened over the ages by the persistence of water and the scouring of ice, kept the passage open. Today it is a strait 4 miles wide that separates the two peninsulas of Michigan and carries a name venerated in Indian lore—Michilimackinac, the Great Turtle, whose back supports the world. The Straits of Mackinac, like all narrow passes, has always been a place of strategic importance in human affairs. The name, still bearing a kind of mystique, has come to encompass a stretch of over 50 miles at the narrowing of the two lakes. And at its apex the three communities of Mackinaw City, St. Ignace, and Mackinac Island still carry, in varying degrees, the aura of their dramatic imperial history.

Cheboygan

Cheboygan is the southern gateway to the straits. It, too, began as a lumbering town, raising a sawdust pile reputed to be 60 feet high over 10 acres of ground. After the Cheboygan River Valley was logged out in the 1890s the mills were sustained from immense log rafts floated across the lake from the still virgin forests of Ontario. After that source gave out Cheboygan languished for a time, but its convenient harbor, its paper mill, a few light industries and growing tourism keep the town of 5,500 people a vibrant place.

About 15 miles from Hammond Bay harbor Fourteen Foot Shoal Light, occulting white from a white tower and equipped with a fog horn, marks the approach to Cheboygan. Don't cut it too closely as you come onto the fixed red range with red and white daymarks on a course of 212° for the river entrance. There is also a flashing white light on the end of the short north pier. The Cheboygan River is subject to severe and rapid oscillations in water level. The first thing you may see after you enter is the big Coast Guard cutter *Mackinaw*, docked at her home berth on the port side. The 290-foot vessel is equipped with six 2,000-horsepower engines to break up the massive ice floes that impede ship passage in late fall and early spring. There is no dockage nearby for pleasure craft, but after you're settled at a marina, walk back by land for a tour of the ship.

The big public launch site, with four ramps, is across the river from the Coast Guard Dock, and near it just below the bridge is **Captains Three Marine Services**, with alongside dockage in 8 to 12 feet and the usual services, except deisel and pumpout. They monitor channels 9, 16 and 68. Downtown shopping is within a block or two. The State Street Bridge, with vertical clearance of

9 feet, opens for six minutes either side of the quarter and three-quarter hour during weekdays and Saturday morning, at other times on demand with one long and one short. Beyond it the **Waterways Commission Marina** has alongside tie-up on the west bank, with all dockside services except showers. A convenient walkway leads directly from it to the downtown shopping area, restaurants and movie theater. The Cheboygan County Historical Museum, at Huron and Court Streets (627-2694) is a few blocks away in the former county jail. The 1877 Cheboygan Opera House has been recently restored and schedules a year-round variety of dramatic and musical offerings (627-9931).

Five miles across South Channel from Cheboygan is the straits' largest island, Bois Blanc, long corrupted to "Bob-Lo." Most of it is owned by the State of Michigan, but there is a settlement of devoted summer residents on the south shore, served by ferry and daily mail boat from Cheboygan. Behind the breakwater where they land the **Waterways Commission** has placed a long dock for pleasure boats, with electricity and water. There is not much of a village here, just a country store, a friendly bar and much nice walking among the rich woods of the island.

The Inland Waterway

While the Straits of Mackinac are strategic and scenic, the Indians in their fragile birchbark canoes used a more sheltered inland route that nature had strung for 36 miles between lakes Huron and Michigan—Cheboygan River to Mullet Lake to Indian River to Burt Lake to Crooked River to Crooked Lake. Where they found it necessary to portage around obstructions, more technologically minded 19th-century business interests made improvements that culminated in the opening of a lock at Cheboygan in 1869. The new waterway was obsolete almost as soon as it was completed because railroads soon supplanted inland boat transport. But 20th-century recreational boaters have fallen heir to the tranquil passage. There's only one problem. Neither man nor nature ever quite completed it to Lake Michigan; the 36 miles never became 38.

Nevertheless, if your boat length is less than 25 feet and its gross weight less than 5,000 pounds, Lake Harbor Marina at Oden will trailer it 8 miles by road for launching at Harbor Springs in Little Traverse Bay, Lake Michigan. Advance reservations are necessary (616-347-3918). If your length exceeds 60 feet, beam 16 feet, height 16 feet, or draft 3 feet, the Inland

Waterway is not for you at all. Those are the controlling dimen-
sions for locks (there are now two), bridges and channel depths.
If you fit, this can be a diverting side excursion into the interior
countryside.

It begins at the Cheboygan River Lock, half a mile beyond the
city dock. This is not the same one that opened in 1869. It was
rebuilt in 1927 and will lift your boat about 13 feet. As you
approach, watch out for swift water discharged at right angles
to the river from the power house adjacent to the Charmin
Paper Company on the starboard side. The lock operates from
0900 to 1900 in summer. On approach, signal the lockmaster
with one long and two short blasts; he will instruct you on the
locking procedure and collect your dollar for the privilege.

The Cheboygan River above the lock is wide and deep, and
rather suburban in the first part of the 5 miles to Mullet Lake.
About halfway along, at the junction with Black River, **Anchor In
Marina** provides slips and alongside dockage to power boats in
10 feet, with all dockside services except diesel, but including
Laundromat; a 30-ton travelift; engine and hull repairs and a
launch ramp. You can take a side trip up Black River to Alverno
Dam.

Mullet Lake is one of the state's largest inland lakes, 10 miles
long by three at its widest, and a popular summer resort. Close to
the entrance at Cheboygan River the venerable Hack-Ma-Tack
Inn offers dockage while you dine on very good food. There is a
marina at the village of Mullet Lake on the west shore, and Aloha
State Park on the east side has a boat basin protected by jetties.
There are also several coves for anchorage, especially on the less
heavily developed east shore.

From Mullet Lake you pass into Indian River at a lighted buoy.
This river is placid and marshy and little developed, a fine
environment for observing wildlife, fishing and duck hunting.
But take care to follow the buoys closely in the twisting channel
for the 4 miles to Burt Lake. There is a marina on each bank at
the town of Indian River. **Indian River Marina** and **Howe's
Interlake Marina** have 5 feet at slips and alongside dockage, with
all dockside services except diesel, engine and hull repairs, a
marine store, and haulout by 40-ton hoist and 12-ton crane,
respectively. They are within walking distance of village shops
and restaurants; Vivios, in the edge of town, is especially recommended for Italian food.

Burt Lake is about the same size as Mullet and also has many
cottages and resorts, with the **Burt Lake Marina** at the entrance,
offering alongside tie-up in 6 to 9 feet for boats up to 30 feet,

with gas, heads, a launch ramp and pumpout. The course of the waterway takes you across the lower part of the lake to the Crooked River. This stream lives up to its name as it twists for about 5 miles through the marshes (and a bridge that swings open to the side) to Crooked Lake. To enter Crooked Lake you must pass the second lock, built only in 1968. It operates from 0900 to 2100 and opens on a signal of one long and one short.

Crooked Lake is a relatively small one, 4 miles by 2 at its widest. Because it lies on an east-west axis, strong westerly winds can kick up a surprising chop. The center of the lake is deep, but its borders are wide shoals, with a dredged channel between Oden Island and the north shore. Near the northeast corner a narrow channel leads into Pickerel Lake, from which there is no outlet. **Lake Harbor Marina**, which provides the portage service and sells gas, is at the village of Oden on the north shore. Here either you are pulled out on the trailer or you turn around and go back the way you came.

Mackinaw City

In the old days of French transliteration of Indian place names this whole area was known as Michilimackinac. And, in the style of the French, the final consonant was unpronounced. This is one of the few French pronunciations of American place names that survives in modern use, and the altered spelling of the town at the top of Michigan's lower peninsula serves as a gentle reminder. It was here, at Mackinaw City, that the soldiers and traders from Quebec began a fortified village in 1715 that grew to be the great emporium of the fur trade. Forty-six years later they were obliged to turn it over to the British, following their conquest of New France. When in 1781 the British moved the fort to the more defensible Mackinac Island, the village and the fur trade went with it.

Revival of the old town site came in the next century when the railroad reached the tip of the lower peninsula. A new Mackinaw City arose where the trains were ferried 4 miles across the Straits to the booming mining settlements of the upper peninsula. After auto ferry service began in 1923 the town prospered as well from the growing number of tourists seeking the salubrious air of the north country. Then, in 1957, the engineering feat previously declared impossible was accomplished. Mighty Mac, the world's longest suspension bridge (measuring between anchorages over water), at last connected Michigan's sundered parts. Railroad car ferry traffic declined somewhat and the ferrying of motor vehicles disappeared. But today tourist passenger ferry traffic to Mackinac Island (where automobiles are prohibited) is brisker than ever, and Mackinaw City glows as a tourist attraction in its own right.

One rarely gets an opportunity to rhapsodize about an engineering structure, but, statistics aside, the Mackinac Bridge soars over the deep-blue waters of the straits with a grace that is breath-taking. Its white towers are visible from 20 miles away in either lake, though you may not recognize the pencil-slim points on the horizon on your first approach. Gradually the suspension cables come into view, the white concrete towers, artfully pierced in geometric design, glint in the sun, and the complex of green steel supporting triangles become life-size in their five-mile leap across the waterway. As you pass underneath, the bridge momentarily shuts out the sun, and the roar of traffic across the grillway at mid-suspension thunders like a great waterfall. In a flash you're past it and can watch its recession as you admired the approach. This is the daylight wonder; at night the bridge sparkles in a halo of light, a tiara on the head of the lakes.

By common consent the great bridge is the divider between Lake Huron and Lake Michigan. Even the wind seems to agree, as it often blows differently on the two sides of the bridge. Nestled under its shadow, 15 miles up South Channel from Cheboygan, is Mackinaw City. (Give the shallow wrecks off Nipigon Point a wide berth as you ascend the channel.) Two projections of land thrust into the straits from the south end of town. On approaching from the southeast you'll see the railroad and automobile ferry installations alongside of them, as you pass both to come around to the harbor entrance from the north. The approach from the bridge or from the main channel is more direct. The first land projection has a fog horn at the end with one 2-second blast every 4 seconds; the second has a fixed red light with a fog horn that emits two half-second blasts every 30 seconds.

At the entrance to the breakwater enclosing the harbor there are flashing red and green lights with matching daymarks. Inside the breakwaters you make an immediate turn to starboard for the **Waterways Commission Marina**, with all dockside services except diesel fuel. That is available at Shepler's Ferry Dock adjacent to the marina. Shepler's Marine Service also provides haulout and repairs if you need them.

Mackinaw City is a busy town, from which hordes of tourists depart and arrive in the constant daytime shuffle of ferries to

Mackinac Island. (Those berthed adjacent to the marina create no wake disturbance as they enter and leave the harbor.) Central Avenue, the main street, begins at the marina, with numerous shops of all kinds, especially gift, several restaurants, and miniature golf. Food shopping and the Laundromat are farther away; taxi service is available. This is one of the few towns on the American side of Lake Huron from which commercial fish tugs still put out, and the prize they bring back can be purchased, fresh or smoked, at Bell's.

A few blocks north of the marina a soft sand beach offers beautiful views of the straits and the bridge along with the swimming. But history is Mackinaw City's biggest attraction. In the marina itself is the reconstructed sloop, *Welcome*, first launched for the fur trade in 1775. The new one makes an occasional voyage from her home berth, so don't be surprised if one fine day you see an anachronism plying the waters of the straits. Upstairs over a tavern on Central Avenue is the Mackinac Bridge Museum, a private labor of love that tells the fascinating story of its construction. Near the beach a few blocks north of the marina the old Mackinac Point Lighthouse is now a marine museum.

But the *pièce de résistance* is Fort Michilimackinac, painstakingly reconstructed as and where it stood 200 years ago from archaeological research that has been going on since 1959. When you pass through the stockade gate you find yourself in the old French village, risen again on the stone foundations that lay so long beneath the soil. As you wander among the fur traders' houses, the church, the commandant's house, and all the other buildings, you will learn of the stirring events that took place here. The most dramatic of these, the ruse and massacre of Pontiac's uprising in 1763, is reenacted every Memorial Day weekend. And July Fourth weekend sees an ancient Voyageurs' Rendezvous.

St. Ignace

Directly across the straits, at the other end of the bridge, is the village of St. Ignace. Here is where the white man's tenure really began, when the much loved Father Jacques Marquette established a mission in 1671. After his tragic death at the age of 38, en route home from the Mississippi in 1675, his remains were brought back here by a special Indian delegation. The final burial site was lost for 200 years until accidentally rediscovered by a local man digging in the soil. Now there is a stone to mark the lonely gravesite overlooking the water (Marquette's bones were later moved again) and a park around it explaining the mission and the lifestyle of the Indians it served. This is at the north end of town, a longish walk from the marina. At the other end, adjacent to the bridge, is the Father Marquette Memorial and National Historic Site and Museum. This is not within walking distance of the marina, but taxis are available. The Michilimackinac Historical Society Museum on Spring Street (643-9570) is a few blocks from the harbor, and St. Ignace's special events—the Antique Auto Show in June, the July Fourth celebration, and the Labor Day Black Gown Tree Pageant, dramatizing the life of Marquette—are all held at the waterfront.

The **Waterways Commission Marina** at St. Ignace is a smaller version of the one across the straits. It gets less traffic, perhaps because it is not very convenient to shopping, although there are many stores and restaurants in the rather sprawled business district beginning a few blocks away. Give Graham Point a fair berth as you come around, to avoid some old dock ruins. There are some land projections here, too, for the railroad ferry docks, and you may see the venerable *Chief Wawatam*, the last remaining railroad car ferry, chugging in and out of its home port. Northwest of the Chief's base is the small boat harbor, with a fixed red light on the end of the east pier enclosing it. The marina is entered from the south, has 6 to 14 feet of water at the slips, and all dockside services except diesel fuel.

Mackinac Island

Despite the attractions of the mainland ports, the magnet that pulls all comers is indisputably The Island—no need even to use its full name. Although not very large, three miles by two, it dominates the straits, physically by its height hundreds of feet above the water and in mood by the mystical spell of the Great Turtle himself. Approaching it from any direction, one can understand why the Indians held Mackinac Island sacred. Its very air is of a different quality from the mainland peninsulas only three or seven miles away.

It's easy to be distracted by the glorious view from the turbulence of your surroundings, as ferries and giant lake freighters churn up the water where the passage narrows. The most constricted place is at Round Island Passage Light, the only deep water passage for ships, precisely where one enters the island harbor. The light is an isophase red, shown from a red and white structure with a fog horn, and the straits are well buoyed throughout. From a distance the old lighthouse on Round Island, recently restored as a historic site, may be more conspicuous.

Somehow the architects of Waterways Commission harbors have never quite figured out how to protect the docks at Mackinac Island from all the disturbance. It can be an uncomfortable place to lie if the wind and sea are anywhere from the east. Yet so insistent is the drawing power of The Island that pleasure craft will race each other for a slip, assigned by loudspeaker to each boat as it approaches the dock, in which they'll bounce and jounce all day in the wash from the ferries and pay a premium dockage fee for the privilege. When those craft are racers from Port Huron or from Chicago the last two weekends in July, dock space for the casual cruiser is virtually impossible to come by—The Island belongs to the fleet.

The harbor is entered east of Round Island Passage Light between two breakwaters with a quick flashing white and a flashing white light with appropriate daymarks. The whitewashed village is spread out before you, dominated by its protective fortress on the bluff, and time warps for a moment to transport you backward over a hundred years with an almost physical sensation. Then the present crowds in as the hustling ferries shoulder past you to their docks on either side of the **Waterways Commission Marina**. The big dock is T-shaped, with slips on both sides of the head of the T; the inside ones are entered from either east or west as the dock master directs you. There are also slips on the street side, generally for boats under 30 feet. Depths range from 6 to 14 feet. Dockside services here include electricity, water and pumpout. For a generous fee you can buy a shower at the yacht club across the street; for gas or diesel fuel you can go to the inside end of the long commercial pier west of the marina, where tie-up is not the most comfortable for a small boat.

But boat service is not what you come to Mackinac Island for. Nor do you want to spend your time on board, bouncing in ferry wakes. There is so much to do and see ashore that an annual stop at Mackinac Island is in the nature of a pilgrimage for all boats that cruise the upper lakes, and a favorite ultimate destination for those who come up from below. Simply wandering and soaking up the atmosphere of the exquisitely preserved 19th-century village is a delightful pastime, for motor vehicles are prohibited and the thoroughfares are given over entirely to the placid pace of foot, hoof and bicycle wheel. During the day the village streets (all two of them) teem with "fudgies." This sobriquet is conferred on the tourists who come over for the day and carry home boxes of fudge from the numerous shops producing and selling that delicacy. Some clever entrepreneur has transformed a mockery into a virtue by producing big round buttons that proudly proclaim, "I am a Mackinac Island Fudgie."

Despite the crowds, and the souvenir shops and restaurants that cater to them, the village manages to avoid the tackiness that has blighted similar places elsewhere. At night, after the last ferry leaves, the quietude at dusk evokes the shades of hoop-skirted ladies and gentlemen in tall hats strolling past these very buildings or clopping home by carriage from a dinner at Mr. Stuart's.

During the day one can walk backward in time inside the buildings of John Jacob Astor's American Fur Company and the home of Robert Stuart, his agent—not reconstructions, but the original structures preserved and maintained. Each has a fascinating and often surprising story to tell. So does the William Beaumont Memorial, the American Fur Company store where in 1822 the doctor got his chance to discover how human digestion actually works. Dominating the village from its bluff is Fort Mackinac, much of it just as His Majesty's soldiers built it. Farther east along the shore are the Indian Dormitory and Ste. Anne's Church. All of these historic places are artfully presented, to captivate the most indifferent nonlover of history. Even the lilacs in the park across from the dock participate; some of them were planted by the French traders.

There are two other sides to Mackinac Island, in addition to historic sites and touristic shopping. Within a very few years of the decline of the fur trade Mackinac was "discovered" as a summer resort by wealthy southern families seeking cool, clear air. By late 19th century it had become one of the most fashionable in the nation, nature's gift to the hay fever sufferer. Elaborate homes were built along the bluffs. One of them is the official residence of the Governor of Michigan. If his flag is up, you know he's there.

In 1887 the Grand Hotel opened its doors and presented the world with its longest piazza. If you approached the island from the west, you got a splendid view of the white collonade. Unlike many resort hotels of its age and style, the Grand has barely wavered in popularity and elegance over the years. Its lobby, grounds, garden-set swimming pool, tennis courts and golf course are open to the public for a fee. (You also pay a fee to enter the lobby if you aren't a guest.) There are four other vintage hotels that have been well restored and maintained. All of them, including the Grand, have dining rooms and cocktail

Mackinac Island, harbor and Governor's Mansion.

lounges open to nonresident guests. A tour around the hotels and cottages away from downtown shows you a different Mackinac.

And then there is all the rest of the island. Most of it is a state park. In 1875 it was the second national park to be established after Yellowstone, but the federal government turned it over to Michigan 20 years later. The largest part of the island is natural, laced by hiking and riding trails, where the forest grows thick and the wildflowers run rampant in late spring. There are geologic wonders to be seen, like the famous Arch Rock and Sugar Loaf, and it is a botanist's delight.

There are several ways to tour Mackinac Island. You might want to try all of them. Before you set out, stop in at the State Visitor's Center next door to the marina, pick up a guide book with information about hours and admission charges, then check the tourist information booth on Main Street. From the latter you can take a carriage tour, whose informed guide tells the stories behind the various sights, while his horse pulls you gently up and down the hills. There are riding stables from which you can charter your own horse. There are countless bicycles for rent by the hour, the day or the week. While the bikes can be hard to manage on some of the steeper slopes, the flat shore road that circles the island is a delightful 8-mile ride. Finally, there are your own two feet to take you on any byway path that suits your fancy.

Mackinac Island, Arch Rock.

Mackinac Island is not a good place to take care of mundane boat needs, like food shopping and laundry. It is a place for recreation—to absorb and enjoy.

Les Cheneaux Islands

A dozen miles east of Mackinac Island a wooded archipelago reaches southeastward into the lake from the north shore. Les Cheneaux translates descriptively to "the Channels," but misunderstanding of the French has been perpetuated in the common designation "the Snows." True, there is a lot of snow on the islands in winter, but it is the maze of channels among them that is their distinguishing feature.

There are three entrances to the group, imaginatively named West, Middle and East. You can begin at the West Entrance to wind along the main, buoyed channel among the low, wooded islands and inlets to emerge 18 miles later at the East Entrance—

or reverse the track. Watch the buoyage *very* carefully. Each of the entrances is buoyed conventionally, reds to starboard, to the nearest town. This causes a reversal of color on some of the channels, notably on the eastern approach to Hessel. The side channels are marked by private buoys maintained by Les Cheneaux Islands Association. Controlling draft in the main channel is 7 feet, except at Middle Entrance where it is 6. The channels west of Middle Entrance are mostly graced with large, old summer cottages, with charming old-fashioned boat houses, while east of that section there are many newer ones more closely built. But scattered throughout are uninhabited coves and islands rich with bird life. Fishing from small boats is the main pastime of the residents. There are a number of anchorages to choose from among the sheltered passages, depending upon the draft of your boat. Marquette Bay on the west and Government Bay near the east end are two favorites.

Two mainland towns serve Les Cheneaux. Hessel, 3 miles from West Entrance, is the better bet for cruising boats. The **Waterways Commission Marina**, behind a breakwater entered from the east, has alongside tie-up in 10 feet or more and all dockside services except fuel and ice. Gas can be obtained at **E. J. Mertaugh Boat Works**, which will also accept transients at its docks in 10 to 14 feet if the public dock is full. Electricity at some of the docks, heads, a 12-ton travelift, engine and hull repairs and a marine store complete the services available here.

Hessel is a quiet little village, but there is a good grocery store, which also sells ice, and the Hessel Bay Inn serves well-prepared food. The Antique Boat Show in early August is the major event of the season.

Cedarville, a few miles east, has more shops and Les Cheneaux Historical Museum, but the only dockage is for small boats and expressly prohibits overnight mooring. For that you might find space at **Viking Boat Harbor** a mile south of town. There is 8 to 10 feet of water at the slips, with electricity, water, pumpout, heads, gas, diesel, a 50-ton travelift, engine, hull and rigging repairs.

Beyond the East Entrance to Les Cheneaux there are no protected harbors along the north shore for another 20 miles or so. Coast at least 2 miles off to avoid all shoals, taking care to spot the green can that marks Tobin Reef, with its nasty rocks and 2-foot shallows. When you arrive at Point De Tour you enter St. Marys River, a different chapter in this tale.

The Sunset Coast

Charts 2290, 2291, 2292

The Canadian side of Lake Huron is the shore of spectacular sunsets, viewed from broad sand beaches for the first 125 miles northward. First settled in the 1830s, the rich agricultural land, known then as the Huron Tract, had to be cleared of its virgin forest. The mouths of the rivers flowing down to the lake became ports, first for the shipping of the timber, then for the cultivated crops of the farms and the bounty the fishermen netted. As elsewhere on the lakes, when the railroads extended westward to the shoreside villages the commercial importance of the harbors declined. By the latter part of the 19th century the shores of the Huron Tract were discovered by people from the growing mid-Ontario cities, who sought relief from summer heat and had accumulated the wealth to build second homes. Summer colonies sprouted and continue their growth to this day.

A cruise up this shore can alternate stops between lively resorts and quaint "working" towns. Then, beyond Chantry Island, the even, sand dune bluffs and soft beaches give way to the irregular, island-studded coast of the Bruce Peninsula, the 55-mile-long promontory that creates Georgian Bay. Here the rugged, coniferous north country begins; agriculture is left behind. The settlements are small and modest. The band of islands and shoals, up to 3 miles wide, speaks of a rugged lifestyle.

In navigating the Canadian shore of the lake keep in mind that you are on a lee shore and watch the weather. Although each harbor is equipped with a lighted entrance range, the daymarks are small, if brilliant, and not readily visible more than 5 miles offshore. It's best to enter in the afternoon with the sun behind you or somewhat below its zenith. In heavy weather the only harbor that should be attempted by a stranger is Goderich. The others are fronted by sandbars, which build and cause breaking seas when the lake is rough. Note that the charts are based on surveys dating from the turn of the century and show depths in fathoms. Furthermore, those depths relate to a water level chart datum no longer in use. To conform to current usage you must subtract from the posted soundings an amount that is stated on each chart. Also note that there is no harbor chart or enlargement for the first three ports at the southern end of the lake.

Port Franks

The 31 miles of coastline between the St. Clair River and the first harbor up the lake is low, with the sand beachfront gradually broadening and rising as dunes here and there. The only obstruction is the reef extending for 2 miles off Kettle Point. Be sure to pass on the outside of the quick flashing red light buoy that marks it. Port Franks is a small harbor at the mouth of the west branch of the Au Sable River. Although there is a minimum of 4 feet in the buoyed entrance channel, the shifting sandbar on the seaward side can shoal to as little as one foot, and in a strong northwesterly there is a dangerous surge at the entrance, which has no breakwater. There is a flashing red light, however, with red and white daymark.

For obvious reasons Port Franks is used mainly by small boats, and the settlement of about 2,000 people is in a lovely natural area with a great deal of bird life. The quiet river is navigable for about 5 miles with draft of 3 feet or less. Just inside the river entrance is the **Pebble Lodge Marina**, with 16 feet at the slips and all dockside services, except diesel but including Laundromat. The beach and two restaurants are close by.

Grand Bend

Ten miles beyond Port Franks, Grand Bend, where the coastline bends northward, is easier to get into, identified by brilliant orange paint on the ends of the piers protecting the dredged mouth of the north branch of the Au Sable River. There is also a range at 098°, showing an isophase green light in front and a fixed green in back, with white and orange daymarks and a fog horn. There is a minimum of 7 feet in the channel and upstream to the highway bridge. About half a mile up the river on the north side is the long town dock, where you can tie alongside in 6 feet. There is electricity, and heads and showers are just beyond the top of the stairs leading up the bluff from the dock. There has been fuel available near the river entrance, but the proprietor of those facilities refused to provide an update on them by telephone.

Grand Bend may drowse in winter with a population of 780, but in summer it comes alive with 10 times that number drawn to its broad beach. The town is then transformed into a lively family entertainment center, which includes a roller rink, mini-golf, kiddy rides, and tennis, as well as shops, restaurants and cocktail bars, some with live entertainment. All of it is handy to

Grand Bend, town dock.

the town dock. Yet the steep river bluff shields the harbor from traffic and helps maintain the quiet of its setting. Grand Bend also offers one of the infrequent opportunities on Lake Huron to attend summer theater. True to the spirit of summer stock, the professional Huron County Playhouse is in a converted barn two miles east of town (238-8451). Closer at hand in the village is the Lambton Heritage Museum (243-2600).

Bayfield

The village of Bayfield, settled in 1830, wears its age with quiet grace in the big trees shading its spacious, dignified homes and carefully preserved old shops and inns. It was "discovered" by prosperous summer cottagers early in this century, and in recent years has been rediscovered by wandering tourists who crowd its excellent restaurants, gift and antique shops. Yet the village of 650 people proclaims old Ontario rather than crass commercialism. And it has some of the best marine facilities on the lake.

The Bayfield River flows into Lake Huron 15 miles north of Grand Bend. It is protected by breakwaters with a fixed green range with white and orange daymarks on a course of 077° on the north pier and a fixed red light with red and white daymark on the south pier. There is 8 feet in the channel, gradually reducing to five at the highway bridge about half a mile up-stream. The **Bayfield Yacht Club** slips are on the south bank. On the north side **Harbour Lights Marina** has four basins, accommodating hundreds of boats. The gas dock and transient dockage are at the upstream end, just before the bridge. The slips have very short side docks, necessitating either backing in or getting on and off at the bow. All dockside services are offered, including Laundromat and full engine, hull and rigging repairs, with a travelift capacity of 45 feet. There are a swimming pool, tennis courts and restaurant, all in a rather resortlike setting. At the extremity of the harbor near the bridge **South Shore Marina** accommodates boats under 30 feet with maximum draft of 3 feet for the approach, although there is 6 to 8 feet at the slips. Electricity and water are available with long lines, and there are heads, showers and ice.

The town was built on the bluff rather than on the river that bears its name. From Harbour Lights it's a pleasant walk of about a mile up the hill and over the highway bridge through charming residential streets to the shopping area; South Shore is closer. The Little Inn and The Albion Hotel are popular restaurants in historic buildings, and there are several others to choose from as well. If you're out for an evening stroll, follow the road to your right, once over the bridge, all the way to the lakefront park and its spectacular view of the setting sun.

Goderich

A mere 12 miles from Bayfield, Goderich is the largest town on this coast of Lake Huron, with a population numbering 7,400. It is also the oldest, founded in 1827 by one of Ontario's most colorful characters, Dr. William Dunlop, known as "Tiger" for his escapades while a British Army surgeon in India. Though he died in 1848, Tiger is well remembered in Goderich, for his long years of influential squirarchy, for the mansion he built on the Maitland River, for his service in the Provincial Legislature, for the unique and beautiful plan he laid out for the town, perhaps most of all for his sense of fun and wit.

Goderich never became the major lakeport its founder envisaged, but the discovery of rich salt deposits in 1866, during a search for oil, gave the town an important industry that flourishes to this day. In fact, the Sifto Salt Mine, which penetrates 1,760 feet and far out under Lake Huron, to produce half of all the rock salt mined in Canada, is the first thing you'll see upon entering the artificial harbor. What is most clearly visible from offshore, however, is the big grain elevator that stands at the head of the harbor. The picturesque mine buildings sit on the spit of land that, together with two breakwaters, forms the inner harbor. Two outer breakwalls give Goderich its double protection and make it the only all weather port on the east coast of the lake.

Goderich has a big lighthouse on shore south of the harbor, a fixed red range with white and orange daymarks on 087°, and flashing white and occulting red lights on the ends of the outer breakwaters. A buoyed channel leads to the inner breakwaters; on the north pier is the range front light and the south pier has 12 equally spaced lights on it, with the end painted fluorescent red. In short, Goderich is hard to miss.

Inside the north inner breakwater, past the mine buildings and close up under them, is the **Snug Harbour Municipal Marina**, with alongside tie-up in 20 feet and all dockside services, except diesel fuel. Despite the breakwaters there is a surge in the harbor in a strong west wind. Under these conditions you may need a breast anchor if you're docked on the outside wall. The mine, which inevitably does sift a bit onto nearby boats, the grain elevator, and the retired lake freighters moved there for grain storage may make Goderich sound like an unappetizing industrial harbor. But the soft municipal beach, crowded with riotous children, just the other side of the south inner breakwater, quickly dispels that impression. And the lake freighter you see tied up on the south side is actually the Marine Museum. Goderich harbor wears its industry very lightly. It is a customs port of entry.

For a more rural atmosphere, to avoid all surge, and to be a little closer to town, however, you might prefer to move a mile up the Maitland River to the **Maitland Valley Marina**. A buoyed channel, leading off to port from the main channel just before the salt mine, carries 8 feet as it follows the outside of a long spit of land, banked by concrete with a grassy peninsula opposite, to the marina. Slips in 8 to 10 feet, all dockside services, and a 15-ton crane for haulout are available at this friendly marina, with mechanics called in if necessary. Goderich is the last port on this side of Lake Huron where big boat haulout and repairs can be obtained. It's 175 miles up and around the Bruce Peninsula to the next such opportunity, at Wiarton.

Although neither marina is very close to town, it's a place you'll want to visit. Taxis are available. Or the walk can be shortcut by a goat track that climbs the bluff directly across the road from the Maitland Valley Marina and exits on a residential street three blocks from the town square. That town square is what makes Goderich unique. The artistic creation of Tiger Dunlop and his literary friend and associate, John Galt, the square is actually an octagon, centering on the County Court-house set amid spacious lawns and shaded by large trees. Radiating from this hub are eight commercial streets. The shopping district is compact and convenient, and there is a hospital. The imposing Bedford Hotel dominates one block on the square; its dining room specializes in a daily buffet luncheon. Half a block off the square the Club Grill really does charcoal broil its steaks. To complete evening entertainment there is a movie theater on the square.

For afternoon recreation, wander the quiet old streets to admire the Victorian homes built of the characteristic local yellow brick. Visit the Huron Historic Jail, built in 1839 in Goderich's favorite octagon shape and used for its intended purpose until 1972 (524-6971). It is an architectural masterpiece where memorabilia of Tiger Dunlop are displayed. Spend as much time as your brain can absorb in the astonishing Huron County Pioneer Museum (524-9610). With 12,000 artifacts on display, centered on the cherished lifetime accumulation of one man, it rivals the collection of Henry Ford in Dearborn. Yet the exhibits are well organized around themes, such as salt mining or flour milling. As the day wanes, walk down West Street to one of the two parks that overlook the lake for your daily view of the sunset. If it's a Sunday night, the strains of the weekly band concert will undoubtedly draw you to Harbour Park. For more active recreation there is golf, tennis, lawn bowling and roller skating in convenient proximity. If you're in Goderich during the fourth weekend in July, don't miss the Annual Festival of the Arts.

Kincardine

Below Goderich the coastal profile rose to high clay banks, topped by the farm buildings and woodlots of a prosperous agriculture and fronted by the continuous beach. This scene continues almost to Kincardine, about 35 miles north. Bad reefs surround Point Clark, where the coast turns northeastward, and you should take care to pass outside the red spar buoy marking Clark Reef about a mile offshore. The big white Point Clark Light, flashing white, shows you where to look for the small buoy.

Kincardine's harbor is the most picturesque on this coast. It is the 1880 lighthouse that makes it so. Although designed in the ubiquitous Canadian lighthouse style, its perch on the side of the Penetangore River bluff at the inner end of the small harbor casts the character of the whole scene. It is now in the loving care of the **Kincardine Yacht Club**, which uses the lightkeeper's quarters in the base for its clubhouse and, in a rather unusual arrangement, operates the light for the Coast Guard and the marina for the town. A detached, unlighted breakwater angled to the shore north of the harbor entrance is designed to reduce surge. Two piers protect the entrance to the dredged river mouth, with a fixed red range front light with white and orange daymarks and a fog horn on the end of the north pier lining up with the flashing red on the lighthouse at 104°. Note that these lights are left to *port* as you enter, in contradiction of the red, right, returning rule. Visitors are moored on the east and west walls of the basin, with 7 to 12 feet of depth, in semi-Mediterranean style—between bollards with either bow or stern to the bulkhead, but no side docks. All dockside services are offered.

The area around the harbor once had a furniture factory and a railroad station, but both are gone now and a park has emerged, with access to the beach. On Saturday nights Kincardine's Scottish Pipe Band marches down Main Street to perform in the band shell. In addition to their club rooms the yacht club operates a marine museum on the upper floors of the lighthouse. With these attractions at the waterfront you'll still want to walk the few blocks up the hill to the main street of this attractive town of 5,800, with shops of all sorts, a choice of restaurants, a Laundromat, a hospital and a movie theater. In addition there are tennis courts, indoor and outdoor bowling and a roller rink.

Port Elgin

About 10 miles north of Kincardine the white dome and towers of the Bruce Nuclear Power Development on Douglas Point, Canada's first nuclear generating plant, are conspicuous against the sky. From this point it's wise to cruise at least 1½ miles offshore, gradually moving 2½ miles off at Logie Rock flashing red light buoy. This should be the start of your approach to Port Elgin, where a fixed green range, with white and orange daymarks, guides you on a course of 109° to the unlighted breakwaters enclosing the artificial harbor. There is a least depth of 5 feet in the buoyed channel. The **Port Elgin Municipal Marina** is in the south side of the harbor, with 7 feet at the floating slips and all dockside services. The **Port Elgin Boat Club** at the north end of the basin also has floating slips in six feet.

Port Elgin, 22 miles north of Kincardine, presents a sharp contrast in style. About the same size, Port Elgin is very definitely a resort town, for both cottage and hotel/motel visitors. The business district is a considerable distance back from the harbor, so it's not a handy place for shopping and such chores. But the waterfront offers a number of attractions, in addition to the ubiquitous fine beach—snack bars, restaurants, a cocktail lounge, tennis courts, children's playground, miniature train and amusement rides, and mini-golf. The port is not especially scenic, but it's a good stop for active recreation. Among special annual events are the Highland Games in June and art and antique shows in July and August.

Southampton

A mere 5 miles beyond Port Elgin, Southampton is a return to small-town Ontario dignity (2,800 people), with good shopping, the excellent Bruce County Historical Museum on Victoria Street (797-3644) and a summer theater season in the Town Hall. It is a customs port of entry at the mouth of the Saugeen River. Unfortunately, its marine facilities don't match the harbors farther south. Just inside the river mouth a concrete government dock has alongside tie-up in 9-foot depths, but no services. There are washrooms in the little park adjacent. Above the fixed highway bridge, with 29-foot clearance, **Saugeen Marina Motel** caters to small boats with gas and pumpout.

On the approach from the south you must pass on the outside of Chantry Island, with its big, white lighthouse displaying a flashing white light, and be sure to clear the long shoal extending north of it before turning for the harbor. The passage between the island and the mainland is foul with old breakwater ruins, and the island itself is fringed with boulders. From the north a flashing red bell buoy marks the end of the long shoal extending from Chantry Island, and a quick flashing green identifies Lambert Shoal. From the latter a buoyed channel and fixed red range with orange daymarks at 095° lead to the mouth of the Saugeen River. The rear light has a fog horn. The channel has 7 feet of depth, but is dangerous in heavy wind and sea from west or northwest.

The Fishing Islands

Southampton, on a straight line with Owen Sound 25 miles east, anchors the base of the Bruce Peninsula, which narrows to

6 miles across at its tip 60 miles north. This remarkable triangle of land presents two totally different faces to the cruising boat that coasts its shores. On the Lake Huron side the land slopes gradually from its limestone spine, meandering seaward in a maze of islands and small peninsulas, as though it isn't certain where land ends and water begins. You've had hints of this change in the coastline from the scattering of boulders that began to appear around Kincardine. Twelve miles beyond Southampton Sauble Beach is the last outpost of the luxurious Lake Huron strand, but there is no harbor there.

The Fishing Islands were first named on a map by naval surveyor Lt. Henry Wolsey Bayfield in 1822. You will see much of Bayfield's work throughout Canadian Lake Huron. He named more than half of the islands, points, headlands, coves, etc., and on the old-style charts the draftsmanship of the land contours is still mainly his. He himself was honored in the naming of several waterways and towns, from the one on Lake Huron to an equally attractive village on the Lake Superior shore of Wisconsin.

The first white man to exploit the incredible bounty of the aptly named Fishing Islands was Alexander McGregor of Goderich. He arrived on the scene in 1831 and erected the first building on the Bruce Peninsula on Main Station Island. No shanty, McGregor's headquarters, from which he supplied the enormous demand of the growing city of Detroit, was built of stone and measured 57 by 18 feet. Its remains can still be found on the island. But McGregor enjoyed his prosperity only a few years before more devious entrepreneurs dispossessed him. He continued to fish at various locations on Georgian Bay, and his name, too, is repeated many times in the region through the numerous progeny he left behind.

Fishing tugs still cast their nets among the intricate channels, reefs and coves of the archipelago, although the catch is nothing like it was 100 years ago. Sport fishermen are far more numerous, putting out in their small boats from resorts on the mainland. These little harbors are not really accessible to the cruising stranger, however. The chart is on a very small scale, its fine print is hard to read, and even where it shows beacon ranges there are too many unmarked reefs and shoals leading in from open water in bands up to 3 miles across. The *Sailing Directions* describes several anchorages among the islands, but I have not visited any of them.

Stokes Bay is the only feasible harbor for cruising boats without local knowledge. A red and white Mo(A) sea buoy marks the entrance to a buoyed channel. There is a range at 069° with a flashing red front light and a fixed red rear light atop white and orange daymarks. Lyall Island Light, flashing white with red and white daymark, also helps to identify the location from offshore of the low rocky coast that seems featureless from a distance. It's a little over 4 miles from the sea buoy to the front range light on Knife Island, where you turn northward to follow another buoyed channel about 1½ miles to the government wharf.

Stokes Bay is not exactly your "easy on, easy off" overnight stop. But it's in a beautiful setting, and if the day is waning and you need shelter, the channel carries a minimum of 7 feet. The government dock has that much at the outer end, and gas, water, ice and electricity are supplied by adjacent Bay Haven Camp. Last time I was there the top planking badly needed repair, but the wharf is sturdy, and the camp sold delicious pies. The village of 175 people, with general store and post office, is about 1¼ miles up a quiet country road. Its big tourist attraction is the roadside plaque on the site of the 45th parallel.

If you want to avoid the long haul into Stokes Bay, the offshore run is a clear passage of 55 miles from Port Elgin or Southampton to Cape Hurd and another 5 miles to shelter after that. By then you're in Georgian Bay.

The North Shore

Charts 2273, 2297, 2298; U.S. 14882

Lake Huron is blessed with two north shores. The inner one follows the north side of the famed North Channel, formed by large Manitoulin Island and small Cockburn Island. The south coast of these two and Drummond Island farther west border the north shore of the main basin of the lake. Just as the open lake side of the Bruce Peninsula differs radically in topographic character from its inner, Georgian Bay side, so the southern shores of these islands present a different aspect from their north faces. On the open lake side their sloping shores have been scourged by the big lake's waves and storms into a ragged fringe of boulder and reef-bound peninsulas. Because of exposure, offlying dangers and a paucity of aids to navigation, this coast doesn't see many cruising boats follow its isolated contours. Yet there are a few harbors to put into if you seek adventure and don't require the amenities of a marina. Canadian charts 2297 and 2298 are in the old style, using an obsolete chart datum, but the rest conform to modern usage.

Settler's Cabin near South Baymouth, Manitoulin Island.

South Baymouth

South Bay is a nearly landlocked inlet at the eastern end of Manitoulin Island, 13 miles long by 4 miles at its widest. At the narrows leading from Lake Huron the village of South Baymouth (accent on the third syllable, please) is the terminus of the big ferry from Tobermory 26 miles southeast on the Bruce Peninsula, and Manitoulin's southern link with the rest of the world. A flashing red bell buoy 1½ miles offshore puts you on the fixed green range at 025°, with a fog horn at the front light. The deep water channel is buoyed.

At the last green spar a turn to port leads through a very narrow, rocky squeeze into a basin with public dockage for small boats. The channel and basin have a controlling depth of 5 feet; the problem for cruising boats is size and turning radius. There are no services at the docks in the basin, and most of the space is occupied by local boats. If you continue past the green spar into South Bay, you pass the massive ferry dock, with no place for pleasure craft.

If you find a place to lie in the small craft basin, South Baymouth has a general store, a couple of restaurants at the waterfront and another at the edge of town on the highway. The local historical museum is in the Little Red Schoolhouse, vintage 1898. But beyond the village there is all of South Bay to explore, uninhabited in large stretches, mostly forested, with big, yet sheltered, water for sailing. There are several small bays on the port shore for anchorage, as well as the deep indentation of Roberts Bay on the southeast side. In McKim Bay, the second one beyond the ferry dock, there is a wharf belonging to the Ministry of Natural Resources with 5 feet alongside. The Fisheries Research Station is open to visitors. This is where scientists developed the splake, a delicious cross between speckled and lake trout.

Providence Bay

From South Baymouth, coast at least a mile to a mile and a half offshore until you pass Michael Point on your way to the next harbor. Seventeen miles west of South Baymouth, Providence Bay is used mainly by fishing tugs and is wide open to west through south. Its entrance is marked by a fixed white light with red and white daymark on the east point, and there is a concrete government wharf near the northeast corner, with a flashing red light on the end. Ease of entry is Providence Bay's greatest virtue. The outer end of the wharf is in a state of collapse, although the inner end is sturdy and has two floating piers extending from it with over 6 feet of water alongside. There are no services, and in a westerly blow there is a lot of surge. The inner end of the bay is fronted by a nice sand beach. The resort village of Providence Bay is about a mile walk from the dock. Once there you can have a good meal at the Huron Sands Motel and browse through its excellent and extensive Canadian craft shop and book store.

To False Detour

From Providence Bay there is 35 miles of exposed cruising along a low, featureless, boulder-fringed, lee shore to the next shelter feasible for a stranger, at Burnt Island Harbour. There is no buoyage to mark either the offshore reefs or the numerous coastal indentations, so keep about 2 miles off to avoid all hazards until you come to the string of Duck Islands extending southward from Manitoulin. Crossing Thibault Shoal can be a tricky business; you must find the 8-foot depth between it and Green Point. If you go around the shoal line, outside Inner Duck Island, you'll be about 3½ miles offshore. The entrance to Burnt Island Harbour, about 2½ miles beyond Thibault Shoal, is also devoid of navigational aids, but Burnt Island, actually a peninsula, shows up well on the approach, and the entrance to the harbor is clear of obstructions. Anchor in the southwest corner in 20 feet, taking care to avoid visible and invisible pilings extending from the small private wharf there. There will be surge in southwest winds.

An alternative to Burnt Island is an anchorage between Great Duck Island and Outer Duck Island, about 10 miles off the Manitoulin coast. This isn't too convenient if you're headed to or from other north shore ports, but if your destination (or departure) is one of the Michigan ports from Rogers City southward, it can be a handy layover. Entry must be made from the north, taking care to avoid the band of shoals fronting the northeast side of Great Duck Island for almost half a mile offshore and the shoals making out northward from Outer Duck. You can anchor off the small wharf, but there are shoals and wrecks south of it. From there it's a 2½-mile walk to the lighthouse, one of the few remaining on the Great Lakes that is still tended by a keeper.

Nine miles west of Burnt Island Harbour, Green Island Harbour offers another sheltered anchorage. Although there are no navigational aids, the low, forested island detaches visually from the mainland, showing the entrance from the southeast. Passage is clear down the middle of the entrance, but there are reefs and boulders on both shores. Best lying is off the northeast corner of Green Island, but take care to avoid the rocks connecting it to Steevens Island. Set your anchor carefully; holding might be poor because of submerged logs.

You are now almost at the western extremity of Manitoulin Island. After crossing Mississagi Strait and coasting most of Cockburn Island, shelter can be found again about 21 miles west of Green Island Harbour in Wagosh Bay at the western end of Cockburn. Alternatively, you could enter the North Channel via Mississagi Strait and find dockage at Meldrum Bay, about 22 miles from Green Island Harbour. If you continue westward, the major hazard is Magnetic Reefs, which thrust about 2 miles offshore and do create magnetic anomalies. By all means pass them on the outside. Wagosh Bay, like all the other harbors on this coast, is unmarked, but it is also unobstructed and wide open to the southeast. It is only useful as a shelter in a blow from west or northwest.

Drummond Island

Drummond Island, Michigan, roughly 20 miles long and 12 across at its widest, is much like its neighbors Cockburn and Manitoulin across the international border. The southern, Lake Huron side is deeply indented with bays, but they are fringed by offlying reefs and boulders, behind which the low shores are quite featureless. Only two of these indentations are identified by an offshore buoy as a reference point for safe entrance. In heavy seas neither should be attempted by a stranger.

About 10 miles west of Wagosh Bay and across False Detour Passage (where you could also enter the North Channel) Scammon Cove opens up. You have to keep almost 2 miles off to get around Big Shoal, but the red nun buoy that marks it is your clue to the harbor. A course of 334° from the nun will carry you past Scammon Point toward Meade Island, but take care not to exceed that course or you'll be too close to the rocks of Big Shoal. When the harbor opens up between the island and the point, enter down the middle and anchor east of Meade Island. There might be a surge here from southwest winds and sea.

From here it's about 14 miles to the other feasible anchorage in Whitney Bay at the west end of the island. Give a wide berth to Horseshoe Reef, Holdridge Shoal and the reefs making out from Grafel island and Espanore Island, all unmarked. Beyond Espanore there is a red nun buoy due south of Arnold Island, one of the group sheltering Whitney Bay. Using this as a reference, you can head up toward Arnold Island, then pass between it and Bellevue into the harbor. There are quite a few cottages here, but a good spot to lie is in the cove beyond Sturgeon Island in 10 feet.

GEORGIAN BAY

Something for everyone is Georgian Bay's gift to the cruising boat, from the simple to the sophisticated, from the worldly to the wild. Three major routes bring maritime visitors—from the main basin of Lake Huron via Cape Hurd, from the Straits of Mackinac and St. Marys River via the North Channel, from Lake Ontario via the Trent-Severn Waterway. A few canoeists still come down the old French River route. There is, as well, a growing fleet in residence on the bay, as southern Ontarians discover how accessible it is by car and how ideally suited to summer cruising vacations. If you're coasting the bay, a harbor is never far away, and its 50-mile breadth can be crossed in a day under sail, although a full passage on the long 110-mile axis would require an overnight. But to cruise only the open waters of the Georgian is to taste merely the appetizer at a banquet. There is no part of the bay that isn't scenic, and each hamlet, town and city has its own special appeal.

The Bluff Coast

Charts 2235, 2245, 2271, 2274, 2282

The Niagara Escarpment attains its most dramatic profile in the long finger of land that creates the western flank of Georgian Bay—the Bruce Peninsula. The ragged slopes of the Bruce that face the open Lake Huron side give little hint of the majestic bluffs that march down the eastern face. Even as you round Cape Hurd that panorama is concealed from you. But you do get your first glimpse of the magical islands that give this part of the world its justifiable fame. They are strung across the 20 miles that separate the tip of the Bruce from Manitoulin Island to the northwest. Five channels wend among the shoals and banks between them, but only three are navigable by strangers. This is where the smooth coasts of the lower lakes give way to the complex ground of the upper.

The first from southward is Cape Hurd Channel, the most direct buoyed route, but it is unlighted. Devil Island Channel, although longer around, may be preferred in rough or thick weather, as there is a flashing green light buoy at the southwest end and a fixed white range with white and orange daymarks to guide you through at 040°. The next two northward, McGregor and North channels, are not buoyed and shouldn't be attempted by strangers. Main Channel, which leads to Georgian Bay north of Cove Island, the largest one in the passage, is used by the ships and ferries. It is buoyed where necessary, with big white Cove Island Light, flashing white and sounding a fog horn. This is the entrance you would use if coming across the top of Lake Huron from Manitoulin Island. Whichever channel you choose to transit, stay with it. Do not attempt to cross from one to another, as they are all separated by treacherous unmarked reefs. Further, there can be strong currents running through all of the channels, up to 5 or 6 knots after a strong wind shift.

Tobermory

Your immediate destination after passing through the channel of your choice is the village of Tobermory, perched at the tip of the Bruce Peninsula. Its two excellent natural harbors served as a lumber port from the 1860s to the 1920s, as a fishing port since the 1880s, and as a ferry port since 1930. Today the ferry business is its most important enterprise, as *Chi-Cheemaun*, the Big Canoe at 365 feet, carries hundreds of cars and tourists (and a few local residents) on four round trips daily to Manitoulin Island. Her huge dock is the first thing you see when you enter Tobermory outer harbor, with fixed red and green lights on the points that flank the wide entrance.

Big Tub opens to starboard immediately past Lighthouse Point, with the typical white hexagonal 19th-century lighthouse, surmounted by a red topknot. A few cottages are scattered along the wooded bluffs of the long and deep harbor. At friendly, informal **Big Tub Lodge** on the north side you can find alongside dockage on floats in 20 feet, with electricity if your lines are long enough, gas, diesel and pumpout. There are heads and showers in the campground associated with the lodge, and with reservations you can enjoy dinner in the dining room overlooking the harbor. In an east wind there is surge in the harbor. It's 1½ miles by road to village shopping from Big Tub, so if you have chores to do, you might prefer Tobermory's other harbor, Little Tub. It opens up to the south from the outer harbor.

Little Tub is virtually Main Street in this village of 400 people. The ferry keeps to the outer end, leaving the rest of the *U*-shaped harbor to the constant stream of small boat traffic. Tobermory is a jumping-off place not only for tourists in cars and on bicycles, but for hundreds of cruising boats that congregate from all points south and west on the Great Lakes. Here they pause to rest, replenish, and wait out the weather if necessary, before scattering to all parts of Georgian Bay and the North Channel. It is a customs port of entry and a place of much yachting camaraderie. The **Township Marina** occupies three sides of the harbor, with alongside dockage in 7 to 10 feet at fixed and floating docks, and all dockside services. The west side has the service dock and shower building, but the east side is a quieter location a bit away from "downtown" bustle.

The stores are concentrated around the harbor—grocery, Laundromat, snack and gift shops. Circle Arts Gallery shows and sells the work of some fine Canadian painters and crafts people. There are still commercial fishermen working out of Tobermory,

The Flowerpot.

and you can buy directly from one of them or at the packing house and store. Night life isn't much—the Ferry Dock Games Room or bingo in the town hall—but there are several places for dinner out. The Garage Restaurant and Tobermory Lodge offer courtesy car service, although neither is a very long walk.

Tobermory may look architecturally unprepossessing, but it has a few unique tourist attractions. The shoals, currents and tendency to fog that surround the tip of the Bruce Peninsula have brought many a vessel to disaster here. Fifty wrecks have been identified in the immediate vicinity, all lying beneath waters of remarkable clarity. This combination has made Tobermory the most popular center for wreck-hunting scuba diving on the Great Lakes. Several dive shops and charter boats provide the necessary equipment and access to the sites. To enhance the experience, Ontario established Five Fathom Provincial Park, its first underwater park, encompassing a 45-square-mile area. All divers are required to register at the Visitor's Center in town.

The federal government has also found the Tobermory area an appropriate setting for a park. Georgian Bay Islands National Park was established in 1929, with island units scattered across 90 miles of the bay. Its northern outpost is Flowerpot Island, 4 miles off Tobermory. A fascinating place geologically and botanically, Flowerpot is well worth a visit. But the island's small harbor entrance is foul, tricky and uncharted, although there are buoys, and the dock is often fully occupied by excursion and diving vessels. It's advisable to take one of the frequent and modestly priced excursion boats that leave from Little Tub. You can spend as much time on the island as you like and return on a later boat. Less than 2 miles of hiking on the self-guided trail will show you the island's attractions, but you may want to linger longer than a brisk walk will take, especially to admire from all angles the two large limestone stacks that give the island its name.

Not exactly a park, but a Tobermory bonus for the hiking enthusiast, is the Bruce Trail. Blazed in sections by members of several hiking clubs along its 430-mile length from Niagara Falls, Tobermory is the northern terminus. You can obtain in town a brief guide to the peninsula section of the trail, for an afternoon stroll or the full 23 hours of backpacking time to Dyer Bay along the most isolated and rugged segment of the entire trail.

Some Anchorages in Between

When you're ready to leave Tobermory you can head in several directions. North by northeast is the route to Killarney and the North Channel, with two island way stations to choose from if the day is late or the weather turns poor. Both lie about 20 miles from Tobermory off the Manitoulin coast. Club Island's harbor is an indentation on its east side that is easy to enter but open to east winds and surge. The beacon range shown on the inset enlargement on chart 2245 no longer exists. Keep the south point of the harbor entrance fairly close aboard as you enter and anchor immediately behind it, as the bottom shoals quickly to nothing.

A more sheltered anchorage, with better holding, can be found in Rattlesnake Harbour at the north end of Fitzwilliam Island. Approach this anchorage from the north, giving a good berth to West Flat. Don't try to shortcut through Wall Island Channel; it is only for those with local knowledge, as it is entirely unbuoyed. The inset enlargement on chart 2235 makes entry clear. The richly wooded cove is perfectly protected, but watch out for deadheads. Whether the harbor deserves its forbidding name is a matter of some dispute. Nevertheless, massasauga rattlers have been seen here, and their venom can be dangerous. Here, as any place where the brush is heavy, it's a good idea to wear boots when prowling the shore.

If you cruise due east from Tobermory, try to pick a clear day and leave with the sun fairly high. Beyond Dunks Point you can follow the steep-to shoreline closely and a good light will show up the colors of the limestone cliffs that form the north wall of the Bruce.

It's 36 miles around Cabot Head to the next village harbor, but halfway along a teardrop in the rock of Cabot Head itself offers perfect shelter. Wingfield Basin isn't easy to enter if the sea is running hard from north through east. But the channel, with controlling 15-foot depth, is buoyed and there is a fixed red range with white and orange daymarks at 180°. As the navigational aids tell you, this was once an important harbor of refuge for lake vessels. Now there are a few cottagers, woods and a country road to walk. The west side is preferred for anchorage in 12 feet or more.

Lion's Head

At Cabot Head the imposing cliffs and bluffs of the Bruce begin their stately march southward for 50 miles to Owen Sound. Each headland is named and its contours shaded in relief on the old-style chart 2282. While this chart shows landforms more vividly than newer ones, its soundings are recorded in fathoms to an obsolete chart datum. Three and one half feet must be deducted to reduce water depths to the present reference plane. The steep-to coast that the Indians feared, because it offered no landing for a canoe, enables present-day pleasure craft to cruise closely for a good look at the forest-topped ramparts of Niagaran limestone. Eighteen miles from Cabot Head the village of Lion's Head nestles beside a small bay under the bluff that resembles the king of beasts when viewed from southeast.

On the concrete breakwater/wharf that shelters the harbor there is an isophase red light with red and white daymark, but the marina building painted red is what you'll spot first from offshore. Sunken ruins extend about 50 feet off the end of the breakwater, marked by a red spar buoy. Tie-up is alongside at floating docks, with the usual services except diesel fuel. Water is available only at the service dock, however. Lion's Head, with about 450 people, is a rather sleepy village, with a few stores about half a mile from the waterfront. Its lumbering days long gone, and even farming dwindling, it is now mainly a cottage resort, with a sheltered sand beach in the harbor. There is also easy access to the Bruce Trail.

Melville Sound

About 10 miles from Lion's Head, Melville Sound opens up into three bays under the projection of Cape Croker. Each affords anchorage. The bottom of Hope Bay is the most scenic, but it is wide open to the northeast. Jackson Cove in the northwest corner of Hope Bay solves the problem when the wind blows from that direction. Around the next headland, the southwest corner of Sydney Bay is somewhat more protected than Hope, but not as scenic. The land is low here, with quite a few cottages and a busy campground on the southeast side. The most sheltered anchorage in Melville Sound is in the third bay, McGregor Harbour. A couple of spar buoys keep you in deep water until you round Harbour Point to set your hook in 12 feet or more. This is Indian reserve, and along the road leading from the harbor there are homes and a church. At one time there was a store and more of a village atmosphere, but there is still pleasant walking on country roads.

Wiarton

Around Cape Croker you might want to cruise a little farther offshore until you pass the big lighthouse with its fog horn and head down the long indentation of Colpoys Bay. The bay is enclosed by three islands. On the west side of the middle one, White Cloud, you can anchor in Kidd Bay, although the water is very deep to within 900 feet of shore, or dock at the government wharf with 10 feet alongside. This is a popular spot for local weekend boaters and may be crowded at times.

It's about a 10-mile run from White Cloud Island down the magnificent Colpoys Bay, lined on both sides with splendid cliffs and protected from the sea by the islands. Wiarton at the far end is a lively commercial and tourist center of about 2,000 people. Although once an important lumber port, mill town and railhead, there is no harbor chart. But there are two marinas behind the unlighted breakwater at the northwestern side of town. **Wiarton Yacht Basin** has 14-foot depths at its slips, with all dockside services (water at the service dock); travelift haulout

Wiarton, house.

up to 40 feet; engine, hull and rigging repairs; marine store and crew lounge. **Wiarton Outboard Marine**, catering to boats under 24 feet, has 5-foot depths at the slips, with gas, electricity, water, a launch ramp and small motor repairs. Wiarton's government wharf, at the very bottom of the bay, is marked by a fixed red light with red and white daymark. Although closer to downtown this is not a desirable place to dock. There is an unmarked shoal at the entrance to the basin behind it, and only 4 feet at the outer end of the wharf, shoaling quickly toward shore. Furthermore, it's usually occupied by local boats, although there is electricity and water at dockside, with heads and showers in the adjacent campground in Bluewater Park. The park also has tennis courts and a swimming pool.

Wiarton has good shopping for boat and crew, restaurants, a hospital, Laundromat, and a game room for entertainment. It's a pleasant town to walk in, with some fine old Victorian homes. On the first weekend in August the annual Village Fair in Bluewater Park features rides, games and displays of all kinds. Wiarton Coast Guard Radio, a familiar voice to all who cruise Georgian

Bay, is located at the airport a couple of miles out of town, where you can take a sightseeing flight in a small plane. There are taxis to get you there.

Owen Sound

Thirty cruising miles around the last arc of spectacular Bruce bluffs takes you to Owen Sound, the largest city on Georgian Bay, with 20,000 people. The sound itself, a long deep indentation similar to Colpoys Bay, runs 15 miles from Cape Commodore. The city is at the end of the bay on the banks of the Sydenham River, with a big grain elevator, a buoyed channel and a fixed green range with red and white daymarks at 195°. Beyond the elevator government wharves line both sides of the river. At one time Owen Sound was the major rail and ship terminus on Georgian Bay. Only a few ships call these days, however, and there is space for pleasure boats to tie up in the quiet harbor. The concrete wharf faces are quite high, and parts of them are rough, but on the east side there is a floating dock for small craft just before the first bridge. There are no services at these wharves, but the east one is adjacent to a supermarket and only a block or two from the heart of downtown.

For a more comfortable boat accommodation you will want to dock at **Owen Sound Marina** on the west edge of town. Its basin is approached through a buoyed channel from the flashing red light buoy at the beginning of the channel to the main harbor. With 6 feet at the slips, all dockside services, Laundromat, marine store, a lounge for boat crews and the Clog and Thistle Restaurant, this is an agreeable base from which to visit the attractions of Owen Sound. There is a bus service into town, and taxis are available. Engine, hull and rigging repairs can be arranged should you need them. The yacht clubs on either side of the marina do not have transient accommodations. Owen Sound is a customs port of entry and has a hospital.

Downtown there is convenient access to all the activities of a city that serves a large hinterland—a full line of shops (there are none near the marina), a Saturday morning farmer's market at City Hall, restaurants, cocktail lounges, movies and bowling. The streets along the river bank above the first bridge are especially attractive, and in this setting is Owen Sound's excellent Tom Thomson Memorial Gallery (376-1932). Named for one of Canada's most outstanding painters, who was born near Owen Sound, the museum features not only his work but a fine collection of other artists as well. The County of Grey and Owen Sound

Museum on the outskirts of town (376-3690) presents exhibits on both natural and human history. Between the marina and the downtown area Kelso Beach offers good swimming and sand castle building. In mid-August it is the scene of the Summerfolk Festival, three days of a wide variety of musical performances and arts and crafts displays.

The Beach Coast

Charts 2201,2202, 2218, 2221, 2222, 2223, 2239, 2282

Beyond Owen Sound the shorescape shifts gradually from the highlands of the Bruce first to undulating meadows and orchards, then to broad sand beaches around the the southern curve of the Georgian, Nottawasaga Bay, then to wooded capes. Towns and cities alternate with agricultural vistas. For Nottawasaga Bay there is no coastal chart; you must use the general chart of Georgian Bay, 2201, with soundings in fathoms. Also note that chart 2202 is a large-scale, small craft folio chart, which can be substituted for the harbor charts 2218 through 2223.

From the flashing green light marking Vail Point Shoal eastward for a few miles orange can buoys define the outer edge of a Department of Defense Air Firing Range. The limits of the range are now smaller than the area shown on the chart, and you can easily pass outside of it. It's a good idea to keep your radio on, however, to receive announcements of firing.

Meaford

Unlike the towns of the upper Bruce, those on the south shore found their destiny not in forests and sawmills, but in the railroad and trans-shipment of western grain. Today Meaford, with 4,400 people, is a commercial center for the apple-growing district surrounding it. Handsome brick mansions, an imposing city hall and the historical museum all speak of the town's prosperous past. Good shopping, restaurants, professional summer theater in the Opera House on the second floor of City Hall speak of a lively present.

The harbor at Meaford, 35 miles from Owen Sound, was developed from the dredged mouth of the Bighead River. Buoys mark the approach from the west side of the breakwaters. There is a flashing green light with red and white daymark on the end of the L-shaped north and east breakwater, and a fixed red light on a building just beyond the short west breakwater.

On the starboard side inside the west breakwater **Cliff Richardson Boats Limited** offers alongside dockage and slips in 12 feet, all dockside services, a 35-ton travelift, and not only full engine, hull and rigging repairs, but a custom built boat if you care to place an order. The museum is next door (538-4381). A few blocks' walk brings you to all downtown facilities. Beyond the marina concrete government wharves line both sides of the river, with alongside tie-up in 7 to 12 feet. The west side is more convenient to downtown, but has no services, while on the east side there are floating slips as well, with electricity and water. The Coast Guard Cutter *Spume* is based here. You'll enjoy a dinghy ride up the Bighead River.

Thornbury

Only 8 miles from Meaford, little Thornbury, with 1,400 people, is another apple-shipping center, but is turning more to tourism, with attractive shops, restaurants, tennis courts and a large new marina under gradual development. There is no harbor chart, but a fixed red range with white and orange daymarks guides you on a course of 212° to the buoyed channel between the breakwaters. A bit of a dog-leg leads into the basin, leased entirely by the **Thornbury Harbour Marina**, and dredged to 15 feet. All dockside services are offered, except diesel; dockage is in slips at the east end. All the commercial facilities of the village, including a Laundromat, are within a few blocks' walk.

Collingwood

One of the nicest cities on Georgian Bay, with an excellent harbor, Collingwood caters to tourists by land but, unfortunately, cares nothing for those who arrive by water. Its government dock has severe disadvantages, and its friendly yacht club is very short on space. But if you want to give it a try, this city of 11,000, 15 miles from Thornbury, has many attractions.

Dangerous ledges and shoals extend northwestward for several miles offshore, but two lighted ranges and a very well-buoyed channel lead past and through all the hazards into the artificial harbor enclosed by breakwaters. The first range, fixed green with white and orange daymarks at 150°, is needed only on the approach from the west. If you're coming from the east, you can head for a quick flashing red light buoy on the harbor approach and turn immediately on the fixed red range with white and orange daymarks at 180° that carries you in. All of this elaborate buoyage leads to the city's major enterprise, Collingwood Shipyards. Collingwood may have begun life as a railroad town, but shipbuilding has carried its name around the lakes on the long freighters that are built, rebuilt and repaired here, and around the world in the naval vessels of World War I and II.

Before you reach the shipyard a turn to port takes you to the government dock extending at right angles from the long causeway that forms the east breakwater. This is a concrete structure, obviously built for small ships, with big bollards and timbers across its face. It is usually occupied by fishing tugs and local boats on its more protected south face, while the north face suffers from bad surging in west and northwest winds. There are no services. The causeway/breakwater leads to a big grain elevator, and nestled under that is the **Collingwood Yacht Club**. Its moorings and slips, with 6 to 10 feet of water, are well protected and have all dockside services except fuel, but the club may not have space for a transient boat. The city is a customs port of entry.

When you do lay over at Collingwood there is plenty to do ashore. Downtown shops are half to three quarters of a mile from the dock. On the way you pass the Collingwood Historical Museum in the old railroad station. Along Hurontario Street and those adjacent you'll find excellent shopping of all kinds, Laundromat, restaurants, a bowling alley and a movie theater. For superior dining the Spike and Spoon in an elegant Victorian mansion is worth the long walk or cab ride; reservations are necessary.

Most of the major recreational attractions of Collingwood are a little too far for walking comfort. You might want to rent a car for a day or so to reach them. Spectator activities range from The Kaufman House displays of furniture in 18 room settings at High and Harbour streets (445-6000) to the renowned Blue Mountain Pottery on Blue Mountain Road (445-3000), where you can observe craftsmen at work and buy their wares, and the Candy Factory across the street, where you can watch confections made in the old way on antique equipment. For more active recreation, with special appeal for children, there are two kinds of mountainside slide rides—one on a bobsled, the other in a stream of water—and a chair lift to get to them, 4 miles out of town on Blue Mountain Road. Blue Mountain is actually a long ridge of the Niagara Escarpment that reaches its greatest height here, 1,775 feet, where it comes close to the bay before swinging west to the Bruce. Nearby Scenic Caves (445-2828) can be explored on a trail that descends, twists and ascends among the escarpment's limestone crags. On the opposite, east, edge of town are the Blue Mountain Go-Kart track, touch and pet park for the little ones and mini-golf course.

Wasaga Beach

The fun continues, or perhaps begins, at Wasaga Beach, 10 miles east of Collingwood. In many ways the archetype of resort towns, Wasaga Beach lies along the banks of the Nottawasaga River that parallels Georgian Bay for 4 miles. Its 9 miles of magnificent hard-packed sand and gently shelving swimming waters make it a natural for the congregation of cottages, resorts, motels and amusements that expand the town of 4,600 people to many times that number in summer. The town and the river are available comfortably only to smaller cruising boats of shallow draft, however. There is no harbor chart, but an iso-phase white light with red and white daymark identifies the river entrance, with 6 feet over the bar. The light is pretty small, so you must coast fairly close to find it. **Sturgeon Point Marina** just inside the entrance has short slips with 7 feet of depth, gas, ice, and a launch ramp. There are one or two small boat marinas in town above the low fixed bridge.

If your boat can meet the conditions of this harbor, and you find crowds, noise and the zipping around of outboards exhilar-ating, Wasaga Beach is a fun place to visit. The beach is just a dinghy push across the way. Downtown is about a mile from the marina (taxis available, or take the dinghy) with shops, restau-rants, night clubs, an amusement park, big slide, and miniature golf. Close to the marina is the Wasaga Fishing and Game Farm, with a petting zoo for children. A cab ride away on the outskirts of town, Waterworld is a theme park with four slides, a wading pool, playground and bumper boats.

But Wasaga Beach wasn't always fun and games. This part of Georgian Bay is also its most historic—Huronia, where French missionaries came in 1615 to live among the Huron Indians, convert them, and teach them modern agriculture; where in 1649 the fierce Iroquois extirpated from the land Indian and Frenchman alike; where the threads of civilization were not picked up again until 1814 when war between two English nations necessitated a secret place for gunboats. And the most secret of available hiding places was 4 miles up the Nottawasaga

Collingwood, Scenic Caves.

River. There the little schooner, *Nancy,* met her destiny. Her story is dramatically retold in sound and light in the theater built in the shape of her sails at the Museum of the Upper Lakes (526-7838). It sits on an island in the river, created by the *Nancy* herself as her neglected hulk dammed the silt. Now her recovered hull is preserved and displayed, along with many other artifacts of maritime history. Wasaga Beach is worth a stop just for this fascinating museum.

At Wasaga Beach the coastline turns sharply north from the southern extremity of Georgian Bay. The foreshore is almost continuous sand beach, lined with numerous summer colonies, but the land back of it begins to rise again to the hills that define the capes northeast of Nottawasaga Bay. At Gridley Point you are officially out of Nottawasaga Bay and also back on a larger scale coastal chart. Three substantial islands, with beautiful wooded bluffs, lie off this shore—Christian, Beckwith and Hope, all Indian reserves. The channel between Christian Island and the mainland carries a least depth of 15 feet and is marked by spar buoys. The island is served by a ferry boat from Cedar Point on the mainland, and there are government docks in both places if you need shelter during this passage. There are no services at either, but depths run 9 to 12 feet, and you might find space in an emergency, provided you keep out of the ferry's way.

Penetanguishene

Penetang, as the locals abbreviate the long Indian name meaning "place of rolling sands," is 42 miles from Wasaga Beach and was the next stop in the march of history. Here, after the episode of the *Nancy*, the British Government established a naval and military base. Its importance and size grew after 1828, when Drummond Island in St. Marys River was awarded to the United States in the final boundary settlement\and the British garrison moved from there to here. But by this time the wheels of international diplomacy had been set in motion to assure peace and ultimate disarmament on the lakes, and the post never saw an engagement. It was finally abandoned in 1856 but has now been meticulously restored and reconstructed from archaeological evidence for the edification and entertainment of sightseeing visitors. The Historic Naval and Military Establishment, as it is called (526-7838), has dockage for waterborne visitors with less than four-foot draft, or you can visit by taxi from one of the marinas in the harbor.

As you follow the coast northeastward past the triumvirate of big islands, hillside farms present a backdrop to the waterfront cottages. And you will see on the horizon the somber shape of the Giant's Tomb, although that representation is more obvious from a northwesterly approach. Legend tells that the giant Kitchikewana, disappointed in love, picked up great handfuls of mainland earth and flung them in wrath into the bay to create the Thirty Thousand Islands. Then, exhausted and lonely, he lay down to die, entombed forever on his isolated island. Past this sad, but important, landmark, Georgian Bay begins to take on a different character again. The southern shores remain relatively smooth, but shoals and islands begin to clutter the offshore waters, and navigation requires careful attention to ranges and buoyed channels. Of these there are many, all designed to guide ships bringing western grain to the cluster of ports in the southeast corner of the bay.

The ranges are just as useful to pleasure craft and are made perfectly clear on chart 2239. Whether or not you use them, make sure to follow the buoys carefully around Pinery Point on the northwestern approach or Watson Point on the southeastern approach to Penetanguishene. From the 2½-mile-long Outer Harbour, the 3-mile-long Penetang (inner) Harbour makes an acute turn around Asylum Point. A flashing white light on the point, with red and white daymark, plus a set of spar buoys in the water, guide you through the narrows between Asylum and Michaud points. The modern Ontario Hospital stands conspicuous on the bluff above the point with the old-fashioned name, which *Sailing Directions* is endeavoring to change to Dalton Point, although the charts still say Asylum. Close under it is the Naval and Military Establishment. And on Michaud Point, opposite, is one of the many monuments on this side of Georgian Bay erected to Champlain's 1615 visit.

Continuing down the harbor, strategically placed buoys and a fixed red range with white and orange daymarks at 186° guides your passage. At Tannery Point on the eastern shore you come to the first of Penetang's marinas. **Dutchman's Cove** has dockage alongside and in slips with 10 feet; all dockside services except fuel; a 30-ton travelift; hull, engine and rigging repairs; mast-stepping for boats that transit the Trent-Severn Waterway; and a marine store. **Bay Moorings**, just beyond, is Penetang's most elaborate facility, with 16-foot depths at the slips; all dockside services, including Laundromat; a travelift up to 50 feet; hull and engine repairs; mast-stepping; marine store; launch ramp; swimming pool; tennis court; restaurant and bar. Both of these marinas are a couple of miles out of town; taxis are available, but not buses.

The **Government Dock** at the foot of Main Street is the most convenient to downtown shopping and restaurants. It offers both slips and alongside dockage in 10 to 20 feet, launch ramp, electricity, water, pumpout, heads and showers. At the foot of the harbor a buoyed channel leads to **Bay's End Marina**, with 9-foot depths at the slips and all dockside services except fuel. Nearby **Hindson Marine** serves mainly powerboats and small sailboats at slips with 9 feet, gas and a launch ramp. Anchorage in the South Basin at the end of the harbor is perfectly protected but is a bit weedy.

The pleasant town of 5,500 people has convenient shopping, Laundromat, hospital, restaurants and movie theater clustered around Main Street ascending the hill from the government dock. The Centennial Museum downtown is a modest one, depicting the town's history. The major tourist attraction is the Naval and Military Establishment. On the way to it, and not far from the Tannery Point marinas, is the Church of Saint James-on-the-Lines. This was the garrison church, built in 1834, still in use. It has some unusual features, such as the variation in pews, each of which was constructed by a different soldier, an aisle wide enough for the men to march in four abreast, and a poignant story behind the double memorial tablet with one half blank. It's worth a visit.

Midland

Penetang Harbour and Midland Bay to the east are separated by a high rounded cape, fringed in part with summer cottages. Ten miles port-to-port, Midland, in the southwest corner, is Georgian Bay's second largest city with 12,000 people. The town got a later start than most in the area, originating in 1872 with the arrival of the railroad. But shipping and shipbuilding under early entrepreneurs guaranteed its prosperity long after the decline of lumbering, in which it also shared. Today Midland is still important as a grain port, where the produce of Canada's prairie breadbasket is trans-shipped from water to rail for the nourishment of the eastern provinces. It is, of course, a customs port of entry.

Its two big grain elevators are conspicuous on the approach, but the downtown waterfront, close to the city's excellent shopping district, is now the province of the pleasure boat. The **Government Dock** has both alongside tie-up and slips, with 18 feet or more, the usual dockside services except fuel and ice, and a launch ramp. **Downer's Yacht Haven**, adjacent on the north, has 25 feet at its slips, gas, diesel, ice, pumpout, travelift up to 50 feet, engine and hull repairs and a launch ramp. Across the harbor in a suburban location, **Sunnyside Marina** caters mainly to powerboats, with 12 feet at the slips, a launch ramp, electricity, water, ice, pumpout and gas.

In addition to its shops, hospital, Laundromat, restaurants and movies, downtown Midland has an interesting historic complex in Little Lake Park on King Street, half a mile from the dock. But the *pièce de résistance* in all Huronia lies a few miles east of town. You can take a taxi from here or get closer by boat.

In the southeastern corner of Midland Bay the private grain port of Tiffin is identified by its elevator. Beyond it is the buoyed entrance to the Wye River. If you draw less than 3 feet, you can follow the placid, willow-draped stream to the place where the white man's history dawned on the Great Lakes. The Mission of Sainte Marie Among the Hurons was established by the Jesuits

Ste. Marie Among the Hurons.

in 1639. A self-sufficient fortified village, which at its zenith housed 66 missionary priests, lay brothers, and servants, it lasted a mere 10 years before the onslaught of the Iroquois destroyed the work and obliterated the Huron nation. As you near the place, the graceful twin spires of the Martyrs' Shrine remind you of the gentle Frenchmen whose lives were sacrificed in torture. For 315 years the ruin lay neglected. Now Ste. Marie exists again, painstakingly reconstructed from archaeological scholarship, using only 17th-century tools and materials. It is, undoubtedly, one of the finest historic expositions on the continent.

On the starboard side, just before the highway bridge, there is a little park with excellent finger docks, but no services. From there you can take a footpath across the river to Ste. Marie. Upon arrival, be sure to attend the film shown in the visitor's center before you do anything else. It's an important overture to your visit. Across the road the Shrine is also open to the public.

Next door to Ste. Marie a totally different kind of opportunity awaits you. The Wye Marsh Wildlife Centre of the Canadian Wildlife Service preserves 2,500 acres of marsh and forest for the visitor who would learn about this natural environment. In addition to programs of various kinds there are self guiding trails. The center's special features include a boardwalk that extends far into the midst of the marsh and an underwater viewing room where you can observe the variety of life forms that inhabit a quiet pond. Access is from the same parking lot as serves Ste. Marie.

If you're cruising in a deep draft boat, you won't be able to take the lovely Wye River approach to this group of institutions. The river and the docks carry 5-foot depths, but the entrance is reported to have silted to 3 feet. There is an alternative, however. A short distance north of the river mouth a dredged canal leads to the **Wye Heritage Marina**. The largest facility on Georgian Bay has up to 9 feet at the slips; all dockside services; a 35-ton travelift; full engine, hull and rigging repairs; a launch ramp; marine and convenience store and a crew lounge. Courtesy transportation can be arranged for downtown Midland shopping and perhaps for a visit to Ste. Marie. Or you can simply go up the Wye by dinghy.

Severn Sound

The southeasternmost corner of Georgian Bay, designated Severn Sound, is its least scenic and, for the cruising boat, its least interesting area. The land around Hog and Sturgeon bays is low and tends to be swampy and shoaly. There is a small boat marina at Port McNicoll on the west side of Hog Bay, once an important railhead but now a residential suburb of Midland. Victoria Harbour on the east side is a resort community with two government docks that have electricity, and a waterfront motel. Sturgeon Bay and its eastern arm, Matchedash Bay, are foul with rocks and shoals, strictly for runabouts with local knowledge.

The only reason for a cruising boat to venture into this part of Georgian Bay is for access to or egress from the Trent-Severn Waterway at Port Severn. Hundreds come this way every summer. Two channels lead to Port Severn from the open bay. Both thread their way among rocky shoals and require very cautious piloting. But they are dredged to 6 feet, are well buoyed, and the tracks are pecked out with precision on large-scale chart 2202.

The Island Coast
Charts 2202, 2203, 2204, 2224, 2225, 2226, 2239, 2243, 2244, 2245, 2284, 2289

Where the coast of Georgian Bay turns northward a cruising adventure begins that is unparalleled anywhere else. The long eastern shore is a world apart—a dazzling array of islands, inlets, coves and bays, laced by complex waterways. Granite reigns on this coast, with pine as its handmaiden. The land and waterscape grow wilder, more austere and more alluring to those who love wilderness as one proceeds northwest for 125 miles toward the white Killarney Mountains that emerge on the distant horizon. The spectacular array of islands come in all shapes, sizes and quantities of verdure. No great heights are achieved by any of them, and from offshore the coast looks deceptively featureless. It is the intricacy of the archipelagoes, the fantastic shapes and colors of the rocks, the symbiosis of rock, pine, sea and wind that weave a spell of enchantment. But this most fascinating part of the Georgian—perhaps of all the Great Lakes—demands a special kind of piloting and navigation from all who might discover its secrets.

The band of offshore islands and shoals ranges from 2 to 10 miles wide, and for every rock that shows above the water there are perhaps 10,000 below. Depths can change from 40 feet to 0 feet in less than a boat length—and frequently do. With so many thousands of potential hazards it isn't feasible for more than a fraction to be marked by buoys. Even where they rise above the surface, when should a rock be called an island? Thirty Thousand is an understatement of gross proportions—100,000 would be more like it. Because of the complexity of this coast, large parts of it have never been sounded, and the charts are replete with empty blue space. Even where soundings have been taken with the most modern equipment, newly discovered rocks introduce themselves to passing propellers every year.

It would seem at first glance that no rational path could be found through the labyrinth. Yet aerial photography some 25 years ago revealed a natural passage behind the offlying band of rocks and shoals that runs virtually the entire length of the coast. The deep water inlets that cross it have been used by generations of small ship captains to reach the ports of the North Shore, as this eastern coast is locally known because it was originally north of the settlements. And parts of the inside passage have been used to reach resorts and summer cottages for 80 years or more. But modern surveys and charts for the full Small Craft Route have been available for only 20. The small craft folios—charts 2202, 2203 and 2204—display an immense amount of detail in large scale and trace a red track line along the twisting 185-mile passage that has been dredged and blasted, where necessary, to a controlling depth of 6 feet.

Highly identifiable port and starboard daybeacons (white

squares with black centers and red triangles bordered in white, respectively) are placed at most major turns and along some of the longer stretches of straightaway. The small red and black spars placed in the water are often harder to see, especially if the sea is at all choppy. Buoyage along the Small Craft Route is directed upstream from south to north. Proceeding from Port Severn to Killarney, red spars and triangular beacons are left to starboard. On the main shipping tracks leading from the open bay, however, the conventional approach from seaward is used. Where the two tracks intersect the shipping route takes precedence and the small craft buoyage may be temporarily reversed. There are few lighted aids to navigation. Most of those are at major inlets and ports, with a few at critical turns on the track. Prudent mariners don't move after dark here. To supplement the buoyage the coast is liberally sprinkled with unlighted ranges of various sizes, mostly red and white, found sometimes in conjunction with other aids, sometimes doing the job alone. All are plotted on the small craft charts, although sometimes hard to read there, especially for those of us who are getting a bit farsighted. Similarly, the port-hand daybeacons don't show up well on the charts, although they're brilliant on the water.

Despite all this cartographic assistance, it is absolutely essential when piloting the Small Craft Route to identify and count all the islands as you pass them, as well as the beacons and buoys. If you lose your place on the chart or the water you might make a disastrous wrong turn. In effect, one pilots with a finger on the chart tracing the course and each of its marks, spotting the next aid well before arrival. In the tight places the track must be followed precisely. That is, the arcs and curves shown between buoys on the chart should be scribed that way by the boat's wake. Don't take any shortcuts. It is usually helpful to pilot these waters in pairs—one person on the helm, the other following the chart and watching through the binoculars to spot the next beacons or buoys. It is doubtless unnecessary to add that in threading the inside passage the watchword is *slow*.

Not all of the small craft track is a squeak between rocks behind sheltering islands. There are numerous stretches on the "outside," and here an additional hazard can crop up. A hard-running sea on this generally lee shore will obscure rocks, shoals and buoys with spray, to make eyeball piloting a nightmare if not impossible. In high winds and seas it's best to stay in port. On the other hand, in fine weather these outside runs can give sailors a chance to shake out the canvas for a while. On the twisting, narrow parts of the route sailing is rarely feasible.

Lake level fluctuations are particularly important when navigating this coast. Rocks are revealed or concealed according to the height of the water above, at, or below chart datum. Anchorages that are feasible for your draft one year may not be the next. Canadian Coast Guard Radio reports the current mean water level on the continuous weather broadcast, so you can adjust your depth readings to conform.

Despite this description of the hazards and intricacies of cruising the Thirty Thousand Islands, you should not be intimidated. It requires no esoteric knowledge or skill, merely care and patience. You will find yourself adjusting to a different time scale, where a slow 15 to 20 miles a day is a good passage, in contrast to your customary speed and coverage. Your reward is scenic splendor and the repose of a hidden anchorage at nightfall. Anchorage is the way of harbor life on the island coast. There is one city, two or three hamlets, a couple of settlements, and a handful of marinas between Midland and Killarney. But there are hundreds of sheltered coves in which to drop your hook. I can direct you in these pages to only a few. Nor would I tell you more if I had space, because the joy of discovering your own special hideaway is another of the rewards of cruising the islands.

Try to enter an anchorage with the sun at your back, or at least beyond its zenith, and a lookout posted on the bow. Water clarity ranges from crystal clear to darkly opaque, but color changes and submerged rocks cannot be observed when the sun's glare intrudes. In many of the anchorages you will find solitude, with no other sign of human intrusion. In others you may find one or more cottages. Regrettably, there is a growing antagonism among cottagers toward cruising boats. We can dispel much of it if we all take care not to plunk our anchors down directly in someone's front yard, not to go ashore on private property, not to leave trash where we do find an uninhabited campsite, and, above all, not to play radios and raise voices into the evening and nighttime quiet, when sound travels much farther and louder than during the day. The same trash and noise courtesies apply, of course, to uninhabited anchorages shared with other boats. Uninhabited anchorages are definitely preferred, in my view, because boaters suffer some inconveniences at the hand of cottagers—primarily their fast-zipping outboards that insist on passing as close as possible to throw the anchored boat into wild gyrations from their wakes. For this reason the descriptions that follow include the presence or absence of cottages.

There are several ways to cruise this part of the Georgian

coast. You can follow the inside track from end to end for intimate acquaintance. You can run offshore to one or more of the five harbors with navigation aids that make them approachable from open water: Parry Sound, Pointe-au-Baril, Byng Inlet, Key Harbour and Killarney. Or, for changes in pace, you can combine the two, alternating inside and outside passages, although in some instances it's a long haul to and from the clear water offshore. When you do go offshore, remember that the indentations, islands and rocks of this low coast are almost impossible to distinguish at any distance; you're committed to the next major inlet.

Whichever way you elect to cruise, start with clean clothes and a well-stocked galley. The only supermarket and Laundromat between Midland and Killarney are at Parry Sound; in between are a few small grocery stores, waters full of fish and shores bursting with blueberries. North of Parry Sound there are places to dine out informally, but no commercial amusements. The blessings of this coast are natural; the only entertainment is what you make of it.

To describe in detail the course of the Small Craft Route would be to reproduce the official *Sailing Directions*, which you should have at hand as you go. Rather, the following pages offer an overview of definable sections of the waterway, present directions for entering a selection of anchorages, describe the settlements and their facilities at the level of detail in preceding pages and explain the routes of access from offshore.

Honey Harbour

The Small Craft Route begins officially at Port Severn, where its character becomes immediately apparent at the narrow Potato Island Channel, with two 90-degree turns; it is enlarged on chart 2202. If you're coming from Midland, however, you'll enter at the red and green spar on Hill Bank, Mile 5. As the passage behind Quarry Island is a bit squeaky you could, alternatively, pass along the buoyed channel between Present and Beausoleil islands to enter the track at Turning Rock, Mile 10, marked by a flashing white light. This is also the most direct route from Penetanguishene. Boats coming from Nottawasaga Bay and the Bruce Peninsula enter at Mile 17, via the south tip of Giants Tomb Island. From there a white and orange beacon range on a course of 053° leads to the Whalesback Channel and junction with the Small Craft Route at Kindersley Island Light, flashing white with red and black daymark. Except for the route from Port Severn, all of these must be navigated on coastal chart 2239 as the small craft chart 2202 shows only their termini.

Honey Harbour is the center of a bustling and rather thickly settled resort community at Mile 12 on the Small Craft Route. The waterway around it throbs with outboard runabouts. The government dock with 10-foot depths, but no services, is right on the track, next door to the attractive Delawana Inn. Reputedly the largest resort hotel in Ontario, this is a good place for dinner, with reservations required. The numerous marinas in and around Honey Harbour all cater to the cottagers' small boats, but most of them sell gas, and Village Marina, with 6-foot depths, has a pumpout. The Town Center, a short walk from the government dock, is a general store-cum-post office-cum-snack bar. Honey Harbour's other establishment is the headquarters of the Georgian Bay Islands National Park, where you can obtain helpful maps and literature. Its largest unit, Beausoleil Island, is just a short channel across the way from Honey Harbour, but only a boat with 3-foot draft can safely pass through Big Dog Channel to get there directly.

Cruising boats can reach Beausoleil via a couple of secondary tracks, however, pecked out in dashed lines on charts 2239 and 2202. The easier one leads from the red and white Mo(A) on the track from Penetang northward between Roberts and Beausoleil islands to Beausoleil Bay. The island's main dock is at Cedar Spring on the east shore near the south end, with 5 to 12 feet of depth. This is where the interpretive center is located, with interesting naturalist programs. The island is laced with hiking trails, and there are three docking areas designated for the use of cruising boats in addition to Cedar Spring—Ojibway Bay in the northwest corner of Beausoleil Bay with 7 feet, Panhawke Dock on Frying Pan Bay on the north side of the island just off the main small craft track, and Lost Bay with 4 feet on the northwest side of the island, reached from a secondary track near Pinery Point north of Penetang. There are no services at any of them. In addition, there are numerous picnic site docks around the island, but cruising boats are requested to anchor off if they want to spend the night.

The park can be as busy as the village, but you can find quietude a few miles farther on up the secondary track of Musquash Channel past Mile 16. Make the turn at Penetang Rock, with its highly visible red beacon. There are a number of anchorages to choose from here and virtually no hazards in reaching any of them. Those indenting Bone Island are free of cottages, as there are two units of the park here, shaded brown

Among the Thirty Thousand Islands.

on the chart. Any of these coves affords an introduction to the haunting natural beauty that intensifies as you move north.

Continuing on your way, every island and inlet will beckon you to linger. On a short, secondary track from Mile 26 is an exquisite little passage known as Indian Harbour. Although there is considerable boat traffic through, it is a lovely spot to anchor. Look for the Indian on the rock at the north entrance. At Mile 35 Twelve Mile Bay opens to starboard, with another unit of the national park and a nice anchorage at its eastern end, about a mile and a half up the bay. Hug the mainland shore as you enter from eastward, to avoid the rocky shoal reaching off the end of the park peninsula.

Sans Souci

On Fryingpan Island at Mile 40 there is a small center of civilization known as Sans Souci. Not a village, it has rather a trading post atmosphere and serves the cottagers scattered among the surrounding islands. For the cruising boat it has several offerings. In Fryingpan Harbour Martin's Sans Souci Marina has gas, pumpout, a 6-ton hoist and repairs, but no transient dockage. There is also on the premises a gift shop and a grocery store that sells produce and frozen meat and serves as a post office. On the east shore of Fryingpan Island, north of

Sans Souci, Henry's Fish Restaurant.

Barrel Point Light, there is a **government wharf** with floating docks on the south side of it for alongside tie-up in 20 feet with electric power. The floating docks on the north side of the wharf belong to **Midway Boat Haven and Restaurant**. Overnight dockage is also available here in 20 feet, with electricity, water, heads and showers; the restaurant serves three meals. Perhaps 400 yards north there is another set of floating slips at **Henry's Fish Restaurant**. These, too, are available for overnight dockage in 20 feet, with electricity, water, heads and showers, or for tie-up for a delicious and generous lunch or dinner freshly caught by the proprietor himself.

After you've taken care of business at Martin's and eaten your fill at one of the restaurants, head eastward along one of the secondary tracks for a selection of anchorages that could keep you right here all summer. Closer to the main track the islands have one or more cottages on them, but as you proceed they thin out, leaving whole islands and big stretches of mainland to the lush forest and the rocky foundations it clothes. The more southerly track gets a bit tricky around Coltman and Carlotta islands, where there are no navigational aids, but if you follow it to the end in Moon Bay, 5 miles from Sans Souci, you can take your choice of places to drop the hook. If you're the explorer type, you can continue on through Captain Allan Strait to the uncharted, but mostly deep, soundings of Woods Bay. From there you have the whole of beautiful Moon River and its wide bays to dinghy around in. There are clusters of cottages in some parts of it, but be sure to follow the river upstream for about 5 miles from Woods Bay to the glittering multilevel cascade of Moon River Falls.

The more northerly secondary track from Sans Souci divides at Pilgrim's Rest Point on Winett Island. You will notice here a dock, picnic table, grill and trash barrel. This is one of some 16 marine picnic sites provided by the Ontario government along this stretch of Georgian Bay. Overnight docking is prohibited, but they are delightful spots for a cookout and a swim. The starboard track from Pilgrim's Rest follows deep water around the north and east sides of Moon Island, with enticing uninhabited coves all along the way. At Burgess Point you can turn northeast again to Port Rawson Bay and a whole collection of additional anchorages. Along the left fork from Pilgrim's Rest there is a smaller selection, but a choice one. Anywhere you go in this entire maze you'll find vistas to catch your breath, rocks to climb and forests to prowl. And for a bonus there is yet another secondary track from Mile 42 past Sans Souci that leads to Spider Bay, with yet another assortment of arms and coves.

Parry Sound

About a third of the way north along the island coast of Georgian Bay there is a respite from the intricacies of the archipelago. Almost landlocked Parry Sound is 36 square miles of deep open water, with a long deep water passage leading to it across the maze. Sequestered within the recesses of the sound is the city that bears its name, where ships have been calling for 125 years. This is where you, too, can make your first approach north of Beausoleil Island from offshore to the inside track. From the Midland/Penetanguishene area, you pass along the southwest side of Giants Tomb and head for the big flashing white light on Hope Island, distinguished by its wooded height against the horizon. Your departure is actually from the flashing red light buoy marking Lottie Wolf Rock. Head first for the Western Islands Light, but leave the islands well to starboard as you reshape your course for the flashing green light buoy on Seguin Bank, 32 miles from Lottie Wolf Rock. From there it's 10 well-buoyed miles at 070° on the fixed green Snug Harbour Range, with brilliant red, white and black daymark, to the Small Craft Route. But it's another 15 miles on the ship channel to the city of Parry Sound.

Moon River Falls.

The Small Craft Route from the south offers two approaches to the city and its sound. The shorter, direct, 13-mile route is via South Channel, which begins at Turning Island, Mile 44, where the main track divides into two main tracks. There are a couple of tight passes, such as Devils Elbow and Seven Mile Narrows, but they are well buoyed and readily negotiated at low speed. There are also several beautiful bays for anchorage, such as Kineras, Five Mile and Menominee. Five Mile Bay has very deep water, but there are a few coves where your hook can find bottom with sufficient swinging room. As you get closer to the city the homes and cottages thicken up and numerous marinas begin to appear, all serving the small boats of the cottagers. At Rose Point the swing bridge, with 15 feet of clearance, connects Parry Island to the mainland. Three long blasts will call the tender, but it's a slow bridge and you should wait until it's fully open before proceeding. On the other side you're just about in the harbor. The picturesque high railroad trestle across the Seguin River beckons you to the dock.

Parry Sound, like the towns on the Bruce, got its start in lumbering and sawmilling, but with its superb natural harbor it grew into the major supply depot for the entire eastern shore and its hinterland. Although most goods come in by rail and truck now, the city still plays that role. Its bustling downtown streets make it seem more populous than 6,000 people. This is the place to stock up and do your laundry if you're planning to explore the farther reaches of the wild North Shore. Supermarket, natural food store, two bakeries, delicatessen, butcher shop, Laundromat, the usual variety of downtown shops and commercial services, restaurants, cocktail lounges and movies are all within easy walk of the waterfront. And the hospital is on the way if you need medical service. This is also the only place on this coast with public transportation for crew changes— middle of the night passenger rail service or daytime inter-city buses. It is also a customs port of entry.

Unfortunately, Parry Sound's marine facilities don't match its commercial opportunities. The concrete government dock was built for ships but is now used exclusively by pleasure boats, including the *Island Queen V* excursion vessel. Alongside berthing on the east side suffers an almost constant wash from outboard runabouts running in and out of the marinas that cater to them along the Seguin River front just beyond the wharf. The west face of the dock is a little more protected and has a float to tie to. There are also some finger slips on that side, but they are mostly occupied by local boats. Nor is the dockage sufficient to meet the demand for it in high season. Rafting is often required. Electricity, water, pumpout and heads are available at the government dock. Ice is obtained at a store across the street.

Parry Sound Marina, with dockage for small boats and gas on both sides of the river, also has diesel fuel and a marine store on the east bank. It can sometimes accommodate a cruising boat for overnight dockage there, at floating slips in 20 feet, and has plans to expand into a full scale, full service marina. It can also haul out by trailer up to 44 feet and offers engine and hull repairs. **Sound Boat Works** is a full service facility on the southeast side of the harbor, about 2 miles by road from downtown. It has very little transient dockage but offers electricity, gas, diesel, pumpout, hoist and railway haulout up to 15 tons, hull and engine repairs.

A stop in Parry Sound has more to offer than fuel, groceries and Laundromat. In fact, you might want to plan your visit to coincide with the Festival of the Sound that takes place the last week in July and the first week in August. Concert pianist Anton Kuerti, who summers in his cottage on the bay, conceived the idea and has brought artists of world renown to the festival, begun in 1980. A varied offering of classical music, jazz, children's programming, cruise concerts on the *Island Queen*, musical potlatches, master classes and who knows what next

Parry Sound, water fountain for man and friend.

year make this an outstanding series. Most of the concerts take place in the high school auditorium, a longish walk from the dock, but there are special taxi fares for concert goers. For advance information and tickets, write to Festival of the Sound, PO Box 750, Parry Sound, Ontario P2A 2Z1, or call 705-746-2410.

In a different entertainment vein, semiprofessional Rainbow Theatre was launched in 1982 and presents a delightful summer-long series of plays at St. Peter's Hall on Church Street, a shorter walk than the high school. Its address is Box 282, Parry Sound, ON P2A 2X4, telephone 705-746-5181. In addition to the performing arts a number of painters and crafts people work, display and sell in studios and at exhibits in Parry Sound. And the Local Architectural Conservation Advisory Committee has printed a historic walking tour of the town.

For before concert or theater dining out the Harbour Light Restaurant serves good food, specializing in schnitzel, and Fish Haven offers excellent seafood in great variety, with a good wine list. Both are on James Street. After the theater the Creamery, over the bridge on Seguin Street, is a cheerful ice cream parlor.

When you've completed your business and entertainment in town you will strike out across Parry Sound on your way northward. The scenery around the sound takes on a softer aspect, as trees cover the rock more generously than on the outer shores and islands, and the shores are higher in elevation.

For sailors who have felt confined by narrow channels there's almost always a good breeze on the sound. And it has its share of lovely anchorages, especially along the north shore—in uninhabited Sawdust Bay behind Huckleberry Island; in Carling, Loon, Collins and Blind bays, with some cottages; and in the cove on the north side of Mowat Island. Depot Harbour on Parry Island was once an ore-loading center. Now there is only the ghostly remains of the big conveyor, a few cottages and Aquacage Fisheries at the entrance, a lake trout raising enterprise that may have a choice one to sell you. You can anchor either in Depot Harbour itself (there are government wharves in deteriorating condition) or in one of the coves just southwest of it behind Cadotte Point.

If back at Turning Island you veer to port, you will follow the other main track around the outside of large Parry Island, the island that effectively encloses the sound. This is still an inside route, however, threading among Parry Island's small satellites along the beautiful Long Sault Channel to Waubuno Channel that, in turn, links up with the main ship channel about 11 miles from Turning Island. The distance to the city this way is 21 miles, but if you aren't planning to stop in town, this is the more attractive way to continue on the Small Craft Route. Cottages are scattered among the islands here, too, but more thinly than elsewhere and Parry Island, being Indian reserve, is wild. You can find secluded anchorage behind Kumfort Island in Hulett Bay, reached on a course of 092° from the beacon on Iron Rock at Mile 50. Hale Bay, indenting the northeast shore of Sandy Island, is another good spot, but note that it's a fish sanctuary and don't try to catch your dinner there. Where you emerge near the ship channel, Rose Island and its channel are thick with cottages.

At Carling Rock, with a big orange beacon, the Small Craft Route from the city of Parry Sound (which coincides with the ship channel) and the Long Sault–Waubuno track join to continue northward. With the shift in charts at Parry Sound from 2202 to 2203 the mileage count begins over, starting from the city dock. Snug Harbour at Mile 16 has a sturdy government dock with 8 feet for alongside tie-up, but no services. **Snug Harbour Marine**, past the red and black spar buoys, has 6 feet at the dock, gas and ice. It is also a grocery store for the small cottage settlement and sells both fresh and superbly smoked fish.

Parts of the next 10 miles on the route are quite heavily developed, with few opportunities for appealing anchorage.

Pointe-au-Baril

Pointe-au-Baril, a summer colony of long standing that extends from both sides of the Small Craft Route from about Mile 30 to Mile 36, is one of the most attractive on Georgian Bay. The cottages are scattered among the islands, most of them painted in browns and greens that harmonize with nature's colors, and are secluded and unobtrusive among the trees. There are bays and coves to anchor in among the islands of the community, but much of the water is unsounded. A better bet for overnight is Shawanaga Inlet, which extends from Mile 25 to Mile 30, is more lightly cottaged and more widely sounded. One good spot is behind Green Island at Mile 28; another is between Nadeau and Black Bass islands just past Turning Island, Mile 30. Shawanaga, by the way, is another broad, unobstructed stretch for good sailing.

At Turning Island, with a flashing red light, you can take a secondary track that leads (with one tight squeeze at Kitsilano Channel) about 7½ buoyed miles to Pointe-au-Baril Station. As the name implies, this is where the railroad once brought nature seekers to their summer homes. Now it's where they park their cars. The fixed government dock, with only 3 feet alongside, is where the islanders tie up their small boats to shop at Kennedy's excellent general store. South of it there is a floating dock, with 9 foot depths, that is better suited to overnight tie-up, but there are no services except heads in the replica of the Pointe-au-Baril lighthouse. The three marinas in the bay west of the government dock cater to the cottagers' small boats, but they do sell gas, and Reid's has a pumpout.

If you continue on the main track at Turning Island, after three miles sight of the imposing Ojibway Club across the channel will jolt you back to the turn of the century when it was built as a hotel. It looks as fresh as ever, with colorful flower gardens in front and bright white trim against the weathered shingles of the three-story turreted structure. It is the social center for the Pointe-au-Baril Islanders Association members. Overnight docking is not permitted at its floating docks with six-foot depths. But cruising boats are welcome to tie up for groceries and ice at the well-stocked store at one end, the attractive gift shop with post office at the other, and the charming snack bar inside the clubhouse. Visitors may also attend the Monday and Thursday night movies in a hall back of the club building. Gas is sold at the far eastern end of the long dock.

As you cruise around the Pointe-au-Baril area you'll notice a good deal of small buoyage, sticks actually, that doesn't appear on the chart. These have been placed by the Islanders Association to mark channels through otherwise uncharted soundings. There is one more place for marine services before you depart Pointe-au-Baril. **Beacon Marina** in Pike Bay, close east of the lighthouse, has little or no space for transients at its floating docks in 8 feet. But there is gas, water, ice, electricity (if you do tie up), a marine store, a marine railway with four-ton capacity, hull and engine repairs.

As you pass the photogenic 1889 lighthouse on your departure from Pointe-au-Baril to continue on the Small Craft Route, make sure the weather is fine and the sea calm. The next 6 miles are among the most tortuous on the entire course, with hairpin turns around Nares Point and Hangdog Reef, and vicious-looking slabs of rock ready to grab you on both sides of the narrow channel all along. There are beacon ranges at the sharpest turns and plenty of buoys, but they can be hard to see if there's a sea running, while a breaking surf makes the hazards look even more frightening. *Sailing Directions* recommends that boats in excess of 40 feet in length and 4-foot draft go offshore to Byng Inlet. Both Pointe-au-Baril and Byng Inlet are quite easily entered from offshore and lend themselves to an inside/outside passage.

Pointe-au-Baril may not be so easy to find on the outside run from Parry Sound, as the mark to head for from Seguin Bank is an unlighted spar 15 miles away on Kennedy Bank. (Give the Limestone Islands en route a fair berth; their soundings go back to 1891.) From Kennedy Bank it's 6½ miles to the red and white Mo(A) off Pointe-au-Baril, and from there you're on the fixed red range at 105° for the last 3 miles to the lighthouse, which is the front light for the range. Heading for (or coming from) Byng Inlet on the outside, you need go only as far as the Mo(A) sea buoy. From there it's an easy 14 miles to the red and white Mo(A) on Magnetawan Ledges off Byng Inlet, then 5 miles to the Small Craft Route through a well-buoyed channel on a fixed red range with white and orange daymarks at 074°.

Byng Inlet

If you continue on the Small Craft Route from Pointe-au-Baril, you'll have a pretty, if cottagy, passage through Hangdog Channel and Alexander Passage, then a 9-mile outside run before you turn inshore again at Gereaux Island. There isn't a large selec-

Pointe-au-Baril, Ojibway Club.

tion of anchorages in this stretch, but one nice bay with only a few cottages is Norgate Inlet. From where the track turns northwest on a rear beacon range just before Mile 53, head east to pass between the north end of Raft Island and the unnamed island opposite. To avoid the rocky shoals off Bourchier Island, take a course of about 092° from the southeast tip of that unnamed island, heading on a flagpole beside a house with a shiny roof up the inlet. Once you've threaded that pass you're in the clear and can follow the inlet through deep water until it turns south. Anchor in 12 to 14 feet just north of the islets that seem to close off the inlet east of the island between Duquesne and Foster islands.

Byng Inlet itself is not a particularly attractive place because there are quite a few cottages and camps lining the Magnetawan River, which forms the inlet. The small craft track has a cutoff west of Clark Island at Mile 58. Unless you need services, you will probably want to continue on this way.

The twin settlements of Britt and Byng Inlet, about 5 miles up the river from that cutoff (via either South Channel or North Channel around Clark Island; South Channel is the buoyed ship route) are fuel depots for the region. As ports of call for fair-sized tankers, their approach is well lighted and buoyed. As a place to shop, neither has anything much to offer. But at Mile 61, below Britt on the north side of the river, **Wright's Marina** is the last one you'll see for 50 miles. There is dockage in 10 feet alongside or in slips, with electricity, pumpout, gas, ice, heads and a launch ramp. There is no drinking water at dockside. Most importantly, Wrights has a railway that can haul out up to 18 tons; many a prop has been changed thereon for those who ply these waters regularly. Engine and hull repairs are also available, and the store sells some basic groceries.

At Byng Inlet you start the mileage count over again, move onto a new set of small craft charts, and enter a new phase of Georgian cruising. Here is where the wilderness part of the bay really begins; no roads come even close. The islands and the coast take on a wilder, sterner aspect that is primeval in mood. The rock is bolder, the soil cover thinner, and the twisted pines bow eastward from the relentless pressure of the west wind. But the fish jump, the blueberries are plump and plentiful and on the mainland the glaciers paved the earth with miles of granite on which to hike. There are some tortuous inside channels, some outside runs open to the sea, and everywhere the vistas are magnificent. There are places where you can just step off the track to anchor—behind Golden Sword Island at Mile 8 or under Rogers Island just past Mile 12—or you can explore the reaches of Sandy Bay and Henvey Inlet.

Key Harbour

It was once a place of modest importance in these parts—an ore-loading port (the only one on Georgian Bay) and later a coal-receiving port, with a spur line of the railroad coming to the waterfront. But all that remains of Key Harbour's past is a derelict masonry power house and a parade of gaunt pilings stretching out into deep water. No road leads to this place, and the permanent population numbers about five. But in summer it is the center of a lively cottage settlement, to which everything and everybody descends 8 miles down the Key River from the highway.

One other thing remains from the past. The big orange day-beacon range on Dead Island that once guided small ships in from the open bay on a course of 058° now brings in pleasure boats. A red and white spar between Cross Ledge and the Bustard Islands Reef lies on the course, which leads after 2½ miles to the Small Craft Route. It's another 4½ miles to Key Harbour by way of the Keefer Island and Dokis Point ranges at 092° and 043°, respectively. The small craft track also leads to the settlement, of course.

Campfire on a rocky shore.

A short distance inside the mouth of the Key River **Key Harbour Lodge** on the north bank has 6 feet at the dock, electricity, water, gas, pumpout, ice and a store with basic groceries and some frozen meat. If you draw more than 4 feet, however, it's a little chancy to try to get over the bar into the river, although there is more depth than the chart shows. Anchor off and go in by dinghy for supplies and local information about water depths this year. If you do go in, the passage upriver (controlling depth three feet) is peaceful and unspoiled once you get past the settlement at the mouth, and there are several spots for a shallow draft boat to anchor. Diamond Key Resort, a short distance south on the first bay west of the river entrance, has a small grocery store and gas at a small boat dock.

Key Harbour is at the precise northeast corner of Georgian Bay. Here the coastline and the Small Craft Route turn west. After coasting the figurative North Shore you have reached the geographic north shore. The cottage community that surrounds the Key is quite compact, and you are in quick retreat from its relative bustle almost the moment you leave it. About 4 miles beyond Key Harbour, at Mile 18, a secondary track leads off to starboard. This is one of the most beautiful of all the Georgian Bay passages. It also has one of its hairiest cuts. Parting Channel, where the brave and the timid part company, is a blasted dog-leg between a rock and a hard place immediately after a 90-degree turn. Less than a quarter of a mile beyond you are rewarded with a wild anchorage east of Obstacle Island. Simply pull off the track and drop the hook.

French River

Somewhere in this northeastern corner of Georgian Bay, Brulé and his mentor, Champlain, emerged from the French River to "discover" the Great Lakes. We can't be certain just where because the French has five outlets. Obstacle Island is at the mouth of the Eastern Outlet. It's a popular canoe route, and if you take your dinghy up the rock and pine-girt waterway, you'll come to the boardwalk maintained by the Ministry of Natural Resources as a canoe portage. Tie up at the small dock and walk across to the poignant ruins of Rainbow Camp, a once elaborate fishing lodge and a glimpse of the inland intricacies of the French.

The Main Outlet of the French River is but a mile and a half on the secondary track from Obstacle Island. Suddenly the scenery loses its dramatic impact as you pull into the wide stream. But, Champlain aside, this outlet is historic in that it was once the site of a lumber and sawmill town of 2,000 people, where schooners and steamers called regularly. Virtually all trace is gone now, except the fixed white range lights with white and orange daymark on the front light at a course of 026° that connects with a range at 041° from the Bustard Lights (described below) and the open bay. There is good anchorage in Macdougal Bay at the head of the outlet, and just beyond you can dinghy or walk the rocks to a boisterous rapids. On the west bank below the anchorage McIntosh Camp is a fishing lodge where you can have dinner out with early afternoon reservations.

If you follow the French downstream, you'll meet the main small craft track again at the Bustard Islands. Not so long ago this archipelago was the summer base for a large commercial fishing fleet. Now only pleasure boats come to join the few cottagers at what may be the richest bass fishing ground on the Great Lakes. There are two harbors to choose from. Coming directly from Key Harbour on the main track, you can head directly into Northeast Harbor and anchor almost anywhere between Strawberry and the outer islands, although the best spot is at the far end. There is only one inconspicuous cottage.

The main harbor is approached from the west side of the island group, along the secondary track that leads through the Gun Barrel. Once inside, turn fairly tightly around the eastern

French River, Main Outlet rapids.

end of Pearl Island and coast its south side closely to avoid a foul area south of it before you turn around the unnamed island off Pearl's southwest tip into the deep clear harbor. There are a few cottages near the top of the harbor, but none where you anchor. The Bustards are not only beautiful but also laced with fascinating little channels to explore by dinghy.

The Western Outlet of the French River divides into three shortly before it reaches Georgian Bay. The easternmost of these, Bad River Channel, offers one of the most spectacular anchorages on Georgian Bay. It is dressed in pink granite cliffs, sprinkled with green pine and carpeted with blueberries. From the red spar at Mile 25 you can take a course directly to the red and white sea buoy off Bad River Channel. There you pick up the daybeacon range at 018° that leads through a buoyed channel into the mouth of Bad River. When you are abeam the middle of Bad River Point Island, turn northeast toward a small group of buildings, to be sure that you clear the nasty rocks on both sides before heading for the next green spar. From here the sounded course is pretty straightforward, except for one narrow spot opposite the *a* in *Bad* on the chart. Until the government sees fit to place a spar buoy, post a lookout on the bow going through. You can drop the hook anywhere in the broad uninhabited bay that opens up, except opposite Devil's Door, where the force of the rapids has scoured the bottom and makes holding

Bad River ridge.

poor. If your dinghy motor is sufficiently powerful to get you through Devil's Door there is a beautiful maze of channels, some with more rapids, beyond it.

The last two outlets of the French River, Fort Channel and Voyageur Channel, have been partially sounded, but there is no buoyage to guide a mariner among their reefs and rocks. From the name it is probable that the westernmost outlet, Voyageur Channel, was the one used by the great fur brigades that plied 1,000 miles from Montreal to Lake Superior between 1660 and 1821. They would take the most sheltered route for their birch-bark canoes, to minimize the open water passage around Point Grondine and through the treacherous shoals of The Chickens.

For today's small pleasure craft mariner, too, there is a hiatus on the sheltered route, which extends for 18 miles between the Bustard Islands and Beaverstone Bay. The first mark is Grondine Rock, its red color made even more conspicuous by a big daybeacon. You could continue from there on a spectacular outside run to Killarney, via Green Island, also conspicuous from the offing. The outside route from Byng Inlet follows a direct course to Green Island. It's 40 miles that way from Byng Inlet to Killarney, 28 from the Bustard Islands. On a bright day this is one of the most magnificent passages on the Great Lakes. At first mauve on the horizon, the Killarney Mountains grow in your sight to reveal the white quartzite of their peaks against a

View from Bad River ridge.

deep blue sky. Then, as you approach closer, the red rock that forms the foreshore and the offlying islands, topped by dark green pines, throws a breathtaking splash of color on nature's palette.

Beaverstone Bay and Collins Inlet

The final segment of the Small Craft Route is a suitable climax to your northbound voyage. First, as a final exam in piloting, the approach to Beaverstone Bay involves no fewer than four daybeacon ranges, each intersecting the next, to thread your passage among the slabs of granite guarding the entrance. Like so much of the track, it sounds worse in the telling than it is in the doing. But it is advisable to make this entrance only on a calm day with good visibility. There is a big red bell buoy offshore, at which you get on the first range of 038° for a little over a mile. A red spar marks the turn to the second range at 081°. After a bit more than half a mile you turn again on 038° very briefly until the final range at 001° comes into focus. Take care not to get off that one too soon, as there are bad shoals to starboard; proceed almost to the port-hand daybeacon before you head up the clear bay. Once inside, Beaverstone is a little reminiscent of Pointe-au-Baril in that the islands are more thickly wooded than those you've been looking at lately, and there are quite a few cottages. But behind Burnt Island there is good uninhabited anchorage, with a stunning cliff to contemplate on the opposite shore.

If your boat draws 5 feet or more, the rest of the inside passage may not be accessible to you. At the top of Beaverstone Bay a very narrow channel, defined by buoys, was originally dredged to 6 feet, but in recent years it has silted up and, depending on water level, there may be spots with less than 5. At the north end of that channel a sharp turn to port brings you into the splendid gorge of Collins Inlet. The passage is deep almost from shore to shore, so if you stay in the middle you can turn part of your attention to the view. At Mile 49 you'll see the wharf ruins of another Georgian Bay ghost town, Collins Inlet. It died when the timber gave out in the 1920s, but there is a fishing camp on the site now that incorporates some of the old buildings. At Mahzenazing River Lodge gas is available at the dock, with 4 feet alongside, and you can have dinner there, with reservations.

A mile beyond Mahzenazing the waterway widens temporarily into Mill Lake, with anchorage at the north end in Second and Third bays, or down at the bottom anywhere beyond Green Island, all secluded from the few cottages that are clustered around the small craft track. The western segment of Collins Inlet has more shoal water along the banks, so a bit more care in piloting is needed. At Mile 57 there is an anchorage behind Keyhole Island. And at Flat Rock, just past Mile 60, the inside passage, begun so many islands ago at Port Severn, is completed. It's a scant 4-mile run across the panoramic top of Georgian Bay to Killarney.

Killarney

Its presence has been heralded for many miles across Georgian Bay as the backdrop mountains have grown larger on the horizon, and from far off the reassuring lighthouse stands out from the bold red rock on which it sits. Killarney, the northern terminus of Georgian Bay, provides a gentle reentry to civilization. The first settlement established on the bay, in 1820, its people have always earned their living from the sea. In fact, Killarney was not connected to the rest of the world by road until 1962. It remains a quiet, "unspoiled" fishing village of about 450 people, with two grocery stores, a liquor store, fish store and two or three gift and craft shops, all in a scenic and unhurried setting. For cruising boats it is a very special place—the nexus

Killarney net sheds and boats.

between Georgian Bay and the North Channel—and they flock to it in multitudes.

Killarney Channel is main street, figuratively and literally. Most of the commercial establishments have dockage and the village has almost more marinas than it has stores. First, after entering the channel past Killarney East Light, isophase white from a white lighthouse with red topknot and fog horn, is **Killarney Mountain Lodge.** The most luxurious of Killarney's facilities, it has tie-up alongside at floating slips in 10 feet or more, with all dockside services and full access to the lodge's activities—swimming pool, sauna, tennis court, shuffleboard, children's playground, excellent dining room, nightly movies, and live entertainment in the Carousel Lounge. The dock master monitors channel 68, and advance reservations are a good idea at the height of the season.

A little farther along on the mile-long channel the Government Dock is taken up on the front face by fishing tugs and the Indusmin Quarry boat, but there is a basin inside, approached from the west, with alongside tie-up in 6 feet, suitable for boats under 30 feet, as the turning radius is short. There are no services. Across the channel from the government dock is the small **George Island Yacht Club**, with alongside tie-up in 5 to 12 feet, electricity, water and pumpout. The steep-gabled Hansel and Gretel cottage on the bluff was Killarney's first schoolhouse, built in the 1840s, now the home of the friendly proprietors. They have sculpted terraces on the hillside, with tables and chairs from which you can enjoy the best view in town.

Proceeding westward, on the north, village, side you come to Killarney's biggest building, the white, verandahed turn-of-the-century **Sportsman's Inn**. Dockage here is also alongside at floats with 6 feet or more, some of them across the channel with launch service, and all dockside services, including Laundromat (at last). Both dining room and bar at Sportsman's are informal, and there is a dive shop with scuba rental and transportation to several wrecks in the area. Beyond Sportsman's **A and R Marina** is a small, older facility with alongside tie-up in six feet or more, and the usual services except diesel fuel.

A few miles out of town, Killarney Provincial Park encompasses much of that spectacular mountain scenery you've been admiring, with chains of lakes nestled between the peaks. Except for a campground at the entrance, it's a wilderness park, equally fascinating to the backpacker and the canoeist. There are no taxis in Killarney, but you can probably arrange transportation at either Killarney Mountain Lodge or Sportsman's Inn for a few hours (or a week) of hiking or canoeing. Pitfield's General Store in town rents canoes, and Killarney Outfitters near the park entrance rents canoes and hiking and camping gear.

THE NORTH CHANNEL

In the North Channel you can continue your idyll of island anchorage and village ports of call. Like Georgian Bay, it is a rhapsody in rock and pine, high bluff and deep bay, but orchestrated in a different key. The scene here is expansive in mood, the channels among the islands broader and (with a few exceptions) untortured, the elevations more dramatic, the forest cover more lush and deciduous, although the exposed rock can be as twisted and barren.

The opposite coasts of the North Channel are as different as eons of separation in geological time can make them. The north shore is composed of pre-Cambrian rock, 2½ billion years old, while the south shore is a mere babe of 400 million years. The island chains and clusters that afford wild anchorage lie along the north shore, while the Manitoulin coast is a series of steep headlands enclosing deeply indented, smooth-sided bays. Here there is little or no anchorage, but each bay has its convivial village dock.

Protected from the full sweep of Lake Huron by Manitoulin

Killarney Sportsman's Inn.

Island and its western neighbors, the North Channel is an almost ideal cruising ground—big enough, at 100 miles in length and almost 20 miles across at its widest, for exhilarating open water passage-making, yet the seas are usually kindly to power and sail boats alike. Winds are generally lighter and less reliable for sailing than they are in Georgian Bay, but they do tend to freshen by mid-morning and die down in early evening. And, despite the protection of Manitoulin, high winds, especially out of the west, can generate a steep chop. Fog is rare, but more than any other place on Lake Huron the North Channel does get a great deal of summer haze. This can make distance-judging and buoy-finding difficult, even as it lends an ethereal blue shade to the mountains of the mainland and the bluffs of Manitoulin.

The techniques for cruising the islands of the North Channel are the same as those for Georgian Bay. Although the passes are often wider and the rocks and buoys only rarely obscured by spray, island counting is a must. And a lookout on the approach to anchorages, preferably with the sun at your back, is a good idea. Buoyage is found where it's most needed, but little of it is lighted, so here, too, it's dangerous to cruise after dark. The village docks, on the other hand, all have lighted aids.

The North Channel is buoyed to and from Sault Ste. Marie. That is, reds are on the right moving westward, or toward the Sault. No single chart covers the whole channel, and two of them, 2286 and 2295, are in the old style—depths in fathoms and soundings to an obsolete datum. Deductions of 4.7 and 2.9 feet, respectively, must be made from their soundings to comply with current practice. And there are still some places in the North Channel that have no soundings at all.

A North Channel cruise can either follow the coast line elliptically around the perimeter, or include diagonal passages back and forth to alternate the isolation of wild anchorages and the camaraderie of village docks. Here we will circumnavigate clockwise, because that course takes best advantage of the scenic splendors of this legendary cruising ground. But not all the anchorages will be revealed; some are left for you to discover.

Manitoulin Island

Charts 2252, 2257, 2258, 2286, 2294, 2295

Manitoulin Island's form is dictated in part by its geologic origin. It is built of limestone, part of the great arch of the Niagara Escarpment. On the North Channel side its bluffs rise high, with wide deep bays between the headlands. Remote from large urban centers, the villages here are small and engagingly old-fashioned. Beyond them there is little that is commercial on the island. It is farm and bush country, with rustic resorts here and there, but little or no commercial entertainment anywhere. The white man's history on these shores is little more than 100 years old.

Manitowaning

The eastern side of Manitoulin Island fronts on Georgian Bay, but there are no adequate accommodations for cruising boats there, either natural or man-made. The first of the island's deeply indented bays is Manitowaning, about 10 miles long, its banks high and forested. From Killarney East Light it's a 25-mile passage to the village of Manitowaning at the foot of the bay. This is where the white man's sojourn first began on Manitoulin Island—in a misguided attempt to establish a government and church managed settlement for all Canadian Indians on the Great Lakes. Few of them accepted the invitation, and the Establishment, as it was called, limped along between 1836 and 1862, when Manitoulin Island was opened for white settlement. But the graceful St. Paul's Church, dating from 1845, is a legacy that remains, and you can learn about the Establishment and the interesting subsequent history of Manitowaning at the Assiginack Historical Museum (859-3977). Although the Establishment failed, there are several Indian reserves on Manitoulin Island and a substantial Indian population.

The pretty lighthouse on the west bluff, with a fixed green light, locates Manitowaning as you come down the bay. The Government Dock beyond it has floating slips in 10 feet or more, but no services at present. There are plans, with some funding commitment, to expand the dockage and introduce them. As you approach the dock, don't be startled into thinking you've made a mistake when you see a big ship moored nearby. The S.S. *Norisle*, built in 1946 for the Tobermory to South Baymouth ferry run, was the last steam-powered passenger vessel on the Great Lakes. At her honored resting place she is now a museum, along with the 1883 grist mill on the site (859-3977).

In addition to a lot of history the village of about 400 people has a sand beach and tennis courts for outdoor recreation, grocery and gift shopping, especially Indian crafts, and a Laundromat. Manitowaning Lodge, about a mile walk around the bottom of the bay, has a very good dining room. (The lodge no longer maintains its docks, but you can find sheltered anchorage there behind Fanny Island.) If you're in town on the right day, you might catch a harness race at the track on the way. The Summerfest Weekend in July includes a midway, contests, food and a dance.

Little Current

Twenty miles up Manitowaning Bay and around the next big hump in the Manitoulin profile the North Channel narrows to a mere 500 feet. Here, at the strategic narrows, sits Manitoulin's largest town, Little Current, with 1,500 people and the bustling air of a metropolis on its two-block main street. All channels lead to Little Current, and all boats cruising this part of the world stop at least once, if not more often. It's a popular place to meet friends and exchange boat crews. Manitoulin's only land connection to the mainland is the elderly railroad-converted-to-one-lane-highway bridge that spans the narrows.

Coming up from Manitowaning, Sheguiandah Bay and Strawberry Channel have no accommodations for cruising boats, and little to recommend them scenically. The east side of Strawberry Island is the preferred route to the lighthouse at its northern tip, followed by a straight westerly run to the bridge. The range and outer buoys of the channel are for the ships that call only occasionally now; in good weather pleasure craft can pass straight across the channel. Closed clearance for the bridge is 18 feet. It swings open on the hour for 15 minutes, so you need to time your arrival accordingly.

Immediately beyond the bridge is a **Government Wharf** a quarter of a mile long. Until 1984 this was Little Current's only dockage. Traffic in and out was almost continuous, and in mid-season the boats might be rafted four deep. Now they are lined up sedately end to end at the alongside tie-up in 10 feet with all dockside services. The service dock and shower building are near the east end of the long wharf, and electricity does not extend all the way to the western end. The little current can occasionally run quite swiftly through here, so before you dock, observe which way the channel buoys are leaning and nose into the current as you come up alongside.

This Government Dock is the handiest location for the shopping, restaurants and Laundromat on the main street that runs parallel to the waterfront. But half a mile farther on, past the flashing white light at Spider Island, is the new **Spider Bay Marina**. Entered between two rubble breakwalls, the marina offers dockage in floating slips, with 6 feet of depth and all dockside services. In 1984 the plumbing was in for a Laundromat, but the machines were not yet installed. This is a large and attractive facility, an easy 15-minute walk from downtown, but unfortunately it was designed for boats only 30 feet or less. The largest slips are just that long, and there is little turning radius between the rows for a bigger boat to get in and out. Steps may already have been taken to correct the problem, but until some changes are made larger boats are better off at the government wharf.

Boyle's Marina, beyond the west end of the government dock has little or no transient dockage, but it is the only full service yard on the North Channel. It can haul out up to 12 tons on a travelift, 68 feet on a railway, and offers engine, hull and rigging repairs. Just before Boyle's, at the west end of the dock, Landfall Yacht Charters has a small marine store with a fair range of stock.

Little Current isn't much to look at architecturally, but it's a lively place with a lot of foot and car traffic on the main street. Its strategic location has long given it commercial importance, and shopping seems to be the main preoccupation. There is a full range of stores and commercial services. Turner's Chart Room, reached through the Stedman Store, carries a full line of charts and marine publications. The town is also a customs port of entry and has a hospital. There is no regular entertainment beyond two bars, but on Haweater Weekend, the first one in August, there are contests and entertainments, and a midway is set up on the outskirts of town.

West Bay and Mudge

As you emerge from the narrows at Little Current the headlands of Manitoulin and a cluster of islands march along the western horizon, while the soft blue La Cloche Mountains hover over the north. Continuing westward along the Manitoulin shore the next bay over is, not illogically, West Bay. There is a government dock without services at the village of Excelsior (known locally as West Bay) at the foot of the bay, 18 miles from Little Current. The village is the center of the West Bay Indian Reserve and the location of the island's only high school; students commute up to 40 miles one way and 60 the other. The Ojibwe Cultural Foundation, a bit of a walk from the dock, has a fine gallery of native art and crafts, some of it for sale (377-4902). The Mission Church of the Immaculate Conception is a unique architectural blend of Indian tradition and Christian worship. Step inside for the full impact.

The next bay over is Mudge, with the hamlet of Kagawong at its foot, about 15 miles from West Bay. Give Francis Point and its shoals a good berth coming around and pass on the outside of Gooseberry Island with its flashing white light. The fixed red light on a white tower is west of the **Government Dock** at Kagawong. There are floating slips on the inside of the wharf, with depths of 5 feet and up and the usual dockside services except diesel and showers.

This harbor has another interesting church to visit, at the head of the dock. Known as the Mariner's Church because of its unusual features, its story is told by displays inside. A short walk around the bottom of the bay brings you to a lakeside park, with beach and playground and a woodland trail to one of Manitoulin's most photographed sites—Bridal Veil Falls. There is also a general store up the road, if you need supplies, and a tennis court next to the dock.

Almost enclosing Mudge Bay on the north is Clapperton Island, with a nearly circular harbor at the southern end. At one time Harbour Island was the site of a popular lodge and marina, but recent years have seen a succession of owners and managers come and go. As of this writing the lodge is not functioning,

Kagawong, Mariner's Church.

but anchorage within Clapperton Harbour behind Harbour Island opposite the lodge buildings is sheltered, if unsensational. Clapperton Island sits on a shallow bank, foul with rocks and shoals, but the channel from east to west is thoroughly buoyed, and lights on Meredith Rock (flashing red with a red and white daymark) and Beverly Island (flashing white with a red and white daymark) and the green spar off Beverly all define the approach to Clapperton Harbour. A big white *H*, the logo of the original lodge, still stands on the west side of Harbour Island to point the way.

Gore Bay

Around the next headland from Mudge Bay, Gore Bay is a relatively shallow indentation, 2 miles long. At its foot, where the bluffs lower to a rolling hillside, is the village of Gore Bay. A lighthouse on Janet Head, the western bluff, with an occulting white light and a fixed red range with red and white daymarks at 189°, make this an easy port to get into at night. A pair of spar buoys guide you around the point of land that shelters the harbor.

Second in size on the island, with about 800 people, Gore Bay is a gracious town of tree-lined streets and wide-lawned homes, the dignified seat of government on Manitoulin. It also has an excellent **Public Marina**: floating docks in 7 to 20 feet, all dockside services, a travelift and marine store operated by Canadian Yacht Charters. Sometimes there is a courtesy car available, but it's an easy walk to the town's several food stores, Laundromat and variety of other shops and services.

For entertainment the beach and tennis courts are adjacent to the marina, the interesting exhibits of the Gore Bay Museum are in the historic jail, at the Community hall you can attend a movie on weekends, and there is an annual folk festival at Janet Head Park in late June or early July. The Twin Bluffs Restaurant on Phipps Street serves nicely prepared home-style food. Finally, Gore Bay has the only car rental on Manitoulin, at McQuarrie Motors. A day's outing among the peaceful country roads can give you a real feel for this pastoral island that, despite the growth in tourism, still exudes the atmosphere of an older time—not museum Victoriana, but the childhood years of those of us who are middle-aged.

Bayfield Sound

Julia Bay, the next one west from Gore Bay, has neither shelter nor facilities for a cruising boat, and the one after that is so different from all the rest as to be called by a different title. A very narrow isthmus separates the east end of Bayfield Sound from Julia Bay and the North Channel, but unless you carry your boat across you must circle around large Barrie Island before you can enter at the western end, 18 miles from Gore Bay harbor. The sound is not the most scenic part of the Manitoulin coast, as Barrie Island is rather flat, but the three bays indenting the south shore become progressively prettier as you move eastward. Take care to give unmarked Jubilee Shoal a sufficient berth as you approach the entrance to the sound between Fishery Point and the red spar off Fanny Island.

At the far end of the sound in Campbell Bay, about 12 miles from that spar, is the main attraction for cruising boats. **Northernaire Lodge**, with dockage in slips with 7 feet, protected by a breakwall, and all dockside services except diesel, extends a warm welcome to cruising boats. The dining room at this American plan resort is excellent, and the beach and playground are ideal for children. There is a nice gift shop on the premises, and you can take your dinghy under the little bridge into Wolsey Lake for good fishing. The best anchorage in Bayfield Sound is under Ned Island at the northwest corner of Helen Bay; there is one house.

Meldrum Bay

Manitoulin Island's westernmost village—almost a frontier outpost 46 miles from Gore Bay by road, with little more than one inhabitant for each mile—is a major crossroad for the cruising fraternity. As a customs port of entry Meldrum Bay is usually the first stop for boats entering the North Channel from lakes Huron and Michigan and often the last for those on the way home. It's actually a shorter distance by water from Gore Bay, only 37 miles, 23 from the red spar at the entrance to Bayfield Sound. Vidal Bay, the major indentation between, gets some protection from Vidal Island for anchorage under its lee or at the foot of the bay, but it suffers from surge in strong winds. Meldrum Bay should be approached from the west side of Batture Island, marked by a flashing white light with red and white daymark and a red spar off its southwest shoal.

At the base of the bluff on which the hamlet is perched the **Government Dock** has a fixed red light on the former freight shed. Some of the floating docks with alongside tie-up in 8 feet have electricity and water, and gas, diesel and ice are available. The heads, showers and a Laundromat are at the campground a short distance from the dock. In fact, everything in Meldrum is a short distance—the two stores, the Net Shed Museum and the Meldrum Bay Inn, where dinner is imaginative and very tasty. Conviviality at the dock and walks along woodsy or pastoral country roads are the major pastimes.

Cockburn Island

Across Mississagi Strait from Manitoulin Island Cockburn Island was actually settled before the western end of the larger island. At first a fishing settlement, Cockburn later thrived on lumbering and finally farming on the cleared land. When the young people began to desert the farm in the 1930s, the island's major landowner, Ontario Paper Company, began reforestation and now ships out a good deal of pulpwood. With the return of lumbering, descendants of the farming settlers have also returned to use the old homesteads as summer cottages or to build new ones. Yet in walking the roads and lanes of the island you may still come across poignant abandoned farms amid the cool, quiet stretches of forest.

The harbor at Tolsmaville, 13 miles from Meldrum Bay, is an easy one to get into, with a daybeacon range at 169°, a flashing white light on the western wharf, used by the pulp boats, and a

Cockburn Island, abandoned farmhouse.

flashing red, with red and white daymark, on the eastern *L*-shaped breakwater/wharf used by pleasure boats. There are floating docks for alongside tie-up in 8 feet, but no services. Anchorage behind the breakwater is sheltered, but the bottom may be foul with old logs to snare your ground tackle.

The North Shore

Charts **2205, 2252, 2257, 2259, 2268, 2286, 2295**

Thessalon

Drummond Island, Michigan, and St. Joseph Island, Ontario, border the western edge of the North Channel, but as there are no harbors on their channelside shores those islands will be described in Chapter 8. Here our narrative crosses the North Channel at its widest, to the westernmost north shore port of Thessalon, about 23 miles from Tolsmaville. Thessalon is also a customs port of entry that is frequently the first stop for American boats entering the channel. Like most of the others in this region, this is a town that lumber built, and there is still an operating veneer mill behind the waterfront. But Thessalon is now mainly a commercial and tourist center.

At long, narrow Point Thessalon, marked with a flashing red light, you get on the fixed green range displayed from masts with white and orange daymarks at a course of 022° for the harbor. Take care not to confuse the daymark on the flashing red breakwater light for the front range. That breakwater is partially submerged, and the area around it is foul. The front range light is at the end of the concrete breakwater wharf, which has floating docks on the inside in 12 to 14 feet for alongside tie-up. **Bill's Marine** supplies electricity, if you have long cables to reach the box, and all other dockside services, including propane refills. There is good shopping and a Laundromat in the village of 1,600 people, a short walk from the waterfront. Restaurants are a bit scattered—two or three downtown, and two more associated with motels on the west side of the peninsula along the beach. The Carolyn Beach Motel, a 1½-mile walk, serves good home-style food, and across the road from it the Cache is a gift shop that features Canadian crafts.

Blind River

A report on this town, 30 miles east of Thessalon along a wooded shore backed by soft hills, must regrettably be mixed. Blind River, the largest town on the North Channel with 3,000 people, good shopping and some entertainment, has barely usable marine facilities at this writing. The tall sawdust burner of the old MacFadden Lumber Mill is a conspicuous mark from seaward. In the booming ground below the burner that was once filled with logs awaiting their turn, dredging and reconstruction a few years ago initiated a small boat marina. Unfortunately, the marina has not been completed nor the docks that were built maintained, and the couple of spar buoys at the entrance to Dorothy Inlet are insufficient to guide a stranger past the remaining invisible pilings of the old wharves. Consequently, I cannot advise readers to put in there at this time, although there is some indication that improvements will be made within the next few years.

There is a government wharf at the north end of the bay, with a flashing green light on a red and white daymark and adequately placed spar buoys to guide you to it. The problem here is the narrow channel and turning radius between that wharf and the old pilings opposite. And in winds from east and southeast the dockface gets a lot of motion. There are no services here, but it is handy to downtown. In addition to shopping, Laundromat, and hospital, there are a couple of restaurants, a movie theater, live entertainment at one of the bars and the well-executed Timber Village Museum, which depicts the old logging days in this part of the world.

The Turnbull Island Group

If you don't plan a stop at Blind River, stock up well at Thessalon, because 8 miles east of Blind River begins the alluring chain of wild North Channel islands that might keep you enchanted for the rest of the summer. First comes a small archipelago composed of Sanford, Turnbull and Bassett islands, and all the little islets on the bank between them. Sanford, formerly called Clara, is low and wooded and somewhat less scenic than the others. But there is sheltered anchorage in a cove at its eastern end, best approached from the main channel north of Sanford. Favor the Sanford shore as you come in, to avoid the shoals off Vaux Island.

A mile farther on is the entrance to Bassett Island harbor. Turn south from the black beacon on McCallum Island, then round the high steep island west of Bassett and its little southwest satellite to head eastward along the Bassett shore into the lovely bay. There is more space than appears on the chart to pass between Bassett and the islands and shoals south of it. There is also more than the 2 feet (usually 6 feet) of depth shown in the

Turnbull Island anchorage.

passage from Bassett harbor into Turnbull harbor between the unnamed island that separates them and the Turnbull shore. Turnbull harbor can also be entered from the south, by turning north from Cherub Rock to leave the entrance rocks to starboard, with a lookout on the bow to direct you past the nasty shoal off your port bow. Anchor in the wedge between the two islands opposite the heights of Turnbull, or you can proceed to Bassett, the more sheltered of the two harbors, by the reverse route. There is delightful dinghy gunkholing among all the little islands in the center of the group.

The Turnbull Island group is approachable from offshore, if you're crossing the North Channel, either through South Passage, with a black beacon on conspicuous Doucet Rock, or via Turnbull Passage, marked by big red and green spar buoys.

Serpent Harbour

A few miles northeast of the Turnbull group the Serpent River flows into the North Channel. There is a rather unsightly lime plant on the mainland just before you get to it, but it's soon out of sight as you pass beyond. Nobles Island almost closes off the river mouth to create a sheltered harbor between the steep banks. And east of the island, at Herman Point, is the hospitable **North Channel Yacht Club**. Although overnight dockage at the floats with 10 feet is scarce, there are often vacant moorings belonging to members off cruising. The usual dockside services are available, except diesel and ice, and there is a railway that can haul out up to 35 feet, although repair people would have to be called in.

The approach to Serpent Harbour between the Fournier Islands and Meteor Rock is quite obvious from the enlarged chart 2268. Keep Meteor Rock and Cross Island fairly close aboard to avoid the shoal water on the north side of that passage. Directly across from the yacht club, round the Morrison Islands, you can enter a beautiful anchorage behind Nobles Island from the east; note the rock off its southeast point. Or you can enter directly from the outer harbor on the west. A dinghy ride up the Serpent River gives you an idea of what the interior looks like.

The Whalesback Channel

One of the frustrations of cruising this part of the North Channel is that some of its most treasured anchorages are in such close proximity that they pose an agony of choice. Barely 5 miles around the corner from Serpent Harbour is the entrance to the Whalesback Channel, one of the most exquisite 9-mile passages in this region of superlatives. Try to make the passage eastward in the afternoon or westward in the morning to get the full effect of the light playing on the consummately artistic placement of islands, trees and undulating rocky shores. You do have to mind the buoys and the beacons as you soak it in, however.

The Whalesback can also be entered from offshore via the flashing white light with red and white daymark on Mills Island. Nearby Scott Island is high and conspicuous from any direction. Within a couple of miles of the western entrance to the Whalesback two superb wild anchorages lie on opposite sides. The red beacon on Turtle Rock is a departure point for entrance to both. Beardrop Harbour on the north is entered on a northeast course close east of the beacons on Wicksteed Point. Approach John Harbour due south between Le Sueur and Gowan islands, then swing eastward down the middle. Both harbors are scenic, with good rock climbing and blueberries. The best lying in each is east of the point or islands making out from the south side. In John Harbour, mind the rock off this point and give it a wide berth. If you draw 4 feet or less, you can get into Cleary Cove, the gem of an anchorage opening from John on the north side of Dewdney Island. Pass between the largest island blocking the cove and all the little islets east of it.

At the eastern end of the Whalesback narrows John Island offers another haven to cruising boats. Moiles Harbour was the site of a substantial lumbering operation early in the century, and you may still see evidence of the old wharf pilings. Enter between Bergeron Point, which looks like an island in high water years, and Aikens Island, favoring the point until you gain the center of the pass. Then head straight into the harbor. Opposite you may see some boats tied up at a dock belonging to the YMCA children's camp that fronts on the other side of the island. Otherwise Moiles is uninhabited. The best spot to anchor is at the northwestern end. Take care that your anchor is well set and doesn't drag on old logs and sawdust.

Beyond Moiles Harbour the Whalesback Channel widens into a broad bay that is of a sufficiently different scenic character that one wonders why it has the same name as the island-studded channel you have just traversed. Nor are there special anchorage attractions along its 8- to 10-mile length (depending upon where you measure). If you need supplies and draw 4 feet or less, you can move off the anchorage-hopping track to the north shore village of Spanish. A flashing red light buoy marks the entrance to the buoyed Spanish River channel, about 9 miles from Moiles Harbour. Although the channel is dredged from time to time, it silts badly and may not measure the reported or calculated depth when you get there. A bit over 3 miles up the river there is a govenment dock with about 5 feet of depth, but no services. Gas is obtainable at Vance's Camp nearby. You are still a mile from the village shops and Laundromat on Highway 17, but taxis are available.

If you continue on along the south side of the wide part of the Whalesback you'll reach an opening between Passage and Shanly islands, marked by beacons, through which you pass to continue eastward. If you're ready to stop for the day, however, there is an anchorage at the western end of the long bay you've moved into, between Jackson and Aird islands. A couple of miles past the beacon on Shanly you come to the tightest pass on the main route of the North Channel, Little Detroit. A lumber town once flourished here, too. The short channel has been blasted to 75 feet in width, and there is an enlargement on chart 2268, but why the government has seen fit to place the helpful (and necessary) ranges to face only westbound traffic is something of a mystery. Rear ranges are harder to steer, but if you're east-bound, that's all you have—one on Green Island on the approach and one in Little Detroit itself on the exit. Because of the blind dog-leg, you are required to broadcast a security call on channel 16 as you enter.

McBean Channel

Passage through Little Detroit brings you into McBean Channel, named for the beautiful mountain that beckons you forward. From now on you will be lured along your eastward course by mountain vistas. McBean Channel can also be reached from offshore between the flashing white light with red and white daymark on Boyd Island and the green spar west of it on Lumsden Rock. And it, too, presents an array of tantalizing anchorages. Shoepack Bay, close north of Little Detroit, is the first of them. It is very deep, but your hook can find bottom in 25 feet at either end.

About 5 miles east of Little Detroit there is an opening in the north shore between Oak Point and Hotham Point. Inside is a long, island-studded waterway that has always been known as

Oak Bay.

Oak Bay until a recent edition of chart 2257 confined that name to the shallow cove at its western end. Watching out for the rocks and islets quite accurately placed on the chart, there are half a dozen anchorages to choose from. Each offers a different vista and a different mix of forest and rock. Each is beautiful. This is a place to explore and find your own special niche.

Back in McBean Channel you can follow three sides of the coast of Frechette Island, opposite Hotham, to a spacious forest-girt anchorage in the north side of Eagle Island. This is one of the few islands named for wildlife whose outline really looks the part. The only hazard is an islet in the center of the harbor, with a shoal making out northward of it. Favor either shore coming in.

At the far end of McBean Channel, virtually under the mountain itself, is McBean Harbour. The red beacon on Bald Rock shows you where to turn north to enter safely past Helen and Black islands and their shoals. There is a settlement in the main harbor, which is not especially scenic, but you can carry 8 feet down the middle of the passage leading to a lovely wild anchorage behind Anchor Island. If you decide to make a try for the summit of Mount McBean from here, be advised that it's farther away than it looks and put on your good hiking boots for the trek.

The Benjamin Islands

Around the corner from the eastern entrance to McBean Channel is the most famous archipelago in the North Channel, the Benjamin Islands. An anomaly of pink granite in a land of gray and black construction, the magnificent Benjamins are beloved of all who cruise these waters. Only one of their three harbors is, in fact, fully protected with firm holding ground, yet few crews fail to stop to render obeisance and refresh their spirits.

The Benjamin group is composed of four major islands—North Benjamin, South Benjamin, Fox and Croker—and all the satellites between and around them. Fox Harbour, in the southwest corner of the island, is best approached from McBean Channel. It's a little tricky. From the middle islet off the northeast tip of Eagle Island, take a course of 099° until the middle of the long narrow harbor comes abeam. While it sounds easy in the telling, there are a lot of rocks on the course and a couple of spots with only 3 to 4 feet at chart datum.

The other harbors are all approached from southward in Main Passage between Clapperton Island and the Benjamin group. If you're coming around from McBean Channel, or coming northwest from Little Current, you'll reach the entrance to Croker and North Benjamin harbors first. To enter Croker, the safest harbor of the lot, pass west of Secretary Island, about 600 feet off, then gradually swing northward around its tip until you can take a course of about 075° into the harbor. The best anchorage is at the south end on either side of the little island there; elsewhere the water is very deep. To enter North Benjamin harbor, which actually lies between the two Benjamin Islands, keep going past Secretary for another 1½ miles until it opens to port. You can anchor at either end, wherever your hook is able to grab the thin mud cover over rock. Many boats tie off to trees in these harbors to overcome the problem of either deep water or poor holding.

South Benjamin harbor, which you reach first if coming from the west or southwest, is a little more difficult to approach from the east, in that you must locate and identify the Sow and Pigs. Leave them well to starboard and head for the southwest tip of the island at the southeastern entrance to the long cove almost bisecting South Benjamin Island. There is a rock, 6 feet high, blocking the entrance. Despite appearances on the chart, leave that to port; there's a nasty shoal extending from the point on the other side of it. South Benjamin harbor is open to the south and southeast, and the holding is sometimes poor, but it is probably the most dramatically scenic of them all.

An Assortment of Anchorages

Six miles southeast of McBean Harbour, about four from Croker, there is an easy to enter layover anchorage between Amedroz Island and its satellite, Bourniot. Best entrance is from the northwest between the two islands. This harbor does get a surge from strong northwest winds. Six miles farther east Bedford Harbour, the anchorage formed by Bedford, West Rous and East Rous Islands, offers complete shelter. Enter from the northwest between Macpherson Ledge and Five Islands, favoring the latter.

 As you pass among these large islands the north shore vista, with its numerous islands backed up by the blue La Cloche Mountains, may call to you with a siren song. Unfortunately, this region is inadequately charted on the old-style, very small-scale, hard-to-read chart 2286. In fact, some of the contours shown date back to the original survey of 1822, and there are very few depth soundings to guide you. The same is true of the Bay of Islands, which lies between Great La Cloche Island and the mountains of the mainland. This is a cottage community, with many scenic island passages, but plenty of rocks and reefs and not a few low slung power lines overhead. Until it is adequately charted, cruising boats are advised to keep clear of the main part of the bay.

But if you want to poke your prow into this region a little bit, there are two anchorages on the north shore of Great La Cloche. Bell Cove and Sturgeon Cove are next-door neighbors. Enter Bell around the east end of Neptune Island, coming down the middle between the island and the east point to avoid the shoals off both. The water is quite deep in Bell Cove, and there can be surge. Sturgeon Cove is a little harder to enter, but there is a beacon range on the far shore at about 138°. Favor the west point at the entrance, as the shoals extend farther from the east side. These anchorages are handy to Little Current, about 8 miles away, if you prefer anchoring to docking or the time is growing late to move on.

Frazer Bay

Some 10 miles east of Little Current, Frazer Bay opens up on the north side of the waterway. Southwest of the entrance there is another anchorage that is ideal with respect to its proximity to Little Current, and whose wild attractions make it a popular destination in its own right. Sheltered on the north side of Heywood Island, Browning Cove is spacious and easy to enter. If you're coming from the east, find the green spar on Shoal Island Spit (from the west you don't need to worry about it), then come in on the west side of Browning Island. You can drop your hook in the main part of the cove or work in behind Browning and its sister islands all the way to the far end.

At Frazer Bay you have left the La Cloche Mountain range behind you, to enter the world of high, sparkling white quartzite ridges, set off by deep tones of pine green. Frazer Bay is a wedge-shaped body of water between two of these. Anchorage in Boyle Cove on its south shore is quite deep, but you can find more comfortable depths at the eastern end of the bay. An island, known locally as Blueberry, divides the cove where Rat Portage terminates. The west side is more sheltered, but the water is very deep; the east cove has a cottage, but you can anchor respect-fully distant from it in 12 to 14 feet. If your draft doesn't exceed 5 feet or your height 33 feet, you can settle into the more bucolic cove at the very end of the bay.

In the northwestern corner of Frazer Bay a buoyed channel leads between Little La Cloche Island and the white outcrop of McGregor Point and very quickly off soundings. This is the entrance to McGregor Bay, a bowl full of beautiful islands that has been a cottagers' paradise for generations. In some ways it matches the Bay of Islands on the other side of the La Cloche Peninsula, but here there has been even less survey work done or recorded on a chart. Without local knowledge it is no place for a visiting stranger in a boat larger than an outboard runa-bout. But the cruising boat has other treats in store, without McGregor Bay.

Baie Fine

About 2 miles east of McGregor Point Frazer Point terminates high, steep Killarney Ridge. Here a buoyed channel leads through the narrows into the magnificent Baie Fine, which some say is the only true fjord in North America. Its high cliffs and green and white vistas present an unforgettable 10-mile passage to The Pool at the far end. This is the second in the triumvirate of must-see anchorages that lure cruising boats to the North Channel. It is often crowded in mid-summer. But by all means, make the passage to the end just to see it. Note the clusters of

Baie Fine, The Pool.

islands at the eastern end of the widest part of Baie Fine and keep to the north shore until the last group of islets before the narrows, which you leave to port. Note also that the controlling depth at the narrows is 5 feet. If your draft is too great, or The Pool overfull, you can return to several equally scenic coves at the western end of Baie Fine to anchor. Mary Ann Cove, west of Frazer Bay Hill, with an island enclosing it, is a popular spot; there is a cottage on the island.

As you pass Frazer Point on the entrance you will see the attractive buildings and docks of a resort lodge. At one time this was a favored stop for cruising boats, but the lodge has been closed for several years and the property posted against trespassers. Apparently the place has recently been sold and there is hope that it may reopen as early as the summer of 1985.

Lansdowne Channel

On the southeast exit from Frazer Bay at Creak Island you enter the last passage on your North Channel adventure. Lansdowne Channel, between another pair of steep ridges, is also an extravagantly scenic waterway, with the heights of the Killarney Mountains pulling like a magnet at the far end. It, like the Whalesback, is a magical 9 miles long, with two narrow places helpfully buoyed. Snug Harbour is aptly named, a woodsy hideaway on the north side. Its obscured entrance opens up when you are precisely abeam the eastern tip of Centre Island. There is a regrettable intrusion on the splendor of Lansdowne's scenery where the heavy machinery of the Indusmin Quarry is busy lopping off the top of Badgely Island; on the opposite mainland shore you can see where a gigantic bite has been taken from the Lion's Rump. But Killarney silica is of fine quality and has been mined here for over 70 years, an important provider of jobs. The mine is quickly left behind as you move beyond Lansdowne into Killarney Bay.

If you follow the buoyed channel at the east end of Lansdowne you arrive at the western entrance to Killarney. If you hug the north shore, taking care to stay outside the 6-foot contour where it shoals out opposite Double Island, you arrive at the third Crown Jewel of the North Channel, Portage Couvert. From Killarney the course from the last red spar buoy is around the east side of Sheep Island and then across to the north shore of Killarney Bay. Stay close to the steep southwest shore as you enter the cove, to clear the rocks and shoals making out from the point on the starboard side. When clear of those, turn immediately northward to the center of the anchorage.

Portage Couvert, whose mellifluous name is so prosaicly translated on the chart to Covered Portage Cove, is cradled in a horseshoe of pine-studded white quartzite cliffs. Those who have voyaged far say it is one of the most beautiful anchorages in the world. Certainly it is a splendid climax to any cruise of the North Channel, Georgian Bay and Lake Huron.

7
LAKE MICHIGAN: METROPOLIS AND VILLAGE, HIGH DUNES AND LOW PRAIRIES

Although only a short, narrow waterway separates them, Lake Michigan is distinctly different in atmosphere from its twin, Lake Huron. Lying wholly within the United States, Lake Michigan's shores are more urban, with a vast range in community size between the nation's third largest city and the lakefront's tiniest hamlet. Four states border the lake—Michigan on the north and east, Indiana and Illinois at the southern end, and Wisconsin on the west. High sand dunes on the eastern shore and the limestone bluffs of the Niagara Escarpment that outline Green Bay on the west are the lake's most prominent natural features. The string of natural harbors on the eastern coast consists almost entirely of formerly land locked lakes whose sandbars have been cut through to create large, sheltered basins. Otherwise, like the lower lakes, Lake Michigan's shores are mainly smooth and most of its harbors are artificial. The large outer harbors function primarily as stilling basins to reduce wave action and are not suitable for anchorage. Only a few islands dot the lake's surface, and there is no wilderness, but every harbor shelters a large resident fleet of pleasure boats. Power and sail seem somewhat more evenly divided here than on the other lakes. Deep sea fishing for salmon and trout is the angler's game and, like Lake Erie, there is a fleet of charter fishing party boats in almost every port.

Shaped rather like a carrot, the 320-mile length of the lake combined with its 50- to 80-mile width through most of that distance, creates some special cruising conditions. It's relatively easy to cross in a day's sail or a few hours of motoring (except at the wide top 118 miles across). But winds blowing along the long axis can kick up high, tough seas. Northerlies are rare in summer, but southerlies have a lot of water to work on before they reach the popular cruising grounds at the north end of the lake. Opposite shores of the lake often experience reverse sea breeze effects. On the east side light (or nonexistent) morning winds blow from east and south, but by mid-day they have swung around to southwest and west to increase speed and make for exhilarating afternoon sailing. On the west side the morning lull is wafted from south and west, with the afternoon lake breeze often coming from northeast through southeast at somewhat lower speeds than on the opposite side. Summer thunderstorms and squalls come in mainly from southwest, sometimes northwest, mostly at night. And Lake Michigan in spring has been known to host an occasional tornado or water-spout. Fog can occur anywhere, especially in early summer, but is likeliest at the north end.

Because of its length, summer weather is quite different at the two ends of the lake. The heat and humidity of a midwestern summer that engulfs the southern shores give way to the cooling effect of northern woods and onshore breezes at the northern end. In fact, weather in northern Lake Michigan can be idyllic—warm, sunny days for water sports and cool, refreshing nights for sleep. As on the lower lakes, the moderating lake effect on climate, combined with the rich soil that surrounds virtually all of Lake Michigan, has created ideal conditions for the growing of produce. Orchards, vineyards and farms flourish the length of the east coast to yield the delicate cherries, strawberries, aspara-gus, blueberries and grapes in sequence, while hardier apples adorn the western shores.

Lake Michigan made its entrance on the stage of recorded history somewhat later than the others, except Erie. It wasn't until 1634 that Champlain got around to sending an envoy to the tribes resident there. So optimistic was he that this lake *surely* led to the Western Sea that Jean Nicolet carried in his baggage a damask coat, appropriate for greeting the Emperor of China. The Indians of Green Bay were suitably impressed, and a new branch of the fur trade took off from there. All through the French and British periods Green Bay was the most important post on the lake, reachable by a partially sheltered passage across the top of Lake Michigan and connected by an inland route to the entire Mississippi Valley. Most of the river mouths around the rest of Lake Michigan also sported local fur trading posts, including the secondary access to the western interior at Chicago.

The two wars by which the United States gained and sustained its independence from Great Britain had little impact on Lake Michigan. But by the first quarter of the 19th century the march of western settlement was transforming its southern shores into frontier prairie farms. Settlement occurred later in Michigan than in Indiana and Illinois, largely because of unfavorable publicity about its climate and fertility. Wisconsin played a major role in the leveling of the great north woods during middle and late century before agriculture took over there too.

The towns around the lake that did not begin life as fur trading posts started out as sawmill sites or farm marketing centers. Then came the railroads, and lake life was transformed. Chicago became the nation's great rail center, linking East and West with bands of steel, and making the critical transfers from ship to rail and back again. At first she received mainly Great Lakes lumber to build the cities of the West and transferred agricultural produce eastward. Then iron ore from northern Lake Michigan and Lake Superior began to come in by cheap water transport to meet the coal brought by rail from the South and East. Together they launched the vast steel-fabricating complex at the foot of the lake. A diverse manufactory grew up in the towns around the lower lakeshore, and today it is part of the Midwest megalopolis that stretches from Buffalo to Milwaukee.

While the lower end of Lake Michigan is densely urbanized, as one moves northward the towns become smaller, farms and orchards take over the scenery between them, and water-oriented resorts fill in among both. For cruising boats Lake Michigan is both a point of residential origin and a vacation destination. All it takes is a passage north. There is perhaps less natural variety here than on Lake Huron, but there are many more cities and villages to visit, some with marine accommodations that more closely resemble a resort lodge than a boatyard. And there is great variation in the level of sophistication you'll encounter at the several ports, from the posh to the primitive. Like Jean Nicolet, we'll begin at the top.

The Island Groups
Charts 14902, 14911, 14912

Each of the Great Lakes has at least one grand bank amid its depths whose heights rise above the surface as a cluster of islands. In Lake Michigan the shoal-skirted archipelago begins at the northeastern entrance to the lake, just beyond the Straits of Mackinac. Extending about 40 miles east to west and 65 north to south, it consists of three distinct groups, separated from one another by deep water. First and largest is the Beaver Island group.

The southern boundary of the Straits of Mackinac straggles westward as the reef-bound extremity of Waugoshance Point (pronounced "Wobbleshanks" locally) and its offshore islands. The abandoned lighthouse that marks safe passage westward of the ragged point is far more conspicuous from any direction than the currently operating lighthouses. Virtually all pleasure boats use it as their navigational reference, although its location is too shoal for contemporary freighters. Although its protective sheathing is falling away, hopefully the structure will stand for a long time yet. Once you arrive at the old lighthouse from the east, three new ones marching in line from north to south show up on a clear day and are brilliant at night—the red and white barber stripes of White Shoal Light, the white square tower of Grays Reef Light, and the slim white tower of Ile aux Galets on its islet of pointy shrubs. (Here, too, the name has evolved into a waggish "Skilly-gallee.") If you're approaching from the west, the gray square tower of Lansing Shoal Light will be the first to greet you. All of these are placed to guide ships through the shallows east and/or north of the Beaver Island group.

The Beavers consist of four major islands, five minors and a number of islets. They take their title from the largest one, Beaver Island, measuring 14 miles by 6. This is also the only one with a true harbor and was the focus of island settlement in the second quarter of the 19th century. A stranger colony was rarely seen on the American frontier, for here was proclaimed the only kingdom within the United States—and the king represented his subjects in the Michigan State Legislature. King James Jesse Strang led his dissident Mormon followers to Beaver Island in 1847, where he ruled in undisputed authority for nine years. Smouldering resentment among his people erupted into regicide, and overt resentment by mainlanders drove the remaining Mormons away. Land on the beautiful island was soon taken up

Lake Michigan, Old Lighthouse.

by Irish farmers and woodcutters, and many of the 200 people living year-round on the island are their descendants.

The Irish cast to Beaver Island is evident immediately upon your arrival at the harbor of St. James, where a sign bids you welcome in Gaelic. The federal government is present in the guise of an occulting red light on a white tower at the harbor entrance and buoys to lead you to the **Waterways Commission Marina**, where you'll find the usual dockside services at the slips, except diesel and ice. St. James is a popular boating destination and, especially on weekends, you may find no room at the dock at all. It's a convivial place, with as much rafting as possible, but if even that fails you can anchor off at the northern end of the harbor.

It's the "unspoiled" charm of St. James that attracts, still essentially a quiet 19th-century village. A substantial summer cottage colony on the island supports a couple of stores and restaurants, however, and the Shamrock Bar offers food as well as spirits and lively *esprit*. To learn more of the fascinating story of King Strang and the fortunes of the subsequent settlers, visit the historical museum in the restored 1848 Mormon Print Shop (448-2254). You can use either your own 2 feet or rent a bicycle to take you down the appealing country roads through forest and field.

If you tire of the whirl of civilization at St. James, each of the other major islands, mostly uninhabited, has a cove in which to anchor with varying degrees of protection and no buoyage. The most sheltered is at Garden Island, a couple of miles north of Beaver. Enter from due west, but watch out for the long rocky spit that extends from the southern peninsula that makes up the anchorage. If you work in behind the island in the middle of the cove, you will have protection from all winds. The cove on the northeast end of High Island, about 4 miles west of Beaver, is wide open to east and south and has very deep water in its most sheltered area. But this makes a pleasant day stop, if a little risky for overnight. Hog Island's anchorage is in the northwest corner and must be approached from the north side. This one is open to the northwest and is not readily combined with a visit to Beaver Island, 6 miles away as the gull flies but a lot farther around the extensive shoal water. But all of the outlying islands are attractive in their natural state with interesting plant and animal life to observe ashore.

The Fox Islands, about 15 miles southwest of Beaver Island, have no harbor and can be admired only in passing. About 25 miles farther southwest North and South Manitou islands are part of the Sleeping Bear National Lakeshore. The pair lies approximately 7 miles off the mainland shore that is dominated by the awesome heights of the Sleeping Bear Dune. The sages of old told the story round the campfire of a mother bear and her two cubs who were trapped on the western shore by a raging forest fire. They had no choice but to attempt the long swim across this widest part of Lake Michigan. The mother made it to the other side and lay down exhausted to await the cubs. But they never arrived. The Great Manitou in pity created two islands where the little bears had sunk beneath the waves, and the great bear keeps her vigil on the mainland to this day. But Mama truly lives, for Sleeping Bear at 480 feet in height is still growing and moving, the largest living sand dune in the world. There is no place for a cruising boat to anchor or dock near the Sleeping Bear, but you can visit her cubs.

South Manitou harbor is nothing more than a large bight in the east shore of the island. Although shown in an enlargement on the chart, for cruising boats it's a pretty iffy harbor—if the wind doesn't blow anywhere from east and part of south. It is also very deep, and there is only a small area toward the northwest side where your hook can find less than 40 feet. It is very easy to enter, however; just come on in. There is a Park Service ferry dock, from which private boats are prohibited. North Manitou has no harbor at all, but it's only 4 miles away,

Sleeping Bear Dunes.

and if you have a fast dinghy, you might want to go over for a look.

Despite its exposure to winds from east through south, South Manitou has sheltered many a lake vessel over the years. Manitou Passage was the main route for 19th-century steamers, and the first islanders earned their living by supplying cordwood to the ships that called. Later, German immigrants came to farm the good soil of South Manitou and the population reached its zenith at almost 100 souls in 1880. By the early 1950s there were only a handful of people left, and in 1970 the island became part of the National Lakeshore. North Manitou has a similar history.

Under National Park Service management the Manitou Islands comprise a wilderness unit. They are not a wilderness yet because much evidence still remains of the farming settlements, especially on South Manitou. But nature is being allowed to take her course with the old buildings as well as the terrain, and facilities for the day-trippers and backpackers who come over on the ferry from Leland are minimal. For nature lovers and history buffs these islands offer miles of delightful hiking on country roads, through lush second-growth forest and along deserted beaches; they, too, have their high dunes on the western sides.

North Manitou is about 7 miles long by 4 wide and South Manitou only 3 by 2½. North Manitou once claimed the biggest

American elm tree in the world, at 180 feet tall and so thick that five men with outstretched arms could not reach around it. A few years ago its life was taken by a bolt of lightning. On South Manitou there is a grove of virgin white cedar in the southwest corner known as the Valley of the Giants. The old lighthouse at the southeast corner of the harbor is open for visitation, and you can view the shipwrecked *Francisco Morizon* on the south shore.

Les Traverses—Grand et Petit

Charts 14902, 14913, 14942

To the voyageurs, who closely followed the shoreline in their birchbark canoes, wide bays indenting a coast where they had no direct business were impediments to cross. The northeast corner of Lake Michigan has two such bays, adjacent and at right angles to each other, logically distinguished by their relative size. They retain the old names but slightly translated as Grand Traverse and Little Traverse.

It may have been the bays that presented an obstacle to paddlers of yore, but for contemporary small boat mariners it's the bulge of high land between the Straits of Mackinac and Little Traverse Bay. Some even refer to it as the Horn of the Great Lakes. Not only is there no harbor in the 50-mile stretch between the Mackinac Bridge, where Lake Michigan semiofficially begins, and Harbor Springs, but the passage includes three cardinal points of the compass. The wind and sea are going to be "wrong" on at least one of them. It's not a dangerous passage (except, like any other, in heavy weather) but often a wickedly inconvenient one. Nevertheless, the rewards at either end are more than worth the trouble.

Harbor Springs

That nefarious bulge was the home of the Ottawa Indians for centuries before white men came and, despite the enormous influx of others, it still is. To guide their canoes they twisted a great pine in the shape of a cross on the bluff and the whole region was known by the French as L'Arbre Croche. That was also the first name given to the mission on the north shore of Little Traverse Bay established by Father Peter DeJean in 1827. By the time treaties opened the area for white settlement in the 1870s the place was known as Little Traverse, and in 1881 it was incorporated as the village of Harbor Springs.

By whatever name, the beautiful, bluff-encircled harbor—the largest, natural, deep water harbor on the lakes—where delicious spring water emerges spontaneously from the ground, has been a favorite resort since men and women first trod here. The first villagers earned their livelihood from forest and field, and at one time the harbor was ringed with sawmills. No evidence of these remains, but at the time they flourished Little Traverse Bay was "discovered" as a summer retreat from the heat and humidity of the cities below. No ordinary resort, Harbor Springs has from the beginning been colonized in summer by families of wealth. Now unto the generations they come from all those states of middle America with low scenery and high temperatures, from as far as Missouri and Oklahoma. With good reason it has been called "the Newport of the Middle West," and on the run in toward Little Traverse Light you'll begin to see why.

Wedge-shaped Little Traverse Bay, 10 miles across and 11½ deep, begins at Seven Mile Point, identified by a tall, white modern house on the bluffside. From there you should keep at least a mile offshore to avoid unmarked shoals until the last mile or so before the light when you can move closer to gawk. The "cottage" mansions that line Harbor Point may not rival the palazzi of Newport in ostentation, but they date from the same era and exude luxury. Take a close look as you round the point and move up the harbor on the deep-to inside, because no stranger is allowed through the landward gates of Harbor Point to invade the privacy of its residents.

But Harbor Point isn't all there is to gaze at as you move eastward into Little Traverse Bay. The sand dunes of Petoskey State Park at the far end point their tips skyward, and the red roof and turrets of the venerable Harbour Inn set on spacious grounds give you a focus for your prow before rounding Little Traverse Light, flashing green on a skeleton tower. On the north shore opposite Harbor Point, Wequetonsing, another colony of elegant summer homes, lines the waterfront. Between them downtown Harbor Springs nestles under the bluff like a picture postcard, the near waters of its superb harbor filled with sailboats dancing on moorings.

Bear closer to the western end of the moorings to reach the **Waterways Commission Marina**, where the slips carry 8 feet or more, and all dockside services are provided except fuel. In season dockage is hard to come by here, but the harbor master monitors channel 16, so you can call ahead to inquire. He may put you on the mooring of an absent boat. The two marinas in Harbor Springs also accommodate transients when they have space available. West of the city dock, **Walstrom Marine** has 15-foot depths at slips and alongside, with all dockside services. This is a full service marina, catering largely to powerboats, with haulout by travelift and elevator up to 50 tons, engine and hull repairs, in-house electronics service, and a marine store. East of the city dock **Irish Boat Shop** caters primarily to sail boats, with 5 to 14 feet at its floating slips; all dockside services; a 20-ton travelift; engine, hull and rigging repair; sail loft and marine store.

The vibrancy of Harbor Springs is evident as soon as you step off the boat. Right at the city dock are the tennis courts, with floodlights for night play, and its three major restaurants are clustered at the waterfront. The Pier serves excellent food in the formal Pointer Room and the informal Chart Room; the New York captures the ambiance of the 1904 hotel it occupies; and Juilleret's has been an informal gathering place since the turn of the century, featuring planked whitefish and homemade ice cream. The town of 1,600 year-round residents is compact. In three blocks Main Street presents an enticing array of shops of all kinds, from the mundane to the elegant. For supermarket provisioning, however, you must ascend the bluff to Harbor IGA, which will provide transportation on call. Also on the bluff on the outskirts of town—but worth the long walk or a cab ride—is an exquisite farm market called Bluff Gardens. Specializing in miniature vegetables, the market features an indoor presentation of delicacies, and the outdoor array of garden rows is a delight to the eye as well as the palette.

Make at least one pass down Main Street from the east end toward the west. The graceful spire of Holy Childhood Church, framed by lofty trees, is a vista that captures the spirit of the town. The mission church dates from 1842, and Holy Childhood School next door still serves Indian boarding students from around the lakes as well as Catholic day students, of both Native and European descent. In further appreciation of the Indian heritage of Harbor Springs the Chief Blackbird Museum on Main Street displays artifacts and the Ottawa story in the former home of the town's longtime postmaster, the literary Chief Andrew Blackbird (526-2104). And in appreciation of boating tradition the annual Antique Boat Show takes place at Walstrom Marine on the Saturday before Labor Day.

Petoskey

On the south shore of Little Traverse Bay Petoskey is the county seat and the biggest city for some distance around at

6,000 people. Petoskey is more of a working city than either of its neighbors, Harbor Springs and Charlevoix, but it, too, has its elegant, historic summer cottage colony. Bay View, in fact, is on the National Register of Historic Places, but can be viewed only in passing, as there is no dockage there. You might want to take a cab out from Petoskey one evening for a concert in the summer series of the Bay View Association.

Petoskey's harbor is an artificial one. It was the arrival of the railroad in the late 1870s that set the town's course as a resort, marketing, government and, more recently, medical center. Behind the enclosing breakwater, marked with a flashing red light (difficult to pick up at night against the city lights), the usual well-built **Waterway Commission Marina** has 8-foot depths and offers all dockside services except diesel fuel. The marina is located in a city park. In the 1892 railroad station at the park's edge the Little Traverse Bay Historical Museum (347-2620) features among its many artifacts and documents memorabilia of two famous authors with Petoskey connections— Ernest Hemingway and Bruce Catton.

Downtown Petoskey has all the stores and commercial services, as well as restaurants and two hospitals, that one would expect to find in a regional center. In addition, what may be the largest collection of elegant fashion, gift and art shops, and boutiques in the Midwest occupies several blocks of the attractive Gaslight District. Whether you love or loathe shopping, it's an intriguing place. All of this, plus a movie theater, is just a few blocks from the marina. The most gracious dining in town is in the Perry-Davis Hotel at the edge of the Gaslight District. Stafford's Bay View Inn also serves very good food in a historic hotel (no liquor), but requires a taxi from the marina.

Additional special activities available in Petoskey are the changing exhibits at the McCune Art Center downtown on Mitchell Street (347-4337) and a tour of Kilwin's Candy Kitchen, which supplies its chocolate shops throughout the Midwest (347-4831). The summer season is kicked off each June with a four-day Historic Festival. Shows, contests and events take place all over town. Highlight is the world's longest tug of war, stretching 2½ miles between the bay's oldest resorts, Harbour Inn and Stafford's Bay View Inn. July Fourth is also celebrated with gusto, including a parade, barbecue and waterfront fireworks. Salmon and trout plantings in the Bear River have been very successful, and during the seasonal runs the river mouth, close by the marina, is crowded with thigh-deep anglers. You might want to try your luck.

Little Traverse Bay has one more uncommon attraction in the finest beachfront hunting ground for the official Michigan state stone, the Petoskey Stone. These are fossilized corals, some 300 million years old, that are highly ornamental when polished. If you aren't successful at finding your own specimens of gray or beige rock imprinted with jagged little circles, you can buy them at many local shops, raw, polished, or transformed into gift items.

Charlevoix

Charlevoix the Beautiful, as its motto declares, is blessed with the waters of three lakes. Its broad beach, backed by lovely homes, faces Lake Michigan, Round Lake forms its main harbor, and the sparkling vista of Lake Charlevoix extends from its back porch. Gilded Age families of wealth followed the railroad here, too, especially from Chicago. Its two gracious enclaves of mansion/cottages are the Chicago Club and the Belvidere Club, flanking the lively downtown.

Charlevoix lies about midway between Little Traverse Bay and Grand Traverse Bay, not really belonging to either. The steep peak of Mount McSauba on the east and the less scenic smoke and stacks of Medusa Portland Cement on the west identify its location from seaward. Parallel breakwaters extend into the lake on either side of the Pine River entrance, with flashing white and fixed red lights and a fog horn. Nevertheless, in heavy wind and sea from north and northwest it can be quite a sleighride getting in. The reversing current in Pine River runs up to 3 miles an hour. But it's less than ½ mile through the pretty, steep-banked river from the pierheads to the Bridge Street Bridge. Closed clearance is 16 feet, but the bridge opens for three minutes either side of the hour and half hour between 0600 and 1800, at other times with one long and one short blast. Through the bridge you're in Round Lake, a bauble ½ mile in diameter set between big Lake Michigan and medium-size Lake Charlevoix.

The town of 3,300 people surrounds the lake, but most of the dockage you see is private. A turn to starboard, past the ferry for Beaver Island 32 miles away, is the **Waterways Commission Marina**. This is the only accommodation for transients in Round Lake, and has at least 10 feet of water at the slips, with all dockside services except fuel. Fuel is available at Bellinger Marine Service on the south shore, which also has a 10-ton hoist, engine and hull repairs. The city dock, separated from Bridge Street, the main drag, by a small waterfront park, is very

Charlevoix, Pine River Bridge.

convenient to all of downtown and just a few blocks' walk to the Lake Michigan beach. But it is usually jammed in summer (the harbor master monitors channel 16, if you want to call ahead) and many visitors to Charlevoix simply anchor in Round Lake. The problem is depth—in excess of 30 feet except for a narrow strip right off the dock faces.

The shops of Charlevoix are less pretentious than those of its sister towns in Little Traverse Bay, but no less appealing, and present a full array of food, beverage, gift, clothing and craft selections. There are several restaurants to choose from; the most gracious for dinner, and serving excellent food, is Grey Gables Inn on Belvidere Street. Night life consists of the movies and a couple of cocktail lounges. You can learn more about the history of this charming town at the Harsha House museum on State Street. Two annual events have long been popular—the Venetian Festival the last weekend in July, with street and boat parades, games and so on; and the Waterfront Art Fair, usually the second Saturday in the month.

Another short stretch of Pine River leads from Round Lake to Lake Charlevoix. The railroad bridge, with 10 feet of clearance, usually stands open. Lake Charlevoix, whose waters run very deep, is enfolded by softly wooded hills through most of its 14-mile length and 1- to 2-mile width. It is a delightful, sheltered cruising ground, with good sailing winds on its northwest-southeast axis. Before you set out, however, there are a couple of marinas near the entrance to the lake that are good alternatives to the crowded city dock. They are more than 1½ miles from downtown, but taxis are available.

A turn to starboard after passing through the railroad bridge brings you first to **Northwest Marine Yacht Club**. This is a condominium, with slips available when members are away. Depths range from 5 to 23 feet and the usual dockside services are offered, except fuel and pumpout, but including Laundromat. There is a swimming pool, and the park next door has a beach and picnic grounds. Just beyond this marina **Irish Boat Shop** is enclosed behind breakwaters with red and green lights at the entrance. It has floating slips with 5- to 20-foot depths, all dockside services, except diesel; a 35-ton travelift; full engine, hull and rigging repair; ready access to the Irish sail loft in Harbor Springs and a marine store.

In cruising Lake Charlevoix there are several choices for stopovers. Pleasant anchorage can be found on the north shore in either Oyster Bay, close to Charlevoix, or Horton Bay, closer to the far end. The lake has two arms, and both are worth exploring. Five miles from the Round Lake entrance South Arm extends another 8 miles to East Jordan. Close to the entrance of this narrow bay the Ironton cable ferry is one of the last of its kind. Quaint and historic to observe, it is hazardous to meet in mid-stream where the cables may garrote your boat. If the ferry is in motion, wait; it doesn't take long for the tiny four-car boat to make the 600-foot crossing. There are some coves in South Arm, where you can pull off to anchor, or you can continue all the way to the village of East Jordan, where there are a few **Waterways Commission Docks** with electricity and water. There are shops and restaurants convenient to the dock.

At the foot of the main stem of Lake Charlevoix, Boyne City offers two choices for dockage. The small **Waterways Commission Marina** is on the north side of town, in a park near the mouth of the Boyne River. There is electricity and water at the dock, with heads in the park, as well as a playground and picnic grills and tables. On the south side **The Harborage** is a large, new marina associated with a condominium development. Inside the sheltering breakwater with a quick flashing red light all dockside services, including cable TV and telephone hookups, are offered at the floating slips with depths in excess of 8 feet. A sand beach is adjacent, and the shops and restaurants of this attractive town of 3,300 people are less than half a mile away.

The Grand Traverse is actually about the same distance

across, 10½ miles, as the Little Traverse. What makes it grand is its 32-mile length, north to south, divided for the lower 17 miles between East Arm and West Arm. Heavy winds and seas from northwest through northeast can raise rough seas as they funnel down the long fetch. The slopes that outline both arms of the bay and the Old Mission Peninsula between them float in spring on a cloud of cherry blossoms. Here, in a happy marriage of soil and climate, are grown one-third of the world's supply of cherries. There was timber to be logged off before the first experimental cherry trees were planted to replace the pine and save the regional economy, and each of the towns around the bay was founded by a sawmill. Now, except for cherry processing, their main business is tourism—by land and by lake.

East Arm

It's 34 miles from Charlevoix around the curve and down the East Arm of Grand Traverse Bay to Elk Rapids. Once past the buoys marking South Point and Fisherman Island it's advisable to stay at least a half mile offshore. The mouth of Elk River is enclosed by breakwaters, marked by quick flashing red and green lights, and dredged to 5½ feet. Inside the basin the **Waterways Commission Marina** has 9-foot depths at the slips, with the usual dockside services except ice and diesel. The attractive downtown shopping area of the village of 1,500 people is only a few blocks away, with full shopping, Laundromat, restaurants and a movie theater.

Near the foot of the East Arm **East Bay Harbor** is enclosed in a breakwater, with flashing red and green lights marking the entrance. Ten-foot depths carry through the channel, and there is 4 to 10 feet at the slips, with all dockside services except diesel, but including telephone hookup. There is a private beach, and the Embers Restaurant is on the premises. A small shopping center nearby has essential stores and Laundromat, but it is a 6-mile cab ride to downtown Traverse City.

Old Mission Peninsula

The first white settlement on Grand Traverse Bay was on Old Mission Peninsula where Reverend Peter Dougherty established his Presbyterian mission to the Indians in 1839. The original Mission Point Lighthouse still stands near the tip almost precisely on the 45th parallel. The current flashing white light on a white tower is placed outside the band of shoals of which it warns. Old Mission Harbor on the northeast end of the peninsula no longer shelters missionaries, but it can protect an anchored boat from all winds except east through south. Its main disadvantage is water depth in excess of 30 feet.

Bowers Harbor, halfway down the west side of the peninsula, is even deeper, though well sheltered except from southwest, but here there is a small marina. **Bowers Harbor Marina**, in a pretty setting, caters mainly to small power boats, but there is 8 feet of depth at alongside docking, with gas, ice and heads. There is a food store nearby and a quarter of a mile away a park with playground and tennis courts.

Traverse City

At the foot of West Arm, Traverse City is not only the cherry capital of the world, but the capital of the northwest lower peninsula of Michigan, with 15,500 people, a rather diversified industrial base, a bustling, well-stocked downtown and extensive tourist facilities. Motels line the shore at the foot of both East and West arms. The **Waterways Commission Marina** is in Clinch Park behind a sheltering breakwater, marked with a quick flashing green light. There is 5 to 15 feet of depth at the slips, with all dockside services except diesel fuel. The waterfront park has much to offer children of all ages—a small zoo, a natural history museum, a miniature train ride and a sand beach. Groceries are available a short distance away, but the closest Laundromat is about a mile.

In addition to its extensive shopping, restaurants and cocktail lounges, Traverse City offers the opportunity to enjoy professional summer theater at the Cherry County Playhouse downtown next to the Park Place Motor Inn (947-9560, or write in advance for tickets to Box 661, Traverse City, MI 49684). The city's civic theater, Old Town Playhouse, also mounts summer productions (947-2210). The region's most renowned center for the performing arts is the National Music Camp, 15 miles south of the city. If you're a music lover and take special pleasure in the performance of young talent, you may want to rent a car to get there. The atmosphere is inspiring at this oldest of music camps, now in its sixth decade of training and showcasing some of the most talented youngsters in the nation. The excellent performances of music, dance and drama are scheduled frequently through the week and weekends (276-9921).

Unquestionably the main event in Traverse City is the National Cherry Festival in July. It originated in 1923 as a Blessing of the

Blossoms, and since then has blossomed into a week of festivities that includes parades, sporting events, amusements, band competitions and, of course, food.

In the suburb of Greilickville on the west side of West Arm there is a basin enclosed by a seawall and a detached breakwater. Flashing red and green lights mark the entrance from the south. The township park, launching ramps and public marina for seasonal docking and mooring are immediately inside the basin. In the northwest corner a red triangular daymark identifies the entrance to a further enclosed basin for **Harbor West Marina**. Catering mostly to sailboats, it has 7 feet through the channel and 5 to 10 feet at the slips with all dockside services; a launch ramp; 30-ton travelift; engine, hull and rigging repairs; sail loft and marine store. The park south of the marina has a playground and beach, and 1½ miles away is a shopping center. It's about 2½ miles into downtown Traverse City.

Suttons Bay

Halfway up West Arm, 15 miles from Greilickville, Suttons Bay indents the coastline for about 3 miles. At the bottom of the bay is a little village of the same name. Unlike the East Arm, this side of Grand Traverse Bay has several buoys dotted along the coast at shoal points. The **Waterways Commission Marina** at Suttons Bay is not quite up to the usual high standard. The alongside dock has fendered pilings, but the side docks at the slips are very narrow and the tie-off bollards are only pipes. The usual services are offered, however, except diesel and ice. But ice, as well as a Laundromat, can be found on the street near the entrance to the park in which the marina is located. The park has a beach and playground, and downtown stores and restaurants are only a few blocks beyond the marina. There are several gift and antique shops in town, and a movie theater, as Suttons Bay's summer population multiplies many times its 500 year-round residents.

Northport

Last stop on Grand Traverse Bay is Northport, a village of 600, also sheltered in its own bay about 15 miles from Suttons. Once an important timber-shipping port, the village now caters to local summer cottagers and wandering tourists with a generous variety of gift, antique and art shops, restaurants and cocktail lounges. There is also a well-stocked general store and a hospital in the realm of essential services, and tennis courts at the schoolhouse.

All of these are within a couple of blocks of the **Waterways Commission Marina**, which at Northport is an excellent facility enclosed behind a breakwater with quick flashing red and green lights at the entrance. All dockside services are offered, and the surrounding park has a children's playground. A mile north in Northport Bay, Northport Bay Boat Yard does not have transient dockage, but if you need repairs, it has a 20-ton crane for haulout with full service to engine, hull and rigging.

The Country Dune Coast
Charts 14902, 14906, 14907, 14912, 14935, 14937, 14938, 14939

When the glaciers were at work molding the terrain of the Great Lakes their loads of debris were often dumped in hills called *moraines*. At one of the earlier stages of glacial Lake Michigan beach sand constantly blown up from shore by the west wind piled up atop a ridge of coastal moraines to create the high dunes of the lake's eastern coast. Geologists have given them the graphic name of *perched dunes*, and in greater or lesser height they border the entire coastline of Michigan and Indiana. You might not always recognize them, for now at 4,500 years of age most are clothed with trees and vegetation. Where the phenomenon known as *blowouts* occurs the raw sand is exposed and is still blowing into the formations we call *living dunes*. Clothed or naked, they present a splendid panorama.

Behind the dune-covered coastal moraines pockets of glacial ice melted into lakes, forming a chain almost the entire length of Lake Michigan. Where an enclosing sandbar has been cut through, boaters enjoy a fine harbor. Most of the lakes are cradled in rolling, wooded and rural hills, with state parks often encompassing the beach and dune areas. The series begins at Michigan's little finger, the Leelanau Peninsula.

Leland

The general rule finds an immediate exception at Leland. The Leland River, just under a mile long, which connects Lake Leelanau with Lake Michigan, is dammed, so there is no navigable connection between the two lakes. The harbor at Leland is an artificial one, dredged from the mouth of the river and

Leland, Fishtown restoration.

protected by breakwaters. It is entered from the south between flashing red and green lights with appropriate daymarks. Controlling depth in the channel and outer basin is 10 feet, but at the inside slips of the **Waterways Commission Marina** it is 5. All dockside services are available. Because this is the only harbor in the 60-mile stretch between Northport and Frankfort, rafting is common during the height of the season. It's accomplished by tying boats off the ends of the slips and linking them up from there; it can be quite a convivial game.

The little village, 30 miles from Northport, became a summer resort at about the same time as all the others in the neighborhood, when the railroad came through and after the timber had been shipped out. Leland has retained one of its older occupations, however—commercial fishing. There are still tugs putting out from the harbor and you can buy fresh fish as well as enjoy it in the local restaurants. Furthermore, the older fishing shanties, net sheds and assorted buildings associated with the industry have been tastefully preserved for a new function as gift shops, bakery, candy store, etc., in addition to the old one of selling fish. Collectively known as Fishtown, these shops are adjacent to the marina, as is a children's playground. Within a block or two there is grocery shopping, more gift shops, restaurants and the Leelanau County Historical Museum in the old jail (256-9343). Leland is also the ferry port for the Manitou Islands, 10 to 15 miles offshore—a possible alternative to taking your own boat across.

Frankfort

From Leland the course southwest leads past the massive headlands and dunes of Pyramid Point, Sleeping Bear Point and Point Betsie, with one of the Great Lakes' most photographed lighthouses, for about 37 miles to Frankfort. If you notice what appears to be giant bats flying from the dune tops on the approach to Frankfort, don't conclude you've been at sea too long. The little town of 1,600 people has passed through its lumbering stage and its period of service as a terminal for railroad car ferries across Lake Michigan to become one of the nation's major centers for hang gliding. Actually, the unique combination of bluffs, soaring winds and soft beach landing places was discovered during the infancy of the sport back in the 1930s. Now Frankfort and its sister town of Elberta host the National Gliding and Soaring Festival every June, but you might see gliders any day in the week that conditions are favorable.

Lake Betsie, 1½ miles long by ½ mile wide, forms Frankfort's ample harbor. A pair of converging breakwaters form an outer harbor to ensure a calm interior, and a second pair of breakwaters leads into the lake. The outer pair has a flashing red and fixed green light, the latter equipped with a fog horn, and the inner south pier has a fixed red. Currents in the entrance channel can run up to 3 miles an hour in either direction.

The **Waterways Commission Marina** is on the port shore about a quarter of a mile past the inner channel, quite far from the beach, as is often the case in these lake-harbors. Fixed and floating slips in 8 feet have all dockside services, and there is a playground in the park surrounding the marina. The town's attractive shopping area is virtually across the street; the Laundromat is about half a mile away. Across the lake in the village of Elberta **Betsie Marina** caters mainly to powerboats in slips with 8 feet, all dockside services, a 30-ton crane for haulout, and engine and hull repairs. Beyond, the lake shoals quickly to swamp. Elberta is a small place, but there is grocery shopping and a restaurant within ½ mile. Rental cars are available in Frankfort if you should care to visit the National Music Camp from this direction, a 30-mile drive through pretty country.

Arcadia

The coast continues steep-to, and 10 miles south of Frankfort, Arcadia Lake has been connected to Lake Michigan by a dredged channel carrying 10 feet. The parallel piers extending into the lake aren't lighted, but there is a black and white Mo(A) light buoy off the entrance. The main part of the small lake is shallow, but deep water extends up the mile-long north arm to the little village, where a **Waterways Commission Marina** provides the usual dockside services at its slips. The town isn't much, but this may be a convenient overnight stop, and there are stores and a tennis court within half a mile.

Onekama

Portage Lake, about 9 miles south of Arcadia, is both larger and deeper, some 3¼ miles long and ½ mile to 1½ miles wide. Depth exceeds 20 feet throughout most of it, except near the vilage of Onekama, where it varies from 4 to 8 feet. This is a good fishing lake, and the marinas cater to the local fleet of smaller motorboats. Parallel piers, with flashing red and white lights, extend into Lake Michigan to protect the channel entrance, dredged to 10 feet. Shoaling is a problem here, however, and currents can run up to 3 miles per hour in either direction.

Impressive dunes and bluffs encircle much of Portage Lake, and Onekama is at the far end on the north side. **Onekama Marina** has two locations. The village side is mainly for small motorboats, although there is 4½ feet at the slips. On the south side of the lake, about a mile from downtown, there are slips for larger motorboats and some sailboats, with all dockside services available, a marine railway, engine and hull repairs, and a courtesy car for shopping. Onekama is a small place, with a year-round population under 600, but it does have essential stores and a Laundromat.

Manistee

The vast forest of enormous white pine that covered central Michigan when the territory first opened up assured the state's fortune (at least while the timber lasted). And it came to glory down the rivers and streams that flowed to the Great Lakes from the deep interior. One of the long ones that tumbled from the spinal ridge was the Manistee, and millions of board feet slid down those waters before the 'jacks were done. The logs piled up in booms around Manistee Lake to feed the 25 sawmills and 12 shingle mills that whined and screeched in the town that grew up on the shore. Then, in a few short decades, it was all over. The mills are long gone and the river that brought giant logs to the lake now brings light canoes. But Manistee survived, blessed with rich salt deposits discovered shortly before the timber gave out, a climate ideal for growing apples and strawberries, and an assortment of industries (including Century Boats) that make the little city a thriving, attractive place today.

The river that flows into Manistee Lake, and even creates a delta in the northeast corner, doesn't quite end there. It exits on the northwest side of the lake to continue another mile and a half before merging with Lake Michigan. Its mouth is doubly protected from wave action, like so many of these east coast ports, with a breakwater on the southwest that creates an outer harbor and parallel breakwaters outlining the channel. The south breakwater carries a flashing red light and the pierheads have isophase white and red lights, with a fog horn on the north pier. Currents here, too, run up to 3 miles per hour.

The **Waterways Commission Marina** is conveniently located on the south bank about a mile upstream in downtown Manistee, but the slips are nicely buffered from traffic. All dockside services, except diesel, are available. At the north end of Manistee Lake **Solberg Boat Yard**, catering to powerboats, has 6 feet at alongside tie-up, all dockside services except diesel, travelift and railway haulout up to 40 tons, engine and hull repairs, a towing service and a marine store. Two highway bridges with a minimum clearance of 23 feet, and a railway bridge with 13 that usually stands open, must be passed before entering Manistee Lake. One long and one short will alert the bridge tender. Solberg's is not close to downtown, but there are taxis available.

Citizens of Manistee are justifiably proud of their downtown Victorian village. This large chunk of the central business district, which is on the National Register of Historic Places, is not only an architectural pleasure to look at, but comprises the range of practical downtown stores that serve a community of 7,500 people rather than cutesy-boutiquey tourist attractions. It begins at the municipal marina, with the 440 West Restaurant right next door. Other restaurants and the movie theater are only a few blocks away, but the supermarket and Laundromat are a bit farther.

Two of Manistee's historic buildings have been set aside as units of the County Historical Museum. The 1881 Water Works Building, a few blocks down River Street from the marina, displays artifacts from the marine, logging and railroad activities of the region; the Lyman Building, on River Street a block from the marina toward downtown, is a big store built after the Great Fire of 1871 and includes replicas of several kinds of 19th-century stores (723-5531 for both). History lives in yet another form in Manistee. The Ramsdell Theatre, an elaborate "opera house" typical of many prosperous small cities of the period, opened with a New York touring company in 1903. What is remarkable about the Ramsdell is that, except for a decade as a movie theater in the 1930s, it has served its intended purpose almost continuously since then. Under management of the Manistee Civic Players (723-9948), it's a short walk from the marina to Maple and First Streets to catch a performance or just to tour the splendid building.

Manistee Lake is 4 miles long by an average ½-mile wide. While it is mostly deep, except for the northeast delta of the Big Manistee River, the bottom is foul with the remains of all those sawmill operations, and anchoring is not advised. But you might like to take a spin or a sail around the lake to see the varied sights of Manistee industry, pretty orchards and suburban villages. And you can, of course, take your dinghy up the river.

Ludington

From Manistee the bluffs continue along the steep-to coast until you round Big Sable Point with its striking lighthouse, where the land flattens out for a while. The harbor at Ludington, 24 miles from Manistee, is formed by Pere Marquette Lake. The beloved French missionary lost his battle with illness at a campsite on the return from his second voyage to the Mississippi in 1675. Both Frankfort and Ludington claim their beachfronts as the site of Marquette's death, and both have planted crosses to his memory. At Ludington it stands as a beacon to incoming mariners, floodlit at night, and the 2-by-½-mile lake is named for him.

Converging breakwaters, marked by an occulting white light on a white tower with fog horn and a flashing red, form an outer harbor, and parallel piers with fixed green and flashing red protect the channel into the lake. Time was when you needed to watch out for the big car ferries plying frequently in and out of the harbor. In those days 13 of the big ships, carrying trains, automobiles and passengers, made the direct connection between several Michigan and Wisconsin towns. Now only one remains, making a daily crossing each way between Ludington and Kewaunee, Wisconsin.

A short way past the entrance to the lake on the port side the **Waterways Commission Marina** offers all dockside services at its extensive slips. A mile or so farther on, where the lake begins to widen, a narrow spit thrusting from the east shore is the site of the **Ludington Yacht Club**. There is dockage alongside and in older fixed and floating slips with 15-foot depths, when space is available. The usual dockside services are available, except diesel, but there is only one water connection near the small, informal clubhouse.

Spar buoys north of the yacht club mark the entrance to the Pere Marquette River, which you might want to explore by dinghy. The east lakeshore beyond the club is taken up by Dow Chemical; anchorage is possible on the west and south sides of the lake, but the water is quite deep.

The municipal marina is the most convenient location for activities in Ludington. In fact, it borders downtown, with all the shops you might need, including a supermarket, several restaurants, a bowling alley and a movie theater within a few blocks. There is a fresh fish market across the street. Although Ludington is a larger town than most of the others on this part of the coast, with almost 9,000 people, it has an intimate atmosphere. You can learn more about its mid-19th-century lumbering origins and events since then at the Rose Hawley Museum several blocks away on East Filer Street (843-2001). Regrettably for boat travelers, Ludington's outstanding historic complex, White Pine Village (843-4808), is located several miles out of town. If you can arrange transportation, however, it's well worth the trip.

For additional outdoor recreation near the marina, there is a playground for children, and a few blocks' walk brings you to the Stearns Park beach. Take a stroll (less than half a mile) over to the car ferry dock when the giant ship is loading. Somehow it creates the expectant atmosphere of an ocean liner preparing to sail from a metropolitan port. On Wednesday evenings you can enjoy a concert in the Lakefront Park bandshell. And if you're here in late August or early September, you might take part in the American Salmon Derby.

Pentwater

At Pentwater, 12 miles south of Ludington, you're again in a charming resort village, with a year-round population under 1,200. Pentwater Lake runs to the standard size of 2 miles by ½ mile. It's reached through a dredged channel between the dunes, which here rise to substantial heights. Flashing green and group flashing white lights mark the parallel breakwaters at the entrance. Although the center of the channel is dredged to 10 feet, it is subject to shoaling and the usual 3-mile-per-hour current.

The several marine accommodations begin immediately past

PHOTO BY FRANK FULKERSIN, COURTESY OF MICHIGAN STATE WATERWAYS COMMISSION

Aerial view of Pentwater harbor.

the entrance to the lake, all on the port side. First comes the **Pentwater Yacht Club**, where members of reciprocating clubs will be accommodated only if the public marina is full. Alongside tie-up with electricity and an informal clubhouse are the offerings. The row of **Waterways Commission** slips comes next, with all dockside services. In a basin opening up beyond, **Snug Harbor Marine** is an attractive facility with an intimate atmosphere. There is 10 feet at the floating slips; all dockside services, including Laundromat (open to the public); a 15-ton travelift; engine, hull and rigging repair; picnic tables and grills. At the end of the basin **The Oar House** serves mainly powerboats up to 23 feet at its floating slips with 5-foot depths, offering gas, ice, motor repairs and a launch ramp.

All these lakeshore facilities wrap around the attractive shopping area, with gift and art shops, in addition to a complete food market, several restaurants and a movie theater. Thursday night band concerts on the Village Green is one tradition. The annual Arts and Crafts fair, held the second week in July on the Green, is another. Longest tradition of all, over 50 years old, is the Pentwater Homecoming, second week in August, with parades, games, band concerts, fireworks and the climactic Fire Department water fight.

Pentwater Lake is deep and free of obstructions if you care to cruise around its scenic shores. You can find anchorage in either Big or Little Bayou on the south side of the lake.

White Lake

Another bulge in the coast at Little Sable Point matches its big brother in style and prominence of its lighthouse. After you round it your course will be southeasterly for a while after its long southwesterly trend, but the shoreline continues scenic, uncluttered, and steep-to. Thirty miles from Pentwater you enter White Lake between the familiar parallel breakwaters marked by flashing red and green lights. The 9-foot channel is subject to the also familiar shoaling and 3 mile per hour currents. But the lake itself gives you a change of pace. First, it's bigger than most of the others—6 miles long by 2 miles wide. Second, its twin ports of Montague and Whitehall are at the far end, where the White River deposited its load of logs in the old lumbering days, rather than close to Lake Michigan.

Just inside the entrance there is a choice of anchorages, if you care to drop the hook as another change of pace. Take care to skirt the flashing green buoy off Indian Point Shoal, then anchor in about 25 feet in Indian Bay on the north side. That's a more secluded spot than the anchorage in the southwest corner of the lake, also in about 25 feet, where the road and houses come closer to shore.

A bit east of that southside anchorage is the **White Lake Yacht Club**, organized in 1903; the handsome clubhouse dates from 1906. The usual dockside services are offered at the slips, except fuel, and there is a swimming pool. The club is 6 miles out of town, but it is as close as you can get to the Great Lakes Marine Museum in the 1875 lighthouse at the end of the road (894-6068).

If you move on up the lake to town, minding the buoys that mark shoal areas on the way, the first marina you come to is **Wesley Marine Service** on the Montague (port) side. Catering mainly to sailboats, the marina offers all dockside services except fuel, at its older, wood slips in 10 feet, haulout up to 20 tons by railway, and all engine, hull and rigging repairs. The yard specializes in restoring wood boats, and there are some handsome antiques to admire as you wander around. Although located a mile and a half from town, the friendly proprietors supply a courtesy car for shopping, and there is a park next door with a children's playground.

The rest of the marine facilities are all located on the Whitehall side of the lake, now the east shore. First is **Skippers**

Landing, with slips in 5 to 12 feet, all dockside services except diesel, a 30-ton travelift, towing service, and engine, hull and rigging repair. There is a small marine store and it monitors channel 16. **Crosswinds Marina**, next in line, has 3 to 10 feet at its older wood slips, all dockside services and an attractive restaurant. At the head of the lake the **Waterways Commission Marina** offers all dockside services except fuel at its slips. There is also a playground and picnic tables on the grounds. This is the most convenient location for downtown restaurants, shopping for necessities and the Laundromat, and there is a bowling alley across the street.

Whitehall and Montague are almost twins in population size, 2,800 and 2,300, respectively. But they are rather different in atmosphere. Whitehall is the more businesslike and workaday, while Montague has more of the tourist shops and the movies. Montague also has the Community Music Shell next to City Hall, the City Museum on Main Street (893-4585) and the roller rink, but Whitehall has the Howmet Theater on Mears Avenue (894-9026). Blue Lake Fine Arts Camp trains youngsters in all the fine and performing arts, and its summer performance season also includes visiting artists. It's quite a distance from town, but fortunately for boaters dependent upon shank's mare or taxicabs, the Howmet Theatre presents Blue Lake performances in addition to other attractions. Even if you're docked in Whitehall, everything is easily reached on foot; Montague is just across the bridge.

The City Dune Coast

Charts 14905, 14906, 14930, 14932, 14933, 14934

A peculiar imaginary line crosses the State of Michigan from Muskegon to Bay City, a kind of geophysical hinge. North of it the land is still rising in rebound from the glaciers; most of it unsuitable for farming; the weather is colder and drier; the main occupations are tourist-related fishing, camping and hunting; and the towns are small. South of it the flat, fertile plains and moist climate support a prosperous agriculture, and medium to large cities support intense industry; more than three-quarters of the state's population lives here. Along the Lake Michigan shore the beaches and the dunes and the orchards continue, but the towns in between are larger, the highways around them busier, and the rivers that flow down to the lake emanate from even larger cities in the interior. The recreational amenities in the lakeports now serve as many or more weekenders and day-trippers from nearby as tourists from afar. For cruising boaters this means more crowded harbor and marina conditions at all times, not only in the height of the vacation season.

Muskegon

They called her the "Lumber Queen of the World" back in the 1880s when Muskegon's 47 sawmills made record cuts from the river of logs that flowed to the blades. A wild town that rivaled Saginaw across the state for sin, Muskegon counted 40 million-aires when the bubble burst about 1890. Most deserted the sinking city. Those who stayed built anew on a diversified industrial base that still serves its 41,000 people and as many again in the surrounding suburbs. Prosperity continued, and the lakeshore bluffs are topped with handsome suburban dwellings.

Muskegon Lake, 4 miles long and up to 2 miles wide, forms the harbor, fed from the east by the Muskegon River. The Lake Michigan entrance, flanked by beachfront parks, looks no differ-ent from the others—converging breakwaters to form an outer harbor, and parallel piers extending from the cut into Muskegon Lake. Flashing red and white lights on towers mark the outer breakwaters, with a fog horn on the south one, while isophase red and flashing green lights mark the pierheads.

Immediately through the cut on the starboard side the subur-ban village of Lakeside has several marine facilities. First is the **Muskegon Yacht Club**, with 8 to 12 feet at its slips, all dockside services except fuel, but including cable TV hookup. The attrac-tive, informal clubhouse has a nice bar, and there is a swimming pool, children's playground, beach and picnic grills. Next door **Torreson Marina** provides all dockside services at its slips with 10-foot depths; a launch ramp; 25-ton open-end travelift; engine, hull, rigging and sail repair; and a marine store. **Balcom Marine Center**, next in line, has 8 feet at the slips; electricity; water; an 18-ton travelift; engine, hull and rigging repairs; and towing and diving service. All of these are about a mile and a half from village grocery shopping, movie theater and tavern, but Lake-side does have taxis.

Diagonally across the lake from these three, **Pointe Marine Association** is a big marina in residential North Muskegon on the channel leading into Bear Lake. Fixed red and white lights with daymarks define the entrance. There is 4 to 7 feet at the slips here, with all dockside services, a 30-ton open-end travelift, and

Aerial view of part of Muskegon harbor.

hull and engine repairs. It's a couple of miles to downtown North Muskegon shopping, but there is a grocery store about half a mile away and a restaurant across the street.

The south shore of Muskegon Lake, fronting the city of Muskegon, is where the commercial port facilities are located. Some of the industry that once lined the waterfront has been removed, and at one location just west of the flashing red Hartshorn Light **Lakeshore Yacht Harbor** was under construction behind a protective breakwater in 1984. When completed, it is expected to have the usual services. The Hartshorn light buoy indicates the approach to the **Waterways Commission Marina** in an enclosed basin marked by red and green lights. The older-style slips with big pilings are arranged in a *U* and offer all dockside services. There are also picnic tables and playground equipment.

The marina is in a warehouse/industrial district, but most of the places you'll want to visit are not many blocks away. Grocery shopping is not handy, but there is a farmer's market Tuesday, Thursday and Saturday on Yuba Street and Eastern Avenue. Muskegon Mall is a large, enclosed shopping plaza between Clay Avenue and Morris Street, beginning at Third. It borders on a historic district that's a pleasure to stroll and has some special attractions. The Muskegon Museum of Art at 296 Webster at Third (722-2600) is widely acknowledged as one of the finest small art museums in the country. You'll see American and European paintings there that you've seen reproduced in books or on loan to others. A few blocks west on Webster, at 484, is the restored home of lumber baron Charles Hackley, the civic leader who didn't desert with the trees and who originated the art gallery and many other cultural institutions in the city. It's a delight to tour (744-8170). A block over on Clay, the Hackley Fire Company Barn has been restored (722-1363), and east again on Clay, at 430, is the Muskegon County Museum (722-0278). The Seaway Festival in July is the city's annual gala with parades, music, food, art fair and a polka contest.

Grand Haven

The Grand River figures importantly in Michigan history, first as interior access for the fur trade, later to carry its share of timber, now as the site of Michigan's second city, Grand Rapids, at the fall line 24 miles inland. There is an appealing set of three small cities at its mouth. Grand Haven, the largest with almost 12,000 people, gives its name to the entire harbor area and breaks the pattern of harbor lakes. Here it's the river that forms the harbor, with Spring Lake an offshoot about 3 miles upstream. The towns of Spring Lake, with 2,700 people, and

Ferrysburg, with 2,400, border Spring Lake, but they form a commercial/cultural complex with Grand Haven, and each has marine facilities. There is industry on the river, although the lake is largely residential, but Grand Haven's setting and spirit are equally devoted to recreational good times.

It's only 12½ miles from Muskegon to Grand Haven, where the river is entered between parallel breakwaters marked by flashing red and green lights, the red mounted on a fog horn building. Immediately inside, a basin carved into the dunes accommodates the **North Shore Marina**, catering mainly to powerboats. Turn immediately to starboard after passing the narrow entrance for the slips with 5-foot depths available to transients, with all dockside services except ice, a 30-ton crane, engine and hull repairs, and a marine store. This is a scenic, residential location, far from town and shops, but there is a swimming pool on the premises.

Continuing upstream, the main channel curves northward around Harbor Island, while South Channel continues east. At the junction on the mainland shore is the **Waterways Commission Marina**, in both a pretty and convenient setting. All dockside services are available, except diesel. If you can get a slip during the busy summer season, the attractive shops of downtown Grand Haven begin only a block away. The Wednesday and Saturday farmer's market is two blocks away. Next door the Tri-Cities Historical Museum occupies an old railroad depot (842-0700). On the river side of the museum is a grandstand for observing Grand Haven's unusual nightly show. But you can marvel from the comfort of your own cockpit at the synchronized sight and sound of the world's largest musical fountain. Against the backdrop of dunes across the river an incredible variety of colored water patterns is played into the air to match the mood of a very high fidelity music system. The show is played nightly about 9:30 (depending upon sunset time) and lasts 15 minutes. The grandstand is also the location of the Big Band concert and dance every Wednesday evening.

Additional attractions of downtown Grand Haven include miniature golf a few blocks from the marina, movies, and the Harbor Trolley, which gets you around town on your business, out to the state park beach, or simply gives you a nice tour. An out of the ordinary restaurant for dinner, a couple of blocks from the marina, is Dansk Kro, featuring tasty Danish food. Among a number of special events the annual United States Coast Guard Festival is the biggest gala. Celebrated since 1938, it's a week-long party, focused on the Coast Guard's August 4th birthday, that includes contests, games, parades, exhibits, entertainment and dances, much of it taking place at the waterfront stadium.

Only small boats can continue up South Channel past the municipal marina because of the 9-foot height limitation on the bridges. The main channel around the west and north sides of Harbor Island leads to the marinas clustered around the junction of Grand River and Spring Lake. The railroad bridge with 9-foot clearance usually stands open, and the highway bridge with 25-foot clearance opens for three minutes before and after the hour and half hour from 0600 to 2100; both respond to a single horn blast if necessary.

Shortly past the pair of bridges, bear to starboard from the main channel to reach **Grand Isle Marina** just ahead. This is a very large establishment that operates almost like a resort rather than a boatyard. With a large staff and an emphasis on service, it offers all dockside amenities at the slips with 6- to 12-foot depths, including telephone hookup. A travelift hauls out up to 40 tons for full engine, hull and rigging repair, and there is a large marine store. Also on the premises are a party store, the Grand Islander Restaurant, a swimming pool with spa and hot tub, tennis courts, game room and children's playground. A social director on the staff arranges social events for both children and adults. With all that is on site one hardly notices that there is no shopping nearby.

If, after passing through the highway bridge, you continue on the main channel, you come to **Holiday Inn**, which has both seasonal and transient dockage in slips with all dockside services. All hotel privileges are also available to marina guests. A turn to port before reaching Holiday Inn leads into the channel to Spring Lake, with a fixed bridge height limitation of 35 feet. Near the entrance to the lake, on the starboard side, **Barrett's Marina** accommodates powerboats at slips with 6 to 12 feet and the usual dockside services, except ice and diesel fuel. There is a 30-ton travelift, engine and hull repair, and a marine store. Both Barrett's and Holiday Inn are actually in the village of Spring Lake, but there is little in the way of convenient shopping nearby. Spring Lake has some beautiful scenery to offer once you get beyond the urban area, and there are a number of nice little coves in which to anchor. The Grand River is also worth an exploratory trip. You can follow a buoyed channel with a controlling depth of 8 feet for a dozen miles or so beyond the Route 31 highway bridge. Boats with shallow draft and less than 19 feet in height can go virtually all the way to Grand Rapids.

Holland

Of the many ethnic communities that were founded on the Great Lakes during the 19th century, few have made a stronger imprint than the Dutch who came to southwest Michigan. The first contingent arrived in 1846, refugees from an unusual period of religious persecution in their native land. Overcoming initial hardships and privations, they prospered to the extent that by the 1920s community leaders feared that the younger generation would lose their cultural heritage. From this concern the annual Holland Tulip Festival was born in 1927, to provide a focus for cultural preservation. The four-day event has placed this city of 26,000 people on the national map. Attendance ranks with New Orleans' Mardi Gras and Pasadena's Tournament of the Roses. Although the festival takes place in mid-May, when hundreds of thousands of tulips bloom in gardens and streetside plantings, most of the cultural attractions that have grown out of the festival operate throughout the summer. This neatly scrubbed and beautifully landscaped city is a pleasure to visit anytime. But Holland lies at the inland end of her 5-mile-long lake harbor, and for those who arrive by boat most of the accommodations are at the Lake Michigan end of Lake Macatawa. A taxi or rental car is needed to reach downtown.

The entrance to Lake Macatawa is 20 miles south of Grand Haven, between the familiar pair of converging breakwaters and inner piers with flashing red and white lights and fog horn on the outer set and flashing red and green on the inner. Two resort communities flank the lake entrance; both have large and well-equipped marine facilities.

On the south shore in the village of Macatawa **Eldean Shipyard** is set in attractive grounds with an unusually good-looking main building, a children's playground, picnic area and The Galley Restaurant. All dockside services are offered at its slips with 15 feet, a travelift hauls out up to 30 tons for engine and hull repair, and there is a marine store. Next door the **Macatawa Bay Yacht Club** welcomes members of reciprocating clubs to its handsome clubhouse set in spacious grounds with swimming pool. There is 10 feet of water at the slips, and the usual services are offered, except pumpout and fuel. The clubhouse has a dining room and bar, and there is a separate junior clubhouse for the youngsters. Macatawa is a residential community with no shopping nearby.

In the north shore community of Ottawa Beach **Parkside Marina** is almost adjacent to the state park and beach—a happy juxtaposition that isn't often found. There is up to 19 feet at the floating slips, with all dockside services. Groceries are available two blocks away.

About a mile and a half from the lake entrance Big Bay opens on the north shore. There are wide-swinging shoals here, so be sure to follow the buoyed channel. **Bay Haven Marina** is a large one in the almost-resort category. All dockside services, including telephone hookup and Laundromat, are provided at slips with 9 feet of depth; a travelift hauls out up to 40 tons for full engine, hull and rigging repairs, with Boston Sails next door; and the amenities include a swimming pool, playground, dog kennel, fish cleaning station and The Hatch restaurant. Just beyond, **Bay Haven Anchorage Marina** is even more luxurious. Its offerings range from all dockside services, including telephone and cable TV hookup and Laundromat; slips with 6 to 10 feet; a 60-ton travelift; full engine, hull and rigging repairs with the same sailmaker next door (between the two marinas); and large marine store to tennis courts, indoor/outdoor swimming pool with sauna, playground, game room, TV room and large convenience store.

The only marina for cruising boats in Holland itself is **Perrin's Marina**, a mile or more from downtown. Take care to follow the buoyed channel up the lake; unlike the others, Macatawa has many shoal areas. The marina is on the south shore just before the big Heinz plant. Catering mainly to powerboats, Perrin's offers all dockside services, except diesel, at its slips, a 40-ton travelift, engine and hull repairs, picnic tables, a swimming pool with Jacuzzi, children's playground and the Captain's Wheelhouse restaurant and bar. There is a Laundromat across the street.

In addition to nice shops and restaurants (and a hospital if you need medical service) Holland's main attractions are associated with its Dutch heritage. Most of them are in a fairly compact area, once you get into town. You might want to start at Windmill Island at the end of Lincoln Avenue (396-5433). Here an 18th-century working windmill, brought over from the Netherlands in 1964, forms the centerpiece for a beautiful park that includes a mechanized miniature Dutch village, a carousel, klompen (wooden shoe) dancing exhibitions and an interesting film about the windmill's history. In addition to touring the mill you can buy the wheat it grinds. The Netherlands Museum at Central and Twelfth streets (392-9084) is housed in an 1889 mansion, but it's not your ordinary local historical museum. One floor relates to the history of Holland, Michigan, but another displays artifacts brought from the Netherlands, including period rooms, and a third contains exhibits from Dutch colonies in the Pacific Ocean. For a change of pace from the Dutch the Baker Furniture Museum on Sixth Street (392-8761) started out as a resource for Baker furniture designers. Its superb collection of period pieces is not artfully arranged in current museum fashion, but if you have an interest in furniture, you can learn and enjoy a great deal here.

Additional attractions are less centrally located, but if you have rented a car, you might want to visit one of the two wooden shoe factories, another miniature Dutch village or a tulip bulb farm. For evening entertainment there are Tuesday band concerts in Kollen Park on the lake at the end of Tenth Street. Hope College Summer Repertory Theater mounts a varied program throughout the season (392-1449).

Saugatuck/Douglas

Seven miles south of the entrance to Lake Macatawa the Kalamazoo River flows into Lake Michigan through a dredged channel about a mile north of its natural outlet. Along its banks is a pair of resort communities reminiscent of those on Little Traverse Bay. Saugatuck and Douglas started out in lumber, like all the others, but around the turn of the century the pretty river, flanked by spectacular high dunes and widening into a lake 2 miles upstream, was "discovered" by Chicago families looking for a summertime retreat and Chicago artists looking for new vistas to paint. Since then the twin villages have grown busier and better as a lively resort for the land-based, the waterborne and the artistic from all over the Midwest.

The river is entered between parallel breakwaters with flashing white and green lights and a fog horn. Controlling depth in the channel is 8 feet, subject to shoaling and a 3-mile current. If you're coming from the south, note that old pilings extend about 200 feet into the lake from the original river outlet; they are marked by a green buoy. The river, which swings south after about a ½ mile, is buoyed almost to its widening into Kalamazoo Lake. The lake, with Saugatuck on its north shore and Douglas on the south, is shaped rather like a wineskin, about a mile long and a half mile wide.

Saugatuck Yacht Services is on the east bank of the river in a very pleasant setting at the north end of town. It has 8 feet at the slips, with all dockside services, a 50-ton travelift, engine and hull repairs, both a marine and a convenience store, a playground, picnic tables, and Clover's Landing Restaurant. At the northeast corner of the lake **Coral Gables Marina** is associated with a restaurant and bar with live entertainment and dancing. There is 8 feet at alongside tie-up and slips with all dockside services, and bicycle and moped rental on the premises. A bit farther on, **Singapore Yacht Club**, with mainly powerboats, has 12 feet at the slips, all dockside services except fuel, a swimming pool and picnic tables. Its informal clubhouse has a bar. Next door **Sergeant Marina**, with 5 feet, offers all dockside services, including telephone and cable TV hookup. These two facilities are conveniently located in downtown Saugatuck, with shopping and Laundromat close at hand.

Across the lake in Douglas **Tower Marine** is a large establishment, with 8 to 14 feet at its fixed and floating slips; all dockside services, including cable TV and telephone hookup; haulout by travelift up to 50 tons; engine, hull and rigging repairs; a marine store; swimming pool; playground and the Tara Restaurant up the hill on the highway. There is a grocery store about a quarter of a mile away. **West Shore Marine** north of Tower caters to powerboats up to 26 feet, with electricity at some of the floating slips, ice, heads, gas, a launch ramp and outboard motor repair.

The two villages have fewer than 2,000 year-round residents, so they are quite compact and easy to get around on foot. There is, in addition, a dial-a-ride transport service, which is handy for moving back and forth between them. You should take at least one ride on the antique chain link ferry that crosses the narrow part of the river from the foot of Mary Street in Saugatuck. It's hand-operated (be sure to avoid it if it's in motion while you're passing up- and downstream in your boat) and is a nice way to get to the beach and the high dune of Mt. Baldhead. Bicycle and moped rental are available at Coral Gables, as we mentioned.

Saugatuck has the larger shopping district of the two towns, with many antique stores, art galleries and boutiques. Both villages have a selection of restaurants; Sir Douglas, a bit down the highway in Douglas, serves fine continental-style cuisine in a charming setting. In Saugatuck the Red Barn Theater, a professional summer stock company of 30 years' standing, offers a varied playbill (857-2105). There are Sunday band concerts in the village park. The Historical Museum is on Lake Street in Saugatuck, but Douglas has the prize historical attraction. The S.S. *Keewatin* served the Canadian Pacific Railway for 53 years on the Georgian Bay to Lake Superior route. A luxury passenger ship, she was retired in 1965 and two years later arrived at her retirement home at the head of Lake Kalamazoo in Douglas, her

PHOTO BY DORIS SCHARFENBERG

Keewatin Ship Museum.

luxury appointments still intact. Be sure to include a tour in your sightseeing rounds (857-2158). Art shows are a feature of Saugatuck/Douglas life, with one scheduled almost every week in summer. The last Saturday in July is the Venetian Festival. If you'd like to see some of the fruitlands of the interior, the Kalamazoo River is navigable for boats of shallow draft and less than 17 feet of height for 24 miles to the Allegan Dam; if your boat can't make it, perhaps your dinghy can, at least partway.

South Haven

Kalamazoo is the last of the lake-harbors. The dunes continue along the coastline, now at lower levels, but the remaining natural harbors are simply dredged river channels. South Haven, 20 miles from Saugatuck/Douglas, has vacillated between commerce and recreation as its main occupation. Less important than some others as a lumber port, it shipped a great deal of fruit in the old days. Then the cruise ships began to call, and by the 1920s South Haven found its destiny as a summer cottage and big hotel resort for Chicago people. With changing tastes many of the hotels faded away, but the summer homes remain, and sport fishing has given a new lift to recreational South Haven. Nor has the town of 6,000 people deserted its blueberry base. The luscious fruit is shipped out by truck rather than steamer these days, but the National Blueberry Festival takes place every July with contests, races, exhibits, entertainments and, of course, a parade.

The big nuclear plant 5 miles south of the harbor entrance is conspicuous from offshore, and the parallel piers that protect the dredged mouth of Black River have a fixed red light with fog horn and a flashing white. Controlling depth in the channel is 11 feet for about a mile to the turning basin below the highway bridge. The bridge has a clearance of 10 feet and opens on the hour and half hour in response to three blasts.

On the north side, about halfway to the bridge, the **Waterways Commission Marina** is in a horseshoe basin, with all dockside services except diesel fuel. Next upriver **All Seasons Marina** has 20 feet at floating slips and alongside dockage with all dockside services; a 30-ton travelift; engine, hull and rigging repair; and canoe rental for exploring Black River. These two marinas are closest to the beach on Lake Michigan. Across the river, closer to downtown, the **South Haven Yacht Club** has 10 feet at slips and alongside tie-up and the usual dockside services, except diesel and pumpout. The small clubhouse has a bar. Above the highway bridge and around a bend in the river **South Haven Marine** offers all dockside services, except diesel, at its slips with 8 feet; a 25-ton travelift; engine, hull and rigging repairs; and a launch ramp. The Black River Yacht Club on the premises has a bar and lounge.

Downtown South Haven is an attractive shopping area, including groceries, although the Laundromat is not convenient. There is a hospital in town. Among several restaurants The Idler, an opulent Mississippi River boat moored near the yacht club, serves excellent meals in the handsome paneled saloons and staterooms of a turn of the century engineless yacht. On the north side of the river at the Dyckman Street bridge the Lake Michigan Maritime Museum (637-8078) not only displays artifacts but sponsors a variety of programs and events, including an annual Heritage Wooden Boat Gathering.

In addition to cocktail lounge entertainment South Haven has a movie theater and a bowling alley downtown. And in addition to the special annual events already mentioned there is a July Fourth Parade and Art Fair and a Labor Day Weekend Crafts Fair.

St. Joseph/Benton Harbor

The last pair of twins on this coast is at the mouth of the St. Joseph River, 22 miles below South Haven. A silver cupola is prominent from the lake. It sits atop an elegant old resort hotel, now a senior citizens' residence, that dominates the bluff on the approach upriver. A fixed white range at 108° leads you to the parallel piers at the harbor entrance. The front light on the pierhead has a fog horn, and the opposite pier has an isophase red light on a red tower.

Half a mile from the entrance the **Waterways Commission Marina** opens up on the port side in a dredged basin known as West Basin. In an unusual arrangement this is a full service marina with a 25-ton travelift, engine and hull repair services, and a marine store, in addition to all dockside services at the slips with 7 feet of depth. Although convenient to the lakefront beach, there is no shopping in this residential area closer than a mile. Taxis are available, however.

The railroad bridge just beyond West Basin usually stands open, but the highway bridge beyond that opens between 0700 and 2000 for three minutes before and after each hour and half hour, otherwise on signal of one long and one short. Just beyond this bridge the Paw Paw River joins the St. Joseph from the northeast, but there are no marine facilities in that direction. The St. Joseph River turns south and divides into two channels around Radio Island. The westerly one is Morrison Channel, with about 6 feet of depth and a fixed bridge limiting height to 36 feet. Most of the channel is industrial, and there are no marine facilities located on it.

At the entrance to the main channel, on the starboard island side, **La Salle's Landing Marina** is a big one with all dockside services, including cable TV and telephone hookup and a Laundromat, at its slips with 12- to 20-foot depths. An open-end travelift hauls out up to 40 tons for full engine, hull and rigging repairs. There is a launch ramp, a marine store, a convenience store, a swimming pool and a lounge deck. There are no stores nearby, and it is about three-quarters of a mile to downtown St. Joseph. Upstream on the island side, past the highway bridge with 19-foot clearance that opens for three minutes before and after the quarter and three-quarter hour, is **Wolf Island Marina**. Catering to boats up to 32 feet, the usual dockside services are available, except diesel. There is a 20-ton travelift, with engine repairs available from Brian's Ship's Store on the premises.

A bit farther upriver and across on the Benton Harbor side **Pier 1000** offers all dockside services, including Laundromat, at its slips with 8 to 10 feet; a 60-ton travelift; engine, hull and rigging repair; a marine store and a swimming pool. There is a party store and a restaurant a quarter of a mile away; otherwise taxis or Dial-a-Ride transit can take you downtown. A couple of miles upstream on the St. Joseph (west) side **Whispering Willows Marina** is an older facility in a pleasant country setting. This is a very large establishment, catering mainly to smaller boats at its slips with 5 to 6 feet of depth. Some have electricity and water, and there is ice, pumpout, gas and a fish cleaning station. The river is navigable for about 22 miles above St. Joseph for very small craft, a pleasant ride all or partway for your dinghy and you.

St. Joseph entered history when La Salle built Fort Miami there in 1679 to await his *Griffon*, which never returned. In despair he turned east to march overland to his base at Fort Frontenac on Lake Ontario, the first white party to cross the future state of Michigan. There is a plaque at the site on Lake Boulevard at Ship Street downtown. In more recent times it was a fruit shipping harbor, along with its former rival across the river, Benton Harbor, and a resort. Now the two cities, with a combined population of 24,000 (Benton Harbor is the larger), have considerable industry. Whirlpool Corporation is based here, and you can arrange for a tour to see how home appliances are made by calling 926-5000.

Downtown St. Joseph has attractive mall-type shopping and restaurants. The Fort Miami Heritage Society offers walking tours from its headquarters at 116 State Street (983-1191 or 983-1375). The Krasl Art Center is a small gallery at 707 Lake Boulevard (983-0271), which sponsors the annual July Art Fair in Lake Front Park. You can enjoy a band concert in that park every Sunday afternoon and evening. And that's also the scene of the biannual Fort Miami Day reenactment of historical events and other appropriate activities. The Venetian Festival in late July or early August features boat races and other contests, music and food.

New Buffalo

A storm-tossed lake captain from old Buffalo started a settlement here in the 1830s, but it didn't take off until Chicagoans turned it into a resort early in this century. Twenty-five miles southwest of the St. Joseph River a pair of breakwaters shelters the dredged mouth of the Galien River. Entrance is from the west, flanked by flashing red and green lights with appropriate daymarks. One extensive enterprise dominates the dredged harbor reached by the first turn to starboard. **Oselka's Snug Harbor Marina** offers all dockside services, except diesel fuel, at its slips with 5 to 12 feet; there is telephone hookup at some of them. A 35-ton open-end travelift hauls out for engine, hull and rigging repairs, and there is a launch ramp and marine store. A game room and easy access to the beach provide entertainment, and the village of 2,800 people about half a mile away has restaurants and a bowling alley, in addition to essential stores.

Michigan City

A few miles past New Buffalo is the state line between Michigan and Indiana, and 10 miles beyond the last Michigan port is Indiana's only small craft harbor, Michigan City. You are now at the southern extremity of Lake Michigan where, if you haven't already noticed, strong north and northwest winds can pile up ferocious seas and storms can be truly hazardous. When the mouth of Trail Creek was first developed as a harbor early in the 19th century Michigan City was intended to be Indiana's major port. Later industrial developments took that distinction elsewhere, but the harbor in the manufacturing city of 40,000 people is a popular place for boaters and fishermen.

Where once there was a giant sand dune, carted away to make glass, the stacks of Northern Indiana Public Service are conspicuous from offshore. The harbor entrance is sheltered from northwest by a detached breakwater with flashing white and red lights on the ends. The east pierhead, marked by a flashing white light on a red-roofed white tower with a fog horn, is angled to give protection from the northeast, and there is a shorter west pier with a flashing red light on it. Controlling depth in the channel is 10 feet.

A break in the east pier, marked by a fixed green light, gives access to the municipal small craft harbor, known as **Outer Basin**. Note that you will leave the green light to starboard on entering. This is a large facility with 8 to 20 feet at fixed and floating slips and all dockside services, including Laundromat. The marina is located in Michigan City's prized Washington Park, where the recreational facilities include beach, gardens, picnic grounds, tennis courts, children's playground, zoo (872-8628) and the 1858 Old Lighthouse Museum (872-6133 or 872-3273). Thursday evenings there are band concerts at the shell. There is also a music festival in the park in late June or early July, an arts festival in August, and the In-Water Boat Show in late August is getting bigger and better every year.

The Barker Civic Center is an opulent 38-room mansion built in 1905 by a local industrialist, at 631 Washington Street (872-

0159) a few blocks from the marina. Across the street from the marina, at the edge of the park, the Michigan City Yacht Club has no dockage, but its attractive dining room and bar are open to members of reciprocating yacht clubs. Canterbury Playhouse, in a restored church at 907 Franklin Street not far from the harbor, is a semiprofessional summer stock company (874-4269).

This unprepossessing city offers little to visiting boaters beyond its splendid waterfront park and the additional attractions mentioned, but if your boat has need of repairs, there are two marinas up Trail Creek. The highway bridge, with 17-foot clearance, opens on signal of one long and one short. **B and E Marina**, on the port side at the next bend in the creek, has 6 feet at its slips, all dockside services except diesel fuel, a 50-ton open end travelift, and engine, hull and rigging repair. A short distance beyond, **South Lake Marina** is dredging its basin and modernizing its facilities and presently offers electricity and water at some of the slips; ice; heads and showers; gas; a 20-ton travelift; engine, hull and rigging repairs and a marine store. There is also tight security here in a rather dubious neighborhood.

Chicago and a Little Beyond
Charts 14904, 14905, 14926
Small Craft Book
14927, 14928, 14929
Industrial Harbors

West of Michigan City the dunes put on one more extravaganza at Indiana Dunes National Lakeshore. But there is no access for a cruising boat. Then, for the next 25 miles, the Lake Michigan coast belongs to the world of giant industry. Here is where those ore boats with whom you've shared the lake are heading—to feed the maw of the immense steel plants that send their stacks skyward beside the bulk of neighboring petrochemical and manufacturing plants. It's an overwhelming display of industrial prowess, but the four major and several minor harbors have no place for a small boat. Recreational craft take a direct 40-mile passage from Michigan City to one of the welcoming harbors of Chicago.

Chicago's industrial brawn, immortalized by poet Carl Sandburg, lies mainly along inland rivers and prairies. To her lake the city presents a necklace of parks, with a halo of glittering skyscrapers arching behind them. And in each of those parks is

PHOTO BY WILLIAM T. SWEDENBERG,
COURTESY OF *NEWS-DISPATCH* OF MICHIGAN CITY

The port of Michigan City, In-Water Boat Show.

one or more harbors, from which the crew of a cruising boat can set out to explore this exciting city. There is so much to do and see here that space permits us to present no more than a few highlights to get you started. Stop in at the Visitors Information Booth at State and Madison streets on the State Street Mall or the Chicago Water Tower (225-5000 weekdays) for information on the full range of opportunities.

Although the portage was used to reach the Des Plaines and Illinois rivers leading to the Mississippi from late in the 17th century, Chicago didn't become much of a settlement until the 1830s. After that it grew rapidly as a transportation hub, and later a manufacturing center, until almost stopped in its tracks. The Great Fire of 1871 is probably Chicago's most famous event. In overcoming the tragic loss, Chicagoans grasped the opportunity to rebuild with an imagination and on a scale that has made it an architectural masterpiece.

A walking tour sponsored by Archicenter at 330 South Dearborn (782-1776) is a good way to get acquainted and learn some of the stories behind the buildings you see. But do some walking on your own, too, especially along the Magnificent Mile of North Michigan Avenue, where elegant shops grace the eloquent structures. A breathtaking aerial view of the marriage between metropolis and lake can be had from the 94th floor of the John Hancock Center (751-3681) or the 103rd floor of the Sear's Tower (875-9696). Prairie Avenue, where Chicago's early millionaires built their fashionable mansions, was left behind in an unseemly warehouse district until resurrected a few years ago as a historic landmark. A visit to the street will give you a glimpse of those years, and a tour of the Glessner House (346-1393) will show you how a famous architect pleased his clients and helped to launch Chicago's architectural tradition.

Museums are legion, from the highly specialized to the comprehensive. Most famous is the Museum of Science and Industry, at 57th and South Lake Shore Drive (684-1414). Housed in the only building that survives from the magnificence of the World Columbian Exhibition of 1893, this is the original hands-on museum, from which all others derive. The Art Institute, at Michigan and Adams (443-3500), has a collection that matches the splendor of its edifice. The Field Museum of Natural History, at Roosevelt Road and South Lake Shore Drive (922-9410); the John G. Shedd Aquarium, at 1200 South Lake Shore Drive (939-2426); and the Adler Planetarium a block away at 1300 South Lake Shore (322-0304) have displays to captivate the imagination while they painlessly educate the mind.

Shopping in Chicago offers an endless variety of merchandise and atmosphere, ranging from the vast and famous Marshall Field Department Store in the Loop to the tiniest boutique in Old Town. Theater, music, dance, sporting events and special shows and festivals can keep you occupied day and night. Consult one of the daily newspapers or *Chicago* magazine to find out what's happening while you're in town. The Hot Tix Booth, at 24 South State Street (977-1755), sells half-price, day-of-performance tickets and full-price, advance-sale tickets. There is also an abundance of night clubs to suit every taste. And for some, above all else Chicago is a gastronome's dream. Impossible to list the opportunities, I will tell you that my most memorable dining experience was at Le Perroquet.

When Chicago won the bid to sponsor the World Columbian Exposition of 1893 the site offered was a 600-acre marsh on the outskirts of town. Landscape design genius Frederick Law Olmsted transformed it into a network of canals and lagoons, while architect Daniel Burnham supervised the construction around them of a constellation of white Beaux Arts exhibition halls. All that remains of the buildings is the Museum of Science and Industry. But the fair's enduring legacy to the city was Jackson Park and Burnham's subsequent success in promoting his grand scheme to adorn almost 20 miles of lakefront with parkland. It required perseverance and the mobilization of civic pride, not to say financial investment, to clear away unsightly development, resist further industrial and commercial encroachment, and extend the shorefront lakeward with landfill where necessary, but the grand plan came to fruition. The lakeshore is perhaps Chicago's greatest treasure, and its citizens know it. Six- and eight-lane expressways may roar between the dense urban cityscape on the one hand and the wide green space on the other. But once inside the parks the din of the city fades, and Chicagoans flock to their playgrounds for every kind of outdoor recreation. Not the least of these is boating.

Thousands of resident boats occupy docks and mooring spaces, while thousands more are launched from the ramps in each of the city's eight harbors. Almost all of the dockage and moorings are under the jurisdiction of the Chicago Park District, but each harbor has one or more yacht clubs as well that supply the graceful amenities. As there are no places reserved for transients, you should call in advance to arrange accommodation. Each harbor has a dock master who assigns temporarily vacant slips; their telephone numbers are given below. Which harbor you choose will depend upon the kind of boat you're in, in which part of the city you prefer to spend your time and how long you plan to stay. You may also have to accept second or third choice during the height of the season. But Chicago's efficient transportation system should enable you to get around quite easily from almost any of them.

Jackson Park

The generally smooth bottom of Lake Michigan becomes more uneven in the southwest corner, but none of the shoals need trouble a pleasure boat, and they're all well marked. Entrance to Jackson Park Harbor, the southernmost of the group, is sheltered from the north by a spit, from which a pier makes out to northward. Both are tipped with flashing red lights on white towers. Entrance to the harbor itself is flanked by fixed red and green lights, with 7 feet or more through the channel. There are two harbors in the park. Outer Lagoon has depths of 8 to 9 feet and is the place for sailboats, mostly on moorings or at star docks—star-shaped sets of floating docks, without services, anchored in the center of the harbor. The rambling, rustic clubhouse of the **Jackson Park Yacht Club** on the east shore evokes the 19th-century origins of the park. It has a few floating slips, with gas, ice, water and pumpout at the service dock, heads and showers in the clubhouse. The dining room is open weekends; bring your own bottle.

Inner Lagoon is dedicated to powerboats, with depths of 4 feet and a fixed bridge with 14 feet of clearance across the entrance channel. **Southern Shore Yacht Club**, with an informal clubhouse lounge, has floating slips with all dockside services except showers and diesel fuel, and there are star docks in this lagoon too. The harbor master for both lagoons can be reached at 312-363-6942. Jackson Park is very large, and neither of the lagoons is near its recreational facilities or mass transportation; taxis can be called, however.

Fifty-ninth Street Harbor is also in Jackson Park, about half a mile north of the others. This one is limited to small powerboats. It is entered between parallel piers, with fixed red and green lights. The channel carries 10 feet, but the fixed bridge that crosses it allows only 10 feet of clearance and there is only 4 feet of depth in the basin. The short slips have electricity, water, ice, pumpout and gas, and there is a launch ramp (312-493-8704). It's a pity that this harbor can't accommodate larger cruising boats, as it is far more convenient to transportation and park activities. Tennis and lawn bowling are nearby, and a walk through a lovely grove of trees brings you to the doorstep of the Museum of Science and Industry.

Burnham Park

The park that honors the man primarily responsible for the waterfront system ironically has less green space than the others, but contains some choice institutions. Its harbor is large and has more conventional dockage than the others, with moorings and star docks as well. There is one substantial disadvantage, however. The harbor was created by a landfill peninsula called Northerly Island, and most of Northerly Island consists of Meigs Airfield. The shriek of aircraft and the stench of their exhaust can be intrusive to on-board life. On the other hand, if you plan to spend most of your time ashore in the city, that may not matter. Burnham Park Harbor is conveniently located.

The airfield requires some careful attention to the approach. Planes take off and land immediately adjacent to the harbor entrance, which opens from the south about 4½ miles north of 59th Street Harbor. A flashing green light at the entrance has a red sector to warn you off the danger zone. White and orange spar buoys mark its southern extremity. Within those buoys, designated Zone A, boats with more than 15 feet of height are prohibited. South of those buoys Zone B is delineated by another set of white and orange spars, within which boats are

PHOTO COURTESY OF THE CHICAGO CONVENTION AND TOURISM BUREAU, INC.

Chicago skyline.

prohibited whose height exceeds 30 feet. Tall-masted sailboats must approach from south and west of all these buoys to enter the harbor in the shadow of McCormick Place, Chicago's big exhibition center.

There are two harbor masters in Burnham Park. The office for the west side is at the docks immediately past McCormick Place (312-294-4615), which have 15 to 20 feet of depth, electricity and water. Toward the northeast corner of the harbor the harbor master for the east side, and most of the moorings and star docks (312-295-4614), is adjacent to the **Burnham Park Yacht Club**. The club has a few spots where visitors can tie up along the wall with electricity and water and runs a tender service for people on moorings and star docks. Gas and ice are also available at the club docks, and the clubhouse has heads, showers, dining room and bar for visitors who obtain a temporary card.

Burnham Park Harbor is a convenient one for public transportation, available at the north end. But the main reason dockage here is desirable is that three of Chicago's great institutions are within walking distance: Adler Planetarium at the northeast corner of Northerly Island, Shedd Aquarium and the Field Museum of Natural History off the northwest side of the harbor. Each of these monumental buildings is set in landscaped grounds, which enhances the walk to reach them even as it lengthens it a bit.

Grant Park

On the other side of the strip of land defining the north end of Burnham Park Harbor is the southern limit of Grant Park Harbor. This vast enclosure in the southwest corner of Chicago's main harbor is the most conveniently located, adjacent to the Loop. It consists almost entirely of moorings and accommodates mainly sailboats. It can be entered directly off the lake if you're coming from the south, or you can pass through the Chicago Harbor outer breakwater and harbor to the inner breakwater entrance flanked by flashing red and white lights.

The harbor master's office (312-294-4612) is next door to the **Chicago Yacht Club** on the northwest side of the harbor, where gas, diesel fuel and ice can be obtained. Club facilities are available only to members of reciprocating yacht clubs and include head and showers, dining room and bar. The plain exterior of the clubhouse is deceiving; it's handsome on the inside. An independent tender service provides transport to and from moorings; call Harbor Tender Company on channel 68.

As you approach the northwest corner of the harbor you may think that the ship you see has lost its way among all the sailboats. This is the new, but not young, home of the **Columbia Yacht Club**. The *M/V Abby* plied the Canadian waters of Northumberland Strait between Cape Tormentine, New Brunswick, and Port Borden, Prince Edward Island, from 1947 until 1982, carrying railroad cars, passenger cars, and unmotorized people. Her lounges and staterooms are being meticulously restored to their original Art Deco splendor. The club offers to members of other recognized yacht clubs not only the ambiance of the ship's dining room, bar and afterdeck, but some alongside dockage in 20 feet, and all dockside services except fuel.

Grant Park has two major attractions for visitors—the Art Institute a couple of blocks from the yacht clubs and the band shell that presents concerts all summer (294-2420). The band shell is at the south end of the park, however, actually a little closer to Burnham Park Harbor dockage.

Here, at Chicago Harbor, is another connection between the Great Lakes and the sea, albeit a circuitous one. The Chicago River, whose course is reversed to flow from Lake Michigan rather than to it, leads to the Chicago Sanitary and Ship Canal and the Illinois Waterway via the Illinois River to the Mississippi and the Gulf of Mexico at New Orleans. If you're headed that way, or from it, you must transit the lock at the Lake Michigan end of the Chicago River on the west side of the outer harbor.

The lift or drop is determined by the level of the lake at the time of transit, as the purpose of the system is to maintain the river level below the lake level. Pleasure boats are locked through with commercial vessels. At both ends red and green traffic lights convey their customary meaning, and you signal the lockmaster with two long and two short blasts. You will also need to transit the lock and the numerous drawbridges, which don't open during rush hours, if your boat requires haulout or major repair, as those services are available only in the river. Consult the harbor master where you dock.

Lincoln Park

Lincoln Park in the near-northside residential part of the city is graced with three harbors. Diversey Harbor, about 3 miles north of the Chicago River entrance, is an attractive one for powerboats. On the north side of the entrance the Lincoln Park Gun Club fires toward the lake. Buoys mark the limit of the range, and red flags are displayed when firing is in progress. A range at 269°, with a fixed red front light and fixed white rear light, will keep you outside the firing area on the approach. Also note, if you're coming from southward, the partly submerged seawall just offshore and take care to avoid it. A highway bridge with 14-foot clearance crosses the entrance channel, which carries 9 feet. Because of the narrow width of the channel, vessel control traffic lights are displayed from the bridge 24 hours a day.

Diversey Harbor fixed and floating slips (call 312-327-4430) have electricity and water. Gas, ice and pumpout are available at the **Diversey Yacht Club**, whose dining room is open on weekends. The major attraction at this harbor is the Lincoln Park Zoo close by (294-4660).

Less than a mile farther on, Belmont Harbor accommodates both power and sail. A flashing red light marks the north side of the entrance with a controlling depth of 17 feet. On the starboard side just inside the harbor the **Belmont Yacht Club** provides gas and ice, but has no clubhouse. The harbor master's office is at the northeast end of the basin (312-281-8587), where floating slips in 10 feet have electricity, water, pumpout and heads. There are also moorings in this harbor. In the southwest corner the Chicago Yacht Club's Belmont Harbor Station is a barge with dining room, bar and showers for members of recognized clubs. This harbor is close to a park playground; tennis and golf are within a mile.

Montrose Harbor is the last in the Lincoln Park triumvirate and the Chicago Park District harbors. It is a pretty basin about a mile and a quarter beyond Belmont, entered from the south between two short breakwaters with flashing red and green lights. A submerged shore protection bulkhead runs south of this harbor entrance too. The channel and harbor have depths in excess of 18 feet, and there are moorings and star docks as well as slips with electricity, water, ice and pumpout. The **Corinthian Yacht Club** on the north side of the basin has heads and showers, a bar and a dining room open weekends. The harbor master (312-878-3710) is based here. Across the street from the clubhouse is the entrance to a public beach.

Wilmette

Second suburb north from Chicago, the village of Wilmette is bordered by the North Shore Channel, controlled by the Chicago Sanitary District. A pair of breakwaters, with flashing red and green lights, encloses the mouth of the channel, which is periodically dredged to 8 feet to accommodate a small craft harbor. The channel is rather narrow, however, and subject to strong currents when the sluice gate at the end of the harbor is open. Another breakwater extends into the lake north of the channel mouth with a flashing white light. When approaching from the north or in poor visibility, take care not to mistake it for the harbor entrance.

The crowded harbor, operated by the Wilmette Harbor Association, has a few slips with electricity, water and ice, but most of the boats are on moorings. The **Sheridan Shore Yacht Club** has attractive lounges and deck and a playground for the children. In Gillson Park, adjacent to the harbor, there are tennis courts, but in the surrounding residential neighborhood there is no convenient shopping.

From offshore the dome of the Baha'i Temple is a conspicuous landmark, and the exquisite building, national headquarters for the Baha'i Faith, dominates the hilltop overlooking the harbor. A pleasant, if longish, walk will enable you to visit (256-4400.)

Great Lakes Naval Training Center

About 17 miles northwest of Wilmette the Great Lakes Naval Training Center is in a large artificial harbor enclosed by breakwaters. In addition to training vessels the harbor accommodates the pleasure craft of base personnel and in an emergency, or with permission, cruising boats may also moor overnight. The harbor master monitors channel 16, or you can inquire at the boathouse in the inner basin. A fixed green range with white and black daymarks guides you on a course of 303° through the outer entrance, flanked by flashing red and white lights. A channel with 12 to 14 feet leads to the inner basin entrance between piers with flashing red and white lights. Ice, heads and showers are available at the docks. Immediately north of the training center harbor entrance a rifle firing practice danger zone extends lakeward for 1 mile and northward for a mile and a half. Its limits are marked by buoys, and red flags are displayed when firing is in progress.

Waukegan

An industrial city of about 65,000 people 21 miles north of Wilmette, Waukegan has extensive new facilities for pleasure boats. Stacks and tanks make the city conspicuous from off-shore, and the harbor is entered between breakwaters with flashing white and green lights and a fog horn. A breakwater northeast of the piers, with a group flashing white light and red daymark, gives additional protection to the entrance. Once through the dredged channel the inner basin opens up, with small boat facilities on the west side. This harbor is subject to extreme changes in water level with sudden shifts in wind direction or barometric pressure.

The **Waukegan Port District** operates the marina, where moorings and slips have 8-foot depths. All dockside services are available, and there is a launch ramp. The Waukegan Yacht Club, almost opposite the harbor entrance, has very little dockage of its own, but the attractive dining room and bar are open to members of recognized yacht clubs. At the north end of the harbor **Larsen Marine Service** has floating slips with 6 to 8 feet, all dockside services except showers; a 30-ton travelift; engine, hull and rigging repair; and a marine store. All of these marina facilities are located in an industrial setting, and city shops and services are some distance away.

For cultural activities the address to find is 1917 North Sheridan Road. There the Waukegan Historical Society has restored an 1853 farmhouse as a museum, which includes the room and the bed in which Abraham Lincoln slept (336-1859). At the same location the Jack Benny Center for the Performing Arts perpetuates the memory of the master comic who always plugged his hometown (244-1660).

Metropolitan Wisconsin
Charts 14904, 14924, 14925

Wisconsin is not a highly urbanized state. Indeed, it's known best for its fine farm products. The lakeshore towns originated not in logging, sawmilling or shipping, as elsewhere, but as farming settlements peopled since the 1830s as much by immigrants from northern Europe as by land-hungry American easterners. In the southern part of the state these solid, enterprising folk moved with later times into industry. Today the 60-mile stretch along Lake Michigan north from the Illinois line is urban and suburban most of the way, and includes the state's largest city, Milwaukee. Having said that, the first harbor we'll describe is remote and rural.

Runaway Bay

Precisely straddling the state line between Illinois and Wisconsin, the small, private harbor of Runaway Bay is surrounded by farmland, nature preserve and some residential development. About 9 miles north of Waukegan, it can be identified from offshore by the nuclear power plant towers a couple of miles south and a large white house immediately north of the harbor entrance. A quick flashing red light marks the entrance between a spit of land on the north and a short breakwater on the south. The channel carries 6 to 8 feet, and there is 4 to 10 feet of depth at the **Trident Marina** slips, with all dockside services, except diesel. A 40-ton travelift hauls out for engine, hull, and rigging repair. There's a beach on the lakefront side of the marina, and half a mile away is the Chiwaukee Prairie Nature Reserve. Here you can wander among the grasses and flowering plants of that almost extinct biological community, the North American prairie.

Kenosha

It's hard to say whether Lake Michigan sport fishing is a more pervasive mania in Wisconsin than it is in Michigan. But in many Wisconsin harbors design and facilities are much more focused on the needs of sport fishermen than those of cruising boaters. In addition to services for small motor boat owners each harbor shelters a substantial charter fishing fleet. And almost every port sponsors an annual salmon fishing contest.

The preoccupation with sport fishing begins at Kenosha, about 15 miles north of Waukegan, 7 from Runaway Bay. This is an industrial city of 77,000 people, but its small harbor was improved for large ships only with the opening of the St. Lawrence Seaway in 1959. Except for some industrial and commercial installations along the entrance channel, it has a pleasant, open atmosphere.

A tank and a stack flanking the entrance help identify it from offshore, and the parallel piers enclosing the channel have flashing red and green lights, with a fog horn on the north light. A detached breakwater, with a flashing red light, helps to dampen northeast seas, but in strong easterlies there is surge in the main body of the harbor. Inside the basin, on the starboard side, the **Kenosha Yacht Club** has alongside tie-up with all dockside services except fuel. The informal clubhouse, with dining room and bar, is open only to members of reciprocating yacht clubs. Between the yacht club and the Coast Guard station there are some municipal floating slips for sailboats, with electricity and water. Where the basin narrows toward the bridge **Gatti Marina** provides dockage in slips with 12 feet of depth and all dockside services except pumpout. A 20-ton travelift; engine, hull, and rigging repairs; and a marine store round out the services. Across the basin **Holiday Inn** has alongside tie-up (watch out for some broken pilings) without boat services, but hotel privileges include pool and showers.

The harbor narrows to a long arm at the north end, crossed by a fixed bridge with 16 feet of clearance. Just beyond the bridge on the port side **Villa Marina** has floating slips for powerboats in 5 feet, with all dockside services except pumpout and diesel. The entire starboard (east) shore of the lagoon is a **City Marina** for powerboats, with electricity and water at the slips. There is also a launching ramp, with a fish cleaning facility and heads.

The marinas on the east side of the harbor, on both sides of the bridge, are all close to or abutting Simmons Island Park with a nice sand beach. Food shopping and restaurants are a few blocks away, downtown about a half mile. The marinas on the west side are a little closer to downtown shopping, restaurants, movies and a bowling alley. Places to visit in the downtown area and a little beyond include the Kenosha Public Museum in a 1908 Beaux Arts post office building at 5608 Tenth Avenue (656-6026), with both natural history and fine arts exhibits, and the Kenosha County Historical Museum in an 1899 mansion at 6300 Third Avenue (654-5770). The mansion at 6315 Third Avenue is headquarters for a unique organization, the Society for the

Preservation and Encouragement of Barbershop Quartet Singing in America, and it gives tours of the house (654-9111). Keep on going down Third Avenue to 6501 and you'll arrive at Kemper Center, once a girls' boarding school, now a county park and cultural center. You can tour the elaborate buildings and grounds and attend a variety of shows and special events (657-6005). American Motors Corporation is Kenosha's largest employer and offers tours of the assembly plant at 5626 25th Avenue (658-7680). Kenosha has a bus system as well as taxicabs.

Racine

Racine has little lake-faring tradition as its early settlers were farmers and there was no natural harbor. By the time the town's industrial development took off, railroad and highway were more important avenues of transport. As a consequence the artificial harbor enclosed by breakwaters is a quiet place, while the city's diversified industry is located along the Root River and inland. There are plans afoot to take advantage of this situation and develop the harborfront into an attractive commercial, recreational and cultural complex. Meanwhile, marina facilities for cruising boats are not conveniently located with respect to Racine's downtown area or its tourist attractions. But there is a bus system, as well as taxicabs.

In approaching the harbor, 10 miles north of Kenosha, care must be taken with respect to Racine Reef, a nasty set of shoals about a mile offshore, marked with a big light and fog horn at its east end and a light buoy on the west. Make sure to pass either side of this area. If you're coming from the north Wind Point is also afflicted with offshore shoals. It's advisable to pass outside both Wind Point Shoals buoys before heading for Racine.

The converging breakwaters enclosing the harbor have a fixed red light with fog horn and a flashing white flanking the entrance channel. The main purpose of the breakwaters is to reduce wave action in the mouth of the Root River, so anchorage in the large outer harbor is ill advised because of surge in northeast to southeast winds. At the north end of the harbor the **Racine Yacht Club** is enclosed behind its own breakwaters with fixed red and green lights at the entrance. Transient boats are accommodated at alongside tie-up in 6 feet or more, with the usual dockside services except fuel and pumpout. The informal clubhouse has a bar and a dining room open on weekends. Next door is a large public beach. The yacht club is distant from downtown at the outer edge of a commercial district, but some of the restaurants will pick up a crew for dinner. Otherwise taxis are required to get around.

At the entrance to the Root River a short pier on the north side has a fixed red light. Just upstream **Pugh's Peerless Marina** offers tie-up alongside and in slips with 7 feet or more; all dockside services; a 20-ton open-end travelift; engine, hull, rigging and sail repair; launch ramp and marine store. The Chartroom Restaurant and Bar is adjacent, and the downtown shopping area is about six blocks away. Past the Main Street Bridge with 9-foot clearance, which opens on signal of one long and one short every 20 minutes beginning on the hour, **Belle Harbor** is on the port side. The slips here have 7 to 11 feet, with the usual dockside services except fuel. There is a 30-ton travelift; engine, hull and rigging repair; and a marine store. On the other side of the State Street Bridge, which opens with three short blasts, **Palmer Johnson Marina** is on the starboard side. All dockside services are available at slips with 9 feet, plus a 30-ton open-end travelift; engine, hull and rigging repair; and a marine store. Both Belle Harbor and P-J, as this famous Wisconsin boatbuilding name is fondly abbreviated, are convenient to downtown shopping and restaurants. Along with other north Europeans Danish people came to Racine in large numbers and brought with them their favorite pastry, called *kringle*. This is a local specialty you should be sure to try, and there are a number of bakeries where you can buy a supply for the galley.

Racine's most famous institution is probably the Johnson Wax Company, whose main office building, at 1525 Howe Street, was designed by Frank Lloyd Wright. On the same property the Golden Rondelle Theater was designed by Wright's Taliesen disciples as the company's 1964 New York World's Fair exhibition hall. Film showings at the theater and tours of the buildings are popular attractions (631-2154 for both). At 701 Main Street the Racine County Historical Museum informs you about local natural and human history (637-8585). Somewhat distant from downtown, at 2519 Northwestern Avenue, the Wustum Museum of Fine Arts has a nice small collection (636-9177), and on the same property the Racine Theatre Guild mounts an annual play series (633-4218).

Milwaukee

Three rivers meet at the "gathering place of waters," called by the Indians something that sounded like *Milwaukee* to white ears—the Milwaukee, the Menominee, and the Kinnickinnic. Together they flow into an indentation of Lake Michigan known as Milwaukee Bay. All of this was conducive to settlement in the 1830s. An influx of refugees from the European Revolution of 1848, mainly Germans, launched a spirit of intellectual liberalism and cultural refinement that pervades the industrial city of 630,000 to this day. Milwaukee is a city for people, for families—clean, safe, prosperous, comfortable, hospitable. Neither flamboyant nor stolid, its ethnic variety gives it color.

From lakeward the 42-story First Wisconsin Center Building, the state's tallest, pinpoints the center of the harbor. Closer approach brings into focus the world's largest four-sided clock tower on the Allen Bradley plant at the south end, illuminated at night. A cluster of tall stacks 3 miles south should not be taken for harbor identification. And if you're coming from Racine, give the coast a 3-mile berth to avoid the firing range a few miles northwest of Wind Point. Milwaukee harbor is enclosed by a series of breakwaters paralleling the shore about 25 miles north of Racine. There are three lighted entrances.

South Entrance, with a flashing red light, is the one to take for the **South Shore Yacht Club**. From there you proceed southwesterly to the entrance to the south shore anchorage area between a flashing red buoy and a fixed green light on a short breakwall. The club accommodates members of reciprocating yacht clubs either on moorings, alongside, or at slips with 6 to 10 feet and all dockside services except pumpout. The attractive clubhouse has a bar and a dining room that serves lunch all week, dinner on weekends. The club is located in a residential area far from neighborhood shopping or downtown attractions, but Milwaukee has buses and taxis, of course.

The main harbor entrance, about a mile north of the south entrance, passes between an occulting red light with fog horn and a flashing green. Almost directly opposite parallel piers, with fixed red and flashing white lights, enclose the merged river mouths; the arch of the I-794 highway bridge shows you just where it is. Currents up to 3 or 4 miles an hour can run through these entrances. This is the industrial part of one of the Great Lakes' most important ports, and a trip up the rivers can be an interesting excursion to show you some of the many ways Milwaukee earns its living. There is also a marina. A turn to port into the Kinnickinnic River brings you to **Milwaukee Marine** with alongside tie-up for transients in 8 to 10 feet; electricity; water; ice; heads; a 100-ton crane; full engine, hull and rigging repair and a marine store. This is a rather isolated, industrial

PHOTO COURTESY OF WISCONSIN DIVISION OF TOURISM

Milwaukee, aerial view of McKinley Marina.

location, but a place to consider if you need work done.

Milwaukee's provision for visitors by recreational boat is at the north end of the harbor in McKinley Park. You can reach it either through the main entrance or a mile farther on at the north entrance, marked by a flashing green light on the break-water. Watch out for fish net stakes at this end of the harbor. A jetty, with a quick flashing white light, partially encloses the small boat harbor. **McKinley Marina**, a Milwaukee County facility, has three dockage areas, with 15 to 20 feet at the slips and all dockside services and a launch ramp. Go to the north area fuel dock for a berth assignment; there is also a snack bar there. Between the north and center piers the **Milwaukee Yacht Club** accommodates visitors from reciprocating clubs in slips with 16 feet of depth and all dockside services. The spacious clubhouse has a dining room and bar. McKinley Park has tennis courts near the marina north piers and the yacht club. These marine facilities are about a mile and a half from downtown, but the number 30 bus runs about four blocks away, and there is some neighborhood shopping there.

Perhaps the most exciting place to shop downtown is The Grand Avenue, a new development that links new structures and four blocks of historic buildings, including the 1915 Plankinton Arcade, by means of connecting, glass-enclosed skywalks. Old World Third Street is a restored area a few blocks away, occupied by small specialty shops. And throughout the city there is a great variety of ethnic (and "American") restaurants and night clubs. The handsome Performing Arts Center at 929 North Water Street is home to the Milwaukee Symphony, Milwaukee Repertory Theater, Milwaukee Ballet Company and others (273-7206). A short distance away at 144 East Wells Street, the restored opulence of the Pabst Theater is a splendid setting for performances (271-3773 for the box office, 271-4747 for tour information). There are many other locations for music, theater, dance and sporting events. The best way to find out what's on while you're here is to call the "Funline," 799-1177, or stop in at the Visitor Information Center at 756 North Milwaukee Street.

The city presents a generous array of historic buildings, including the 1895 Flemish Renaissance City Hall at 200 East Wells Street (278-2221) and the Milwaukee Grain Exchange Room at 225 East Michigan Street (272-6230), which provided the city's prosperous burghers an extravagant Gilded Age, Italian Renaissance setting for their wheeling and dealing. The ornate Captain Frederick Pabst Mansion, built by the beer baron in 1893, is farther out at 2000 West Wisconsin Avenue (931-0808), but close by is the St. Joan of Arc Chapel on the campus of Marquette University at Wisconsin Avenue and 14th Street (224-7039). It was moved here in 1964 from its original location near Lyon, France. It is believed that Saint Joan worshipped in the Chapel during her period of wartime struggle against England.

Also more distant from downtown, but not far from the marina, the Charles Allis mansion, built in 1909 at 1801 North Prospect Avenue (278-8295), is actually an art museum, housing the large collection of the first president of Allis-Chalmers. Chamber music recitals also take place here. Nearby is Villa Terrace at 2220 North Terrace Avenue (271-3656 or 271-9508). A relative newcomer, the Italian-style villa was built only in 1923, but is now a museum of decorative arts and also sponsors concerts. It is, in fact, a branch of the Milwaukee Art Museum, which is housed in the beautiful Eero Saarinen War Memorial Center that dominates the park at the opposite end from the marina (271-9508).) The Milwaukee Public Museum, downtown at 800 West Wells Street (278-2700), is probably the city's favorite. Its life-size dioramas and walk-through exhibits are outstanding.

Finally, you may not want to leave the city that beer made famous without a tour of one of the breweries. There are two to choose from: Pabst at 901 West Juneau Avenue, not far from the

Public Museum (347-7300); and Miller farther out at 4251 West State Street (931-2000).

In addition to all the sights to see, Milwaukee can keep you busy all summer with an almost continuous series of festivals. Most of them take place at the Summerfest grounds, a large waterfront site set aside for the purpose, which you may have noticed if you entered the harbor through the main channel. The Lakefront Festival of the Arts, which opens the season in June, is held on the grounds of the Art Museum. Summerfest Music Festival follows in late June and early July on the Summerfest grounds and includes contests, exhibitions and sporting events as well as the entire range of music performed from 10 stages, culminating in Independence Day fireworks. Bastille Day, July 14, is celebrated downtown, with puppet shows, magicians, exhibits, dancing and sidewalk cafes; it actually goes on for two days. Late July sees the German Fest on the Summerfest grounds, with food, exhibits and dancing. The Italians also celebrate for four days in July, with cultural exhibits, entertainment, food and fireworks. The Irish take over three days in August, with crafts, music and food. Near the end of the month Fiesta Mexicana has music, dancing and food, and the season is topped off during the first week in September with the four-day Polish Fest of music, dance, crafts, exhibits and the sine qua non of ethnic food.

Small Cities and Smaller Villages
Charts 14903, 14904, 14910, 14922

As Milwaukee's suburbs fade in your wake, the farms and orchards one expects in Wisconsin begin to appear along the low bluffs of the coast, with small cities and towns spaced 5 to 20-odd miles apart. Fresh and smoked fish markets appear at the waterfronts, and shops specializing in Wisconsin cheese multiply as you move north. Each of the towns along this stretch has a hospital.

Port Washington

Port Washington has traditionally been a commercial fishing harbor, although now a variety of small manufacturers employ some of the town's 9,000 residents. It's also making a bid for tourism, and the recently completed **Port Washington Marina** should attract cruising boats to a harbor that was previously untenable. Power plant stacks south of the harbor, 25 miles north of Milwaukee, are prominent from offshore, and flashing red and green lights on white towers, with a fog horn at the north light, guide you through the breakwater entrance. The large marina occupies the northwest side of the artificial harbor. For added protection from surge it is enclosed within a pair of breakwaters that overlap slightly and are marked with flashing red and green lights at the pierheads. Slips with 10 feet of depth are set aside for transients, and all dockside services are available, including Laundromat. There is also a six-lane launch ramp. The harbor master monitors channel 16.

The attractive downtown shopping area is only a block away and includes a supermarket. There are several restaurants, including the popular Smith Brothers Fish Shanty. The Smith family began fishing from Port Washington in 1848, and the restaurant, still in family ownership, has an interesting history. You can stock your galley with fresh fish from their adjacent retail store, and they will smoke your catch if you so desire. Among sights to see in town are the Sunken Treasures Maritime Museum around the harbor (285-5614) and the restored 1872 Eghart House at 316 West Grand Avenue (284-4918). "The World's Largest One-Day Outdoor Fish Fry" takes place the third Saturday in July and includes rides, games, exhibits and a parade to enjoy while you're munching your fish 'n' chips.

Sheboygan

Sheboygan is one of the few towns along this stretch of coast with a lumbering background, which also included furniture manufacture. But it was the Kohler Company, manufacturers of bathroom fixtures, that put it on the industrial map. After Kohler established his own company town 4 miles west there were still strong connections, but Sheboygan, with almost 50,000 people, now has a diversified industrial base.

The harbor, 26 miles north of Port Washington, is flanked by two firing ranges that pose a hazard up to 3 miles offshore. The Sheboygan Police practice their shooting 2 miles south of the harbor, while the Sheboygan Rifle and Pistol Club operates 5½ miles north. It's best to keep about 3 miles off until inside the 7-mile distance between these target areas. If coming from the north, also note Sheboygan Reef and pass outside the nun buoy that marks it.

Breakwaters enclose the artificial harbor and dredged mouth of the Sheboygan River, with an occulting white light on a red tower with fog horn on the north breakwater and a flashing green on the south. North of the river entrance the **Sheboygan Yacht Club** offers a warm welcome to visiting boats, with 8 feet at the slips, all dockside services except pumpout, and a launch ramp. Pumpout is available, however, at the club's service yard upriver, where haulout and repairs can also be arranged. The attractive clubhouse has a bar and dining room open for dinner. Downtown shopping and restaurants are several blocks away. For powerboats with less than 14 feet of height to pass an overhead power line and a fixed bridge, **J.P. Marine** upriver offers short slips in 7 feet, all dockside services except diesel, haulout and repairs. The Eighth Street Bridge, with 10 feet of clearance, opens on the quarter hour, except at rush hours when the schedule is half-hourly.

Sheboygan is not a tourist town, but the Italianate villa, built in 1882 by John Michael Kohler at 608 New York Avenue is now the Community Arts Center (458-6144). In addition to exhibits and classes, there is an art fair here the third week in July.

Manitowoc

Unlike its sister cities in southern Wisconsin, Manitowoc has been a lake-faring town since the beginning. The first wooden sailing ship built on Lake Michigan was launched here in 1847, and with it a shipbuilding tradition that endured until yesterday. Burger Boats continues, as it has since 1863, with its regal line of motor yachts, but the city of 36,000 people now has a more diversified industrial base. And, like Port Washington, it's putting in a heavy bid for the tourist trade with a brand new public marina.

Twenty-four miles north of Sheboygan a grain elevator and a stack about half a mile south of the harbor, both lighted at night, identify Manitowoc from offshore. Shoals both north and south of the harbor are marked by buoys, and the converging break-waters carry an isophase white light with fog horn and a flashing green. The city and its commercial piers lie up the Manitowoc River, but for access to the new **Manitowoc Marina**, head for the opening in the north breakwater between the shore and a large diked spoil area. It may look as though you'll be moving out of the harbor, but a new breakwater connects the north end of the spoil area to the shore, completely enclosing the marina. Watch out for a short rubble extension from the spoil dike projecting into the harbor on the east side of the marina entrance. The basin has been dredged to at least 6 feet and all dockside services are or will soon be available at the floating slips.

The marina is about half a mile from the downtown area, which, in addition to stores and restaurants, has two movie theaters. But the main attraction downtown is the excellent Manitowoc Maritime Museum on South Eighth Street at the riverfront (684-0218). Its scale models include one of an 1854 wooden vessel under construction, and tied up at the museum dock is the submarine *Cobia*, to represent the 28 that came off the ways here during World War II. Close to the marina, in an 1891 mansion at North Eighth and Park streets, the Rahr-West Museum displays local historical artifacts, including an authenticated piece of *Sputnik IV* that landed on a Manitowoc sidewalk one morning. Farther out on Eighth Street is the Lincoln Park Zoo.

Two Rivers

Less than 6 miles from Manitowoc, Two Rivers is also an industrial town now, with about 14,000 people. Its maritime tradition stems from commercial fishing, however, preserved at the outdoor Rogers Street Fishing Village Museum, a two-block-long site on the East Twin River at 22nd Street.

There is still commercial fishing from Two Rivers, as the net stakes offshore remind you on the approach. You aren't likely to miss this small city, heralded with conspicuous stacks and tanks, one of which proclaims "Twin Rivers" in bold black letters. Parallel breakwaters, with a fixed red light and fog horn on the north and a flashing white on the south, protect the small harbor at the confluence of the Twin Rivers. East Twin is the more industrial side; the two marinas are in West Twin.

A turn to port as the harbor opens up brings you to **Two Rivers Sports Marina**, with alongside tie-up and short slips in 9 feet, with all dockside services. The highway bridge immediately beyond has closed clearance of 14 feet. Its opening schedule is complicated and requires a telephone call to the Two Rivers Police Department, so for all practical purposes it's a fixed bridge. Therefore, **Twin Cities Marine** just beyond has only powerboats at its floating slips with 20 feet. There is gas, pumpout, a launch ramp and outboard motor repair here. Across the street, and also easily accessible from the other marina, is a park with tennis courts, and a short walk across the park Lighthouse Inn is a very pleasant setting for a good dinner. There is a public beach on the lakefront. Downtown shopping is also handy to both marinas, just over the bridge. Both Twin

Rivers are navigable for several miles upstream, and you might want to take a dinghy ride into the pretty countryside.

Kewaunee

At the mouth of the Kewaunee River, about 24 cruising miles from Two Rivers, the village of Kewaunee is a marketing center for surrounding farmlands and a sport fishing port for charter boats. It is also the Wisconsin terminus for the last car ferry operating across Lake Michigan. The first one steamed from here in 1892. Kewaunee Shoal, a couple of miles offshore, is marked by a flashing green light with a fog horn. The harbor is enclosed by breakwaters with a flashing red and a fixed white light with another fog horn, and an inner pier, enclosing the river mouth, also has a flashing red light on it.

On the port side, beyond the widening of the harbor basin, there is a **City Dock** with alongside tie-up in 6 feet, gas, diesel, ice, pumpout and a launch ramp. Downtown shops and restaurants are a couple of blocks away, and there is a fish market next door. A short distance up the river, past the highway bridge with closed clearance of 9 feet that opens on signal of one long and one short, is a new **City Marina**. Here there are floating slips, with short side docks in an open setting with picnic tables, heads and a launch ramp. It's about a quarter of a mile walk downtown. The river is navigable from here for about 6 miles with drafts of less than 4 feet.

There are two main sights to see in downtown Kewaunee. The world's largest grandfather clock stands in front of the Svoboda Industries shop, a century-old family enterprise, which manufactures furniture as well as clocks and clock kits. On the Court House Square the Kewaunee County Historical Museum and Old Jail was in official use from 1876 to 1969. In addition to preserving the sheriff's living quarters, jail cells and other artifacts, there is a stunning wood carving of Custer's Last Stand and a model of the *Pueblo*, the notorious U.S. spy ship captured by Korea in 1968; she was built here in Kewaunee.

Algoma

Algoma got a later start than the other towns in the neighborhood. The first permanent settler didn't arrive until 1851, but the town grew on wood-processing and fishing to its present size of 4,000. The fishing has switched from commercial to sport, but the wood-processing is still here.

The harbor is entered, 11 miles north of Kewaunee, between an angled north pier with an isophase red light with fog horn at the outer end and a fixed red at the angle, and a flashing green on the south pierhead. Heading straight through the harbor basin to the mouth of the Ahnapee River, **Algoma Marina** is in an enclosure just past the entrance. Alongside dockage in 8 feet, electricity, water, ice, pumpout, gas, an open-end 20-ton trave-lift, engine and hull repair and launch ramp are all available here.

Downtown shopping, restaurants, movies and bowling alley are only a few blocks away across the river. At the waterfront on Navarino Street Von Stiel Winery offers tours and tastings of its cherry and other fruit wines (487-5208). Algoma hosts an unusual annual event the third weekend in July—the Antique and Contemporary Doll Show and Sale at the Algoma Dug-Out Knudson Hall and Youth Center, 620 Lake Street. Exhibitors from all over the country congregate here and display other kinds of antique toys as well as their artistic collections of dolls.

The Door Peninsula
Charts 14902, 14909, 14910, 14919

After 200 miles of smooth-shore cruising between artificial harbors west Lake Michigan mariners are rewarded with the Door Peninsula and its island extension. Little brother to the Bruce Peninsula on Lake Huron, the Door is the western leg of the Niagara Escarpment's great arch. It, too, encloses a beautiful bay that is a sailor's delight and a cruiser's goal. Like the Bruce, its lower reaches present a tranquil, gently sloping face to Lake Michigan and a bold succession of stunning limestone cliffs to Green Bay. Its name is a direct translation from the somber Porte des Morts, which the French conferred on the treacherous passage at its northern tip. But the Door today is a gateway to the pleasures of cruising in relatively sheltered waters to inviting harbors. Its villages are informal resorts, with few "sights" to see but much of the simple life to enjoy.

The peninsula, like much of the rest of Wisconsin, was pioneered by Scandinavians alongside westward-seeking Americans, and they cultivated the lime-rich soil, bathed by a lake-moderated climate, to bring forth fruit. Today many of those farms and orchards are being replaced by summer homes, as resorts creep inland from waterfront villages. For some inexplicable reason, the Door Peninsula is frequently compared to New

Algoma fishing boats.

England, Cape Cod in particular. I, for one, see nothing reminiscent of Cape Cod's sand dunes and beaches in the forested limestone bluffs of the Door. As for the villages, they speak to me not of prim Anglo-parented New England, but of open-hearted Wisconsin and its Scandinavian heritage. Technically, the peninsula begins at Kewaunee, but its distinction as a recreational area and the individuality of its atmosphere begin at Sturgeon Bay.

Sturgeon Bay

The bay itself is an indentation of Green Bay that originally penetrated to less than a mile and a half from Lake Michigan. From ancient Indian times the portage was used as a shortcut to save almost 100 miles of dangerous paddling around the peninsula. In 1878 the barrier was finally breached with a canal that would permit the passage of ships. Fourteen miles north of Algoma the Sturgeon Bay Ship Canal is entered between converging and detached breakwaters. Flashing red and green lights on the detached piers and a fog horn on the north side are followed by a fixed red on the north side of the entrance and a big lighthouse with a flashing red behind that. Additional lights and buoys carry from beyond the entrance all the way through the 8½-mile channel to Green Bay. If you're coming from the west, there's even a range before the canal entrance at 120°.

No, all these aids to navigation have not been placed to serve the fleets of pleasure boats that use the passage. Sturgeon Bay has been a shipbuilding town for 100 years and still is. Bay Shipbuilding and Peterson Builders between them construct ships of every description from naval vessels, through fishing and research craft, to ocean freighters, passenger liners and lakers up to 1,100 feet, and Palmer Johnson is one of the nation's most honored names in custom yacht building.

There is a 5-mile speed limit in the canal, but the current can run up to 7 miles an hour in either direction. Note also that the entire channel is buoyed from seaward in Lake Michigan; if you transit from Green Bay eastward, reds will be on the port hand. Passage through the canal and Sturgeon Bay itself is very pleasant. The shores are bordered by woods and attractive homes. Despite giant ship construction and a number of other industries, Sturgeon Bay does not have a heavy industrial atmosphere. Rather, the city of 8,800 people evokes a sense of unhurried good living in salubrious surroundings.

About 3 miles from the canal entrance **Orbit Resort** on the north side introduces you to the resort qualities of the Door Peninsula. Dockage is alongside in 6 to 10 feet, with electricity and water; finger slips are in the planning stage. Hotel privileges are extended to visiting boats and include the swimming pool and tennis courts, as well as the dining room and lounge with live entertainment on weekends. The resort is about a mile and a half from town, but taxis are available.

Immediately west of Orbit the Bayview Bridge, with 42-foot closed clearance, opens on the hour and half hour during the day, otherwise on signal of one long and one short. The same regulations apply to the downtown Michigan Street Bridge, which has a closed clearance of 14 feet. On the east side of that bridge, north side of the bay, **Palmer Johnson** accepts transient boats. The slips and alongside tie-up are aging, but all dockside services are offered, and it hardly seems necessary to add that any conceivable type of repair can be made, including a complete remodeling of your boat. You might even be inspired to that after observing operations in the simple, uncluttered, unflappable yard that turns out masterpieces of the boat builders' art. P-J is the closest facility to downtown shopping, restaurants, bowling alley and movies. There is also a hospital.

Across the bay, and a little eastward, **Sturgeon Bay Yacht Harbor** is a large marina with excellent slips in 7 to 8 feet, all dockside services; an open-end travelift to 50 tons; full engine, hull and rigging repairs; a launch ramp and a marine store. There is a Laundromat and some shopping two blocks away. The Sturgeon Bay Yacht Club adjacent has little dockage but extends reciprocal privileges in the dining room and bar.

There are three museums to visit in Sturgeon Bay. The Door County Historical Museum, at 18 North Fourth Avenue (743-5809), and the Miller Art Center at Fourth and Nebraska (743-6578) are both downtown. A bit of a walk west on Third Avenue to Georgia Street brings you to the Sturgeon Bay Marine Museum (743-5809). This is on the doorstep of Bay Shipbuilding, whose enormous crane looks like a gargantuan erector set and is labelled "Golieth" [sic].

Baileys Harbor

For convenience we will circumnavigate the Door Peninsula, now actually an island, counterclockwise. There are only two harbors for cruising boats on the Lake Michigan side. If you've been circling around lower Lake Michigan and are lulled into complacency by the regular and uncluttered shoreline, now is the time to reestablish vigilance. The lake side of the Door is fringed with shoals and reefs making out from the headlands, and some are detached. The worst spots are marked by buoys, but most of them are unlighted. This kind of bottom configuration is ideal for fishing, so the area can also be thick with commercial fish net stakes. Lay your courses carefully and keep a sharp lookout.

Baileys Harbor, 20 miles northeast of the Sturgeon Bay Ship Canal Entrance, is fringed with shoals, but a black and white Mo(A) bell buoy a couple of miles outside the horseshoe-shaped harbor places you on the beam of the directional range light, with fixed white, red and green sectors. The white sector, at 339° to 340°, is the one you want through good water until you're fairly well into the harbor. There are some additional buoys to help. At the red and black buoy BHYC you can turn to starboard for the **Baileys Harbor Yacht Club**, actually a gracious resort hotel. A breakwater encloses the basin with a fixed red light on the end and a quick flashing green light buoy opposite.

This is perhaps the most attractive facility on the peninsula, with dockage alongside and in slips, with 5-foot depths and all dockside services, including Laundromat. There is a silting problem in the harbor, so boats with 5-foot draft should keep close to the entrance, but the showers are the most luxurious this side of Florida. I can't speak for the men, but the ladies have furnished, carpeted, private dressing rooms with a vase of flowers on the dressing table. The dining room is excellent, the lounge has live entertainment, and on the grounds there are tennis courts and a swimming pool. Both car and bicycle rentals are available to get you into the orchard-studded countryside or to the village a couple of miles around the harbor, which has a few stores and a movie theater. Nearby, the Ridges Sanctuary preserves the native flora and fauna, including 25 species of orchid, for you to enjoy from well-maintained hiking trails.

Rowley Bay

About 15 miles from the sea buoy off Baileys Harbor **Wagon Trail Resort** in Rowley Bay is another very attractive resort, secluded in a more rustic setting, but offering almost everything a cruising boat might want. Hazardous unmarked shoals border the good water for about 4 miles on the approach from the south. Make certain you identify the red nun "8" on Four Foot Shoal and leave it well to starboard as you move up toward N "2." If you're approaching from the north, you can follow a line of red nun buoys from south of Spider Island on a westward course to the channel into the bay.

Wagon Trail is on the west side of the bay, with slips enclosed in a basin carrying 5 to 8 feet and all dockside services except pumpout and diesel, but including Laundromat. The list of amenities at this complete resort is long: convenience store, bakery and snack shop, gift shop, picnic tables, tennis courts, indoor pool, sauna and whirlpool, game room, dining room (bring your own bottle), bicycle and moped rental, canoe and fishing boat rental, sand beach nearby. Mink River, which flows into the north end of the bay, is unspoiled and navigable by dinghy for a couple of miles, and reputed to be excellent for fishing.

Washington Island

The tip of the Door Peninsula is 9 miles from Rowley Bay, where the infamous Porte des Morts Passage separates it from the string of islands that march 28 miles northeastward to Michigan's Garden Peninsula. A combination of shoals and strong currents, setting either way, have conferred on the passage its wrecks and its reputation. On a fair day it's beautiful, but as the *Coast Pilot* laconically reminds us, "The shores are rockbound and almost certain destruction to vessels going aground." The passage is well equipped with aids to navigation, however and, except in thick weather, should present no problem. From Lake Michigan a black and white Mo(A) bell buoy puts you on the fixed red Plum Island range with white daymarks at 330°. A very conspicuous lighthouse on Plum Island and buoys marking the shoals help you through to the Green Bay side, where you can turn either way. Three other passages thread the island chain between open Lake Michigan and Green Bay. Rock Island Passage, the state boundary between Wisconsin and Michigan, and St. Martin Island passage are well buoyed; Poverty Island Passage is not, but on a good day is easily navigated by small craft.

Washington Island is the largest in the barrier chain, mainly a summer resort that has remained rustic and natural. It has two harbors on the south coast. One is at the southeast corner and is approached on a northward course directly from the red and white sea buoy on the Porte des Morts range. It can also be approached from north or east. A red spar identifies the channel into the private harbor of **Njord Heim**. The pretty little basin has been carved out of the limestone and is perfectly protected by its two peninsulas and breakwall. But the entrance is narrow, and there isn't much turning radius at the slips. Channel depth is 8½ feet, with 9 to 10 at the alongside tie-up and floating slips. Some of them have electricity and water; ice, pumpout and gas are offered, and there is a washroom with shower. The island village is 5 miles away, but restaurants will pick up for dinner, grocery delivery is available, the marina has a courtesy car, and there are taxis.

Detroit Harbor is entered from the west or southwest side of Washington Island via Detroit Island Passage. The buoyed channel is dredged to 13 feet, and the flashing white entrance light has a fog horn. **Kap's Marina** is just off the entrance channel, with 7 feet at the slips, all dockside services, a 25-ton travelift, engine and hull repair, launch ramp and convenience store. The Ship's Wheel Restaurant is on the premises, and the marina rents mopeds for getting around the 5½-square-mile island. The village, with grocery, drugstores, hardware stores and restaurants is 2½ miles away, and the Laundromat is about 1 mile. At the ferry dock next door there is bicycle rental and a cluster of gift shops. On the other side of the ferry dock **Island Outpost Marina** offers alongside tie-up in 10 feet with electricity and water.

Detroit Harbor is mostly 7 to 10 feet deep, but there is a 3-foot spot in the middle. The bay that indents Detroit Island on the south side of the harbor is a good place to anchor. On the east side of the harbor **Shipyard Island Marina** is in the process of expansion. A buoyed channel, with 7½-foot depth, leads to the marina, which has the same depth at its slips. They expect to have all dockside services in place by the 1985 season. At present not all the slips have electricity and water, and there is no diesel fuel. There is a 35-ton travelift; engine, hull and rigging repair; a launch ramp and the Sailors Pub Restaurant. The village is 3 miles from here, but the marina plans to offer both moped and car rental.

Washington Island was the first and last port of call of La Salle's ill-fated bark *Griffon*. Here was where she took on her load of furs, to sail east across Lake Michigan and into oblivion. In later, happier days the island was settled by a large contingent of Icelanders. Their story and that of their predecessors is told at the Jacobsen Indian Museum and Washington Island Museum near Little Lake in the northwest corner of the island. You can also learn more about the island on the Washington Island Tour Train, with narrated commentary during the 1½-hour tour of the island (854-2972). Another unique way to tour the island is behind the historic 1916 steam locomotive that has been placed on a truck bed to pull old railroad cars refitted with rubber tires. This new service also provides regular transit; you can get on and off anywhere on the route.

There is one more sheltered harbor in Washington Island, Jackson Harbor in the northeast corner, which must be approached from the west. A red nun buoy helps you into the channel with a controlling depth in the center of 7 feet; all the rest of the harbor is foul. You can follow a straight line from the entrance to the town dock, the southernmost of the docks. But between the ferry and the fish tugs you're not likely to find space. If you do, there is electricity, water and heads.

The main reason for going to Jackson Harbor is to catch the ferry for Rock Island (wilderness) State Park opposite. This is a beautiful island, laced with hiking trails, graced with virgin forest and embellished with some fascinating buildings from its days as the island retreat of a Chicago millionaire. There is no place for a pleasure boat to dock, however.

Gills Rock, at the tip of the mainland in Hedgehog Harbor, doesn't offer much shelter. The small breakwater is inadequate to its task in strong north and northwest winds, and the few slips at **Weborg's Wharf** are largely taken up by charter fishing boats. Gas and ice are the only services available, but there is a fresh fish store and a couple of gift shops.

Detroit Harbor.

PHOTO COURTESY OF WISCONSIN DIVISION OF TOURISM

Ellison Bay

Green Bay extends officially for 118 miles from the head of Big Bay de Noc to the mouth of the Fox River. But it's the 72-mile stretch between Porte des Morts Passage and the river that one generally associates with the name. Regrettably, not a single harbor on the beautiful Door Peninsula side is adequately protected from west to north wind and sea. All of the bays are open to those directions, and such breakwalls as there are are mostly inadequate. Despite the discomfort, and occasional hazard, this is a popular cruising ground and every one of those harbors is crowded in season.

Ellison Bay is a hamlet in the bay of the same name about 10 miles from Detroit Harbor and 6 from Gills Rock. Like all the others it's open to winds from west through north and deep-to almost to shore. There are two places to dock in the village. The first is **Cedar Grove Resort**, with an *L*-shaped dock and slips on the inside. Electricity, water, heads and gas are the only services. The resort consists of housekeeping cottages, but a grocery store and restaurants are close by in the quiet village. The **Town Dock** is in a small basin south of the resort, with short slips suitable to small boats; there are electric outlets and heads. If you want to get into the countryside, mopeds and bicycles are rented at the Grandview Motel, and there are public tennis courts in the village.

An outstanding tourist attraction in all the towns of the Door Peninsula is the traditional Wisconsin Fish Boil. Its origins are ambiguous, but majority opinion seems to favor the lumberjacks of 100 years ago and more as the inventors. Hungry after a long day in the woods, they prepared the plentiful whitefish and trout at their disposal by boiling it in a big cauldron with an equally generous quantity of potatoes. Sounds simple, doesn't it? Yet somehow, in the hands of the aficionados who have refined the art, a well-executed fish boil is a matchless gastronomic experience. The ceremony is performed out of doors, where first the fresh, peeled potatoes are plunged into the steaming cauldron over a wood fire. At precisely the right moment the pieces of fish are added (onions are a matter of controversy between the purists and the innovators), and at the next critical moment a splash of kerosene is thrown on the fire. The flames leap high for the spectacular boil-off, and in the overflow from the pot the fat is skimmed away. Served with cole slaw, home-baked bread, and topped off by apple or cherry pie baked with the fruit of local orchards, the fish boil is an event to remember. Each town on the peninsula has at least one restaurant that presents fish boils on a scheduled basis with reservations—they're also popular at church suppers—and the Viking at Ellison Bay claims to have been the first to do so.

Sister Bay

With 564 permanent residents Sister Bay is the largest town north of Sturgeon Bay. And to serve the explosion in summer population it is one of the two main shopping areas on the peninsula. In addition to the necessities of groceries and hardware, there is a long street of trendy and elegant gift and fashion shops, some of them grouped in attractively designed clusters. There are a number of restaurants in town. One of the most colorful is Al Johnson's Swedish Restaurant, where goats graze on the thatched roof and delicious Swedish foods are served in addition to traditional American fare. The Fish Connection and J.J.'s Restaurant do fish boils. For active recreation there are tennis courts, a public beach and a bowling alley. In late July the Village Hall is the scene of the Door County Folk Festival.

No aids to navigation appear along the steep shore on the 6-

Fish Boil, Door County.

mile run from Ellison Bay to Sister Bay. None of the harbors along this coast have any, nor are they needed. Several islands, reefs and shoals offshore are suitably marked, however. On the north end of town, about half a mile from the shopping district, **Anchor Marine** has a small basin with older wood slips in 7 feet. All dockside services are offered, and there is a travelift with 12-ton capacity, engine, hull and rigging repair service. The **Village Dock** downtown consists of an angled steel breakwater, with a few shallow draft slips behind it, but transient boats are generally moored alongside the inner face of the breakwater in 5 to 6 feet. Boats with more than 4-foot draft should keep close to the breakwater. There is electricity, ice, heads and a launch ramp.

Ephraim

Five miles around Sister Bluffs on the east shore of Eagle Bay is the village of Ephraim. The Biblical name recalls its origin as a settlement of Moravians who dissented from the parent colony in 1853. Now, like its neighbors, it's a resort village that consists almost entirely of motels, restaurants and condominiums circling the harbor, with very little shopping. The Edgewater Restaurant is the one for fish boils here, and the Ephraim Shores Motel is where the bicycle rentals are located. There are two charming historic buildings in town to visit—the 1857 Thomas Goodleston House, one of the first permanent homes on the peninsula, and the Pioneer School House, built in 1869. And the first marina you come to from the north is a historic site.

Anderson's Dock and Store were built in 1858. The dock has been modified a bit since then. The wharf shelters a few slips, and there is also alongside dockage, with some electric outlets available. The store at the head of the dock has been restored to its original general store appearance, and the warehouse on the dock is now the Francis Hardy Art Gallery, with an annual juried show as well as regular displays of local work. South of Anderson's **Ephraim Yacht Harbor** has slips in a basin with some shelter, with depths to 10 feet and all dockside services. This is a busy facility, so it's wise to call on channel 9 for a slip reservation. Beyond this marina and the private docks next door the bay shoals severely.

Just west of Eagle Harbor, 2 miles from Ephraim, there are two popular anchorages in Peninsula State Park. Shanty Bay on the mainland side is open to north and northeast, but in settled weather it's a pretty spot, with anchorage in 10 to 12 feet over sand, and a sand beach at the head of the bay. The bay in the underside of Horseshoe Island, which explains the name, affords shelter from all winds west through north to east—an unusual attribute around here—in a wooded setting. The bottom, 4 to 8 feet down, is weedy, so make sure your anchor is truly set.

Fish Creek

On the 7-mile run from Ephraim to Fish Creek there are shoals making out from the offshore Strawberry Islands. Lights on Horseshoe Island and Eagle Bluff and buoys on the shoals all help you on your way through Strawberry Channel, however. Fish Creek harbor is as open as any of them, yet there are many boats on moorings in this busiest harbor of them all. There are

Aerial view of Fish Creek.

also two marinas. The first one you come to is **Alibi Marina**, with slips and alongside tie-up in 8 feet with all dockside services. Transients are usually placed along the inner side of the so-called breakwater, which is all right for dockage, but totally inadequate in mitigating any sea from west through north. The **City Dock**, a little farther into the bay, has slips in 8 to 20 feet, with all dockside services except diesel, and is very little better protected.

Fish Creek is the liveliest of the peninsula towns, with many gift shops, craft shops, artists' studios, boutiques and restaurants in a variety of architectural settings. Mixed in among them is a general store and a grocery store. The log cabin of original settler Asa Thorp can also be found nestled among the shops. The White Gull Inn, an attractive 1896 hotel, has one of the most famous fish boils on the peninsula; The Cookery is another restaurant with very good food. Fish Creek is the place to enjoy theater—if you can get there. Much of the Door's entertainment activity is geared to its automobile-driving cottagers, and there is no public transportation or taxicabs. At any rate the Peninsula Players are the oldest resident professional summer stock company in the country and perform in an all-weather pavilion set in lovely gardens 3 miles south of town (868-3287). The Peninsula Music Festival takes place in August at Gibraltar High School (854-4060). One mile north of town there is an amusement park.

The village has tennis courts, and the usual moped and bicycle rentals are available at Bayside Tavern and Cottages.

Egg Harbor

In the last (or the first) of the bluff-sculpted bays indenting the east side of Green Bay the village of Egg Harbor offers the best breakwater protection at its **Village Dock**. The floating slips are supplied with electricity, and there are heads and a launch ramp, swings and picnic tables. This is a quieter village than some of the others, but has a grocery store, bakery and restaurants; the Villager has fish boils. There is a riding stable half a mile south of town, but the major attraction here is the Chief Oshkosh Indian Museum.

Sawyer Harbor

A dozen miles south from Egg Harbor, Sturgeon Bay opens off from Green Bay. Immediately inside the entrance, on the southwest shore, is a shallow bay called Sawyer Harbor. No navigation aids lead into the harbor, but good water can be found for anchorage close to the north point. The city of Sturgeon Bay is about 4 miles southeast along the channel.

Green Bay—The Other Side
Charts 14909, 14910, 14917, 14918

There was a time when Green Bay was the second most important place west of the 74th meridian, which runs through Montreal and New York. Mackinac was first. The sheltered waterway, which receives the flow of a river system from deep within the continental interior, was ideal for the fur trade. When Father Claude Allouez established the first mission to the Indians in 1669 at La Baye du Puans, as it was then called, there were already a few traders there ahead of him. In the years that followed they congregated in increasing numbers at the mouth of the Fox River, trans-shipping trade goods and furs between the big *canots du maître* that came from Montreal via Michilimackinac and the smaller *canots du nord*, which could negotiate the rivers and portages that penetrated to the Mississippi. The post that flourished there for 150 years was known simply as La Baye. Father Allouez removed his mission upriver, away from the fleshpots, to the present townsite named simply De Pere, to honor the beloved missionary who labored 26 years in the vast territory between Lake Michigan and the Mississippi River.

Little Sturgeon Bay

It's about 40 miles from the entrance to Sturgeon Bay to the city of Green Bay at the Fox River mouth, and 25 miles to the beginning of the channel to Green Bay. If you're bypassing Sturgeon Bay, leave the flashing white Mo(A) bell buoy off Sherwood Point to port. Six miles beyond the buoy Little Sturgeon Bay opens to port. You can pass between the red and black buoys to starboard beyond the entrance and move down along the west side of the bay to anchor in about 8 feet. Or you can head west between the buoys for **Little Sturgeon Inn** with alongside dockage and slips in 8 feet, all dockside services, except diesel, and small engine repair. The inn is a tavern that serves sandwiches and has live entertainment two weekends a month.

Green Bay

By the time the fur trade petered out in the 1830s Wisconsin was a territory and settlers had moved in to farm in summer and log the surrounding forests in winter. The river system that facilitated the fur trade also kept the pulpwood flowing, and in time the city of Green Bay became the "Tissue Paper Capital of America." Some 16 paper mills line the Fox River, along with several other industries, to keep this city of 88,000 people more active industrially than others of its size. Smoke still rises on the river front, and it's a busy Seaway port. The bay becomes increasingly shoal toward its lower reaches, however, and the heavily buoyed ship channel begins about 10 miles north of the harbor. Pleasure boats are wise to follow it, as there are no other harbors to put into in this area. At Long Tail Point and beyond there is no choice.

Not that there could be any doubt, but you know you're at Green Bay when you see the big power plant with its attendant coal pile. Just before the high fixed bridge that crosses the river mouth, in a basin opening to port, you'll find the friendly, informal **Green Bay Yacht Club**. Take the first opening in the pier that crosses the end of the basin, with a fixed white light on the piling. The channel into the club carries 6 to 8 feet, and there is 5 feet at the slips, with all dockside services except diesel fuel. The club has a 50-ton travelift, and repair people can be called in. The small informal clubhouse has a bar and weekend snack service. Its location is isolated, far from downtown and off the bus routes, but there are taxis available. A healthy walk from the yacht club is the Bay Beach Wildlife Sanctuary, with hiking trails and a naturalist program (497-3677) and the public beach is adjacent. Bay Beach also has an amusement park with nostalgic 10-cent rides.

About a mile up Fox River, at the confluence with East River and closer to downtown, **Holiday Inn** offers alongside tie-up with electricity and water and hotel privileges that include showers, pool and sauna. The Fox River is crossed by numerous opening bridges, with clearance ranging from 7 to 31 feet. They open on a complicated signal pattern—consult the *Coast Pilot*—except during rush hours. A mile and a half and four bridges past Holiday Inn **Longtail Marina** is located in a residential area. Their floating slips are mostly occupied by seasonal boats, but there is electricity, water, heads, and gas, a 12-ton open-end travelift, and engine and hull repairs.

Green Bay has all the commercial activities you'd expect to find in a city of its size that is central to a large service region—shops, restaurants, night clubs, movies, bowling, hospital. It also has the Packers. This renowned football team actually started in the 1920s as a packing company "sandlot" team. Their devoted hometown has immortalized them in a Hall of Fame on Lombardi Avenue at the outskirts of downtown (499-4281). A somewhat more eclectic museum is the Neville Public Museum in a splendid new building at 210 Museum Place (497-3767), featuring natural history, local history and art. If you're a railroad buff, you might want to take in the impressive collection of locomotives, railroad cars and other memorabilia at the National Railroad Museum, 2285 South Broadway, on the river a bit distant from downtown (494-9507). Closer to the center of things, at 1008 South Monroe Street (not far from Longtail Marina), is Hazelwood, the city's historic house museum (497-3767).

The Fox River is dredged and buoyed for 7 miles to the city of De Pere where, unless the federal government decides finally to close the system, you can enter the locks and continue for 37 scenic miles to Lake Winnebago. The controlling depth is 6 feet.

Oconto

The west side of Green Bay is strikingly different from its eastern shore. Here the land is low and often marshy; shoals and shallows make out for some distance into the bay. For the 27 miles from Green Bay to the next port that can accommodate cruising boats it's best to follow the ship channel, so you're in line to take the outside of Pensaukee and Oconto Shoals before heading in to Oconto. The marshy mouth of the Oconto River is protected by a pair of breakwaters with fixed red and flashing white lights. An occulting red light is placed midway along the entrance channel that carries 6 feet. The river is subject to silting and shifting sandbars, but current depths are 7 to 11 feet to the two marine facilities. First is the **Oconto River Marina** in a basin on the north shore dredged to 8 feet. The floating slips have all dockside services, except showers and diesel, and there is a 15-ton travelift for engine and hull repairs, and a launch ramp. Opposite the lower point of Ajax Island the **Oconto Yacht Club** has floating slips in 6 to 8 feet, with all dockside services except diesel; the informal clubhouse has a bar. The club is in a placid river setting about a mile from town. There are no taxis, but you might want to walk up to look at it.

The town of 4,900 people is a quiet workaday place, but rather historic. This was the site of Father Allouez's Mission of St. Francis Xavier, where Father Jacques Marquette spent one winter in a vain attempt to recover his health after his first voyage to the Mississippi River. St. Peter's Catholic Church is said to be on the spot. Another interesting piece of church history of a different kind—a quaint little edifice at 102 Chicago Street is the first church building ever constructed for the purpose by Christian Scientists; it dates from 1886. The West Main Street Historic District contains a number of handsome historic homes, several built by lumber barons. The Beyer Mansion Oconto County Museum at 917 Park Avenue (834-2266 or 834-2430) displays artifacts not only from historical times, but from important discoveries in the area of a prehistoric copper culture dated at 5500 B.C. Oconto also has the usual compliment of necessary shops and a hospital.

Marinette/Menominee

About 20 miles north of Oconto the twin cities of Marinette and Menominee flank the Wisconsin/Michigan border, defined by the Menominee River. On the way you must stay several miles offshore to avoid the reefs off Peshtigo Point, guarded by a big flashing white light with fog horn.

Marinette and Menominee are more twinlike than most paired cities in that they have almost the same population, 12,000 and

11,000, respectively; both grew up in lumbering; and both today manufacture a variety of products, including paper. One difference between them is that Marinette developed along the river front, while Menominee extends along the bay shore. Each has a pleasant downtown area and a hospital. Scheduled airline service is available for crew changes.

Stacks and a radio tower help to identify the harbor from the open bay. The Menominee River entrance, which leads to Marinette's marine facilities, is flanked by parallel breakwaters with fixed red and flashing green lights. The red forms a range at 245° with an inner pierhead fixed red light. A deep water, dredged channel leads a couple of miles upriver to the **Menominee River Marina** just below the bridge on the port side. Floating slips in 12 feet; all dockside services, including Laundromat; a 35-ton open-end travelift; engine, hull and rigging repairs; a marine store; a TV lounge and a picnic area with grills complete the offerings at this full service marina. It is located right downtown, convenient to shops, restaurants and movies. Almost adjacent to the marina, in the park on Stephenson Island, is the Marinette County Historical Logging Museum (732-0831). One of the outstanding exhibits is a handmade replica of a logging camp.

Almost directly across the river in Menominee The Mystery Ship Seaport Museum (863-8721) is devoted to the 1864 schooner, *Alvin Clark*. The story of her discovery and resurrection from the depths of Green Bay off Chambers Island in the late 1960s is as fascinating as the vessel itself. It began with snagged fishing nets, continued with volunteer divers who found a perfect ship and raised it, followed by the search for her identity before she was confirmed as the *Alvin Clark*, oldest merchant vessel afloat. The story is not concluded yet, as the man who has devoted 15 years of his life to her continues to seek financial support to restore and preserve the ship in proper style.

At Menominee you know you're back in Michigan when you enter the basin of the **Waterways Commission Marina**. It is located a mile northwest of the entrance to the river, with a flashing red light on the east breakwater. There is 6 feet of water at the slips, with all dockside services. The marina is about half a mile from the supermarket and shopping mall in downtown Menominee, but there is a bowling alley and game room nearby.

The Michigan North Shore
Charts 14902, 14908, 14911, 14915

Before Michigan could become the fourth state carved from the Northwest Territory in 1837 her boundaries had to be determined. Her leaders insisted that the southern line should run through the lower reaches of the Maumee River, thereby placing the new city of Toledo in Michigan. The citizens of Toledo thought otherwise, and fisticuffs, if not shooting, erupted as irate militiamen faced each other in the "Toledo War." As Ohio was already a state with political clout, Congress awarded her the Toledo Strip. Michigan, on the other hand, was compensated with a vastly larger piece of wilderness that became known as the Upper Peninsula. A glance at the map shows this as more logically belonging to Wisconsin, but as a new territory Wisconsin had even less political influence. Besides nobody, least of all the disgruntled Michigan beneficiaries, placed any value on this hunk of real estate. Less than a decade later the enormous mineral wealth of the U.P. came to light.

Mining, lumbering and fishing built the port towns of the Upper Peninsula fronting on two Great Lakes. When the timber gave out and the fish fell victim to the invading lamprey eel and the mines became unprofitable in competition with newer enterprises elsewhere, many of the towns died. Some of those that remained shrank, and today they are quiet, friendly, unassuming places, welcoming the tourists who are renewing their lease on life. There are more of them on Lake Superior, where the scenery is also more dramatic, but the ineffable U.P. spirit prevails everywhere.

Little Bay de Noc

Named for a gentle and readily extinguished Indian tribe, Little Bay de Noc is entered some 50 miles north of Marinette/ Menominee. The shoreline along this entire coast, including the bay, is low and mostly wooded—pleasant, but not especially scenic. As you approach the bay, shoal areas extend in wide bands from both the west shore and Peninsula Point, which divides Little Bay de Noc from Big Bay de Noc. Big Minneapolis Shoal Light with fog horn, and buoyage at the critical points, keeps you in deep water on the approach to Escanaba, 5 miles into the bay.

The first timber cruisers arrived in Escanaba in the 1830s, and lumbering for pulp continues to this day. But the natural harbor behind Sand Point made Escanaba a logical shipping port for Upper Peninsula iron after mid-century, when the rail connections were laid. By 1890 the town claimed to be the largest iron ore port in the world. Today the city of 15,000 still loads ore, in greatly diminished quantities, engages in some manufacturing, and plays an important regional commercial and governmental role.

On the approach a red brick building and the projection of Sand Point are conspicuous. Pay strict attention to the buoyage as the unmarked shoaling of the west shore is sudden, with depths shifting from 50 feet to 3 in a twinkling. Also be aware that there are magnetic disturbances to the compass in this iron-bound region. Sand Point, which shelters the industrial harbor northwest of it, sports a big isophase white light with fog horn on its bordering shoal, but the entrance to the small craft harbor, which is enclosed on the south side of Sand Point, is marked by a fixed red light. The channel carries 9 feet, and inside the basin the **Waterways Commission Marina** slips have up to 12 feet of depth. All dockside services are available here. There are also moorings in the harbor belonging to members of the informal and friendly Escanaba Yacht Club.

The marina is located in Ludington Park, which includes much of what you might want to see and do in town. There is a beach, tennis courts, the Delta County Historical Museum, and Wednesday evening band concerts. Adjacent to the park the historic House of Ludington has been restored to turn-of-the-century opulence, with gracious dining room and bar. Downtown shops are not far, and the William Bonifas Fine Arts Center is at Seventh Street and First Avenue (786-3833). This is also where the Players de Noc perform. Escanaba has scheduled airline service and a hospital.

Six miles up the bay Gladstone occupies a point of land that is almost an identical twin to Escanaba's. This town of 5,000 was founded in 1887 by an admirer of the British Prime Minister who was looking for a good lakeside railhead site. Lumber and grain shipment brought prosperity to Gladstone for many years, but times have changed and, except for some oil receiving, Gladstone is a pretty quiet little town. Its small boat harbor is about a mile southwest of Saunders Point, the entrance protected by a pier and detached breakwater with an isophase green light. The entrance is rather narrow but carries 7 feet, and there is 6 to 10 feet at the **Waterways Commission Marina** slips, with all dockside services except diesel fuel. The Gladstone Yacht Club on the premises typifies the informal friendliness of the people in this area. This marina, too, is located in a park with a children's playground and safe swimming beach. Downtown shops, restaurants and a bowling alley are a few blocks away, with tennis courts en route.

Big Bay de Noc

When you round Peninsula Point and all its shoals to enter Big Bay de Noc a dramatically different scene confronts you. The limestone bluffs of the Door Peninsula are picked up again in the beautiful, forested headlands of Big Bay de Noc's eastern shore. There are no towns to speak of, and much of the landscape is quite wild. The west side of the bay is quite foul with unmarked shoals and rocks. From the flashing red light buoy on Corona Shoal off Peninsula Point, head northeast for Burnt Bluff. If entering Big Bay de Noc from the east, you can pass between Summer Island and Poverty Island with its lighthouse, or take Poverty Island Passage.

At Burnt Bluff a small private harbor has been carved out of the limestone. It's a little hard to see, and rather tricky to negotiate the narrow entrance, but there's a warm welcome awaiting you at the rustic resort docks. The harbor is entered from the north. The water is very deep here right up to shore, and you can steer for the bluff just north of the harbor entrance, minding the shoal off the point. When you're quite close to shore you make a 90-degree turn to starboard through the narrow, rocky channel dredged to 8 feet. Usually an approaching boat is noticed and someone will appear at the dock to gesture you in. In addition to local conviviality, the reason to visit Burnt Bluff is to see the Indian pictographs, estimated to be 1,500 years old. A long flight of stairs leads down the bluff to the paintings on the sheer rock face. The bonus for your climb back up is a superb vista, especially at sunset.

Three miles north of Burnt Bluff the next headland conceals exquisite little Snail Shell Harbor. At its base is Michigan's most celebrated ghost town, now a state park. Fayette was considered an ideal site in 1867 for a blast furnace to produce pig iron. The ore could be brought into the safe harbor by boat from Escanaba, while the surrounding forest provided hardwood for charcoal and the bluffs yielded limestone for flux. The Jackson Iron Company established an elaborate smelting operation here, with charcoal ovens spotted around in forest clearings, and a model company town at the harbor. For 24 years Fayette produced high-grade pig iron in substantial quantity, but by 1891 it couldn't compete economically with Pennsylvania coke iron and the hardwood resource was beginning to peter out. The company closed the works and Fayette was left to the not-so-tender mercies of nature until acquired by the State of Michigan in 1959. Now much of the town has been restored, and there are both guided and self-guiding tours available. Start at the Visitors Center, with an orientation model of this fascinating place.

A flashing white bell buoy marks the entrance to Snail Shell Harbor. As you round the point the gaunt chimneys and gaping archways of the brick blast furnaces evoke the mood of a medieval castle ruin. Then you spot the wooden stores and homes in the background and recall that this is frontier Michigan. The thick woods surrounding the rustic harbor confirm it. There are no docks, as such, in Snail Shell Harbor. But the old pilings from the glory days are still there, many of them still sturdy, and planks have been laid across some sets to serve as docks. Chances are you won't find "dockage" space at them anyway, as this is a popular boating destination. But you can anchor in 12 to 14 feet in the shelter of the shell. The bottom is very weedy, however, so make sure your hook is well set. There are, of course, no marine services.

Five miles farther into Big Bay de Noc there are several coves for anchorage east of Garden Bluff. All are exposed to north and northwest winds. Although the fetch across the bay is not very long, surge can be uncomfortable.

Manistique

From the Poverty Island Light, where you officially exit Green Bay, it's about 37 miles northeast to the next port, Manistique. Adding 15 miles from Fayette to the light makes a pretty long run, for a sailboat at any rate, so pick your weather carefully. You're now back in the open lake, with its full sweep of 320 miles to bear down on you in strong southerly winds. Nor is there adequate shelter along the shoal-bound coast between a cove on the north side of Summer Island, where you would be protected from southerlies, and the harbor at Manistique.

Like the others, this, too, was a lumbering town; now the town of 4,800 has a paper mill and a good harbor of refuge. The mouth of the Manistique River is protected by converging breakwaters marked by an isophase red light with a fog horn and a flashing white. The pierhead at the river mouth has a flashing green light on it. Controlling depth is 9 feet for about a quarter of a mile upriver to the **Waterways Commission Marina** on the east side. All dockside services, except diesel, are offered at the slips with 6-foot depths. Downtown shops and restaurants are only a block or two away. Manistique's major attraction is the unusual bridge that carries U.S. 2 across the river. Called the Siphon Bridge, it was built by the paper company in 1916 to accomplish the dual purpose of damming the river and providing a crossing. The roadway sits in a concrete conduit, actually at a lower level than the river.

Naubinway

About 30 miles east of Manistique you enter the Lake Michigan island and shoal area with which this chapter began. Lansing Shoal Light, occulting white on its big gray square tower, marks the north edge of it. About 15 miles northeast of that, past some well-marked reefs, the hamlet of Naubinway has a small craft harbor. There is no chart enlargement for it, but shelter can be found at the small **Waterways Commission Marina** behind a short breakwater. The usual services are available, except diesel fuel. There is a general store and a restaurant in the village.

From here it's 80 miles to the Mackinac Bridge, the northeastern limit of Lake Michigan, with no shelter for a cruising boat on the way. The north shore of Lake Michigan, between Seul Choix Point and Point Saint Ignace, is lightly inhabited, with pristine stretches of beach and forest. It is the most natural, but least accessible, part of the lake and best bypassed by voyaging boats. For a break in the distance across the top of the lake the Beaver Island group is a better choice.

8
LINKAGE:
SAINT MARYS
RIVER

Charts 14882, 14883, 14884;
Canadian 2288, 2295

Descent of the Great Lakes staircase begins at St. Marys River, where Lake Superior's vast waters squeeze into a narrow channel, drop 21 feet through a mile of rapids, and flow 63 miles to Lake Huron. But the river you see today is quite different from the one that greeted the 17th-century French explorers. Of all the watercourses on the inland seas, St. Marys River has been altered the most by human engineering.

For 200 years fur trading paddlers and their successors in sailing ships struggled upstream and sleigh-rode down. When Lake Superior mining became a multi-million dollar business in the 1850s it was time to make some improvements. First the terrible bottleneck of the tumultuous rapids—the Sault de Ste. Marie—had to be unstopped. The State Lock and canal opened in 1855. Rebuilt many times, it now consists of 5 parallel locks across the ½-mile-wide river. The awe-inspiring rapids that once evoked the artistry of paint brush and verse are now properly restrained in a narrow channel between lock systems, most of their energy siphoned to electrical generating systems on both banks.

As the ships grew larger and more numerous the smaller

rapids downstream were tamed by channel straightening or enlargement. Dredging has been almost continuous to accommodate the steady increase in vessel draft. Even the flow of the river is regulated by manipulation of 16 sluice gates above the locks. All of this work has altered the banks of the narrow passes and the broad lakes that punctuate the river's course. Although the waterway is far from primeval, much of the countryside through which it passes is wild or but lightly developed. The riverside scene is generally placid and soothing.

If you haven't met many ships on your Great Lakes cruising so far, you're sure to do so in St. Marys River. It is one of the world's busiest shipping lanes—more tonnage passes through the Sault Locks than through the Panama and Suez canals combined. Ship traffic on the winding river is carefully managed through channel separation, speed control, elaborate buoyage and Coast Guard radio voice communication. All the small boat mariner need do is keep out of the way. He's likely to be invisible from a ship's bridge, and even at their slow river speed a laker requires a couple of miles to stop. Nor is there room for one to turn aside. But there is enough room for small craft to hug the side of the channel and take advantage of the buoys and ranges. Current on the river isn't as strong as you might expect from the discharge of 75,000 cubic feet of water per second. It varies according to the relative levels of Lake Superior and Lake Huron and manipulation of the control gates in response, but rarely exceeds 1½ miles per hour.

Four major islands, and many small ones, occupy or border on the river. Their presence creates a selection of channels for pleasure craft. The main ship channel is the most direct route from one end to the other, 63 miles, but is the least scenic, with no harbors in the lower 50 miles. The other alternatives lengthen the passage up to 10 miles, but are more attractive and offer some interesting harbors to visit. You might want to cruise upriver one way, and down the other.

The Ship Channel to Sault Ste. Marie

DeTour Reef Light welcomes you to St. Marys River. Four miles upstream the village of DeTour is the base for pilots conning the ships up and down, the mainland terminus for the Drummond Island ferry, and a customs port of entry. There are a few shops and restaurants. At the north edge of town a new **Waterways Commission Marina** is enclosed by a rubble breakwater with a flashing red light at the entrance, which is approached from the south. As of this writing all dockside services are in at the slips, except fuel. That may or may not be available by 1985. The basin is dredged to 6 feet or more.

Opposite DeTour Drummond Dolomite is a big mining operation on Drummond Island. Otherwise the shores are quite rural as you move up between St. Joseph Island and the mainland along the international boundary. Beyond Point aux Frenes the river widens into Munuscong Lake, formerly called Mud Lake. Its shallow depths and marshy shores make the reason obvious and the fishing and duck hunting extraordinary. At the entry to the lake ship traffic is separated into an upbound channel passing between St. Joseph and Neebish islands for 17½ miles, while downbound traffic passes between Neebish and the mainland for 16½ miles. Both channels are quite narrow, but the downbound, West Neebish Channel includes a massive artificial rock cut, 9,000 feet long and 300 feet wide. The low stone walls have a rather Roman look about their precisely cut blocks, while behind them is a gray Sahara of conical broken rock piles. Neebish Island, 8 miles long, is mostly a summer resort, with a ferry connection near the head of the west channel. Beyond the island Lake Nicolet is another wide place in the river, but its 9-mile length and maximum 2-mile width isn't very lakelike. It flows between the mainland and Sugar Island, which is 15 miles long and also mainly a summer resort with a ferry at its north end. About halfway along, the two channels join and continue as one past the twin cities of Sault Ste. Marie to the head of the river.

If you take the upbound course east of Neebish Island, you have the opportunity to leave the ship channel at Stribling Point on St. Joseph Island. From there you can either continue eastward through St. Joseph Channel, leading to Lake Huron's North Channel, or turn northward through Lake George between Sugar Island and the Ontario mainland to the Sault. This is a more scenic route than the one west of Sugar Island and only a little less direct. It is described in a later section. The full course of St. Joseph Channel is limited to boats that can clear the 38-foot fixed bridge 7 miles from Stribling Point.

Potagannissing Bay

The commissioners charged with the task of defining the international boundary during the 1820s had a hard time deciding where to place it on St. Marys River. The 1783 Treaty of Paris had decreed that it should pass through the middle of the Great

Lakes and their "water communications." Where was the middle of St. Marys River? Which islands should go to whom? In the familiar style of government decision-makers they defied geographic logic to place St. Joseph Island in Canada and Drummond Island in the United States. Even the British Army was confused. They had, reasonably, built their base on Drummond after evacuating Mackinac Island at the close of the War of 1812, and now they had to abandon it and find a new home. They finally left in 1828.

Drummond Island, 12 miles by 20, is today mainly a summer cottage resort, although there is still some farming, as well as the big limestone quarry and dock on the St. Marys River side. Harbors on the south shore were described in Chapter 6. The north side is favored by Potagannissing Bay, filled with round wooded islands. Most, but not all, of the shoals and reefs among them are marked by buoys, and you have to keep count and identify the islands as you pass them in order to find your way through. Centered in the largest one, Harbor Island, is a large land-locked cove for anchorage in 10 feet. Although there is a cottage at the entrance, the island belongs to the Nature Conservancy, to be preserved forever wild. Otherwise Potagannissing Bay is a well-developed colony of attractive summer homes.

When the main channel of St. Marys River turns northwest past DeTour, you keep going straight for a couple of miles, then turn east into Potagannissing Bay at Sims Point. From there it's 4½ miles to Drummond Island Village, where **Drummond Island Yacht Haven** provides alongside dockage and a few slips in 10 feet and all dockside services, including Laundromat. A hoist hauls out up to 36 feet for engine and hull repair, and there is a marine store. The proprietor is a customs officer. On the approach to the marina, note the long shoal making out just east of it, marked by a red nun and two white barrels with orange bands. A walk around the harbor brings you to a general store, and to reach the supermarket, bakery and restaurants at the inland village center there is bicycle or short-term car rental at the marina. Other than anchorage behind some of the islands in Potagannissing Bay there are no additional suitable harbors on the north and east shores of Drummond Island.

The north edge of Potagannissing Bay is skirted by the international boundary, and on the other side of it the long, narrow inlet of Milford Haven penetrates the St. Joseph Island shore. From the main channel of St. Marys River, head north past Squaw Island, with a flashing red light on it. A buoyed channel leads northeast, right along the boundary line, aiming for Koshkawong Point, 8 miles away. On the other side of the point, with a flashing red on it, is the entrance to Milford Haven. Sheltered anchorage can be found northwest of Sandy Point in 10 to 12 feet. There are a couple of scattered cottages on the wooded shores, but this is a mostly wild and peaceful place. If you have just entered Canada from United States waters, you are not authorized to go ashore until you have cleared with a customs officer; there is none here, of course.

St Joseph Channel

If you're headed up St. Marys River for Lake Superior, the route around the south and east sides of St. Joseph Island is certainly the long way around. And if your mast exceeds 38 feet, you can't get through on the far end. On the other hand, this passage takes you along the edge of the North Channel and through St. Joseph Channel, where the scenery is unmatched for splendor anywhere else on the river. There are also some quaint ports to visit.

The panorama of granite and pine begins on the east coast of St. Joseph Island. You are now navigating on Canadian charts that are still published in the old style. Depths are recorded in fathoms to an outmoded chart datum; you must deduct 2.9 feet from the soundings to arrive at the current reference plane. Departing from Milford Haven it's best to pass between the flashing red and green light buoys off O'Donnell Bank and Seine Island, respectively. Leaving the red spar beyond them well to port, you can turn northward for the 12-mile run to Bruce Mines at the mainland entrance to St. Joseph Channel. On the way, make sure to spot the red spar on Prout Rock and keep clear of it.

A church spire in Bruce Mines helps to identify it from offshore, and McKay Island on the approach to the harbor has a fixed white light with red and white daymark. The brand new **Bruce Mines Marina** has a flashing red light on the service dock, behind which floating docks in 10 feet are well protected. All dockside services are available; dockage is alongside tie-up. There is also a launch ramp.

Bruce Mines is the site of Canada's first successful copper mine. It opened in 1848, and the town was settled by experienced Cornish miners brought over to work it. Before the mines closed in 1876 they were managed by a rather notable person, the Marquis of Queensbury. Not the boxing marquis—that was his father, whose title he inherited after he returned to England. The town's history and a lot of other things are nicely preserved in the Bruce Mines Museum (785-3705), an 1894 church with a distinctive Norman tower. The village of 500 also has good shopping for food and drink, a Laundromat, a restaurant at the head of the dock, and tennis courts.

Departing from Bruce Mines, it's best to cross toward the St. Joseph Island side of the channel to avoid the shoal area off the north shore. There are some isolated, unmarked rocks among the otherwise adequate depths. Note that buoyage is placed leading toward Sault Ste. Marie, reds on the starboard side as you head west and north. And most of the buoyage through the rock and shoal-studded channel is unlighted. The course line is pecked out on chart 2288, and there is buoyage where it's most needed, but it's inadvisable to cruise St. Joseph Channel after dark. The distance from McKay Island to the main channel of St. Mary's River is only 18 miles, but this stretch of waterway entices you to linger.

When His Majesty's government finally turned Fort Mackinac over to the United States in 1796 the British Army base was removed to St. Joseph Island. From Fort St. Joseph, at the southwest corner of the island, a surprise attack against Mackinac was launched in 1812, which succeeded in the island's capture without a shot. (The National Park site is accessible only by car.) After the war the place was more or less abandoned until 1835, when Major William Kingdon Rains arrived with plans and authority to establish a settlement. He also brought an unconventional marriage—one wife and one consort. They were devoted sisters, apparently content to share a husband and each other's companionship as they raised two sets of children in the desolate wilderness. Milford Haven was the site of their first home, and you'll notice the name Rains at many other places on the island. Despite the peculiar domestic arrangements, the educated family was well respected. People with names other than Rains came to farm the fertile island as the 19th century wore on, and today there are many summer residents as well. The island is a quiet place, with peaceful country roads to walk and no commercial entertainment.

The first harbor on the island side of St. Joseph Channel is Hilton Beach, about 6 miles from Bruce Mines. The L-shaped government wharf, with a fixed red light on the old freight shed, shelters floating docks with 5- to 8-foot depths, most of which are fully occupied by local boats. **Hilton Beach Marine and Sports** supplies electricity, water, gas and pumpout. A general store and a couple of restaurants complete the commercial operations, and there is a sand beach adjacent to the dock.

Directly across the channel from Hilton Beach is beautiful Portlock Harbour. A course of 030° from the Hilton Beach Light directs you to the pair of spar buoys that marks the approach. From there a series of daybeacons guides you between Colby Island and Woodman Point into the anchorage. Portlock Harbour is a summer cottage colony of well-concealed homes, but you can find fairly secluded anchorage between Portlock and Dawson islands or behind Wurtele Point on Dawson Island in 8 to 12 feet. There is no safe passage westward between the islands that enclose Portlock Harbour. You must go out the way you came in, to continue on the main channel.

From the flashing red light on Plummer Bank a westward course takes you into Gawas Bay, where there is a government dock without services in 6 feet of depth, or you can anchor. From Graveyard Point on Campement D'Ours Island you can strike off in several directions. A course of 060° will lead you to a lovely anchorage on the northwest side of Dawson Island. If you're in a powerboat, you can aim for the buoyed channel into the Desbarats River, identifiable just east of the high bluff on Walker Island. Note the rock off the little island off Walker and leave all of that well to port. It's only a mile to the head of navigation, with a small government dock and a nearby store, but a power line of unreported height crossing the pretty river limits the excursion to low-profile boats.

Crossing the channel northwesterly from Graveyard Point brings you to **Holder Marine** at Kensington Point, catering mainly to small boats, but with 12 feet at the dock and a gas pump. Perhaps the favorite anchorage in St. Joseph Channel lies on the west side of Campement D'Ours Island, in an uninhabited, cliff-sided bay enclosed by Picture and Sapper islands. The water here is very deep, but shoals gradually in the notch cut into Campement D'Ours; you might want to tie off to trees after dropping the hook.

From here it's only 2 miles to the 38-foot bridge. Narrow Wilson Channel is well buoyed and ranged, and enlarged on the chart, so it should give you no trouble. A couple of miles beyond is the major town on St. Joseph Island, Richard's Landing. Its population is 300, contrasted to the 200 at Hilton Beach. But Richard's Landing has the hospital, library, liquor store and several restaurants, including one at the government dock, as well as a general store. It also has Courtney's, an excellent

Canadian craft and import shop, and a tennis court. The first weekend in August island artist Doug Hook shows his expressive paintings in the Town Hall.

A fixed green light marks the government dock, with alongside tie-up on the inner face in 10 feet. Electricity with long lines, water, gas, pumpout and heads are supplied by **Paul's Marina**. Richard's Landing is a customs port.

Two and a half miles past Richard's Landing is the trickiest part of St. Joseph Channel. The short, tight passage off Boulanger Point is well buoyed, but a strong current from St. Mary's River can complicate the piloting. Make sure you have the right amount of power on to overcome it without too much to avoid the rocks. Another mile and a half and you're at Stribling Point and the connection to the main ship channel described earlier. Just before you get there, at the flashing green light buoy "3" off Harwood Point, you can enter the East Neebish Channel between East Neebish and Sugar Islands. Although narrow, it is well buoyed for the 3½ miles to Lake George. This is another wide place in the river, 10 miles long and 4 miles across at its widest, between Sugar Island, Michigan and the Ontario mainland.

The lower end of Lake George is very shallow, but there is a closely buoyed channel into deep water, from which a course of 025° can be followed to the exit channel at the north end. The east and west shores are low and dotted with farms and summer resorts, but the passage across the lake is made scenic by the upthrust of high hills to the north. As the river curves around the north end of Sugar Island the channel is fairly narrow again, but not hard to negotiate for the remaining 12 miles to the Sault.

Sault Ste. Marie

The name refers to the rapids of St. Marys River and to each of the cities that face one another across the international boundary in the narrowest part of the river. And for each of them, as you may have noticed, the name is often abbreviated simply to The Sault, sometimes spelled *Soo*. The first French missionaries visited here in the 1640s. Twenty years later there was a permanent settlement of missionaries and traders at the strategic portage, where Indians congregated in great numbers in spring and fall for the massive whitefish runs in the rapids. Because the portage was shorter on the south side of the river, that's where settlement began, making Sault, Michigan, the older community by 100 years. But for 40 years around the turn of the 19th century the people of both villages considered themselves one community—British and oriented to Montreal. Sault Ste. Marie, Michigan Territory, didn't really become American until the U.S. Army and a U.S. Indian agent arrived in 1822.

After that the two towns developed quite independently. By the turn of the 20th century, Sault, Ontario, began to industrialize in steel and paper and soon far outstripped her southerly neighbor in population and importance. Over 81,000 people live in the Ontario city, while Sault, Michigan, has only 14,400. Both cities are customs ports and have commercial airports. The major industry on the American side is operation of the locks. Since the first tandem pair opened in 1855, additional locks, enlargements and replacements have been constructed regularly. Now there are four, side-by-side, the newest one completed in 1968 at 1,200 feet in length, 110 feet in width and 32 in depth, to accommodate the largest lakers built. The Canadian lock opened in 1895 and is the one usually used by pleasure boats because there is less ship traffic there and no formalities in locking through.

If you take the main ship channel up the river, you arrive first at the Michigan **Waterways Commission Marina** in a side channel entered at Frechette Point southeast of the city. There's plenty of buoyage to direct you, but a considerable current can run through this narrow channel, especially in a strong west wind. Getting into a slip may be tricky, but the islands that create the channel also protect the marina from surge. Depths run about five feet at the aging docks, which have electricity, water, pumpout and heads. Fuel is available at Lawrence's next door to the south. There are two serious disadvantages to this marina, however. It has not been as well maintained as the other public marinas in the state, and it's a 4-mile cab ride to town.

Continuing in the main channel, as you swing westward around Mission Point the two cities are laid out before you. Sault, Ontario, has more of a skyline, but Sault, Michigan, has the impressive Romanesque masonry of the Edison Sault Power House, 1,500 feet long and housing scores of turbines fed by water rushing through the power canal behind it. Beyond the power house there is dockage in a basin just below the canal and lock entrance. It's identified from the river by the museum ship S.S. *Valley Camp* moored immediately east. Tie-up is alongside, with electricity and water provided. One peculiar feature that may be troublesome for your boat is that every other post facing the dock is cut off short at the waterline. There is remarkably little surge in this basin, but whatever there is may cause problems with those posts.

Downtown shops and restaurants are only a few blocks from this yacht basin, although grocery stores and the hospital are a bit farther out. There are taxis available. Many of the sights to see are close by, however. The *Valley Camp*, across the grounds, was built in 1917, and most of the ship remains as it was when she was in service (632-3658). In one of the cargo holds there is a marine museum with a variety of artifacts, including a lifeboat from the *Edmund Fitzgerald*, most recent freighter to "sail away" with all her crew in 1975. On Water Street, about a block away, the home of John Johnston, gentleman fur trader and early settler, has been restored as the Chippewa County Historical Museum (632-6255). The Historical Society is also working on the Agency House, the home and office built by Johnston's son-in-law, Indian Agent Henry Rowe Schoolcraft in 1828; it may or may not be open. Of similar uncertain status is the home on Portage Avenue of beloved 19th-century missionary Frederic Baraga. Across Portage Avenue you can't miss the 21-story Tower of History (635-1211), built for the city's 1968 Tricentennial to honor the Jesuit missionaries who founded the town and to offer visitors a splendid panoramic view of the river, the locks, and the Canadian highlands beyond.

The biggest show in Sault Ste. Marie is the canal and lock system. The Army Corps of Engineers hosts thousands of lock watchers every year in the reviewing stands in Government Park, a few blocks west of Ashmun Street, the main shopping thoroughfare. Even though you may transit the locks yourself, you can learn a great deal about their operation at the visitors' center, and it's a fascinating spectacle to watch the big ships pass through, up to 80 per day. There are also lock tour boats, originating in both cities, and a "toonerville trolley" Tour Train covering both cities from a depot across the street from the locks.

Sault Ste. Marie, Ontario, also has two municipal marinas. Where the ship channel just west of Mission Point turns, a buoyed channel leads to **Bellevue Marine Park**. A big apartment house west of it helps identify the location, and quick flashing red light buoy "104" is a useful point of departure from the channel by whichever route you've taken up the river. Protected by a breakwater from the wash of passing freighters, there is 8 feet in the channel and at the slips, with all dockside services except showers. The marina was designed for boats up to 30

Sault Ste. Marie, American locks.

feet, so the slips are short and closely spaced, with little turning room at the gas dock. Transient boats are usually asked to tie up along the inner wall, where turning radius is also tight and dust from the parking lot settles on the boat. But this location is closer to the electric outlets, which are placed only at the base of the floating piers. There are plans to expand the marina and add services; perhaps its shortcomings for larger boats will be overcome as well. It is located at the edge of spacious Bellevue Park, with colorful gardens, a children's zoo and an imaginative playground with fixtures like a tugboat sandbox. At the far end of the park The Great Lakes Forest Research Center, 1219 Queen Street East, offers interesting displays and tours (949-9461).

It's a mile by foot, taxi or half-hourly bus from Bellevue Marine Park to the heart of downtown, with its excellent shopping, restaurants, cocktail lounges and movies. Cesira's is recommended for Italian cuisine in a gracious setting. On the way you pass the city's two hospitals, and at the edge of downtown, 831 Queen Street East (949-1488), is the Old Stone House, built in 1814 by prosperous fur trader Charles Ermatinger. It's a fine example of how some people managed to live graciously in the wilderness. More local history is offered at the Sault Ste. Marie Museum in the dignified old post office building at 107 East Street (256-2566).

The downtown waterfront is still in the process of an impressive redevelopment, anchored by the handsome Civic Center. A block or so east of it, at 10 East Street, the Art Gallery of Algoma presents a variety of exhibits (949-9067). About two blocks west the S.S. *Norgoma* entertains visitors at her retirement berth (942-6984). The last overnight passenger ship built on the lakes, she served Georgian Bay, the North Channel and the Sault from 1950 to 1974. Between the *Norgoma* and the Civic Center another municipal marina occupies a basin with 12 feet at the floating slips, which accommodate boats to 36 feet, without services. And immediately west of the museum ship **Holiday Inn** has alongside tie-up with electricity and water, hotel shower and swimming pool privileges. If you can get a spot in the basin, rather than along the front face, you will be well secured from the wash of passing ships.

Who would expect a railroad in this day and age to be a major tourist attraction? Yet the Algoma Central Railway's day-long excursions through the magnificent wilderness to Agawa Canyon are so popular that a new station was recently opened on Bay Street to serve the traffic. The tour runs from 8:00 A.M. to 5:00 P.M., with a two-hour stopover at the canyon, and dining car or box lunch service. Tickets go on sale only one day in advance, but it's advisable to buy them a day ahead to prevent disappointment (254-4331).

There are additional tours available in town. Algoma Steel Corporation, at the far west end of the city (945-2228), will show you how the Sault's most important enterprise functions. The tour of the Abitibi-Price Pulp and Paper mill near the lock (942-6070, ext. 202) takes you from the vast log stockpile through the entire process to the gargantuan rolls of paper that come off the line. On the tree-shaded grounds of the mill, near the handsome Georgian administration building, is a replica of the first Sault lock, built by the fur-trading North West Company in 1797. The present Canadian Lock is now a part of Parks Canada. When the lock was built in 1895 the site was designed like a traditional boarding school might be conceived—solid, red sandstone buildings with limestone trim, on spacious lawns bordered by flower beds. And so it remains, essentially a park. Even if you're planning to transit the lock, it's worth visiting by land, to see the informative display in the administration building (which is also a marine post office and chart distribution center) and take the self-guided walking tour (942-6262). If you cross the lock on the footbridge at the upper gate, you will find a trail leading straight across Whitefish Island for the best close-up view of the rapids you can get. The frothing waters are still an impressive sight.

Sault Ste. Marie, Canadian lock.

The Locks and Beyond

Most pleasure boats transit the Canadian lock both because there is less traffic and because the procedure is simpler. At each end there is a Small Craft Landing, designated by a sign, yellow markings and a blue light. You can dock there to pick up a special telephone for instructions, or you can call the lockmaster on channel 16, call sign VDX 23, on your way to the lock. Traffic signals carry the usual color-coded messages, a flashing red meaning the lock is being readied for you. Do not proceed past the Limit of Approach sign until the light is green. Tie-up is usually on the north wall, whichever direction you're locking, so have your fenders placed and two 50-foot lines ready. (Boats under 22 feet need only one.) If you're upbound, the lock attendants will drop lines to you to bend onto your own, which they will then haul up and secure. If you're downbound, you simply pass your lines to the lock attendant. The railroad bridge at the west end of the lock has a closed clearance of 15 feet; three long blasts is the signal for opening the draw.

When you transit the American locks you must turn in to the lockmaster a Waterway Traffic Report form. If you send for it in advance from the Army Corps of Engineers and have it all ready, you can arrange lockage by radio, call sign WUD 31, on channel 16, working channel 14. Otherwise you must dock at an inconvenient ship's pier to obtain the form. This is the East Center Pier when upbound and the Southwest Pier when downbound. The American system is divided into two canals, with two locks each. The lockmaster will assign you to one of the four, which you will enter ahead of any ship that might transit with you. Which wall you moor to depends upon which lock you're assigned, so you should be fendered on both sides to be ready. Line handling procedures are the same as in the Canadian lock, but the American authorities recommend 75 feet of line.

There are various currents in this part of the river that you should be aware of. The rapids don't have as much effect as the swift currents often found at the inlets of both the Michigan and Ontario power canals below the locks. Above the locks a very strong current sets toward Vidal Shoals, its speed dependent upon how many sluice gates are open. Because this is the busiest two miles of waterway in the world, and somewhat complicated at that, you should be thoroughly familiar with the text of the *Coast Pilot* as well as the chart.

Once past the locks there is another 15 miles of river cruising before entrance to Lake Superior between Gros Cap and Point Iroquois. Algoma Steel dominates the skyline on the north, forming an intriguing silhouette, along with the bridge, as the city recedes or as you approach it downbound. Beyond the steel plant both sides of the river are residential. Pointe aux Pins Bay, on the north side, is actually a resort area with a sand beach. The Pointe aux Pins range, at 233°, leads you to an anchorage behind Pointe Louise, about 5 miles from the locks. From here on you don't need to keep so closely in the channel as you did in some lower stretches of the river. You can give yourself to admiration of the bold contours of the Algoma Hills as they grow in your view. If the day is too far gone, or the weather is deteriorating as you approach the entrance to Lake Superior, you have another opportunity to anchor in Waiska Bay on the Michigan side, 11 miles above the locks. Most of the bay is shallow, and there is a dangerous submerged railroad bed running across it, but you can find good shelter in 10 feet immediately behind Bay Mills Point.

9
LAKE SUPERIOR: THREE SETS OF TWINS AND THE WILD SPLENDOR BETWEEN

The biggest lake in the world has the widest reputation and is the least understood. "Everyone" knows of its size, its remoteness, its tempestuous behavior, its toll in ships and men—but few have ever been there. Mention Superior to experienced boaters elsewhere and they conjure up visions of perpetual storm, fog and even ice in mid-summer. Those who have found out the benign secrets of the big, bad lake have mixed feelings about revealing them—a desire to share the joy, tempered by fear of invasion by the thundering hordes. For, above all else, Lake Superior is the last outpost of navigable North American wilderness south of the 50th parallel. Serene solitude is the reward for seeking its distant anchorages. Yet there are also sophisticated cities and quaint villages to enjoy along with the natural wonders on this vast inland sea.

Although Lake Superior is not the portal to peril that some people make it out to be, cruising there is different from the other lakes. And most of those differences are attributable to its immense size, 400 miles long by 160 across at its widest. Its 32,000 square miles of surface—about the size of New England minus Maine—combines with its great depth, averaging 500 feet but reaching as low as 1,300, keep the water very cold. In mid-lake it varies little from 46° throughout the year. The contrast with warm continental air moving up from the south and west in summer produces the legendary fogs, which on this lake are worst in the summer months. Inshore the fog often burns off by noon, as elsewhere, but it can also persist for days at a time. Most resident boats carry radar.

Because of its enormous expanse Lake Superior can generate its own weather systems, which modify the succession of cyclonic lows and anti-cyclonic highs moving across the continent. The seasonal pattern is a bit complicated, but the most significant characteristic for cruising boats is the relatively moderate winds of summer. Contrary to much popular belief, "windspeeds are most often in the 10- to 20-knot range with gales and near gales uncommon," to quote from the *United States Coast Pilot.* As a consequence of moderate winds, seas rarely build over five feet in summer, despite the long fetch in almost any direction. Statistics indicate waves of two feet or less 60 to 70 percent of the time, which is not to say it can't get pretty rough part of the remaining time, especially on a lee shore. On the other hand, Lake Superior, unlike its siblings, does develop a long swell in the aftermath of tempestuous weather even if it has occurred at a distant place.

The shape of Lake Superior has been described in fanciful ways—as a wolf's head with his long snout leading to Duluth and Isle Royale for an eye, or as a bow, arched on the north shore, with the Keweenaw Peninsula poised as the arrow on the bowstring of the south shore. In any case, the lake is rather pointed at both ends, so that it seems to have only two coasts—the curving north from the American lakehead around to the Sault, and the straight south connecting the same two places.

Wind and sea conditions vary remarkably with location. As an example of lake modification, the prevailing westerlies experienced in the eastern half become prevailing easterlies toward the western end. At the southwest end of the lake southwest winds coming in on a weather system from mid-continent often collide with the northeasterlies from Superior's own weather system to produce windless and glassy seas. The lion becomes a pussy cat here. The Keweenaw Peninsula seems to be the dividing line, windwise, between the eastern and western segments of the lake.

In summer thunderstorms are no more frequent on this lake than on any of the others, but they can be vicious, generate severe squall lines and even tornadoes and waterspouts. They are likeliest to occur between midnight and 3:00 A.M., when most pleasure boats are secure in harbor. They are also more frequent and more severe at the western end of the lake, whence they come off the hot land. By the time they travel across hundreds of cold miles to the eastern coasts they often peter out.

The wind and weather conditions I have described refer to the summer months, June to August. The rest of the year it is a different story. Because Lake Superior conditions can be rough through May and begin to get that way again in September, the ideal cruising season here is shorter than on the other lakes. Warm summer air arrives later because of the larger, colder lake, so that June can be a pretty chilly month. Full body tans must be acquired in July and August, and those are the months for swimming in the warmed-up shallows of sheltered harbors. Most days you'll wear warm clothes for sailing, including cap and mittens, even when you might peel down to a bathing suit in harbor. You also need warm bedding, sometimes cast off during occasional hot nights. In short, carry a full range of clothes, but no more than one dress-up outfit for a night out in one of the large cities; elsewhere dress is casual.

As the two ends of Lake Superior display different weather conditions so its two sides are topographically disparate. The north shore edges the Laurentian Shield, composed of some of the oldest rocks known to science at about 2½ billion years. Bold cliffs plunge steeply into the sea, backed by ranges of ancient mountain stumps clothed in boreal forests of spruce and pine, where wildflowers explode in profusion and variety in the open patches. Yet the bases of these walls are ragged, cut by streams, etched with bays and fronted by islands that afford sheltered harbors to small boats. They are quite closely spaced, from 5 to 25 miles apart, although not all of them afford full protection and the water is often very deep for anchorage. It is always advisable to enter these anchorages with the sun at your back and a lookout on the bow; some cannot be attempted with a hard sea running. The shores of the much younger south coast are generally smooth, with few natural harbors, and feasible artificial ones are up to 50 miles apart. Sand and sandstone are the main ingredients here, heaped into steep bluffs and spectacular dunes in some places, cut into fantastic formations in others. The Keweenaw Peninsula is a south shore anamoly—ancient, folded, metamorphic rock reaching toward its brethren across the lake.

The first explorers of record on Lake Superior were Médard Chouart, Sieur des Groseilliers, and his young brother-in-law,

Pierre Radisson. They opened the fur trade here in 1659 and were followed six years later by the first missionary, Father Claude Allouez, whom we met on Lake Michigan. Allouez's map of the lake was the standard reference for the next 100 years. Forbidding though these vast waters might be, Lake Superior was the most important source of fur among the Great Lakes. Here the beaver grew bigger, with thicker coats, and every stream feeding the lake was the site of a trading post at one time or another. Those at the far end led, by series of streams, lakes and portages, deep into the interior, ultimately to the Rocky Mountains and the streams that flowed in other directions to the Arctic and the Pacific Ocean. This difficult fur trade route was the Northwest Passage sought so long by European explorers, and it began at Lake Superior.

The fur trade continued to thrive here until well into the 19th century. By then the lake had been politically divided—the north shore Canadian, the south coast American—and each began to move toward a different destiny. Most of the south shore was assigned to Michigan in the deal that gave the new state its Upper Peninsula in recompense for relinquishing claim to the Toledo strip on its southern border. The far west end was divided between Wisconsin and Minnesota when they became states. Discovery of rich lodes of copper and iron in the 1840s spawned a fringe of towns and settlements along the Michigan shore. Several grew quickly into sizable cities; three have remained so. But only Marquette gives a glimpse of the fortunes made on the mineral ranges. Most of the successful mines were financed by eastern capital, and the enormous profits were shipped out of the lake along with the ore, to endow cityscapes elsewhere. On the Ontario side mining came later, on a much smaller scale, without the development of port cities.

Timber was the next bonanza on Lake Superior. Between the 1880s and the 1930s both shores were denuded. Second growth has flourished, however, and there is still a good deal of logging around the lake, especially for pulpwood. But the lumber barons didn't stay on Lake Superior to enjoy their wealth; they retired elsewhere. So there are no fine cities built with lumber wealth either. Commercial fishing has been significant on both sides of the lake for 100 years or more, but fishermen don't grow rich; their base of operations is usually the quiet village or small town.

What has built the cities of Lake Superior is transport. The two sets of twins at the western end, Fort William and Port Arthur (now Thunder Bay) in Ontario and Duluth/Superior on the U.S. side, were both launched on the flood of western grain. The cheapest way to move the bounty of the prairies to eastern cities and a hungry world is by rail to the lakehead and then by bulk carrier to another railhead or its ultimate destination. Growing rich on storage and the carrying trade, the two sets of cities later industrialized and became the centers of urban sophistication on the lake.

But the rest of Lake Superior continues as it always has, dependent upon its natural resources to earn a living. The north shore remains mostly wild, with only two port towns in the 325 coastal miles between Thunder Bay and Sault Ste. Marie. On the south side the fortunes of the little villages, and even the three cities of Marquette, Hancock and Houghton, rise and fall with the profitability of minerals, fish and timber. But many of them have come to recognize new opportunities for fame and fortune in the visitors who arrive to play. Tourism has not yet "spoiled" the Lake Superior coast, but it has promoted some conveniences and attractions.

Lake Superior's long history as a commercial waterway has endowed it with a plenitude of lighthouses and fog signals. Buoyage, too, is generous in most parts of the lake, but because the rugged northeast shore gets very little traffic it is scantier there and eyeball navigation is necessary. One hazard that can be encountered anywhere on the lake doesn't lend itself to buoyage. This is the legacy of partially submerged logs and deadheads left by 100 years of lumbering. It is worst on the north shore, but requires watchfulness everywhere.

Charts, like buoyage, are more detailed and more up to date on the American side than on the Canadian. Except for the large-scale harbor charts, all of the Canadian coastal charts are printed in the old style and show soundings in fathoms reduced to an obsolete chart datum. Necessary corrections are printed on each chart. Although old, these charts are quite reliable, as natural features change little in this area. But they are displayed in very small scale, making them difficult to read. Many of the dozens of harbors barely show up.

There are local magnetic anomalies at several places on the lake. Strongest disturbance of the compass is found at the western end, between the Apostle Islands and Minnesota's "north shore" and between Thunder Cape and Pic Island on the north coast. LORAN and radio direction finding are invaluable navigational tools in these conditions, as well as in fog. The western end of the lake is well supplied with radio beacons; they are more widely spaced toward the eastern end.

Recreational boating on Lake Superior is increasing, but it is concentrated in only a few locations—Marquette, Houghton/ Hancock, the Apostle Islands, Duluth/Superior and Thunder Bay. Emergency repairs can be found in these places, but are hard to come by elsewhere. When you cruise this lake you are very much on your own, whether coasting the long distances of the south shore or the isolated north shore. Make sure all systems on your boat check out before embarking, and carry essential spare parts and marine stores with you. Food and personal necessities can, of course, be purchased in most harbors on the south side, but selection is often limited, so bring from home those amenities that are dear to your comfort. The one comestible that you can find almost everywhere, to the joy of seafood lovers, is fish—very fresh or delectably smoked.

The north shore presents its own special kind of cruising. Here self-sufficiency is essential, in operations as well as in stores. There are virtually no fuel pumps for cruising boats between Sault Ste. Marie and Thunder Bay, although delivery by truck can be arranged in a few places. The weasel word *virtually* is used here because there are one or two gasoline pumps, if you have a boat that can get to them. The only shower you'll get is the one you bring with you. Nor do you find any Laundromats, except at Nipigon. Whenever and wherever you cruise in Lake Superior, preparation is the essential requirement; on the north shore it is crucial: sturdiness of boat and gear, with backup at hand; knowledge of coastal navigation and attention to your position at all times as a precaution against sudden fog; strong ground tackle with plenty of scope for deep water anchoring (an all chain rode is very helpful here); above all, time to wait out the weather if necessary, and the fog.

In cruising Lake Superior you have a choice between isolated, rugged, wilderness anchorages or convivial village and city docks—or both, if you circumnavigate. Lake Superior is not one to cross back and forth. We will circumnavigate counter-clockwise here and will begin with the north shore for logistical reasons. If you're coming up from the lower lakes, or start out from one of the boating centers at the western end to circle in the opposite direction, you will be more fully supplied with all the essentials enumerated earlier than you will in mid-cruise. Carry enough food to last the period you plan to spend on the north shore, plus 15 to 25 percent extra. With little or no opportunity to shop, you may have plenty of opportunity to linger longer than anticipated while waiting out the weather—or because you can't tear yourself away. The simple pleasures reign here—fishing, hiking, wildflower identification, some swimming and, above all, the regional pastime of rock hunting. Agates abound on many of the beaches, with more localized gems such as greenstone, Thompsonite and amethyst.

East of North
Charts U.S. 14962; Canadian 2304, 2306, 2307, 2308, 2309, 2310, 2315, 2318

While still in St. Marys River you get a preview of the dramatic scene that will frame your entire north shore voyage. As soon as you emerge from the river at the unusual Gros Cap Reef Light you are confronted by challenge. Whitefish Bay, beautiful to look at, can be the roughest, meanest part of Lake Superior. Approximately 25 by 35 miles in dimension, it is where the lake waters begin to narrow before they squeeze into St. Marys River. The opening is only 15 miles across between Whitefish Point and Coppermine Point. Furthermore, this is a lee shore that gets the full force of all westerly winds and seas. The chances are good that your passage across Whitefish Bay will be exhilarating, if not tumultuous, although in the perverse way of all the lakes it could be totally calm just because I said that. In any event, you should try to pick good weather before leaving the river because it's about 30 miles to the first harbor.

Batchawana Bay

In Batchawana Bay you can enjoy a splendid view of the Algoma Hills, but you are still within the exurban orbit of Sault Ste. Marie, 40-odd miles away by road. Much of the bay is surrounded by not particularly attractive cottages. Close to the lake, however, a mile north of Corbeil Point, there is an L-shaped government dock, with 5 to 15 feet of water, where you can tie up for an overnight stop. Note the submerged pilings off the end of it, marked by a buoy. There are no services, nor does the Indian village strung along the road have anything to commend it.

If you find yourself weathered in, you might want to explore a little deeper into the 8-by-10-mile bay. You can take the dinghy up the Batchawana River, about 3 miles from the dock. It is quite unspoiled for several miles upstream. Just beyond the low highway bridge near the mouth the Batchawana Hotel serves good food, and there is a supermarket next door. Batchawana Island is uninhabited, and there is a restful, if rather deep, anchorage in the cove on the north side. The narrows separating it from the mainland on the north carries 9 feet. The rest of Batchawana Bay is either very deep or foul and is quite thick with cottages.

Maimanse

Shortly after leaving Batchawana Bay you emerge from White-fish Bay at Coppermine Point. There are rocks and shoals up to half a mile from shore here; farther on you can glide right under the cliffs. Note the offshore Steamboat Island shoal and Pancake Shoal, both marked by spar buoys, and give them a good berth. At Maimanse Harbour, about 15 miles from Batchawana Bay, is the last government dock for many a long mile. It even has electricity. But this is a major fishing station and the dock may be crowded with fish tugs when you get there. There is no village, but Ferroclad Fisheries is a big operation, with a store where you can stock up on the fresh or smoked variety and top off your ice box.

On the approach from the south, note Hibbard Rock, 12 feet high and 1 mile offshore, and keep well clear of its shoal. The harbor is entered from the north, between Maimanse Island, with a fixed red light and red and white daymark, and the unnamed island immediately east. Mind the islets off the middle of Maimanse Island as you come down between the two, then move around the south end of the unnamed island to the government dock on the mainland. A breakwater north of the dock shelters it from that direction. Shoal water and a power line with 20-foot clearance close off the south end of the harbor. Controlling depth in the channel is 5 feet, with 6 feet at the dock. The 3-foot depth shown off the end of the island on chart 2315 has been deepened by blasting.

Agawa

Continuing north from Maimanse you will encounter very few boats between here and the northernmost point of the lake. The high, steep hills come close to the shore, and you can examine from deck the twists of pink and gray granite along the shore and on the cliff faces. Theano Point is especially beautiful. Highway 17 appears now and then through the trees, so this isn't yet wilderness country, but it is Lake Superior Provincial Park, which runs for 50 miles along the coast and stretches 25 miles inland. Camping, hiking and canoeing share the park's rugged

Trail to Indian pictographs.

terrain, but its rare and special attraction is the Indian picto-graph site on the sheer face of Agawa Rock. Remarkably well preserved, the paintings tell the story of a voyage across Lake Superior. The marvel is that the artist worked his skill in such a precarious place. The viewer must sidle out on a narrow ledge and then, with his back to the sea, look up. It's not quite as difficult as it sounds merely to look, but I wouldn't want to try to paint there.

There are two ways to view the pictographs—by land, with other park visitors, or from the dinghy. You do get a better look from the land, especially of those segments which have faded. If you decide to see the paintings only by dinghy you can anchor in 15 to 20 feet behind Ganley Island, about half a mile south of Agawa Rock. Enter from the north. This spot is rather open, however, and there is a sometimes busy cottage compound on it. A better anchorage for overnight, or a longer visit, is a half mile north of the rock, around the next headland in Sinclair Cove.

Sinclair Cove is about 23 miles north of Maimanse. Montreal Island and Montreal Shoal on the way are of little concern to a pleasure boat, but the Agawa Islands, lying close offshore just short of your destination, do have some submerged unmarked rocks among them. A flashing white light with a red and white daymark on Sinclair Island identifies the entrance. Anchor down in the cove in 10 feet over sand. There is a park launch ramp here and a dock with 8-foot depths that may or may not be in good repair. In any event, it's useful as a dinghy landing, from which you can walk up the road to the trail for the pictographs. Sinclair Cove looks as though it is a well-protected harbor, with high sides and islands closing it off from the north. But, surprisingly, it does develop a surge in even moderate winds from northwest to north.

Gargantua

A cluster of anchorages lies 20 to 23 miles northwest of Sinclair Cove below the long headland of Cape Gargantua. If you coast fairly close inshore, the only hazards to be concerned about are the reefs surrounding the Lizard Islands. Rowe Island Light, flashing white with a red and white daymark, helps you to navigate easily around them. The rounded, forested hills continue close to shore, with red rock bases and patches of gray granite on their higher faces.

The first harbor you come to is Gargantua Harbour itself, easily entered from the south, leaving Gargantua Island, with its flashing white light and red and white daymark, to port. Entrance is also possible north of Gargantua Island, but there are unmarked shoals making out from both the mainland point and the island. Best lying in the harbor is at the far end near the sand beach, in 10 to 20 feet. This is quite an open bay and will get surge from south and southwest winds. A cozier anchorage lies a few miles northwest in Warp Bay. There is a hiking trail between the two, if you want to take a look at one from the other.

To enter Warp Bay from the south, take the deep water passage between the Devil's Warehouse and Dixon Island. Leave

The Devil's Warehouse.

the smaller Wilde Island between them to port and Wadena Shoal at the far end to starboard. The harbor can also be entered from the north past Pearson Island and the mainland point, leaving both Alexander Reef and Wadena Shoal to starboard. Unfortunately there is no chart enlargement of this harbor, but the small-scale coastal chart is readable and shows the anchorage in 14 feet over sand. This is a more scenic spot than Gargantua Harbour, with vistas of both the mainland hills and the rock and forest islands.The sand beach is a broad one, with a little step-dune, and beyond it a stream to explore by dinghy. There is both flat walking and rock climbing in the woods back of the beach. Devil's Warehouse is a fascinating island you might want to explore by dinghy. The east face is very high and bare, with rock cleavages that break it into blocks colored by traces of iron. A few trees and shrubs grow straight out of the steep rock. On the north side there is a cave, but I haven't been there.

Warp Bay, too, is open to south winds, although the islands afford some protection. For an even cozier anchorage you can move into the unnamed bay west of it. By keeping the east side of the mainland point close aboard as you round it and move into the long bay, you will avoid the shoals making out from the first little island. There isn't a lot of swinging room for the 20-foot depth at the widest part, but there's just enough for one boat, and you'll enjoy almost perfect protection here.

Brulé Harbour

As you exit from the Gargantua harbors, stand off the islands that surround the cape, then take the light on Hursley Island as your point of departure to head first north, then northeast. Beyond Grindstone Point the first of many north shore waterfalls will come into view, shimmering slim and high on the mountainside between velvety undulations of forest. A little later you pass the curved strand of pink rock and beach around Old Woman Bay. Shortly beyond is the entrance to Brulé Harbour, about 18 miles from Warp Bay. It tends to blend in with the surrounding hills, so don't expect to see the entrance until you've arrived at it—if your navigation and piloting are accurate.

Brulé is a double harbor, entered north of Entrance Island, a gull rookery with deafening sound effects. Both harbors are very deep, but the the outer, or north, harbor is likely to surge in southwest winds and seas. The inner harbor, on the other hand, is one of the few totally land-locked anchorages on this coast; elsewhere it would be called a *hurricane hole*. Passage through its narrow entrance channel carries 25 feet; stay in the center to avoid some shoaling on the sides. To starboard, just inside the harbor there is a shoal, and old pilings foul the south shore. The eastern end is ill advised for anchoring because of deadheads; best lying is in the northwest cove in 25 feet. Because of depth and limited swinging room, you may want to tie off your stern to a tree or lie to bow and stern anchors.

Falls of the Magpie River.

Michipicoten

At one time the Michipicoten River was an important artery of the fur trade, with a substantial post near the mouth. Now the river is so badly silted, with shifting bars and strong currents, that no stranger should attempt it. A mile upstream, however, there is a government dock, with 6-foot depths, and next door is **Buck's Marina**, with 5-feet at alongside tie-up, gas and diesel. Buck's is an exceedingly friendly place, and if you call Brad Buck by radio-telephone through VBB Sault (705-856-4488), he will meet you at the river mouth and guide you in. Controlling depth is supposedly 5 feet, but there may be a 4-foot spot or two. There's not much at the settlement of Michipicoten River, but there's a fine view of the lower falls of the Magpie River from Buck's dock, and reportedly great salmon fishing in the river.

There are no navigation aids to steer you to the Michipicoten River mouth, 10 miles from Brulé Harbour—you'll have to rely on your own navigation and piloting—but the river empties into Michipicoten Bay, and there is a flashing white light with a fog horn on Perkwakwia Point enclosing the northwest corner. Oakes Cove behind the point offers shelter from all winds except east to southeast, in 5 to 10 feet. Michipicoten got a second lease on economic life when the famous Helen Mine opened up about 10 miles inland just before the turn of the century. Algoma

Central Railway built a spur line from the iron mine to Michipicoten Bay and a big ore-loading dock on the north side. It has now fallen into disuse, but the fixed red range lights on a course of 355° may still be operating as a further assist in getting into the bay.

A Row of Harbors

At Michipicoten the coastline turns a sharp corner to follow two sides of a square bulge for the next 100 miles. This is true wilderness—the most remote and uninhabited part of the lake. The highway is 50 miles inland, and only the skimpiest of forest tracks occasionally come down to the lakeshore. Undulating mountaintops, blue on the horizon, continue to pace the lakeshore, but they are a little less steep at the waterside than they were. The vertical slabs of twisted rock give way to a ground floor of granite outcrops, interspersed with alternating pink sand and gray gravel beaches. Although the terrain looks forbidding from offshore and on the small-scale chart, there is a surprising number of anchorages along this entire stretch of coast. The trick is to find them, as most are unmarked.

Dog Harbour lies 16 miles west of Michipicoten. A triangular, slatted daymark, painted white, sits on the point to bid you welcome. The point is fringed with rocks, however, so keep off as you round it into the harbor and anchor toward the west end in 10 feet over sand. This harbor is open to east and southeast, and gets a surge in any winds with south in them, but there is a broad sand beach fronting the flower-bedecked woods.

Pilot Harbour, 18 miles farther on, offers shelter from all winds, but the stone cairn that marks its entrance, sometimes painted white, is not as readily picked up from offshore; from the west it's pretty well obscured by trees. A big shoal makes out from the east side of the entrance, so favor the port shore until you're fairly well between the peninsula and the islands east of it, then move to the west end to anchor in 10 to 15 feet.

Only 7 miles west of Pilot, Ganley Harbour is an attractive alternative. Its two entrances are also hard to locate, especially if you're coming from the west and have to swing wider offshore to avoid two unmarked shoals 2 and 3 miles west of the harbor. There is, however, a bare rock, about 10 feet high, lying a quarter of a mile off the west entrance that helps identification. Take care not to confuse it with another one, 6 feet high, about a mile east. If you're approaching from the east, the triangular red daybeacon on an island just inside the east entrance will show up as you come around the outside of the easterly bare rock just mentioned and the shoal leading shoreward from it. Either entrance around the pair of islands that encloses the harbor has good water. Someone seems to have set up a range of sticks and rock slabs for the west entrance, based on an interesting rock slope in the northeast corner of the harbor; it may or may not still be there when you arrive. Whichever entrance you use, favor the north shore as you head to the eastern end to anchor in 10 feet over sand. A rock shoal makes out from the island that creates the protection, but you can go beyond it to set your hook.

There are some signs of habitation at the head of the anchorage—an old dock and camp shelter. Nearby a beautiful woodland trail leads eastward to the next bay. The islands at the western end of the harbor provide an opportunity for some dinghy exploration, and a shallow draft cruising boat might find anchorage behind one of them. In the cobble beach of the western point there is an interesting local phenomenon. Obviously man-made depressions have been found in the cobble beaches all along this coastal bulge, measuring up to 9 feet in diameter or 10-by-20-foot rectangles, and up to 4 feet deep. The anthropologists call them Puckasaw Pits, but only a little cultural material has been found in them, making positive identification as to origin or purpose a difficult task. The most plausible explanation is that they were used by the Indians as shelters from wind and cold during ice fishing expeditions, their varying size determined by the size of the group that scooped them out of the cobbles.

Richardson Harbour, the last in this group, 14 miles beyond Ganley, is, in some respects, the most interesting. Its location is relatively easy to identify because La Canadienne Point, a mile and a half southeast, is high and bold. There are two entrances here, too; the eastern one is a little easier to negotiate as both sides of it are steep-to. There are no daymarks to help you here, however. You must find the entrance by eyeball navigation. The east end of the anchorage is good for dinghy-tripping, but as an anchorage it's open to the west, unless you are in a shallow draft boat and can move well down into the southern bight. Anchorage behind Richardson Island in 15 feet over gravel is far better protected than it looks. (Watch out for some old sunken cribs near shore when you set the hook.) You can hear wind in the trees and the surf pounding on the rocks outside, with nary a ripple around your boat. From the cockpit you enjoy a vista of islands and mountains, with twisted rock faces again on the steep bluffs that alternate with low forests of spruce, fir and birch. A couple of trails back of the mainland gravel beach lead to inland lakes reportedly good for fishing. Puckaskwa National Park, devoted to wilderness, begins here and extends for 80 miles up the coast.

Michipicoten Island

All the time you've been coasting this shore—since Cape Gargantua, in fact—an alluring shape on the horizon has been calling you out to Michipicoten Island. From the east shore its profile alternates highs and lows, with a flat pâté shape at the north end. From the north the 17-mile-long island shows up as a serrated bluff in blues and grays. You are closest to it at Ganley Harbour, should you care to pay a call. Although the island is but 10 miles offshore from here, its only totally protected harbor is on the south side, 25 miles from Ganley.

Quebec Harbour is sheltered by an offlying chain of islands. A fixed white range with orange daymark at 001° leads between the easternmost pair, Davieaux and Hope, into the harbor. But if you're approaching around either the east or west end of the island, you will pass on the inside of the island chain. This is easier to manage from the east, where there are no obstructions. From the west, Antelope Rock and The Breeders, an unmarked ledge, stretch westward from Green Island. With care these can be avoided, but note Black Rock and another unnamed one that will be on your port side coming through. In either approach the big flashing white light with a fog horn on Davieaux Island will orient you. This is one of the few manned lighthouses left on the lakes, and the lightkeepers are friendly people who welcome visitors. The small dock has less than 5 feet alongside, so you may have to come over from the harbor by dinghy.

A well-buoyed channel, backed up by a daybeacon range at 050°, takes you into Quebec Harbour itself. These aids are critical as there is a strong magnetic disturbance to the compass right at the entrance. You should also be aware that in strong northwest winds a fast easterly current sets at the entrance, which can sometimes submerge the buoys. This harbor should not be attempted by a stranger in thick weather. The most sheltered anchorage is at the eastern end in 14 to 18 feet. Quebec Harbour has a long history as a fishing station, and while some of the old docks are in ruins, others are in good repair and used by Ferroclad Fisheries operating out of Maimanse. If their boat is not expected for a while, you may be permitted to tie up at the dock. There are also a few private fishing camps around the harbor and some old wrecks to explore by dinghy at the south side of the anchorage.

The Northbound Strand

At La Canadienne Point you began to make the gradual turn northward again around the corner of the bulge. At Otter Head, 6 miles beyond, you complete it. High Otter Island extends another 2 miles beyond the head itself. You can pass between the headland and the island to reach one of the most appealing anchorages on the north shore, but only in good weather, because there is a band of shoals around Otter Head that is inaccurately placed on the chart. Favor the steep island shore on this approach.

But if you aren't in a hurry, go the extra couple of miles and treat yourself to the approach from the northwest end of Otter Island. As you turn toward shore beyond the big lighthouse on Otter Island, the radiance of Cascade Falls draping the cliffside opposite will draw you across the bay. This waterfall, unlike others on the mountainsides, falls directly into the lake. After you've made certain to clear the shoals extending from the lighthouse base, you can approach within a couple of hundred feet, camera clicking all the while. Later you can beach a dinghy nearby and climb up to view it even more closely.

The first of two anchorages here is in the northwest corner of Otter Island, known as Old Dave's Harbour. It is actually a passage between Otter Island and the small island lying north of it. Entrance is made from the east through an *S*-shaped channel that shoals out from both sides but carries 8 feet in the center. Once inside the elliptical harbor the water becomes very deep. Your anchor can most easily find bottom on the southwest side, in about 35 feet, but there isn't room for more than one or two boats to swing here on adequate scope. On the island side there are some fishery buildings with a private dock, and in the southeast corner is the lightkeeper's dock. You may tie up your dinghy there and follow the woodland trail, which the lightkeeper's wife has salted with waggish signs, up over the hill to the lighthouse complex. From there the vistas all around are spectacular. If you're in luck, you'll get a tour.

The wide bay between Otter Island and the mainland gradually narrows as you follow it southeastward for about 4 miles to the fjord-like Otter Cove. It may come as a pleasant surprise to find some spar buoys marking the channel; at the pair off the southeast end of Otter Island is where the channel leading directly from the lake comes in. Just beyond it you turn more easterly to enter Otter Cove around a bit of a dog-leg between the two long islands at its mouth and the point on the starboard side. The long cove, sheltered by high, rounded bluffs and thick forest, is very deep, but there is ample room to swing in 35 feet. The cove shoals quickly beyond a stream entering from the mainland side about halfway down, but if you sound carefully and proceed slowly, you can find safe bottom at 10 feet between the stream and the park buildings on the north shore.

At one time Otter Cove was the site of a private fishing camp/ summer cottage complex. Those buildings were purchased by the government when Puckaskwa National Park was established, and the largest group of them is now a ranger station, with dock, generator and radio tower. When the rangers are there, the amenities of wilderness are somewhat reduced in this otherwise splendid harbor—but not much. At the mouth of the stream mentioned earlier there is a tiny old cabin, where you can beach the dinghy. Follow your ears as you walk up through the forest to the pretty waterfall tumbling over the rocks. The far end of Otter Cove is good dinghy cruising territory. The last of the abandoned buildings was once a boathouse with a marine railway. Rather than detract from the setting, these old structures are a nostalgic whisper from summers gone by. You might also want to take a long dinghy ride back to the south end of Otter Island, where there is a large site of Puckasaw Pits.

On the generally northwesterly course from Otter Head the coastline becomes much more ragged than it has been, with hazardous isolated rocks and rocky banks fringing the shore or extending up to a mile offshore. Triangle Harbour is only 3½ miles from Otter Island Light, but if the weather should be deteriorating, it's easy to get into and affords fair protection. There is a white, slatted triangular beacon on the south point of the entrance. Holding to the center of the channel, you can move about a third of the distance down the bay to anchor in 6 feet. There will be surge in winds from west to northwest.

About 8 miles farther on, Simons Harbour is a more attractive alternative, though a little more complicated to enter. Note the offshore shoals southeast of English Fishery as you come up the coast. There is a white triangular daybeacon at the harbor entrance, but the islands immediately offshore can obscure it on the approach from both directions. The approach from the south between the islands is quite clear from the chart. The northerly entrance is ill advised for a southbound boat because

Hidden waterfall at Otter Cove.

of unmarked Stench Rock a mile offshore and the unmarked rocks and shoals in the northerly entrance itself. There are two coves to anchor in at the south end of the harbor. The easterly one is preferable both for shelter from surge in northwest winds and for lesser depths of 15 to 20 feet.

In proceeding north from Simons Harbour, Stench Rock and the line of rocks and reefs extending northward from it should be given adequate berth. Oiseau Bay, 10 miles beyond Simons Harbour, is a large island-studded bay with expansive views of the hills ranging back in the interior. The easiest anchorage to get into is at the north end behind the innermost island. This entrance is not so easily identified from offshore; you must rely on dead reckoning and landmark identification. Pass midway between the north point of the bay and the islands southeast of it, and proceed toward the curve of beach at the far end. There is good holding behind the island in 9 feet over sand, but there is surge in strong winds from south through west. Other coves toward the south end of Oiseau Bay may offer better protection, but they are difficult to reach through the shoals and are best explored by dinghy.

The beach here is an especially fine one—hard-packed at the water's edge, soft and powdery inshore, and enclosed in a riotous wildflower garden. The park rangers are much in evidence here, with tasteful little signs reminding you that some of these blooms belong to endangered species and the park service is making an effort to encourage their propagation. Trails lead through the spruce/birch woods, carpeted by more flowers. You may see an odd-looking floating dock in the middle of the harbor; it's used for off-loading supplies. There's also a good deal of canoeing in this vicinity, as you're approaching the entry facilities for Puckaskwa National Park.

You should pick your weather carefully when you leave Oiseau Bay as there aren't many good choices for anchorage nearby. Playter Harbour, 14 miles north, is a long narrow, bay, enfolded by hills, readily identified by its prominent north point, but wide open to the west. Anchorage can be found in 10 feet about halfway down the cove. From there it's 15 miles to the next desirable harbor, 28 from Oiseau Bay. There is an undesirable one in between.

By now it may be apparent that you are approaching civilization again—park activity in Hattie's Cove, its northern extremity a mile north of Playter Harbour, evidence of logging activity in the Pic River, and smoke signals from Marathon in the southwest corner of Peninsula Harbour, a dozen miles northwest of Playter. This pulp and paper company town sprang like Venus from the sea in the late 1940s. There are only two reasons why a cruising boat might want to visit—either the boat needs emergency repairs or a member of the crew does. Although Marathon is a reasonably attractive "model" town, with shops and a hospital, the commercial wharf serving its big mill is high, rough and dirty. And even though one can fender from a wharf, there is no defense against the air pollution here that will eat through the finish on your boat as fast as locusts through a field of corn. Finally, once you do tie up, assuming there's space, you have to tramp a mile or two through the mill and up the bluff to reach the urban services you came for. If you must go in, the flashing white light on Hawkins Island is the beacon that directs you. But unless you're desperate, Peninsula Harbour is best bypassed entirely.

The Island Coast

Charts 2302, 2303, 2304, 2305, 2312

When the coastline turns west again from its final northeast corner at Peninsula Harbour, it takes on a different character. Up to now there has been an occasional offshore island, but from here westward the islands appear in clusters or in chains, to create somewhat more sheltered cruising conditions in the channels behind them. While the procession of harbors continues along the mainland shore, there are pockets of civilization there, where the highway has returned to the lakefront. The wild island anchorages are the feature attractions for the next 100 miles.

Allouez Island Harbor

Pic Island is the most dramatic in Lake Superior. Only 2 by 2½ miles in dimension, and lying less than a mile off the north shore, it is entirely mountainous. Its towering slopes, with massive bare batches among the trees, plunge sharply to the lake. Nestled in the shadow of Pic Island's southeast end, tiny Allouez Island offers an exquisite harbor, whose smooth rock faces look like a quarry mined by nature.

Allouez is 10 miles from Marathon, 18 from Playter Harbour, and 28 from Oiseau Bay. While a good compass course will get you there from the latter two harbors, there is severe magnetic disturbance in the entire Peninsula Harbour–Pic Island area. You need good visibility to ensure your landfall. The anchorage is actually an almost circular bay between Allouez Island and an unnamed island adjacent. Its opening on the northeast side is not easy to spot, as it is blocked by a huge rock, mostly under water, with only a narrow gap for access. Keep the south point close aboard and you should carry 15 feet through the channel. There is just enough room inside for one boat to swing at anchor in 18 to 20 feet. To accommodate more would require bow and stern anchors or the stern tied off to a tree. The sea may rage all around, but you'll feel no disturbance in here.

In embayments on the mainland shore on either side of Pic Island there are alternative anchorages, but be aware of magnetic anomalies as you approach them. Port Coldwell, about 5½ miles northeast of Pic Island, is the site of an Indian village, but a well-sheltered anchorage. There are numerous unmarked rocks and shoals on the approaches from both east and south— note especially McKay rocks—but the western passage between Detention Island and the mainland is clear. A white beacon identifies the entrance, and you can find anchorage in 10 to 12 feet in the western arm of the harbor. McKellar Harbour is about 6 miles northwest of the north side of Pic Island, 14 from Port Coldwell. The approaches through Ashburton Bay are clear. Keep to the island side when entering the harbor, to avoid the extensive shoal bank to port, then round up behind the island.

Most of this passage is very deep, but you can find 10 to 15 feet under the north shore just east of the little hook.

The Slate Islands

Jackfish Bay, the next one west on the mainland shore, has its own harbor chart, dating from the days when there was a port town here, but there is nothing to attract a cruising boat. The two arms of the bay are open to winds with any south in them, and the water is extremely deep. The Slate Islands, on the other hand, 6 miles offshore, 18 miles from Allouez, have a number of delightful coves and passages to explore among the eight islands and several islets that make up the group.

From the east the Slate Island group is best entered at Delante Island. The easiest course is between Delante and Mortimer islands, although the passage south of Delante, between Dupuis and little François, is also clear. Once inside, the course follows the east and south shores of Mortimer Island like a mountain road, with sweeping vistas of steep slopes in ranges. Mortimer Island is almost bisected by Lambton Cove, which is too deep to swing at anchor, but in the indentation halfway up on the west side you can tie off your stern to trees and enjoy the rock and beach landings.

On the southwest corner of the east half of Mortimer Island is a two-way beacon range. The range facing southwest brings you into (or out of) the west entrance to the Slates, safely past the major channel hazard of Kate Rock. The range facing southeast carries you down the passage between Bowen and McColl islands into McGreevy Harbour. The northeast corner, between Bowen Island and the tip of Patterson, has good depths for anchoring, but it also has some cottages. And there is a conspicuous compound at about the middle of the southeast shore. On a weekend this harbor can be quite busy (by lonely Lake Superior standards) with local people coming over to fish and camp.

But if you head toward the house on the south shore, and then turn to starboard alongshore, you can pass into the southwest arm, which is wild and has the least depth for anchoring in the entire island group. The entrance is quite narrow, made even more so by an island in the middle. This island can be passed on either side in 6 to 10 feet, but the south pass is preferred because of an overhanging pine, which will shower you with needles if your mast catches in it. Favor the port side of the south channel, because there is a shoal making out from the island. Toward the far end of the cove you can find comfortable mooring in 10 to 15 feet. This anchorage is less spectacular scenically than many of the others you've been visiting, but its gentle wooded shores and grassy shallows at the far end give it a homey feel. And if you watch the shore carefully and quietly, you may see one of the herd of caribou that still lives on the islands.

Rossport

As you realize from the small boats you encounter in the Slate Islands there are a couple of towns on the north shore, where Route 17 now comes quite close to the lakeshore. Terrace Bay and Schreiber are not ports, however; they're relatively new places, oriented to the highway. The bulk and belching smoke of the Kimberly Clark plant shows you where Terrace Bay is located, and Schreiber is neatly ensconced in a fold of hills. Rossport is a port, however, about 25 miles from the western entrance to the Slate Islands, where you might welcome the opportunity to dock for a change of pace.

One of the nicest things about Rossport is the route to get there. The entrance to wide, deep Schreiber Channel is about 15 miles northwest of the Slates. Here begins the chain of big islands that closes off Nipigon Bay and its extensions and creates a cruising ground sufficient unto itself. All of them are wild. The only unmarked obstruction in Schreiber Channel is the shoal making out from Cat Island, easily avoided. To reach Rossport, or to continue to the anchorages beyond, you should take the passage between Channel Island and Healey Island. The shoal off Channel is marked by a spar; the one descending from Healey is not. If westbound you can take a shortcut to Rossport between Healey and Quarry islands. The chart shows a rock in the passage, although boats going through have not been able to find it. Nevertheless, prudence suggests that you hug the steep-to Healey Island shore, then head for the passage between Nicol Island and Whiskey Island southwest of it. Favor the Whiskey Island shore right in the pass, after you've made certain to clear the shoal on the east side of the island. Whiskey is not named on the chart, nor is the little wooded islet connected to it on the north, known locally as Blanket. In using this shortcut, take care not to mistake the pass between Whiskey and Quarry Islands for the one between Whiskey and Nicol. It isn't much farther to avoid the problem altogether by passing around the outside of Quarry Island, which is high and steep on its west side though shoal on the south, to the main entrance to Rossport harbor.

This is the one to use if you're coming from the south or west, and here you'll find a flashing white light with red and white daymark on Whiskey Island.

Whichever way you come through, you'll see all of Rossport (population something less than 100 souls) spread out on the hillside before you. At its feet is an *L*-shaped **Government Dock** with a fixed red light on it and 16 feet alongside. Electricity and pumpout are available, and by the time you read this, water may be, too. Gas in a tank, diesel in cans and ice in blocks is brought down on order from Mac's Service about a mile down the road. Mac's Service, in fact, represents virtually the entire commercial enterprise of Rossport. You can obtain a few basics there, like bread and milk, and if Juris Zdanovskis is still smoking fish, you have a great treat to buy as well. The Rossport Inn, which opened in 1884, has been renovated to modernize its accommodations and dining room, while retaining the country ambiance of its old woodwork and furniture. Dinner out will no doubt be welcomed by your resident galley slave. Rossport has also revived its annual fish derby in recent years. It's scheduled for whenever the water temperature reaches 50° to 52°, usually mid-July. Three days of hard fishing, sales and exhibit booths, and food attract several thousand people.

A Bounty of Anchorages

If the social whirl of Rossport is overwhelming, you can escape quickly back to the serenity of wilderness. But more boats cruise this area from urban centers at the west end of the lake, so you might not always have them to yourself. The islands that enclose Nipigon Bay, to which Rossport is the eastern gateway, are mostly steep and smooth-sided on the bay side. But their southern rims are etched with bays and coves and enclosing small islands to produce such an abundance of beautiful harbors in such close proximity as to confound choice.

Wilson Channel is the easternmost passage between the islands, leading southeast opposite Rossport Point with its flashing white light. In the southwest corner of Wilson Island, Boat Harbour offers complete protection from all winds. Keep all the islands and islets to port as you enter, and once past the shoal off the starboard point, keep that shore close aboard until the narrows. Then move down the center into the second cove, to anchor in 15 feet. You are only 6 miles from Rossport.

Across Wilson Channel is Salter Island, with a group of smaller islands closing off Chubby Harbour indenting its south coast.

The name is, apparently, a corruption of Chummy, which the *Sailing Directions* is trying vainly to correct. By whatever name, Chubby is a lovely harbor, but deep for comfortable anchorage. Entering from the west, between Salter and Harry islands, you'll find a cove north of Harry Island that is known as Old Man's Pocket. This, too, is very deep where there is sufficient room to swing; unless you are on chain, you will probably want to tie off your stern in shallower water at the far end. Another alternative is to continue east, leaving the long, narrow island north of Harry to starboard, and find bottom at 20 to 30 feet between Harry and Minnie islands.

Simpson Island gives its name to Simpson Channel, from which you entered the Salter Island anchorages. This is one of two fully navigable channels leading into Nipigon Bay from the open lake, with big Battle Island Light, flashing white with a fog horn, at its entrance. In the southeast corner of the island is Morn Harbour, easy to enter between the high bluff of Morn Point and the island that shelters the harbor from the sea. Pass through the narrows to the inner harbor and anchor anywhere in 20 feet over mud. At the far end you can follow a stream bed to a pretty inland lake or pick up a blazed trail that circles easterly around the end of the harbor through cool spruce woods.

Simpson Island's other prize, only 6 miles west, is Woodbine Harbour. Stay ½ to ¾ of a mile offshore until you round Grebe Point. Woodbine, too, is entered between the east side of its protective island and the mainland shore, but the passage isn't so easy to spot from offshore. Mind the rock shoal making out from the island in the pass. A dog-leg turn—favor the east shore— brings you to the most sheltered, far end of the anchorage, where you can drop the hook in 20 to 25 feet. Here there is also a trail from the anchorage to an inland lake. Although Morn and Woodbine may sound similar in the prosaic facts, their poetic beauty is quite different.

Moffat Strait between Simpson and St. Ignace islands is passable into Nipigon Bay, but because of unmarked rock shoals protruding into the channel at the northern end it is not advisable for strangers. St. Ignace Harbour, indenting the southeast coast of St. Ignace Island, is beautiful, but inadequately sheltered from southeast. Armour Harbour, on the south coast of the island, offers good shelter but is, regrettably, too deep for anchorage.

The best anchorage on the St. Ignace coast is off the northwest shore of Paradise Island in 15 to 20 feet. But don't expect waving palm trees. Paradise here is gravel beaches, alluring rock climbs and a haunting remoteness. Whether from east or west, the anchorage is approached from the channel inside the long narrow chain of islands that extends for 10 miles between Talbot Island and Cedar Island. When abreast of Angelica Island, turn northwest to pass up the west side of Owl Island, giving its offlying shoals a wide berth, and around its northern end to Paradise. There is a dock on Bowman Island, across from the anchorage, whose generous owner hasn't minded lending it to visiting boats when he isn't using it.

If you're continuing westward from here, you can enjoy the sheltered passage inside the island chain just mentioned to the entrance to Nipigon Strait. This is the second deep water channel leading to Nipigon Bay, guarded by big Lamb Island Light, flashing white with a fog horn. In these pages we'll backtrack to Simpson Channel to look at the bay, then emerge again through Nipigon Strait.

Nipigon

Nipigon Bay is a large body of water, 26 miles by 12 at its widest. Therefore, while it is sheltered from the full sweep of Lake Superior, it's quite capable of kicking up a sea of its own. Encircled by rolling hills fronted by low woods or sand beach on the mainland, with steep cliffs on the island side, the westward vista presents the serrated ridges of Vert Island, Ile La Grange and the mainland beyond. In brief, it's a magnificent passage, but there are no fully protected anchorages, except the relatively unscenic cove between the Anguros Islands in Pays Plat Bay at the eastern end. Another alternative, open to southwest, is behind Kama Point in Mozokamah Bay toward the western end of the north shore. The main reason for traversing Nipigon Bay is to visit the town at its northwestern extremity. You know you're approaching a place of some importance hereabouts when you come to the flashing white lights on Vert and Crichton islands and several buoys thereafter. What you're headed for, however—the big Domtar wood products plant at Red Rock—is not what you want. You will turn to starboard to enter the Nipigon River.

An interesting change in the landforms of Lake Superior takes place here. The east bank of the Nipigon River is a series of mesas—flat-topped, bare, vertical cliffs, jointed to look like columns, standing on slabs of red, sedimentary rock. Eons ago dark igneous rock intruded into the sedimentary layers, then shrank into columns when it cooled quickly. Subsequent exposure and erosion accomplished the rest. This kind of geological formation heightens the drama of this entire region of Lake Superior; it extends westward from here for 90 miles to the American border.

Nipigon is as far north as you can get on Lake Superior, almost on the 49th parallel. Its recorded history goes back over 300 years to the first visit of Father Allouez in 1667. Thereafter it became an important post in the fur trade, later a logging center. Although the days of immense log rafts are gone, you might keep a lookout for strays that have escaped over the years and still meander up and down the river. Nipigon, with 2,500 people and wooded hills all around, seems to exude the atmosphere of the far distant north—especially if you don't see the motels and chain stores out on the highway. Like so many towns in the north country, this one, too, is now bidding for tourists. But "downtown" Nipigon combines a nostalgically old-fashioned look with all of the essential modern products stocked in its stores. It's comforting to know that the Hudson's Bay Company has been in continuous operation since it opened a trading post here in 1859. So has the railroad for almost as long, and there is still a daily passenger train if you want to change crew. There is also a hospital.

The Nipigon River is well buoyed for the 5-mile passage to the excellent government dock in least depths of 5 or 6 feet, with 8 feet at dockside. The only dockside service is pumpout, but both gas and diesel can be obtained by truck. If you've been cruising the north shore for a while, you'll undoubtedly make a beeline for the Laundromat—clean, friendly and only a couple of blocks away. Another block or two, and you have all the stores you need—groceries, hardware, pharmacy, liquor.

But Nipigon isn't all mundane chores. The Nipigon Museum on Second Street presents very good displays of the geology, Indian history, logging, mining and railway history of the area. The railroad is still important in this part of the world, and you can watch the trains from your cockpit as they curve around the harbor into town or go on down to the station in the evening and welcome the passenger train coming through. A dinghy trip farther up the river makes an interesting excursion, but the current increases as you proceed upstream; you may not get past the high railroad bridge unless you're fairly well powered. There are several restaurants, but Trader John's, through the

Sportsman to the back, is the place to dine in a bit of style. After dinner you can either take in a movie at the Plaza or join the crowd at one of the three bars in town.

Nipigon is a good place to ease back into civilization, but you get a chance to ease back out again for a while before hitting the big city. After leaving the Nipigon River continue on a southerly course through Nipigon Bay—buoyed where the deep water channel makes a couple of turns—to Nipigon Strait. This part of the bay and the upper reaches of the strait are not as scenic as the rest of the area, but as you approach the massive, high knobs of Fluor Island the drama returns. The narrows between Fluor and the mainland is buoyed, and a flashing red range with red and white daymarks, guides inbound boats at 014°. Opposite the southern end of Fluor, Moss Island shelters anchorages at either end. Which one to choose depends largely on wind direction. Both are pretty and easy to get into, provided you watch out for some shoal water around the tips of Moss Island. Here you are 30 miles from Nipigon.

The Last Bit of Wild

On the exit from Nipigon Strait it's better to favor the Spar Island shore to avoid shoals making out from Lamb Island, but the light and fog horn on Lamb provide helpful guidance. There's a passage of about 8 miles southwest through open water until you gain an inside track among the islands again. About 6 miles along another Otter Cove opens up to the north. Follow the deep, open bay for 3½ miles to the eastward turn through narrows that carry 9 feet down the middle. Anchorage in either arm at the far end, in 15 to 20 feet, is well sheltered. From the extremity of the northern arm you can take the dinghy partway up a stream, followed by a short walk to the waterfall. A blazed trail leads from the east side for another mile to an inland lake.

Another half dozen miles beyond Otter Cove along the track among the islands that is pecked out on the chart is the entrance to Loon Harbour. This is deservedly one of the favorite anchorages in the area, and you aren't likely to have it to yourself. In fact, someone has built a crude, but sturdy, dock of spruce logs and a few planks next to the open rocky campfire setting on Spain Island, and you'll often find a boat or two docked there. Nevertheless, there's plenty of room in the main anchorage between Spain and Borden islands in 20 feet. This is an ideal base for dinghy exploration of neighboring islands and coves.

Nipigon River railroad bridge.

Continuing southwest, the protective island chain thins out a few miles past Loon Harbor and ends at Shaganash Island. The number of unmarked rocks and shoals surrounding the magnificent Black Bay Peninsula also increases, and you enter another area of magnetic disturbance. Scenic as it is, this segment of the passage is hard to negotiate in fog or heavy weather. Nor are there many harbors for refuge. The best of them is Edward Harbour in the southwest corner of Edward Island, 24 miles from Loon Harbour. Give Point Porphyry and its nasty reefs off the southeast side a wide berth. The big flashing white light with fog horn on the point helps to orient you, but remember the reef is ½ mile lakeward of the light. Heading northward, you can take either side of Hardscrabble Island, avoiding the reefs that make out from each end. The entrance to Edward Harbour is perfectly clear from the chart. The most sheltered spot to anchor is in the southeast corner behind the little island in 20 feet. In northerly winds you might want to move to the northeast end, taking care to avoid a shoal making out from the northwest side. Either spot will get surge in strong winds.

Point Porphyry is less than 15 miles from Isle Royale, the closest mainland point of departure to that island. Edward Harbour is a good place to wait out the weather for the transit. Point Porphyry also marks the entrance to Black Bay, a 35-mile indentation of the north shore. Although the bay is relatively free of natural obstruction, and has some scenic stretches along its shores, there are no well-protected anchorages. Furthermore, the upper coves have long served as collection points for pulp-wood logs, which don't always stay in their booms. Black Bay tends to be foul with floating logs and deadheads. Most cruising boats pass it by.

The Canadian Lakehead
Charts 2301, 2314; U.S.14968

Nanabozho was a gentle and playful giant, son of the West Wind and guardian angel of the Ojibway people. When he scratched a rock one day and found silver he knew that it would bring greed and bad luck to his people, so he made them bury it deep beneath the lake and swore them to secrecy. But somehow the secret got out, and when Nanabozho saw enemies leading white men across the lake in a canoe he caused a storm to arise that sank the boat. The Great Spirit, angry at the demigod for usurping authority, turned him to stone where he lay at the lakeshore. To this day the Sleeping Giant keeps watch over the lake and the vein of silver. His form, 3 miles long, dominates the skyline whichever way you approach the Sibley Peninsula, his bed 1,000 feet above the lake. And from far offshore his majestic figure beckons you to Thunder Bay.

As for the silver, nature (or Nanabozho) played a sly trick on man's cupidity when she placed a 20-foot-wide vein of pure silver on an islet 90 feet in each dimension and 10 feet above the lake, then extended it unknowable fathoms into the lake bottom. Ingenious mining engineers rose to the challenge, constructed cribbing and coffer dams to keep Lake Superior off their new "land" with pumps, and thereby enlarged the islet to 10 times its original size. A whole community of machine shops, pump-houses, offices, boardinghouses, clubhouse and lighthouse was built on it, and in 15 short years, between 1869 and 1884, $3,250,000 worth of silver was extracted from the bonanza. But the mighty lake was not to be subdued by mere men. The expense of keeping it at bay eventually became unprofitable as the shaft sank deeper, and for 100 years now Lake Superior has had its way with Silver Islet. It's just about back to original size, and to see the scraggly trees and tiny gravel beach one would hardly know that men had been there.

On the mainland the village of Silver Islet, which provided a base of operations for the mine three-quarters of a mile off-

Loon Harbor, my son David removing bread from the oven he built.

shore, is now a summer cottage resort. There is a government dock there, with 7 feet at the front face, much less on either side. Although protected somewhat by Burnt Island, this dock is untenable in strong wind and sea from southwest. It should be approached from that direction, in line with the beacon range at 053°. There are no services, either at the dock or in the settlement.

Tee Harbour, 3 miles southwest, is much preferable for overnight mooring in 10 to 20 feet. As the name implies, this double harbor offers shelter from any wind direction, depending upon which side of the T-stem you choose. Nestled under the mesa of the Sleeping Giant (for that's what he is in geological terms), both harbors enjoy a magnificent backdrop in the vertically jointed cliffs, fringed by cool woods and a curve of sand beach. Most of the Sibley Peninsula, of which the Giant is only the tip, is a provincial park of the same name. One of the hiking trails skirts the harbor. Tee Harbour provides a fitting conclusion to the wilderness part of a Lake Superior circumnavigation. While it isn't actually a wilderness anchorage, it feels like one.

Thunder Bay

The gateway to Thunder Bay is nothing short of magnificent, as befits so important a place as the Lakehead. The spectacle of

brooding, flat-topped mesas here reaches a climax, from the
Sleeping Giant at Thunder Cape on the east to the incredible
shape of Pie Island guarding the bay on the southwest and
Mount McKay standing sentinal over the city on the west.

The bay itself is 25 miles long by 15 at its widest, extending
northeasterly from its broad entrance. The east side is formed
by the steep-sided Sibley Peninsula, with no suitable anchorage,
while the north shore, fringed by a succession of beaches, is
fairly well developed with cottages and resorts. There is only one
sheltered anchorage, in Amethyst Bay, about 17 miles from
Thunder Cape. Caribou Island and a red and green spar on
Temple Rock west of it help identify the approach from southward. Be sure to find the spar in order to avoid the unmarked
shoals off Buck Island. Aim for the southwest tip of Lambert
Island, then follow its shore about 150 feet off, to avoid all the
other shoals in the entrance. Pass between Lambert and the little
island north of its center, to anchor behind Perry Point in 15 feet.
This harbor is only 16 miles from the city and is quite built up
with cottages, but there is a beach and a government dock
where you can land your dinghy.

It's not the suburbs that attract cruising boats to Thunder Bay,
but the city itself. Its site has been drawing men of European
descent since the 17th century, when the first fur trading post
was established on the banks of the Kaministiquia River. The
city actually dates from 1803. The elaborate western headquarters and supply depot of the great Montreal trading firm, the
North West Company, had grown up at the grand portage of the
Pigeon River, some 40 miles southwest of the Kaministiquia. As
it lay in United States territory, vulnerable to heavy taxation, the
partners decided to build a new depot at the outlet of another
route into the vast interior they controlled as a virtual fiefdom.
Fort William, named for General Superintendent William McGil-
livray, was even more splendid than its predecessor and thrived
until the company's merger with the Hudson's Bay Company in
1821.

While the little settlement of Fort William languished for a
while afterward, a farming community and military staging area
was growing up a few miles north at Prince Arthur's Landing
(later called Port Arthur). The coming of the railroads in the
1880s launched both settlements on the road to cityhood. Trans-
shipment of western grain was, at first, the major occupation of
the exploding port area. Iron ore and other bulk cargoes were
soon added, followed by industrial development and an expanding role as service center for 200,000 square miles of northwest-

Thunder Cape.

ern Ontario. The twin cities of Fort William and Port Arthur were about equal in population when they merged in 1970 and took the name of Thunder Bay. Old urban patterns die hard, however, and the two segments, now designated Thunder Bay North and Thunder Bay South, still convey differences in atmosphere and loyalties.

The vast harbor and its dockside installations render the impression of a much larger city than 120,000 people. It lies on the western side of Thunder Bay, on the first plain you've seen for almost 400 miles, 15 miles from Thunder Cape. From the Kaministiquia River to Bare Point, a distance of almost 5 miles, the harbor is entirely enclosed by breakwaters, punctuated by three lighted entrances. The southeast entrance to the bay has lighted aids to navigation on the two shoal areas that pose any hazard, Angus Island off Pie Island, with a fog horn at the flashing white light, and Hare Island Reef with a flashing red light buoy. Pass north of the aptly named Welcome Islands, also marked by big lighthouse, flashing white with a fog horn. The southwest approach, between Pie Island and Flatland Island, is less well buoyed and should not be attempted in thick weather. On this route you pass west of the Welcome Islands, where lighted buoys are placed where you need them.

The only adequate accommodation for transient boats is at **Prince Arthur's Landing Marina**, close to the middle breakwater entrance. Flashing red and green lights with a fog horn flank the entrance, and there is considerable buoyage inside. Bear to port as you cross the harbor to the marina, which is enclosed in sections by a series of breakwalls. The service dock is in the westernmost basin, where you obtain all the dockside services, including Laundromat, except the electricity and water furnished at the slips in the other basins. You can call customs from here. A floating breakwater at the northern end of the marina is reserved for transient boats but has no services and is very far from the service building. When there is space available at seasonal slips, transient boats are assigned to these more comfortable moorings. The marina monitors channel 68, so you can call in advance to find out what's available. Depths throughout are in excess of 10 feet. If you require haulout and repair, Morton's Marina in the northwest corner of the harbor, near the Current River, can lift up to 40 feet.

The other alternative for haulout is at McKellar Marine on the McKellar River, with 15-ton capacity and a small marine store. The Kaministiquia River has three outlets south of the long breakwater, around and between McKellar and Mission islands. All are well buoyed. The northernmost, main outlet is entirely industrial; the McKellar, in the middle, is rather rural. The southern outlet, called the Mission River, is also quite industrial, but here are located the Thunder Bay Yacht Club and the Kam Boating Club, both primarily for powerboats. (The sailing members of the Thunder Bay Yacht Club have moved to Prince Arthur's Landing.) Neither has sufficient dockage to accommodate visitors, except in emergency. Their docks are small and rather elderly, with little or no service, and they are very far from any shops or city amenities.

Prince Arthur's Landing is not only located in a landscaped park but is also within two blocks of the main downtown thoroughfares of Thunder Bay North. But you may have to time your crossing of the railroad tracks; a procession of trains, including passenger, continues round the clock in both directions. The railroad station next to the marina makes this an ideal place to change crew. A supermarket on Court Street, beer and liquor stores on Cumberland are all in close proximity, not to speak of department stores and specialty shops of all kinds, restaurants, night clubs and a choice of movie theaters. The restaurant in the Prince Arthur Hotel is excellent, with an elaborate smorgasbord, as is the Valhalla Inn on the outskirts of downtown Thunder Bay South.

The biggest tourist attraction in Thunder Bay is Old Fort

William, a masterful reconstruction of the North West Company headquarters on the Kaministiquia River (577-8461). Unfortunately, the original site was covered over by the railroad yards of the Canadian Pacific about 1902, so the reconstruction is located 9 miles upstream. But the rural setting here is actually a more authentic environment. A self-guided nature trail explains how the Indians and voyageurs used the plants you see. The fort itself, with more than 30 buildings and installations, is worth several hours of your time. Docents will put you into the midst of the action as they play the roles and keep firmly in the character of men stationed here or attending the rendezvous of a specific year. Guided tours are available, or you can guide yourself, lingering as long as you wish at the artisans' sites and enjoying an authentic fur trader's lunch at the canteen. Canada Day weekend the fur trading rendezvous comes alive again in an annual reenactment.

Although Old Fort William is a long distance from the marina, there is an intriguing way to get there. From the northern dock of Prince Arthur's Landing the harbor excursion vessel *Welcome* offers a package cruise. It includes a very well-narrated tour of the harbor with its fascinating array of grain elevators (Saskatchewan Pool Number Seven is the world's largest), docks, terminals, wood products plants, and ships, and tranquil passage up the Kaministiquia River from the heavy industrial complex at its mouth, past downtown Thunder Bay South and some retired old ships dozing in the sun, through a quiet residential area under the brow of Mount McKay. You arrive at Old Fort William's dock much as the voyageurs did in their time. Three hours are allowed for a tour of the fort and lunch before you board the bus for a quick half-hour ride back to the marina. It may sound like a busman's holiday, but this five-hour excursion is the best way to see the best of Thunder Bay.

Thunder Bay is a sprawling city, and you might want to rent a car to take in some of the additional sights. Before you do, stop in at the quaint Pagoda that houses the tourist information bureau at the head of the marina's east wharf. Among other useful items, pick up a city map. Thunder Bay is a city of parks. In addition to Hillcrest Park, with its colorful sunken garden, within walking distance of the marina, there are two special places to visit in Thunder Bay South.

The Centennial Conservatory, at Dease and Balmoral streets, specializes in tropical plants and cacti. The International Friendship Gardens, at Victoria and Hyde Park avenues, is a set of individually landscaped gardens that represent the cultural and floral traditions of the many ethnic groups in the city's population. Not far from these two the Thunder Bay Historical Museum, at 219 South May Street (623-0801), displays the natural and human history of the region. While you're on the south side of town, drive up Mount McKay for a thrilling view of the city, the bay and the lake. Across the city on the northern outskirts Centennial Park on Arundel Street features a 1910 logging camp and museum, a little railway tour around the park, a children's log playground and a bush camp lunch at the camp cookery.

Eighteen miles west of the city Kakabeka Falls drops the Kaministiquia River 128 feet over broad ledges of varied rock formations. The complex cascade, known as the Niagara of the North, is at times subjected to an indignity of modern technology, when the demands of hydroelectric power generation shut them off completely. It's a good idea to call Kakabeka Provincial Park headquarters (475-1531) to find out if the faucet is open or closed.

Border Country

Much of the 20 miles between the western entrance to Thunder Bay and the international border at Pigeon Bay can be run inside a chain of sheltering islands. It should not be attempted by a stranger in poor visibility, however. Not only are there unmarked hazards, but one cannot rely on the compass here. Magnetic disturbance continues throughout this area. Sturgeon Bay is the first anchorage southwest of Flatland Island, a 20-mile run from the marina in Thunder Bay. Sister and Mink islands opposite help to identify the entrance. Favor the Sturgeon Point shore as you enter. There is 8 feet through the center of the narrows and 12 in the completely protected anchorage. Cottages ring the west and north shores, so the east side is a preferred spot to set your anchor. Ten miles farther on, Cloud Bay is not quite so land-locked but offers fair protection on the northeast side in 10 to 15 feet. Little Trout Bay, adjacent, is perhaps more scenic, but it is very deep and open to the northeast.

From here, if you're continuing southwest, you should pass around the outside of the islands off McKellar Point and the outside of Pigeon Point. If you're crossing to Isle Royale, on the other hand, you can take your departure from McKellar Point or through Spar Channel between Victoria and Spar islands, marked by a flashing white light on Jarvis Rock. This would be the preferred route coming from Isle Royale, with the light to aim for. In passing through, favor the steep-to Jarvis Rock side.

Isle Royale

Charts 14968, 14976

When canny Old Ben Franklin negotiated the Peace of Paris in 1783 he used an inaccurate map of Lake Superior (at the time there weren't any that were correct) as well as his wits to place the U.S./British boundary "through Lake Superior northward of Isles Royal [sic] and Philipeaux." No one has ever found Isle Philipeaux. Isle Royal turned out to be a lot farther north than the middle of the lake and, therefore, much closer to British Canada. Then, to make Isle Royale's position even more anomalous, 50 years later it was assigned to Michigan as part of its gift of statehood. Yet it lies less than 20 miles from the Minnesota coast and almost three times that distance from the state to which it belongs. Finally, to cap the climax, the entire island became federal property in 1940, with the establishment of Isle Royale National Park.

Its curious political history aside, Isle Royale is a rather special place. Formed over a billion years ago, it has been carved by volcano, ice, water and wind to form a striated pattern of ridges and valleys, lakes and streams, on a northeast to southwest axis. This pattern has fostered a remarkable variety of botanical habitats on an island 44 miles by 9, and animal life tells a fascinating story about the symbiotic relationship between moose and wolf. Some 4,500 years ago an ancient race found the copper hidden in the island's rock folds, mined it with Stone Age tools and fire, and sent it out as a symbol of wealth and art to people living as far distant as the New York coast and southern Indiana. Modern copper mines operated from about 1840 to 1900.

Isle Royale affords a rich experience to the geologist, the biologist and the historian, whether professional or amateur. Carefully managed as a wilderness park, the interior is accessible only to hikers. There are 160 miles of trail, with campsites strategically placed for minimum impact. Boat camping is also encouraged in that the Park Service ferry from Houghton will carry any kind of boat of 20 feet or less, and the smaller ferries from Copper Harbor, Michigan, and Grand Portage, Minnesota, will carry canoes. Its geological formation has created a complementary marine environment. Isle Royale is not one island, but 200. The big island is virtually encircled by smaller ones of all sizes, most of them lying on the same northeast to southwest axis, to create numerous hideaway harbors. Secluded anchorage can be had in most, and many are equipped with small park docks, with depths ranging from 5 to 10 feet at their outer ends.

For boaters who like to hike, Isle Royale offers an ideal environment—safe harbors with direct access to trails of environmental variety and several levels of challenge. Except near the larger campgrounds you aren't likely to encounter many people on the trail, but at any time you may see a member or two of the island's famous moose herd. But if hiking is not of interest to you the island's harbors are less scenic and less interesting than those of Superior's north shore, and, other than fishing, there is little else to do here. To safeguard the wilderness there are three prohibitions imposed by the Park Service: no wheeled vehicles, such as bicycles; no pets, *even if kept on board;* and no wood campfires, only self-contained camping stoves. They do patrol.

Having emphasized the wilderness quality of Isle Royale, we'll begin a counter-clockwise circumnavigation at the center of island civilization—Rock Harbor, at the northeastern end of the island. Here, where the ferries dock and deposit their campers, is the park's only marina, with alongside tie-up at finger docks in 4 to 8 feet and all dockside services. A grocery store, Laundromat and showers serve everybody, and this is one of the few dockside locations on the lakes where you can fill your propane tanks. But there is no ice. At the park information office across from the store you can pick up a helpful map and some interesting literature and check into customs. A short walk from the marina Rock Harbor Lodge is the only hotel accommodation on the island, and its family-style dining room offers plain cooking to all. Read the plaque near the park headquarters office to learn the interesting history of the resort. The rangers offer excellent afternoon and evening interpretive programs. There are some hiking trails that begin here, which are usually well populated, but the bustle of Rock Harbor is not repeated elsewhere on the island.

Passage Island Light, flashing white from a big gray tower with a fog horn 3½ miles offshore, identifies the approach to the northeast end of Isle Royale. Rock Harbor, 13 miles long, is easy to enter from the northeast, either between North and South Government islands or through the wide deep passage northeast of Gull Rock. There is another buoyed entrance, Middle Islands Passage, near the southwest end of the harbor, with a group flashing white light displayed from a gray tower on the inner side of the entrance. Park Headquarters is on Mott Island, where emergency repairs can be obtained, with a haulout capability of

Isle Royale, on the trail.

60 feet. The west end of the harbor is the best spot for anchorage, with several campground docks on both the mainland and island sides. At each of them one or more hiking trails lead to the interior.

Around the corner from Rock Harbor, 6 miles southwest from Middle Islands Passage, Chippewa Harbor is carved out of the hillsides. Its opening isn't easy to find from offshore, but the coast is steep-to here and you can follow it closely; there is a daybeacon high up on the eastern entrance point. Chippewa is actually a double harbor, with a dog-leg at the first narrows. Keep the first islet on your port side, then hug the port shore as you leave the next islet and its offlying rocks to starboard. The first harbor is very deep, but there is a dock, with campground and trailheads. The best anchorage is in the second harbor at the far end in 20 feet.

Beyond Chippewa the coast continues steep for about 5½ miles, then shoals out with unmarked rocks and the islands that make up Malone Bay. A beacon range on a course of 311° will carry you safely between buoys and dangerous reefs into the harbor. A dock is located around the point in the northeast corner, from which a short trail leads to Siskiwit Lake, the island's largest. The fishing is good, but unfortunately the inland lakes are no good for swimming because of leeches. Approach the dock from the east to avoid a shoal south of it. There is a protected anchorage in Malone Bay behind Malone Island.

Malone Bay is an inlet of the much larger Siskiwit Bay, 12 miles long and up to 3 wide. It can get very choppy in east winds, but toward the southwestern end there are some good mooring spots. If you coast the north shore, Hay Bay is easy to enter inside of the reefs on the point and around Little Siskiwit Island. There is a deep passage between those hazards, but it's unmarked and you must feel your way with the depth sounder. Hay Bay has a dock, or you can anchor in 9 feet. There are no trails here. Siskiwit Campground dock at the western end of the bay, with 8 feet at its outer ends, is sheltered by a breakwater from the long fetch. From here there is a trail around the harbor as well as paths to the interior, one of which leads to an abandoned copper mine, and you can take the dinghy up the Big Siskiwit River.

Siskiwit Bay makes a good landfall or point of departure for boats passing between Isle Royale and the Keweenaw Peninsula on the mainland. Isle Royale Light, flashing white from a big white tower, is conspicuous from offshore and marks the shortest distance across, 43 miles to Eagle Harbor. Menagerie Island on which it sits is surrounded by shoals, however, so care must be taken not to approach too closely. If you're continuing southwestward around the island, you can exit Siskiwit Bay through the buoyed channel at Point Houghton. You have 20 miles to go to the next harbor, around the southwest end of the island, with some unmarked shoal areas extending offshore in between.

Grace Harbor is wide open to the southwest and not recommended for anchorage, but if you want to duck into shelter quickly you can enter the more protected Washington Harbor from Grace through a buoyed channel east of Washington

Island. In approaching Grace Harbor from the south, be sure to give Cumberland Point and its nun buoy a good berth. Washington Harbor is approached more directly from the southwest, in the vicinity of Rock of Ages Light, whose white group flash and fog horn on a big white tower is one of the major navigational aids on the lake. Its surrounding shoals are infamous. Be sure also to avoid the islets and shoals off the west end of Washington Island, then head straight up the middle of the harbor toward Beaver Island. There is also a shortcut entrance between Thompson Island and the "mainland" on the north side of Washington Harbor, marked by a buoy and a daybeacon.

There is a campsite and dock on Beaver, with less than 4-foot depth, or you can go on to Windigo at the head of the harbor. The ferries from Grand Portage dock at the outer end of the large wharf, with a quick flashing red light on it, but there is alongside tie-up in 15 feet farther in on either side, with water available. The service dock for gasoline and pumpout, a bit north of the main dock, is not in very good condition. Windigo was once a lodge, but now it is merely a ranger station, with a small store up the hill, a welcome new shower and Laundromat building at dockside, and evening interpretive programs. One of the hiking trails emanating from here leads to an abandoned copper mine. The best anchorage in Washington Harbor is in the cove west of Beaver Island in 12-foot depth.

Another long passage awaits the circumnavigator around the north side of Isle Royale—27 miles from Windigo to Todd Harbor. Once past McGinty Cove the shore is steep-to and can be followed closely, but mind Finlander Reef, the 3-foot spot near Thomsonite Beach, and the shoal making out from the shore opposite Gull Rocks. Todd Harbor can be entered between Wilson Point and Wilson Island, but there is a 6-foot shoal in mid-channel. If you enter northeast of Wilson Island, note the unmarked 1-foot shoal in the middle of the harbor. The dock here is best suited to small boats, but there is anchorage in either Florence or Pickett Bay at the southwest end. Pickett is not quite as deep; you can find 15 feet about halfway down. There are no trails at these anchorages.

Only 8 miles beyond the entrance to Todd Harbor, McCargoe Cove is the most sheltered anchorage on the island. But the entrance is tricky—a circuitous pass between and around a pair of spar buoys, with another dog-leg beyond. The dock at Birch Island is a small one, but at the far end of the cove is a large campground and dock, with 4 to 8 feet alongside, not so attractive for boaters seeking seclusion. Among the several trails here, one leads to an abandoned mine site, with some prehistoric Indian mining pits on the route.

Beyond McCargoe Cove the shoreline becomes ragged again. A series of long narrow islands runs parallel to the main island, with deep water channels between. The vista along this entire north shore is commanded by the Sleeping Giant and Pie Island brooding on the horizon. From Amygdaloid Channel a course of approximately 125° from abeam the middle of the opening between Amygdaloid Island and Captain Kidd Island should carry you safely between a couple of rocks and shoals into the protected anchorage of Lane Cove, 7 miles from McCargoe's entrance. This is one of the most scenic island groupings off Isle Royale, with deep water channels running between the long, narrow islands. Lane Cove itself is deep, but in the southwest cove you can find 20 to 30 feet over mud. The northeast side of the cove is foul. Pickerel Cove, a beautiful passage, extends 4½ miles southwestward from the entrance to Lane Cove. Most of it is too deep for anchorage, but the narrows about two-thirds of the way down has only 5 to 8 feet. Robinson Bay is both deep and cluttered with unmarked rocks and shoals, but there is a dock and campground under Belle Isle. The Lane Cove area is strictly for enjoyment by boat; there are no hiking trails here.

Rounding the northeast end of Isle Royale, 4½-mile-long Duncan Bay offers anchorage about 8 miles from Belle Isle. On the way around, give a wide berth to Locke Point and its nasty shoals, marked by a buoy. In approaching the narrow entrance to Duncan Bay, favor the south (port) shore until past the long shoal with a rock pile on top of it that shows brown in the water when the sun is past its zenith. Immediately past the narrows there is a small dock and campground, with another at the far end of the bay. A pretty spot to anchor is the cove northeast of the farther campground in 15 feet over mud. There are no trails here, either, but the high ridge dominating the southeast shore is quite scenic.

Around Blake Point there is one more harbor before you complete the circuit. Tobin Harbor is best entered as though you were heading for Rock Harbor. From the red and green buoy on Five Foot Reef, pass between North and South Government Islands. Then at Scoville Point, marked by a beacon, turn north to round the small islands and come down into the main body of the harbor. Stay in the middle as you move down toward the bottom of the bay for anchorage. Tobin Harbor was the center of the summer cottage colony established on Isle Royale before it became a national park, and the surviving owners retain the privilege of using their cottages during their lifetime. These are concentrated at the eastern end of the harbor, however, and the western end is both more scenic and more secluded, with 10-foot depths. Several trails emanate from here.

Had you continued past Scoville Point, you would have arrived back in Rock Harbor, with only 2 miles to go to the marina. Circumnavigation of Isle Royale is just about 100 miles.

Minnesota's North Shore
Charts 14966, 14967

One hundred and fifty miles of coastline between the extreme southwest corner of Lake Superior and the international border at Pigeon River is known to its native Minnesotans as the North Shore. It is a region of stunning views, from both the land and the sea, where sheer cliffs plunge into the lake, immense dark boulders bounce the surf into spray at the base, beaches of pink sand or gray gravel front the coves between headlands, and the forest of birch and spruce at the top is backed by even higher ridges or the sharp peaks of the Sawtooth Mountains. On this beautiful, but forbidding, coast there are few harbors, and of those there are only two, separated by 95 miles of lee shore, that have small craft accomodations. To cruise the Minnesota shore one must be prepared for long passages or poor mooring conditions.

Grand Portage

In the unremitting quest for beaver the traders of the 18th century pushed ever westward on the waterways of North America. By the second quarter of the century they had found the intricate canoe route that led from Lake Superior by river and portage, first to Rainy Lake, then to Lake of the Woods, then to Lake Winnipeg and ultimately to the Rocky Mountains and the Arctic Ocean. Every outpost yielded more and better beaver skins, while it stretched more tautly the lines of communication and supply.

At the western extremity of Lake Superior, the logistics of the fur trade changed with the nature of the terrain. Le Grand Portage, where the tortuous rapids and falls of the Pigeon River must be overcome by a 9-mile carry, was the natural location for a depot. Supplies for the west could be stockpiled and incoming peltry trans-shipped in larger canoes, so that men traveling 1,000 miles into the interior wouldn't have to make the additional

1,000-mile journey to Montreal. For this purpose, in the last quarter of the 18th century the North West Company built the biggest and most important trading post of all. Here every July the canoe brigades from Montreal met the brigades down from the Saskatchewan, Churchill, and Red River, and as far away as the fabled Athabasca country, to exchange peltry for supplies and Indian trade goods. For one short month hundreds of traders and voyageurs exchanged news and gossip of business and family, danced and gambled and relaxed, before each group turned once more to the arduous journey ahead—back to civilization for the Montrealers, back to another year of snowbound isolation in the wilderness for the Nor'westers.

After the Pigeon River was declared the international boundary, and after the company moved its western headquarters to Fort William, the elaborate complex of buildings gradually decayed and disappeared. Today Grand Portage is only a place— an Indian settlement, a few summer cottages around the bay and a United States National Historic Monument. Since its establishment in 1960 some of the buildings have been reconstructed from archaeological remains and are open to visitors, but not much of a budget allocation has been made to this site. The Canadian flag also flies here, and the Ontario government has erected a marker too, for by the Webster-Ashburton Treaty of 1842 the Grand Portage was declared an international thoroughfare.

The famous portage itself never fell into complete disuse. You can hike the 9 miles today and find conditions much the same as when the voyageurs toiled through muddy marshes and across slippery rocks with two 90-pound packs on their backs. The pleasure hiker with modern insect repellent, and carrying only a camera and a water bottle, can enjoy the beauty of the wooded trail in a way his predecessor never could. But this is an isolated trail with rough conditions. Wear sturdy hiking boots and sign in and out at the registration boxes located at each entry point. Camping is prohibited on the trail, but if you don't want to return the same day there are two campsites at the site of Fort Charlotte on the far end. A trail map for the Grand Portage and for the self-guided, half-mile Mount Rose Nature Trail near the monument can be obtained from the ranger office.

Grand Portage Bay is a relatively sheltered harbor 20 miles from the southwest tip of Isle Royale as the ferry goes. Mount Josephine helps identify it from offshore, and there is a flashing white light on Hat Point, with a black gong buoy marking a shoal off the point. If you enter the harbor here, you will come first to

Grand Portage, watergate to restored fur trading post.

the **Voyageur Marina** on the east side of the bay, with 5- to 6-foot depths, gas and diesel, electricity, water, and heads. The marina is on a country road with nothing else nearby, but you could get to the National Monument across the harbor by dinghy. The harbor can also be entered on the west side of Grand Portage Island, with some shelter for anchorage behind the island in about 10 feet.

The National Monument stockade is on the far shore, fronted by a sturdy dock with a flashing white light on the end. That dock is not for private boats, however, but is reserved for the Isle Royale ferry. To visit the monument you can anchor off in settled weather and take your dinghy to the dock. There is also a general store up the hill. The Grand Portage Band of Chippewa, which owns most of the land around the bay, operates a handsome lodge and conference center south of the monument, with a dining room open to the public and a shop selling Indian art and handicrafts. Associated with the center is **Grand Portage Marina**, with a tight entrance and dockage suitable only for small or very shallow draft boats.

When you arrive at Grand Portage from Ontario or Isle Royale, note that Minnesota is on central time.

Grand Marais

Thirty-five spectacular cruising miles southwest of Grand Portage is the only natural harbor on a forbidding stretch of coastline and the only small craft marine facilities for the next 95 miles. Severe magnetic disturbance continues all the way down the Minnesota coast, however, and it's advisable to cruise about a mile offshore, although the coastline is deep-to. Breakwaters complete the enclosure of the natural harbor at Grand Marais, with flashing white and green lights at the entrance. An inner breakwater on the northwest side, with a flashing green light on it, shelters part of the town waterfront. The **Grand Marais Marina** is at the west end, adjacent to the Grand Marais Recreation Area, with its campground, playground and indoor swimming pool. Alongside tie-up at finger docks in 4 to 6 feet and all dockside services are offered, but fuel and pumpout are at the innermost dock, which may be too shallow for some boats. The commercial fish tugs dock near the marina, and the area is alive with aquatic birds. The flocks of ducks and geese that congregate are so much a part of the Grand Marais community that feed for them is sold in the campground.

Grand Marais history is typical of Lake Superior towns: first a fur trading post, then lumbering and commercial fishing, now tourism. Strategically situated between the big lake and the Boundary Waters Canoe Area, the town of 1,300 is an important outfitting center for both. It's about a half-mile walk to the supermarket and Laundromat, but there is a convenience store close to the park. Downtown there are shops of all kinds, several restaurants and the Cook County Historical Museum, all within easy walking distance around the harbor. There is also a hospital in town. For evening entertainment the Grand Marais Playhouse presents live theater and concerts in an old church, and the rangers at the U.S. Forest Service headquarters near the marina present evening slide and movie programs. On the first weekend in August Grand Marais celebrates summer with a Fisherman's Picnic, complete with carnival, dancing, food and fireworks.

Harbors of Refuge

Try to pick a spell of good weather for your departure from Grand Marais. While the coastline continues impressive to look at, with its steep cliffsides backed up by high peaks, it is also inhospitable. The only shelter for the next 95 miles is two private industrial harbors, with marginal protection, and one ore-loading port. Thirty-one miles below Grand Marais, Taconite Harbor is where Erie Mining Company loads taconite pellets. Stacks and the big power house identify the artificial harbor from offshore. An impressive array of lighted aids to navigation assists you through either the north entrance between two breakwaters, which is the exit channel for the ships, or the south entrance between Gull Island and the shore. Small boats are not welcome here but are tolerated if they need shelter. The water is very deep, with the shallowest place for anchorage an 18-foot shoal off Bear Island.

Twenty-three miles farther on, Silver Bay is a harbor of the same ilk. This one is owned by Reserve Mining Company, and its immense taconite beneficiation plant is highly conspicuous. Lighted aids and buoys also facilitate entrance here, but this harbor is far more exposed than Taconite. The more sheltered northeast end is too deep for anchoring, and you won't be permitted to dock. The southwest corner, with 15- to 25-foot depths, gets some protection from the east behind the little islands extending from the breakwater, but it's wide open to northeast. Silver Bay is for the truly needy.

Two Harbors, 29 miles from Silver Bay, was one of the earliest iron ore ports in Minnesota. It is a very nice town, but there is no place in it for you. The city has built an attractive waterfront park for shoreside observers to watch the ore-loading, but a cruising boat can't be part of that scene. The only place for refuge here is anchorage on the east side of the harbor, but watch out for old dock ruins. If you must come in, entrance is made between breakwaters with flashing red and white lights and a fog horn.

Only 7 miles farther on there is at last a small boat harbor close south of Knife River. On the northerly approach, take care to pass on the outside of Knife Island and the long shoal extending southwest from it. Magnetic disturbances continue here. Entrance to the artificial harbor is protected by a breakwater with a flashing white light on it. **Knife River Marina** offers slips in 8 feet with all dockside services and monitors channel 16 if you want to call ahead. An open-end travelift can haul out up to 20 tons for engine and hull repairs. Knife River isn't much of a town, but there is a general store nearby and two places to buy the smoked fish for which the place is locally famous.

The American Lakehead
Charts 14966, 14975

In the far southwestern corner of Lake Superior the St. Louis River spreads a wide delta where it meets the lake. It, too, became an early highway of the fur trade, connecting with other streams to the headwaters of the Mississippi. But nature gave this river mouth a gift bestowed on few others. She cast a sandbar, 9 miles long, across and beyond the St. Louis and the smaller Nemadji River to create an immense harbor. When the riches of mine and prairie began to flow from the west the harbor at the lakehead was ready and waiting.

The villages at either end began to vie for the carrying trade. The natural pass through the sand spit, named Minnesota Point, was at the southeastern end, fronting Superior, Wisconsin. But the citizens of Duluth, Minnesota, had no intention of being upstaged. They dredged a canal at their end, and ultimately Duluth became the larger and wealthier city. By whichever entrance you gain access to the harbor, you are plunged into an entrepôt of astonishing size, complexity and variety. Western grain, Minnesota iron and, more recently, Canadian oil have built a port and the twin cities to support it that is second in the nation in the tonnage it handles from 50 docks, a succession of immense elevators, and one of the longest pipelines in the Western Hemisphere.

Approaching from the north, the lacy network of steel triangles that composes the Aerial Lift Bridge rises ethereally on the horizon. The symbol of Duluth, it spans the Duluth Ship Canal to connect downtown with the residential strip and beachfront park on Minnesota Point. So eyecatching is the operation of this bridge, as the long lakers pass underneath, that Canal Park was laid out beside it for the pleasure of shorebound boat watchers. If your height exceeds 15 feet, or you follow a ship into the harbor, you, too, can be part of the show. The unusual bridge was basically constructed in 1905. In 1929, with increasing

Ore dock at Two Harbors.

automobile traffic to the point, the old cable car ferry was replaced by a lift span added to the bridge. It is the largest and fastest of its type in the world, rising to its full 141 feet in 55 seconds. But it can be stopped at any intermediate point, so if you need only 50 feet, that's all you'll get. The signal is one long, one short, repeated a second time. But you can also call the bridge tender on channels 16, 10, 12 and 68, call sign KAN 388.

Needless to say, the entrance and the harbor itself are brilliantly lighted and heavily buoyed. The Duluth Ship Canal is enclosed by long parallel piers, with the bridge at the inner end. Moderate currents set in and out of the canal, but when heavy northwest seas collide with an outflowing current the entry can be turbulent.

There is only one marina in Duluth Harbor, **Lakehead Boat Basin**, ¼ mile south of the bridge on the inside of Minnesota Point. Enclosed in its own basin, this full service marina offers all dockside services, including Laundromat, at its slips in 6 feet or more; a 50-ton travelift; engine, hull and rigging repair; and a marine store. There is little or no shopping in the immediate vicinity of the marina. It is fairly convenient to downtown, but the bus system does not extend to Minnesota Point and you will probably want a taxi.

Duluth is an oddly shaped city. It stretches for 30 miles in a narrow riband rarely a dozen blocks wide under the high bluff of the Minnesota North Shore. The contrast of its compact downtown conveys a metropolitan atmosphere unexpected in a city of 93,000 people, with an excellent selection of shops, restaurants, night clubs and movie theaters. The Top of the Harbor and the Chinese Lantern are both recommended for dinner.

Duluth is a city that coddles its tourists. Your route downtown from the marina will take you first to Canal Park. The Marine Museum there, operated by the Corps of Engineers, tells the story of the lake's formation and its shipping history through excellent audiovisual displays and artifacts (722-6489). While you're wandering inside you need miss none of the action outside. Ship arrivals and departures are broadcast over a loudspeaker, informing both insiders and park-strolling outsiders of the identity and some of the specifications of the vessel coming through.You need only move to an immense window-wall on the canal side to see it all.

A few blocks from the Canal Park Museum is the impressive waterfront Arena-Auditorium, where many special events take place (722-5573). Adjacent to it the Visitor Information Center will supply you with good maps and detailed information. From here you can get a bus tour of the city (722-4426), a boat tour of the harbor (722-5573) or a combination of the two that includes some special stops. A block or two west, the 1892 Norman chateau railroad station has been transformed into the St. Louis County Heritage and Arts Center, which houses an amazing variety of attractions and activities: an art gallery, a children's museum, a historical museum, a railroad museum, a recreated 1910 street, and theater, ballet and symphony performances (727-8025). Each of the museums presents its exhibits imaginatively, with special care for the attention of children. The annual summer Festival of the Arts is partly staged here, partly at the Arena-Auditorium and at other locations around town.

In the opposite direction from the Visitor's Center, follow Superior Street, the main shopping street, northeast past the hospital to London Road and Leif Ericson Park. There you will find the replica of a Viking ship that was sailed from Bergen, Norway, to Duluth in 1926. Next to the park is the beautiful Duluth Rose Garden. Both are high on the bluff, with a magnificent aerial view of the lake and harbor. About a mile farther, past the stately homes on London Road, is Glensheen. The 39-room Jacobean mansion and estate was completed in 1908, with all of the exquisite architectural, decorative and landscaping detail that a mining fortune could buy. Now owned by the

University of Minnesota, tours include the gardens, grounds and outbuildings, as well as the residence (724-8864).

Whether you elect to take an informative, narrated boat tour of the harbor or do it on your own, tour the harbor you must. It is spacious enough for you to meander among the docks and terminals, watching the lakers, salties, tugs and workboats at their tasks, without getting in the way. There is even room for the Duluth Keel Club to race when it's too rough outside. Continuation up the St. Louis River will take you out of the industrial district, past suburbia and through the marshes beyond Spirit Lake, where the walleyes wait for your hook and some 275 species of birds await your binoculars. Only a few years ago this river was foul with industrial and pulpwood waste; its recovery via a pollution control program has happily exceeded expectations. The river is buoyed and navigable for about 14 miles, with a controlling depth of 9 feet to the village of New Duluth, 5 for the remaining 1½ miles to the junction with Mission Creek at Fond du Lac. There are side bays to turn into, depending upon your draft. It's advisable to follow the outside of the curves between buoys.

Although Duluth has more sights to see and a more sophisticated downtown than its "twin" with one-third the population, Superior has, by far, the superior accommodation for cruising boats. **Barkers Island Marina** offers luxury at its specially reserved transient slips, with 7-foot depth, all dockside services, a marine store, three tennis courts, swimming pool, dining and entertainment at the Radisson Inn on the premises. The dockmaster monitors channel 16. At the opposite end of the large property a 30-ton travelift and full engine, hull and rigging repairs are available. You can reach the marina from the inside through the harbor or via Superior Entry from the lake at the south end. The entry is flanked by generously lighted converging breakwaters. The marina is approached from the south end of Barker's Island, between flashing red and white lights and through a buoyed channel.

Barker's Island is not only distant from the sights of Duluth it is also far from downtown Superior or any shopping for supplies. Taxis are, of course, available. There are two attractions within longish walking distance, however. Barker's Island is a city park, and at its landward entrance, about three-quarters of a mile from the marina, the S.S. *Meteor* is docked. This 90-year-old vessel is the last of a unique breed that was built in Superior and Duluth—the whaleback ship. Brainchild of a self-educated Scottish lake captain, these ships were designed to take the short, steep waves of the Great Lakes more gracefully, and safely, than conventional designs. Forty-three of them were built between 1888 and 1898, but for various reasons the revolutionary design wasn't adopted by others. Now only the *Meteor* is left for you to tour (392-5742). There are also craft and gift shops at the site and a harbor excursion boat. Across the highway from the park entrance, the Fairlawn Historical Museum (394-5712) is in the 42-room Victorian mansion built by lumber baron Martin Pattison.

The Wisconsin Shore

Charts 14966, 14973, 14974

At the lakehead you turn a corner, both geographically and scenically; your course now points eastward. The steep bluffs you've been following for so long terminate at Duluth. Superior is set on a plain, and the land continues low for the next 35 miles. Small streams flow into the lake at regular intervals, but there is no opening in the smooth shoreline.

Port Wing

About 33 miles northeast of Superior Entry, the harbor at Port Wing has been recently improved for the accommodation of both resident and transient boats. There is little to identify it from offshore, except the hills that begin to rise east of the harbor. Entry is made between parallel piers, with a flashing white light on the east pier, to the dredged mouth of the Flag River. Controlling depth is 8 feet to the transient docks immediately to port inside the entrance. These docks are about 22 feet long, so that larger boats will protrude from the end. Electricity is available on a long cord. Additional new dockage in the east basin is occupied by local boats, but one of those slips may, on occasion, be available. Stay close to the docks as you move eastward in the harbor, as the rest of it is shallow and foul.

The village of Port Wing is a mile away, around the harbor. There is a general store, and if you can cadge a ride, the Quarry Inn on the highway west of town has good food in a homey small-town atmosphere. If you need to stop for the night between Superior and the Apostle Island area, this is the place to pull in. The next harbor has even less to offer.

Cornucopia

For the cruising boater it doesn't live up to its name. Dredged from the mouth of the Siskiwit River, the harbor is well protected by an angled breakwater northeast of the entrance with a flashing green light. But the two basins that branch southwest and east from the inner end of the channel are crowded with local boats. Some alongside tie-ups for transients may be available in the east basin in 6 to 7 feet, without services. Gas is sold at Jones Marina in the west basin, and there is a general store a few blocks away.

The Apostle Islands

Nobody seems to know who named the Apostle Islands, but whoever it was didn't count very well. There are 22 of them. Flung off the end of a peninsula they once were attached to, these smooth-sided islands of sandstone extend 20 miles into the lake. At one time some of them were inhabited by fishermen and quarry workers, but now the 21 that comprise the Apostle Islands National Lakeshore are wild. Mostly wooded, some with beaches, others with intriguing caves and sandstone formations, none of them has a harbor. Yet together they form a delightful, sheltered cruising ground, and this area is *the* boating center of Lake Superior—mostly sail.

The Apostles are best explored in day trips, however, from a secure base in one of several marinas. You can anchor in the shelter of any of the islands, according to which way the wind is blowing, and many of them have park docks to tie up to. But to remain overnight you court discomfort at best and disaster at worst if the wind shifts. Many people do risk it, but the whole area is small enough that it isn't much trouble to return to base at dusk each day. One more caution: this is an active commercial fishing ground and you must watch out for net stakes.

You got a preview of the sandstone cliffs and red clay bluffs of the Apostle Island area back at Port Wing, but they rise to a scenic crescendo as you continue northeast. Unless you're in a very shallow draft boat, you can't follow the mainland shore the whole distance because of the shoal building a land bridge to the Sand Island. The north tip of Sand Island has a lighthouse with a flashing white light. From there a buoyed passage takes you southeast between the inner islands and the mainland to Red Cliff Point, 27 cruising miles from Cornucopia.

Under Red Cliff Point **Schooner Bay Marina Inn** is the first potential base for cruising the islands. A small breakwater protects the slips, with the usual dockside services except fuel. This marina caters mainly to shallow draft boats less than 30 feet long. The restaurant and tavern feature live entertainment. A couple of miles south the **Red Cliff Marina** is enclosed in a breakwater with a flashing red light. It is entered from the south through a buoyed channel carrying 6 to 12 feet. There is similar depth at the slips, with all dockside services except fuel, but including Laundromat. This marina is operated by the Red Cliff Chippewa Band in connection with their campground. The Center for Arts and Crafts on the premises is a striking museum of both fine and folk art rendered by the Chippewas.

Bayfield

Another 3 miles south, the village of Bayfield is the "capital" of the Apostle Islands region. Nestled against the hillside, this pretty resort town, with about 900 permanent population, is one of the few on the lake that didn't originate as a fur trading post. It was founded in 1856 and prospered during the latter part of the 19th century in lumbering, fishing and quarrying. Sandstone from here built a large portion of the fashionable brownstone houses in the eastern cities between 1880 and 1910. There is still a score of commercial fishing license holders operating from Bayfield, and now it is also a marketing center for the apple orchards and berry farms in Bayfield County. The town was "discovered" by summer residents by the turn of the 20th century, and one of its classic hotels, the Old Rittenhouse Inn, has been restored as a fine restaurant (reservations required).

The harbor at Bayfield is enclosed by a rather unusual breakwater arrangement. The City Dock projects from the shore and a breakwater across the end of it forms a T. In the basin thus sheltered on the north side the docks are private. The City Dock itself is usually fully occupied by fish tugs and local craft, although theoretically there is transient space at the inner end in 6 to 7 feet. The southern arm of the T forms the north breakwater for the main harbor, with a more standard breakwater further enclosing it on the south. These are marked by flashing red and white lights with a fog horn. In the south end of the harbor the **Apostle Islands Marina** offers all dockside services at its slips in 10 feet; a 25-ton open-end travelift; engine, hull, and rigging repair and a marine store.

The marina is close to the appealing village shops, restaurants and night spots. The gift and art shops are supplemented by the annual Tri-State Arts and Crafts Fair held on the grounds of Memorial Park at the harborside. The July Commercial Fishermen's Festival features a famous Wisconsin fish boil. In the impressive 1883 County Courthouse (the government was moved to Washburn in 1891) the headquarters and visitors' center of the National Lakeshore can supply you with helpful materials to enhance your cruising among the islands.

Three miles southwest of Bayfield **Port Superior Marina** in Pike's Bay offers all dockside services, including Laundromat, in slips with 6 to 8 foot depths; haulout up to 25 tons; full engine, hull and rigging repair; and a marine store. Much of the bay is shoal, but the marina is approached in 8 to 10 feet through a buoyed channel to the north end of its sheltering breakwaters, which have flashing red and green lights. Port Superior is connected with a condominium development, and the additional amenities available to visiting boaters include a playground, swimming pool, tennis courts and the Fore and Aft Restaurant. Its only disadvantage is the 3-mile cab ride to town.

Madeline Island

The one island that is not included in the National Lakeshore is Madeline. A mere 2 miles offshore from Bayfield, it has the most interesting story to tell—of ancient Indian villages and medicine men gone berserk, of French and English and American fur traders, at least one of whom also went mad at the close of winter, of missionaries and teachers, of fishermen and farmers, of summer residents and boating tourists. Madeline, named for the wife of fur trader Michel Cadotte, has always evoked a sense of mystique among its devotees. As you approach the clapboarded village of La Pointe—a name enduring since Father Claude Allouez established the first mission of La Pointe du Saint Esprit in 1665—the ghosts of this oldest settlement on Lake Superior seem to reach out. Their story is to be learned in the Madeline Island Historical Museum complex (747-2415), in the Greek Revival Town Hall and in the ancient lakeside cemetery. There the remains of little wooden houses protect the Indian graves as they have since time remembered, and Michel Cadotte sleeps under his conventional tombstone. It is revealing of the island's character that this humble burial ground is adjacent to the sophisticated marina.

The **Madeline Island Yacht Club Marina** is enclosed in a basin, with its entrance further protected by an angled breakwater. Flashing red and white lights flank the entrance. Seven to 10 feet carry through the channel and the basin, where all services are offered at the slips; a 25-ton travelift hauls out for full engine, hull and rigging repairs; and there is a well-found marine store.

Madeline is a quiet residential resort, unto the third and fourth generation. The shops to meet their needs and supply a few souvenirs to the day-trippers are clustered around the ferry dock, half a mile from the marina. There are also a couple of restaurants. In the opposite direction from the marina The Club has tennis courts and a golf course open to the public. The island, 12 miles long and 1 to 3 wide, is a place for bicycling (rentals available), walking and beachcombing—when you aren't out there cruising among the other islands.

The Island Park

Stockton is the largest island after Madeline and affords good protection in Presque Isle Bay, where there is a dock in 7 feet and the only safe place for overnight mooring. Tie up at the north face; the south side is foul with boulders. Because of the great demand for space at all the park docks you are obliged to use a Mediterranean moor, with either bow or stern tied to the dock and the other end of the boat anchored off. The island has campgrounds and several miles of interesting hiking trails. One leads to an old brownstone quarry.

The outer islands, which take the brunt of lake waves and storms, have interesting caves and cuts in their sandstone bases, and some of them—Cat, Ironwood, Rocky, Raspberry and Outer—have sand beaches. The most impressive cave formations are found in Devil's Island, the outermost of the group. There is also a dock with 5 feet and a hiking trail on this island, as there is on Otter (5-to 7-foot depths). Rocky and Oak islands each have several trails and their docks have 6 feet alongside. Outer Island has a trail, but no docks, while docks at Sand Island (4 to 5 feet), Manitou (5 to 7 feet), Raspberry (5 to 6 feet), Basswood (4 to 5 feet) and South Twin Island (4 to 5 feet at the north dock, 6 to 7 at the south) are not yet complemented by trails. Little Eagle Island is a rookery for gulls and blue herons and should not be approached too closely during nesting season. Finally, the Apostle Islands probably have more lighthouses per square mile than any other place on the lakes.

Washburn

Almost due south from the Apostle Islands Chequamegon Bay is a 12-by-5-mile expanse of relatively shallow water, enclosed by a long sand spit. It is not particularly scenic, can get rough and nasty in a northeaster, has no anchorage to offer, and the industrial city of Ashland at the bottom of the bay has no facilities for cruising boats. But halfway down its western, deep water shore the city of Washburn has hung out the welcome sign in the shape of an attractive new marina. Enclosed behind breakwaters, with red and green lights at the entrance on the south side, the **Washburn Marina** offers all dockside services at its slips. The largest travelift on the Great Lakes can haul out up to 150 tons for full engine and hull repairs; there is also a launch ramp and a marine store.

Washburn, 10 miles from Bayfield, is a relative newcomer to Lake Superior. The town of 2,000 was founded in 1883 as a lumber and sandstone port. Now it's devoted mainly to county government and tourism. Shops, restaurants, tennis courts and a hospital are all within convenient walking distance of the marina.

Saxon Harbor

Twenty-eight miles eastward from either Washburn or Bayfield the Montreal River forms the boundary between Wisconsin and Michigan. A mile west of it, where Oronto Creek flows into the lake, Saxon Harbor has been artificially dredged. A pair of converging breakwaters, with flashing red and white lights, is entered from the west, with a controlling depth of 7 feet in the channel. There is 6 feet at the slips that rim the basin opening to the west inside the harbor. They are fully occupied by local boats, so that transient dockage may not be readily available. If it is, you will find the usual dockside services, except diesel and showers. There are no shops or services at the harbor, as the town of Saxon is several miles inland along the highway. For a cruising boat this is simply a harbor of refuge.

The Copper Range
Charts 14964, 14965, 14971, 14972

From the earliest days of French contact with the Indians of the Great Lakes tales of copper haunted the European mind. To

Native Americans the metal was sacred, and they tried to conceal its whereabouts. But Father Allouez found nuggets of float copper lying free in the shoreside shallows, and the government at Quebec sent more than one explorer to seek its source. But 125 years of intermittent attempts at commercial mining under three flags didn't turn up much until a trained scientist came exploring in 1840.

Douglass Houghton, a brilliant wisp of a young man, with an irrepressible sense of humor—botanist, physician, chemist, geologist, professor, politician—knew where and how to look. He found hidden in the rumpled ridges of the Keweenaw Peninsula, 60 miles by 10, one of the richest lodes of copper the world has ever known. The Copper Rush that ensued brought more men to the forbidding ridges and brutal winters of this remote frontier than California gold would lure a few years later. In the next half dozen decades of feverish prospecting, speculating, drilling, swindling, hauling and consolidating the best of it was torn out of the hills and carried off to electrify a nation. Eventually western copper, cheaper to retrieve, came to dominate the industry, and the red ore is no longer mined on the Keweenaw, although one lode is still in production on the Ontonagon Range to the southwest.

Black River

The copper range begins some 60 miles inside the Michigan border, and there is only one harbor on that sometimes steep and forbidding stretch. The mouth of the Black River, 20 miles northeast of Saxon Harbor, is protected by a pair of converging breakwaters with flashing red and white lights. Eight feet carries through the channel to a dock on the southwest side of the river with 5 to 6 feet alongside. There are no good landmarks to identify the harbor from offshore; you have to rely on dead reckoning. Immediately past the west breakwater light you must turn sharply to starboard to avoid the shoal area in the outer harbor, marked by a buoy. The alongside dockage is usually crowded with local boats, but with no alternatives close by a transient will not be turned away. Electricity, water, gas and diesel are provided.

The harbor is part of the Black River National Forest Recreation Area. There are no commercial services here, but the setting is one of tranquil beauty, with tall trees shading the river. You can take your dinghy up to the rapids beyond the bridge with 18-foot clearance. And there are several hiking trails to follow; on either bank of the river they lead to a series of waterfalls. There is a picnic area with restrooms in the park.

Ontonagon

The largest hunk of pure copper the world has ever known, a 3½-ton bauble, lay 30 miles up the Ontonagon River for millions of years before an enterprising promotor hauled it away in the early 1840s. The federal government immediately claimed this national treasure, and the Ontonagon Rock resides today in the Smithsonian Institution. Although robbed of its rock, the river advertises its copper-rich origins in the red color of its waters. So intense is this hue that it continues beyond the breakwaters into Lake Superior. At a precise distance out it would seem that the hand of God took a stylus and etched a sharp line—on one side the water is deep red; on the other it is deep blue.

Black River is a harbor of refuge it's a pleasure to be stuck in, so you can be choosy about the weather when you leave. The 40 miles to Ontonagon offer no refuge. The land continues to rise after you leave Black River, ultimately to the pointed peaks of the aptly named Porcupine Mountains. Their slopes plunge steeply to the sea for about 15 miles; then they terminate abruptly in a level plain. Fifteen miles farther on you reach the parallel breakwaters protecting the mouth of the Ontonagon River, with a flashing white and an isophase green light. There are stacks and tanks to identify the harbor from offshore. Controlling depth is 5½ feet to the highway bridge with 7-foot clearance. It opens on signal of one long, one short. A short distance beyond you turn westward into the enclosed basin of the **Waterways Commission Marina**, with depths of 7 feet at the slips and all dockside services, except diesel. There is also a large open-end travelift, but no repair personnel on site.

Downtown Ontonagon is half a mile back over the bridge, with all the necessary shops, a Laundromat and several restaurants. Stubb's Bar doubles as an intriguing museum, and the official Ontonagon County Historical Museum on River Street (884-2342) has an extensive local collection. The fortunes of this town of 2,400 people wax and wane with the level of operations at the White Pine Copper Mine and Mill southwest of town, although Champion Paper near the marina operates quite consistently. Nevertheless, it's a friendly place, and tourism is growing. You'll want to stay until the weather is settled. The next leg of an eastward voyage is 40 miles or 70, depending upon your destination.

The Keweenaw Waterway

Ontonagon anchors the copper range on the west, but the heart of it is the Keweenaw Peninsula, pointing like an arrow 60 miles into Lake Superior. The topography here is the most rugged on the south shore of the lake, much older geologically than the surrounding landforms. It is in the interstices of the tortured Keweenawan rock strata, folded into steep ridges, that the mineral wealth lies hidden—silver and some gold, as well as copper. In designing the Keweenaw nature also gave a thought to the frail humans who might need to pass from one side of its base to the other. She placed a natural waterway there that would save 100 miles of exposed voyaging around the outside of the peninsula.

The Keweenaw Waterway didn't go all the way through, but Indians traveling in birchbark canoes had no trouble carrying them across the land bridge. But portage wouldn't do for the sailing ships of the white men when they began coming to collect the copper in the 1840s. The first dredging of the sandbar at the southern end of the waterway began in 1859. In 1873 the 2-mile land cut was completed at the northern end, and since the Army Corps of Engineers took over the Waterway in 1891 they have made continual improvements. The main shipping track across Lake Superior lies north of the Keweenaw Peninsula, and in summer few ships come through. But when the fall storms begin the lakers are as glad to cut through the shelter of the 25-mile waterway as the Indians were long ago.

Upper Entry to the Keweenaw Waterway is sheltered by converging breakwaters, with flashing red and white lights and a fog horn, 40 miles from Black River. There are no distinguishing landmarks from offshore. Lights and buoys continue where needed throughout the length of the Waterway. Anchorage is possible behind the breakwaters but is not comfortable because of surge. From here it's only 10 miles through serene, rolling countryside dotted with homes to the comfortable accommodations at Hancock.

The twin cities of Hancock and Houghton, 5,000 and 7,500 people respectively, were founded early in the copper rush days at the steepest and narrowest part of the waterway, to serve the needs of mining adventurers. They continue today to serve mainly commercial and governmental functions and to provide for the growing tourist trade. Scenically, historically and culturally, the copper range is arguably the most interesting part of Michigan, and the historic ambiance of the twin cities is a good base from which to explore it. In the narrows between steep bluffs each climbs upward, with steeples and clock towers punctuating the scene. They are joined by a double-deck vertical lift bridge, much like the one at Duluth. Its closed clearance is 7 feet, and on a signal of one long and one short it will rise to whatever height you need short of its full opening of 103 feet.

Immediately past the bridge the **Michigan Waterways Commission Marina** occupies a graceful curve in the north shore at Hancock. All dockside services are offered in this well-managed marina, with 10 feet or more at the slips. Houghton is the customs port of entry, and there is some alongside tie-up for pleasure boats a quarter of a mile east of the bridge, but no services. The walk across the bridge is so short, however, that the downtown shops, restaurants and movies of both cities are equally accessible on foot from the marina. A Laundromat (located in the basement of a garage and scrupulously clean) and a supermarket in Hancock are a few blocks from the marina, which has a courtesy car for transport of your loads. Hancock has the hospital.

Copper work is the regional specialty to buy here, but look carefully at labels. A lot of it comes from California, and you often must inquire about the work of local coppersmiths. The shops in Houghton are a bit more sophisticated than those in Hancock, and The Library is an unusual restaurant serving good food. Highly recommended for dinner is the Onigaming Supper Club, south of town in the 1926 clubhouse of a yacht club that was organized in 1894. They will send a car to the marina for you, or on your way down the waterway you can anchor among the boats of the more recently formed successor yacht club just below Pilgrim Point and go in by dinghy.

Although there is at present no active mining on the Keweenaw there are several opportunities to see at firsthand how copper has been mined in the past. The Arcadian Copper Mine, less than a mile walk from the marina, is the closest one that conducts underground tours. It's a somewhat bigger hike up the hill to see the Quincy Mine Hoist, the largest steam-powered hoist ever built, which reached 9,000 feet down to pull up 10 tons of ore at 40 miles per hour when it was operating. The hoist is worth the walk, and so is the spectacular view from the top of the ridge.

Another attraction on the Hancock side is Suomi College, the only Finnish institution of higher education in the United States. It was founded in 1895 to educate children of the thousands of Finnish immigrants who worked the mines alongside the Cousin

Jacks, as the miners from Cornwall were called. (Everyone had a cousin, Jack, to sponsor as an immigrant from depressed Cornwall to booming Michigan.) The Finns and the Cornish have made an important culinary impact on this part of the world, and you should be sure to sample their art. The Suomi Bakery and Restaurant in Houghton excels at both Finnish sweets and Cornish pasties—the hot, hearty, lunch-in-a-pie-crust that a Cornish miner carried to work inside his shirt, where he and it could share a mutual warmth until mid-day. While you're on the Houghton side the A. E. Seaman Mineralogical Museum at Michigan Technological University exhibits one of the nation's finest collections of mineral specimens (487-2572).

Although there is a good deal to see and do in and around Houghton/Hancock, the Keweenaw Peninsula is rich in ghost towns and historic sites accessible only by car. You should consider renting one. Among the many places to visit on a driving tour, I'll mention only two. Central is a ghost town conveniently adjacent to the highway with a special appeal; the descendants of its original Cornish miners return every July for a one-day reunion and service at the Methodist Church. Calumet is no ghost town, but an architectural gem that boasts an impressive turn-of-the-century big cityscape. The Calumet and Hecla Mine was one of the most successful on the range, and the Coppertown U.S.A. Museum and Visitors Center is in one of its handsome buildings on Red Jacket Road (337-1976). But the prize is the resplendent Calumet Theater on Sixth Street, where Sarah Bernhardt, Enrico Caruso, Maude Adams, Otis Skinner and Harry Houdini, among many theatrical luminaries, once trod the boards. The 1,000-seat theater has been meticulously restored, and its stage is lit again for a variety of performances (337-2610).

Continuing southeast on the Keweenaw Waterway, the shoreline lowers as you round Pilgrim Point into Portage Lake. On the north side of that curve, at the entrance to Dollar Bay, Julio's Contracting has a 20-ton travelift should you need haulout. They will change wheels and shafts and call in mechanics as needed. Portage Lake, with many cottages on its west shore, offers no anchorage. Torch Bay leads off from the northeast end through a narrow but deep water canal to Torch Lake, which is mostly too deep for anchoring. On the shores of both these lakes there are big barren flats of tailings from the stamping of copper ore, and throughout the region mine and stamping mill ruins are a constant reminder of past glory and prosperity. Yet the spirit of

Hancock from ridge top.

the Keweenaw people is not one of defeat. Those who have not emigrated retain a strong pride in their heritage and hope that the mines may open again as they have sometimes done. And many of those who emigrate find a way to return, so intense is their loyalty to this beautiful land.

The lower end of Portage Lake dissolves into marsh, filled with wildlife. Anchorage can be had in Pike Bay in the southwest corner in 10 to 15 feet, although this is not very secluded; the highway runs right along the shore through the village of Chassell. The Portage Canal is buoyed through attractive grassy marshes, mostly undeveloped, and just before the exit into Keweenaw Bay there is a smooth concrete wharf to tie up to, with picnic tables on the grassy embankment. This is a pleasant place to lay over if the bay looks rough or the day is far gone; it's about 15 miles from Hancock.

Keweenaw Peninsula Harbors

Although the Keweenaw Waterway provides a convenient and scenic shortcut, there are harbors all around the perimeter. The northwest side is scenically more dramatic—bold and steep, with pink sand beaches between rocky outcrops. The southeast side is more gently sloping and forested, with the high ridges rising as backdrop. Exposure on either side depends on the direction and strength of the wind; the northwest side is likely to be a little riskier in this regard.

It's 28 scenic miles from the Upper Entry of the Keweenaw Waterway to Eagle Harbor, 38 from Hancock, almost 70 if you've come directly from Ontonagon. Give the unmarked hazard of Eagle River Shoal a good berth. Eagle Harbor is an elliptical bay, 1 mile long by ¼ mile wide, with a difficult entrance. A big lighthouse, with an alternating white and red flash, and a fog horn, identify the harbor, but hazardous shoals immediately outside require that you enter with care on the range at 150° shown from a quick flashing green front light with a white daymark and a fixed green rear light. A black gong buoy at the approach limit helps to orient you, but the range is sometimes hard to see at sunset or if foliage has grown up around it. Stay precisely on it until you thread two partially submerged stone cribs in the middle of the harbor entrance. You should carry a least depth of 11 feet. Strangers should not attempt Eagle Harbor with a heavy sea running. When you reach deeper water inside the harbor, turn to port for the **Waterways Commision Marina** at the site of the old Coast Guard Station on the northeast peninsula. Alongside tie-up in 6 feet and all dockside services, except diesel, are available. It's almost a 2-mile walk around the harbor to the village, which has one historic general store, one restaurant and a pink sand beach. You could dinghy across, although a landing place isn't so easy to find when the beach is busy. Anchorage is poor in Eagle Harbor, for both protection and holding.

Copper Harbor

Fourteen miles farther on, Copper Harbor offers better possibilities. It's cradled by steep hills in a much larger elliptical bay, 3 miles long by half a mile wide. Here is where the copper boom began. In 1843 the first land office was opened to register claims, and in 1844 the first copper ore was brought up. By the close of the decade Copper Harbor had the second largest hotel and the second largest newspaper circulation in the state. In 1844 the War Department sent a garrison to build Fort Wilkins and keep law and order between the miners and the Indians. The post turned out to be a quaint candidate for the Golden Fleece Award of current times. No real trouble ever developed, and the fort has been garrisoned for only 5 of its 138-year history. It became a state historic park in the 1920s, and today you can visit the restored site, with vivid interpretation of army life at a remote outpost by role-playing docents (289-4215). Unfortunately, it's almost 3 miles from the marina and there are no taxis in Copper Harbor, but your dinghy could get you fairly close and your thumb could take you to the gate.

The entrance to Copper Harbor, too, is partly foul with unmarked reefs. As at Eagle, a big white lighthouse with a flashing green light sits on one point. Here a black and white bell buoy helps put you on the quick flash and fixed white range at 190° with red and white daymarks. The lighthouse, while still in active use, is also a state historic landmark, and can be visited on a special park boat that leaves from the marina dock. The **Waterways Commission Marina** is at the west end of the harbor, with alongside tie-up and the usual services except diesel. If you draw more than 4 feet, however, you may have trouble at the fuel and pumpout dock, where severe shoaling has occurred. There is also good anchorage at either end of the harbor.

The marina is in a pretty wooded setting but is a half-mile walk to the beginning of the village, which sprawls for quite a distance along the road. There are two general stores at the far end of town, a fish market closer, numerous gift and craft shops and several restaurants. The town is almost entirely devoted to the tourist trade, which is considerable because of the ferry service from here to Isle Royale. Up on the mountaintop above town Keweenaw Mountain Resort is a handsome complex, sponsored by the WPA when the Great Depression virtually wiped out what little mining was left on the range. Still operated by the county, the lodge offers golf and tennis and a very good dining room. They will send a car to the marina for you, if you request it when you call for reservations.

A Pair of Refuges

The 25-mile passage around the tip of the Keweenaw from Copper Harbor to Lac La Belle is scenically splendid, but cross-winds and currents can make it a rough one. At Bête Grise Bay the mountainous ridges come down to the shore, and a beautiful little channel, first cut in 1866, leads from the bay into Lac La Belle. Parallel piers, marked with flashing red and white lights, enclose the entrance. The canal is about ¾ of a mile long and carries a controlling depth of 8 feet past a quaint abandoned lighthouse into the deep water of the 2½-by-1-mile lake. A hundred years ago this was a busy port for the shipment of copper brought over the hills by a narrow gauge railroad. Today it is strictly a summer resort, with a T-shaped **Waterways Commision Dock** in the northwest corner. There are no services, and depths at the outer face probably don't exceed 4 feet. Anchorage is good almost anywhere in the lake; avoid the heavily traveled area close to the entrance canal. Because of intense cottage development, the lake is not as pretty as its entrance canal. Nor are any supplies or services available. This harbor is a good refuge or a useful overnight stop, but that's about all.

The next harbor, Grand Traverse, 20 miles southwest, isn't any better, however. A tall stack at the village of Gay, 5 miles from the harbor, is the identifying landmark, and the breakwaters are marked by group flashing white and flashing green lights. A controlling depth of 10 feet carries to the **Waterways Commission Dock,** with alongside tie-up in 6½ feet and no services. That assumes that you can find space at this small dock, usually fully occupied by local boats.

Keweenaw Bay

Another 18 miles and you're back at the lower entrance to the Keweenaw Waterway. Keweenaw Bay is a tapered indentation of the coast that extends southwesterly for 15 miles and measures about 13 across the top. Strong winds from northwest through northeast funnel into the bay, making it a very rough body of water. It is also a beautiful one, rimmed with red sand bluffs and beaches in startling contrast to the often brilliant blue water.

There are two towns at the bottom of the bay. L'Anse on the east shore is the larger and more interesting, but is devoid of facilities for a cruising boat. Baraga across the way on the west shore has a **Waterways Commission Marina**, with a least depth of 9 feet at the slips, electricity, water and gasoline. Entrance is between two land projections, with some submerged ruins extending from them. After passing the red nun off Sand Point, stand off until you can come directly into the basin between the jetties. It is several uphill blocks to town for shopping, but there is a restaurant across the road.

On the east side of Keweenaw Bay a mushroom of land juts out into the bay, forming a semisheltered natural harbor. A sawmill town was built here at Pequaming in 1877, and in 1923 it was taken over by Ford Motor Company to supply the Rouge Plant with wood for station wagons. By 1942 the place was abandoned; no station wagons were produced during World War

II, and after the war wood paneling had gone the way of the
dodo bird. In recent years the former ghost town site has been
revived as a summer resort and many of the homes attractively
restored. The ruins of the old Ford plant still stand on the south
point, however, with the company's logo identifiable on the tall
tank. There is a private dock for small boats on the inside of the
point, where you can bring a dinghy to explore the ruins. The
best spot to anchor is off the beach toward the northeast end,
but watch out for a line of randomly spaced cribs off the west
and north shores. If you anchor in no less than 18 feet, you
should be all right. In southwest winds you'll roll with the surge.

Given the limitations of Keweenaw Bay, you're best off on an
eastward voyage to wait out the weather inside the waterway
and then head northeast on the next leg.

Stone and Sand
Charts 14962, 14963, 14964, 14969, 14970

East of Keweenaw Bay the long coast of Michigan is bordered
successively by mountains tailing into rock formations, grinding
into high sand dunes, leveling off to sand bluffs, lowering to flat
beach. The succession comes into view around Point Abbaye
and its extenuating reef, where the high crags of the Huron
Islands stand sentinel a few miles offshore, their great gray
lighthouse a lonely castle. You pass close to the islands on the
direct course eastward. Although there is no harbor among
them, the water is deep and they lure you to circle for a closer
view.

Alternatively, you can find shelter in Huron Bay, a miniature
version of Keweenaw Bay, indenting the shoreline for 10 miles
but only a mile or so wide. Best anchorage lies east of the point
marked by flashing white Huron Bay Light in about 10 feet. If
the little marina there is operating, go in by dinghy first to
inquire about depths; shoaling has been severe in recent years.
The village of Huron Bay at the far end no longer exists, and
anchorage there is risky because of old dock ruins and shoal
water. Huron Bay is quiet, pretty and thinly settled with farms
and summer cottages.

Beyond the Huron Islands the Huron Mountains rise in back
of the succession of rocky bluffs and points. The entire range is
owned by the Huron Mountain Club, established in 1889 by
wealthy sportsmen. Their descendants still have summer cottages there, but now the property is maintained as a nature

preserve, where many rare and endangered species provide an important laboratory for biological research. A long shoal makes out from Huron River Point, but its least depth is 8 feet and you can follow the lovely mountain shore quite closely to Big Bay near the eastern end of the range.

Here there is a **Waterways Commission Marina** behind converging breakwaters in the southwest corner, with a flashing red light on the west pier. The harbor of refuge is 27 miles from the anchorage in Huron Bay, 40 miles from the lower entry to the Keweenaw Waterway. The usual dockside services, except diesel and showers, are provided for at the alongside tie-up in 6 feet, but in recent years not all of them have been functional. The village, about a mile away, isn't much—a general store, hotel and tavern, still basking in its moment of glory as the movie set 20-odd years ago for local author Robert Traver's *Anatomy of a Murder*.

Marquette

On a cool September morning in 1844 United States surveyor William Austin Burt and his crew were running lines in the Upper Peninsula when the compass suddenly went crazy. The first of Michigan's three rich iron ranges was thus revealed. Within a few years mining crews were hacking out the ore, but a harbor was needed from which to ship it to the forges and mills below. The city of Marquette was born with the first 10 tons of ore shipped in 1850. Its future was assured as a river of red rock continued to rumble by the trainload onto the skeletal trestles of the ore-loading docks at lakeside. The city grew rapidly, and its prosperity spawned millionaires. Fortunately for future generations, these iron tycoons took great pride in their city and endowed it with fine parks and cultural institutions. Although the flow of iron has slowed to a trickle in recent years, Marquette remains a vibrant and attractive place to visit. With 23,000 people it is the metropolis of the Upper Peninsula, and a customs station.

There is no natural harbor in this part of Lake Superior, but two artificial harbors serve Marquette. Each is sheltered by a peninsula with a breakwater extending from it at the appropriate angle. Both are approached from the northwest around the red-rock-bound Presque Isle Peninsula, about 28 miles from the harbor at Big Bay. On the way it's easy to mistake Granite Island, about 6 miles offshore, for a ship headed your way.

Through the efforts of Peter White, one of Marquette's founders and most important philanthropists, Presque Isle became a city park back in 1886. Eighty years later, the **Waterways Commision Marina** was built at the edge of the park opposite one of the two ore docks in Presque Isle Harbor. On the approach from the east the stacks of the power plant at the south end of the harbor are prominent. From Presque Isle Breakwater Light, flashing red with a fog horn, you head northwesterly for the marina breakwater with its flashing red light. All dockside services are offered here, but the basin, originally dredged to 6 feet, has shoaled badly. If your draft exceeds 5 feet keep to the outer slips. If it exceeds 5½, you'll have to take your chances at the main Marquette harbor, 3 miles south.

On the approach, mind the shoals making out from the big Marquette Light, flashing white; there is only a can buoy to mark their outer edge. The breakwater has two lights, an outer occulting white with a fog horn and an inner fixed red. There are local pleasure craft moored here in the shadow of the ore dock, which lease their space from the Soo Line Railroad, and the Marquette Yacht Club has a small property here. But there is rarely space for a transient boat.

The disadvantage of the Presque Isle Marina's 3-mile distance from downtown is more than compensated for by the attractions of its immediate surroundings. The 328-acre park offers a swimming pool, tennis courts, a zoo, band concerts and a rustic self-guided nature trail. There is rich rock hunting on the agate beaches around the peninsula, and from the cockpit you have a front row seat for the ore dock. Art on the Rocks, a large juried art show and sale, takes place in July. Outside the park gates, a short walk from the marina, the Marquette and Huron Mountain Railroad recaptures the age of coal-fired steam engines. A 2½-hour excursion trip on a 1910 train from the restored depot (228-8785) carries you back into the past and through the forest and lake country beyond the city. The morning run includes a delicious old-time lumberjack breakfast at long trestle tables in the bright yellow wood caboose.

Taxis are readily obtained to take you to downtown Marquette, or, if you carry bicycles on board, there is a separated bike path all the way. On the route a new Maritime Museum has opened in the old waterworks building on Lakeshore Boulevard. The solid red sandstone buildings of downtown Marquette retain an aura of dignified 19th-century prosperity. But the shopping is convenient and modern, including Thill's fish market at the waterfront. There are several restaurants, two movie theaters, a hospital and a commercial airport for crew changes.

The Marquette County Historical Museum on Front Street (226-6821) presents a well-mounted exhibit of Indian life and local history. The building also houses the excellent Longyear Research Library, and next door is the Peter White Library with its own special collections. A walk down nearby Arch Street displays some of the city's handsome Victorian mansions. Two other Marquette attractions are more easily reached by car or taxi than on foot. The first house built in town by pioneer John Burt is at 200 Craig Street on the south side of town (226-6821). The Shirras Planetarium in the Marquette Senior High School presents a show two or three evenings a week in summer.

Munising Area

Munising, 40 miles east of Marquette, could be a good harbor for cruising boats, if Munising only cared enough. The natural protection afforded the harbor by Grand Island, the forested hillsides surrounding it, its equal distance between Marquette and Grand Marais should add up to a recommended stop. But all the town can offer a cruising boat is a miserable public dock, faced with corrugated sheet metal with holes in it for your lines, and no services—if you can find space among the assorted local craft, fish tugs and excursion boats. Fortunately, there is an alternative that allows you to come in off the big lake short of a straight passage of 65 miles between Marquette and Grand Marais.

Murray Bay on the south side of Grand Island affords sheltered anchorage off the east shore. You may see scuba divers in the harbor working from small boats. The Alger Underwater Preserve encompasses 113 square miles of lakeshore, including Munising Bay, with 10 shipwrecks identified for the looking. The island, owned by the Cleveland Cliffs Iron Company and maintained as a nature preserve, is more scenic on the outside than it is in Murray Bay. The approach from the west is impressive—pass around the north end of Wood Island and come down toward the harbor between Wood and Grand islands—and the thumb of the island east of the harbor has some complex sandstone bluffs.

It is sandstone bluffs that brings you to Munising in the first place, even if a 65-mile passage direct to Grand Marais from Marquette is easy for you. Munising's real treasure is the Pictured Rocks, stretching almost 15 miles northeast of the town. The water is deep very close to shore, so you can get an excellent view from your own boat at dead slow while the camera shutter

Pictured Rocks.

clicks along. But there is a problem of timing. The shapes of the rocks, sculpted by Superior's wave action and the down-cutting of streams from the forested bluff top, are fascinating enough. It is their remarkable colors that make them outstanding. Caused by the leaching of minerals, iron shows up red, copper blue and green; lime is white. But when the sun is overhead those marvelous colors wash out completely. To fully appreciate the Pictured Rocks you must see them with the sun low at your back, early in the morning if you're westbound, late in the afternoon if you're eastbound. Unless you're in a very fast boat, however, you can't get to the next harbor east before dark, or you have to set out westbound at some ungodly hour in the morning. A third alternative is to spend two nights at Murray Bay, returning there after a cruise along the Pictured Rocks in late afternoon aboard either your own boat or the excursion boat from Munising. The excursion includes an explanatory narrative and some poking into caves that you might hesitate to enter. The spectacle begins northeast of Sand Point and its shoal, as you move beyond the shelter of Grand Island. Each of the formations has a name, some of which are shown on the chart; the most dramatic of them are at the eastern end, culminating in the Grand Portal. If you do put in at Munising, you can obtain information about the formations from the headquarters of the Pictured Rocks National Lakeshore in town.

Grand Marais

After the Pictured Rocks recede in your wake there is only a little time to muse on them before the next spectacle appears around Au Sable point—the glowing undulations of the Grand Sable Dunes, capped by a forest of birch. The dunes, 350 feet high and spread over 5 square miles, anchor the eastern end of the Pictured Rocks National Lakeshore. You'll get the chance for a closer look after you dock at Grand Marais.

The approach to the harbor is quite straightforward. Note the unmarked shoal off Au Sable Point. Once an important fishing port because of its natural harbor, Grand Marais is now a quiet rustic resort village, off the beaten highway track, with a few commercial fish tugs still operating. Parallel breakwaters protect the channel leading across the sand spit that encloses the harbor, with a flashing white light and fog horn at the outer end of the west pier, a flashing green light buoy opposite, and a fixed green light on the inner end of the west pier. The red schoolhouse and a chimney in town are the identifying features from seaward. The **Waterways Commission Marina** is in the northwest corner of the harbor, with alongside tie-up in 6 feet, electricity, water, pumpout, gas and diesel.

At the turn of the century Grand Marais had a population of 3,000, many stores, a dozen hotels and 29 saloons. Today it is home to only a few hundred, but has a good grocery store (with ice), general store, fish market, hardware, and gift shops; no Laundromat. Alvorson's Restaurant renders the old-time flavor, enhanced by its handsome bar and old pictures. As you wander, stop at the imaginative tourist information booth in a barrel. Welker's Lodge, a ½-mile from the marina out toward the breakwater, serves good plain food and has a nice gift shop.

There is a choice of places to swim in Grand Marais between the pebbly beach on Lake Superior or the sand beach on the south side of the harbor. National Park naturalists offer interpretive programs at Woodland Park, a campground a couple of blocks from the marina. But the main tourist attraction is the Grand Sable Dunes. They begin only a mile from the town, accessible by road, on foot or by thumb. It is also possible to walk the beach to the outlet of Grand Sable Lake and follow a trail up the stream bank to Sable Falls and the dunes beyond. Once there you can lose yourself among the quiet, grassy, windblown slopes. For an unusual experience, roam these hills in the early morning or just before dusk, with no sign of humanity within view and only the sounds of the wind and the wildlife within hearing.

Grand Sable Falls.

Little Lake

Sand bluffs continue to border the 30 miles from Grand Marais to Little Lake. This exquisite little harbor was created by dredging through the sandbar that separates Little Lake from Lake Superior. That sandbar doesn't want to stay dredged, however, and the process must be repeated annually. If you draw more than 4 feet, you probably can't get in until after the dredge has done its work, usually in August, and if you draw more than 5½, you probably can't get in at all. In that case you have no alternative to a 50-mile run between Grand Marais and Whitefish Point.

There is no way to identify this almost-wild harbor from offshore. The longer west breakwater is angled to overlap the shorter one on the east side of the channel, which is entered from northeastward. The breakwaters are marked by flashing white and green lights. Favor the west breakwater as you follow the curving channel into the half-square-mile lake. The **Waterways Commission Dock** is on the north side, with 6 feet at the alongside tie-up. The proprietress of the small, friendly cottage resort on the point is the dock mistress. In addition to gas and pumpout, if you request her to turn on the generator, there is electricity and water.

Little Lake harbor has only unspoiled nature to offer in the way of entertainment—the nearest town is 37 miles away. If you're just starting out on a Lake Superior circumnavigation, it's a good taste of what lies around the other side, and if you're approaching its conclusion, it's a happy reprise. You can walk across the narrow neck of land dividing the big and little lakes, to roam for miles along the beach, swim in the surf and hunt agates along the water's edge. You can hike an alluring network of forest roads and find acres of blueberries in recently cut-over patches. You can fish the little or big lake. You can read or reread Ernest Hemingway. This was the country in which he loved to fish and hunt, and he wrote about it.

Whitefish Point

Twenty miles more along the forested sandy shores and you turn the corner back in to Whitefish Bay. If it should be acting up in its usual fashion, or you've had a long passage from Grand Marais, there is a harbor of refuge 1 mile south of the point and its big group flashing white light with fog horn. The artificial harbor is protected by an angled double breakwater on the north and east overlapping the breakwater on the south. All three are marked by flashing lights, red, white and green. The channel, which carries 7 feet, is entered from the south. When past the south breakwater, turn to port to pass around the inner north breakwater, then to starboard to head for the **Waterways Commission Docks** at the north end. There are only a few slips, with 6- to 8-foot depths and no services. No matter what's happening beyond the breakwaters, you're snug in here, but the harbor is in a rural area with no town nearby. The soft sand beach and a mile walk to the lighthouse, in process of becoming a shipwreck museum, provide entertainment, while Brown's Fishery provides fish, both fresh and smoked.

At Whitefish Point we've come almost full circle around Lake Superior. There is neither harbor nor anchorage on the south and west sides of Whitefish Bay to provide an alternative to the direct 25-mile crossing to St. Marys River. And here we conclude as well the voyage we've taken together through this book— where the fresh waters of the inland seas begin their long journey to the ocean.

APPENDIX A: RADIO BROADCASTING STATIONS

PUBLIC CORRESPONDENCE AND WEATHER

STATION	CHANNELS
LAKE ONTARIO	
VDQ Cardinal, via Kingston	24, 26, 85, weather 83B
VBG Toronto, via Cobourg	26, 27, 88, weather 21B
via Fonthill	26, 27, 28, weather 83B
KLU 788 Rochester	25
LAKE ERIE	
WBL Buffalo	26,28
KIL 929 Ripley	86, weather 17, 6:02, 12:02
KLU 745 Erie	25
WXY 934 Ashtabula	28
KQU 440 Cleveland	87, weather 17, 6:02, 12:02
WMI Lorain	26, weather 17, 6:02, 12:02
KIL 928 Oregon	84, weather 17, 6:02, 12:02
KAD 806 Toledo	25
VBE Sarnia, via Leamington	26, 27, 88, weather 83B
via Port Burwell	24, 26, 85, weather 21B

DETROIT RIVER, LAKE ST. CLAIR, ST. CLAIR RIVER

KQB 666 Detroit	26, 28
KIL 927 Algonac	86, weather 17, 6:02, 12:02
KAD 836 Marysville	25
VBE Sarnia	26, 27, 88, weather 21B

LAKE HURON

KIL 926 Harbor Beach	87, weather 17, 6:02, 12:02
KUF 718 Bay City	28
WLC Rogers City	26, 28 weather 26, 6:17, 12:17
KIL 923 Pickford	84, 86, weather 17, 6:02 12:02
VBE Sarnia, via Kincardine	26, 27, 88, weather 83B
VBC Wiarton	26
via Tobermory	24, 26, 85, weather 21B
via Meaford	24, 26, 85, weather 83B
via Pte. au Baril	26, 27, weather 21B
via Killarney	24, 26, 85, weather 21B
VBB Sault Ste. Marie, via Silver Water	26, 27, 88 weather 83B

LAKE MICHIGAN

WLC Charlevoix	26, weather 6:17, 12:17
KQU 546 Muskegon	86
KQU 438 Saugatuck	28
KIL 924 Benton Harbor	86, weather 17, 6:02, 12:02
KSK 283 St. Joseph	24
KLU 757 Michigan City	25
KQU 578 Portage	28
WAY 200 Chicago	26, 27
KTD 564 Waukegan	84
KVY 605 Port Washington	85, weather 17, 6:02, 12:02
KVY 604 Sturgeon Bay	87, weather 17, 6:02, 12:02

ST. MARYS RIVER

WLC Sault Ste. Marie, MI	26, weather 6:17, 12:17
VBB Sault Ste. Marie, ON	26, 27, 88, weather 21B

LAKE SUPERIOR

VBB Sault Ste. Marie, via Bald Head	26, 27, 88, weather 83B
VBA Thunder Bay	24, 26, weather 21B
via Horn	24, 26, weather 21B
KVY 601 Duluth	84, weather 17, 6:02, 12:02
KIL 922 Ontonagon	86, weather 17, 6:02, 12:02
KVY 602 Copper Harbor	87, weather 17, 6:02, 12:02
KVY 603 Grand Marais, MI	84, weather 17, 6:02, 12:02

UNITED STATES COAST GUARD WEATHER
AND MARINE INFORMATION

	CHANNEL 22A
Group Buffalo	Every 3 hours, commencing 0255
Group Detroit	Every 3 hours, commencing 0135
Group Muskegon	Every 3 hours, commencing 0235
Group Milwaukee	Every 3 hours, commencing 0255
Group Sault Ste. Marie	Every 3 hours, commencing 0005

APPENDIX B: COAST GUARD STATIONS AND RESCUE UNITS

LAKE ONTARIO

Kingston, Rescue Cutter
Trenton, Inshore Mobile Unit and Air Rescue
Cobourg, Rescue Cutter
Youngstown
Rochester
Sodus Bay (seasonal)
Oswego
Sackets Harbor (seasonal)

LAKE ERIE

Buffalo
Erie
Ashtabula
Fairport
Cleveland
Lorain
Marblehead
Toledo
Port Dover, Rescue Cutter

DETROIT RIVER, LAKE St. CLAIR, St. CLAIR RIVER

Detroit
Amherstburg, Rescue Cutter
Mitchell Bay, Inshore Mobile Unit
St. Clair Shores
Clinton River
St. Clair Flats
Port Huron

LAKE HURON

Harbor Beach (seasonal)
Saginaw River
East Tawas
St. Ignace
Goderich, Rescue Cutter
Tobermory, Inshore Mobile Unit
Meaford, Rescue Cutter
Port Severn, Inshore Mobile Unit
Britt, Inshore Mobile Unit
Whitefish Falls, Inshore Mobile Unit

LAKE MICHIGAN

Charlevoix
Traverse City
Frankfort
Manistee (seasonal)
Muskegon
Grand Haven
Holland
South Haven (seasonal)
St. Joseph
Michigan City
Calumet
Glenview (Chicago)
Wilmette
Kenosha
Milwaukee
Sheboygan
Two Rivers
Sturgeon Bay
Plum Island (seasonal)
Green Bay (seasonal)

St. MARYS RIVER

Sault Ste. Marie, MI

LAKE SUPERIOR

Batchawana Bay, Inshore Mobile Unit
Thunder Bay, Rescue Cutter
Grand Marais, MN
Duluth
Bayfield
Keweenaw Waterway
Marquette
Munising (seasonal)
Grand Marais, MI (seasonal)

APPENDIX C: GOVERNMENT MARINE PUBLICATIONS

UNITED STATES

Order from: Distribution Branch (N/CG33)
National Ocean Service
Riverdale MD 20737

Nautical Chart Catalogue 4, Great Lakes and Adjacent Waterways

United States Coast Pilot, Number 6

Order from: Superintendent of Documents
U.S. Government Printing Office
Washington DC 20402

Light List, Volume IV

Order from: Commander, Ninth Coast Guard District
1240 East Ninth St.
Cleveland OH 44199

Local Notices to Mariners

CANADA

Order from: Hydrographic Chart Distribution Office
Department of Fisheries and Oceans
1675 Russell Rd. PO Box 8080
Ottawa ON K1G 3H6

Catalog of Nautical Charts and Related Publications, Great Lakes

Sailing Directions, Great Lakes, Volume I

Sailing Directions, Great Lakes, Volume II

Georgian Bay, Small Craft Guide

List of Lights, Buoys, and Fog Signals, Inland Waters

Radio Aids to Marine Navigation, Atlantic and Great Lakes

Navigation Canals

Notices to Mariners

Order from: St. Lawrence Seaway Authority
Place de Ville
Ottawa ON K1R 5A3

or

St. Lawrence Seaway Authority
PO Box 520
Massena NY 13662

Tickets for the Welland Canal and an excellent handbook, *Pleasure Craft Guide*

APPENDIX D: SELECTED READING ABOUT THE GREAT LAKES

A great deal has been written about the Great Lakes, individually and collectively. In addition, many of the cities, counties, villages, islands and regional areas have been the subject of histories, memoirs and novels. The following list is highly selective, limited to general works about broad segments of the region, and by no means exhaustive of those. Some of them are out of print and available only in libraries. Some of them have bibliographies to guide you further. In many of the ports around the lakes you will be able to buy locally published books and booklets about the area.

Barry, James P. *Georgian Bay: The Sixth Great Lake*. Toronto: Clarke, Irwin & Company, 1968.

Bayliss, Joseph E. and Estelle L. *River of Destiny: The St. Marys*. Detroit: Wayne State University Press, 1955.

Bogue, Margaret Beattie, and Virginia A. Palmer, *Around the Shores of Lake Superior: A Guide to Historic Sites*. Madison: University of Wisconsin Sea Grant Program, 1979.

Boyer, Dwight, *Great Stories of the Great Lakes*. New York: Dodd, Mead & Co., 1966.

———— *True Tales of the Great Lakes*. New York: Dodd, Mead & Co., 1971.

Brazer, Marjorie Cahn. *Well Favored Passage: A Guide to Lake Huron's North Channel*. Revised Edition. Charlevoix: Peach Mountain Press, 1982

_____ *The Sweet Water Sea: A Guide to Lake Huron's Georgian Bay.* Charlevoix: Peach Mountain Press, 1984.

Cantor, George. *The Great Lakes Guidebook.* Three volumes in paperback. Ann Arbor: The University of Michigan Press, 1978–1980

Dahl, Bonnie. *The Superior Way: A Cruising Guide to Lake Superior.* Ashland: Inland Sea Press, 1983.

Hatcher, Harlan. *The Great Lakes.* New York: Oxford University Press, 1944.

_____ *Lake Erie.* New York: The Bobbs Merrill Company, 1945.

Havighurst, Walter. *The Long Ships Passing.* New York: The Macmillan Co., 1953

Holling, Clancy. *Paddle-to-the-Sea.* Boston: The Houghton Mifflin Co., 1969. (For children 6 and up.)

Hough, Jack L. *Geology of the Great Lakes.* Champaign: University of Illinois Press, 1958.

Landon, Fred. *Lake Huron.* New York: The Bobbs Merrill Co., 1944.

Nute, Grace Lee. *Lake Superior.* New York: The Bobbs Merrill Co., 1944.

Pound, Arthur. *Lake Ontario.* New York: The Bobbs Merrill Co., 1945.

Pye, E.G. *Geology and Scenery, North Shore of Lake Superior.* Toronto: Ontario Department of Mines, 1969.

Quaife, Milo. *Lake Michigan.* New York: The Bobbs Merrill Co., 1944.

Richardson, J.A., and K.D. Card. *Geology and Scenery, North Shore of Lake Huron Region.* Toronto: Ministry of Natural Resources, 1972.

Scharfenberg, Doris. *The Long Blue Edge of Ontario.* Grand Rapids: Wm. B. Eerdmans Publishing Co., 1984.

_____ *The Long Blue Edge of Summer.* Grand Rapids: Wm. B. Eerdmans Publishing Co., 1982.

Wells, Kenneth McNeil. *Cruising the Georgian Bay.* Toronto: Kingswood House, 1961.

_____ *Cruising the North Channel.* Toronto: Kingswood House, 1960.

INDEX

All proper names are indexed, with a few exceptions. Cities, towns and villages also carry the state or province name. All bodies of water on which ports or anchorages are located are included, as are channels that border more than one place. The five Great Lakes, minor channels traversed in passing, aids to navigation, and identifying landmarks are not indexed. Nor are shops and non-marine business establishments, theaters, events and parks, except those that can be toured.

491

Amedroz Island, 293
American Fur Company, 217
American Motors Corporation, 352
American Revolutionary War, 28, 71,
    101, 190
Amethyst Bay, 432
Amherst Island, 35–36
Amherstburg Channel, 170–71
Amherstburg, Ontario, 170–71
Anchor Bay, 174, 179–81
Anchor In Marina, 211
Anchor Island, 291
Anchor Marina, 105
Anchor Marine, 371
Anchor Point Boat-o-Minium, 143–44
Anchorages, 19–21, 255, 414
Anchors Away Marina, 133
Anderson's Dock and Store, 372
Apostle Islands, 405, 406, 452, 453–56
Apostle Islands Marina, 454
Apostle Islands National Lakeshore,
    453, 455, 456
Aquatic Park, 54
Arawanna II, 146
Arawanna Princess, 146
Arcadia Lake, 318–19
Arcadian Copper Mine, 461
Arch Rock, 218
Archicenter, 341
Armour Harbour, 425
Arney's Marina, 81
Arnold Boat Works, 205
Art Gallery of Algoma, 396
Art Gallery of Hamilton, 67
Art Gallery of Northumberland, 46
Art Gallery of Ontario, 52
Art Gallery of Windsor, 173
Ashbridge's Bay, 55
Ashbridge's Bay Yacht Club, 55
Ashland, Wisconsin, 457
Ashtabula River, 114
Ashtabula Yacht Club, 114
Ashtabula, Ohio, 101, 114–15
Assiginack Historical Museum, 279
Astor, John Jacob, 217
Au Gres River, 199–200
Au Gres, Michigan, 200
Au Sable, Michigan, 202
Au Sable River, Michigan, 202
Au Sable River, Ontario

B

B and E Marina, 340
Bad River, 271–72
Baha'i Temple, 348
Baie Fine, 294–95
Baileys Harbor Yacht Club, 365–66

Baker Furniture Museum, 333
Balcom Marine Center, 326
Baraga, Father Frederic, 394
Baraga, Michigan, 466
Barcelona, New York, 108
Barclay, Commander Robert Heriot,
    170
Barker Civic Center, 339
Barkers Island Marina, 451
Barnes Winery, 70
Barrett's Marina, 330
Bassett Island, 287–88
Basswood Island, 456
Batchawana Bay, 407–8
Batchawana Hotel, 407
Batchawana Island, 407–8
Batchawana River, 407
Bath, Ontario, 36
Battery Park Municipal Marina,
    130–31
Bay Beach, 376
Bay City Yacht Club, 198
Bay City, Michigan, 197, 198–99, 325
Bay Harbor Marina, Bay City, 198
Bay Harbor Marina, Erie, 111
Bay Haven Anchorage Marina, 332
Bay Haven Marina, 332
Bay Moorings, 249
Bay of Islands, 293, 294
Bay of Quinte, 35–44
Bay of Quinte Yacht Club, 40
Bay View Association, 309
Bay View Yacht Club, 145
Bay's End Marina, 249
Baycrest Marina, 39
Bayfield River, 223–24
Bayfield Sound, 283, 284
Bayfield Yacht Club, 224
Bayfield, Lieutenant Henry Wolsey,
    229
Bayfield, Ontario, 223–24
Bayfield, Wisconsin, 454–55, 457
Bayshore Marina, Caseville, 197–98
Bayshore Marina, Erie, 111
Bayview Yacht Club, 168
Beacon Marina, 226
Bear Island, 447
Bear Lake, 326
Beardrop Harbour, 289
Beausoleil Bay, 257
Beausoleil Island, 256, 257, 260
Beaver Creek, 125
Beaver Island State Park Marina, 104
Beaver Island, Isle Royale, 441
Beaver Island, Lake Michigan, 302,
    310, 383
Beaver Park Marina, 125
Beaver Park Yacht Basin, 125